The Complete Guide to

HUNTER SEAT TRAINING, SHOWING, AND JUDGING

ON THE FLAT AND OVER FENCES

ANNA JANE
WHITE-MULLIN

INTRODUCTION BY CHRYSTINE TAUBER
FOREWORD BY MARIA SCHAUB

PHOTOGRAPHS BY BILL JOHNSON

T
TRAFALGAR SQUARE
NORTH POMFRET, VERMONT

First published in 2008 by
Trafalgar Square Books
North Pomfret, Vermont 05053

Printed in China

Disclaimer of Liability
The publisher shall have neither liability nor responsibility to any person or entity with respect to any loss or damage caused or alleged to be caused directly or indirectly by the information contained in this book. While the book is as accurate as the publisher can make it, there may be errors, omissions, and inaccuracies.

Library of Congress Cataloging-in-Publication Data

White-Mullin, Anna Jane.
The complete guide to hunter seat training, showing, and judging—on the flat and over fences / Anna Jane White-Mullin.
p. cm.
Includes index.
ISBN 978-1-57076-408-0
1. Hunt riding. 2. Hunter seat equitation. 3. Hunters (Horses)—Training. 4. Jumping (Horsemanship) 5. Hunter horse shows—Judging. I. Title.
SF295.65.W45 2008
798.2'5—dc22
2008012710

Photo credits: All photos in this book by Bill Johnson (www.horsepixphotography.com) **except** p. 10 (Ronald B. Blackwell, DVM); pp. 52, 53, 54, and 57 (Dwayne Deesing); pp. 55 and 56 (Randy Cutter); pp. 104, 206 *left*, and 258 *right* (Lili Weik); and pp. 226 and 230 (Roy Ramsey).

Illustration credits: Cathia Mooney Strickland (pp. 7–177); Sharon Ashby (pp. 199–200, 234–240, 243, and 245–8); Anna Jane White-Mullin (pp. 207, 221, 231–3, 241 *left*, 243 *bottom*, 249, 270–333).

Book design by Carrie Fradkin

Typefaces: Rotis Semi Sans, Myriad, Kennerly

10 9 8 7 6 5 4 3 2 1

This book is dedicated to

Frank Madden of Frank Madden Show Stable

for his unfailing friendship through the years.

Contents

Foreword

Anna Jane White-Mullin's newest release, *The Complete Guide to Hunter Seat Training, Showing, and Judging*, is an updated, all-inclusive version of her two previously released books. The text bridges the gap between the principles of horsemanship for the trainer and the student and the rules that govern how a horse and rider are judged at horse shows. The book has two sections, the first on training and the second on judging.

With diagrams, sequential pictorials and detailed instructions for training horses and riders, the first section uses principles of instruction the author learned while working with equestrian icons Gordon Wright, George Morris, Ronnie Mutch, and Bertalan de Nemethy. Exercises for the horse and rider that coincide with the questions a rider faces while executing a course, pointers on how to choose the best equitation horse, and tips on how to deal with the anxiety that sometimes accompanies competition are highlights of the first section.

In order to become an accomplished equestrian, or to become an accomplished athlete in any sport for that matter, an individual competitor has to adopt a long-term view to skill building. As a junior competitor, I found that mastering the necessary skills from one level of the sport helped in the transition to the next level. The skill sets presented in the book are clearly written and well illustrated. The complex aspects of the skill sets are made understandable and are extremely useful to junior riders interested in improving their performance.

One of the highlights in the second section is how a standardized system of judging hunters and hunt seat equitation determines how one round may receive the top score over another. Additional areas of importance include how to distinguish a beginner from an intermediate and advanced rider, how to identify correct form in a flat or over fences class, and how to demonstrate correct rider position in hunt seat equitation. The author explains the process of judging so that anyone interested in the sport can understand its standards.

The book is a necessary read for anyone interested in equestrian sport. It reinforces the value of repetition and practice, and acknowledges the need for a thorough understanding of all aspects of competition. As a young equestrian professional with the responsibility of training horses and teaching riders, this current and up-to-date guide about both sides of the horse show world will prove invaluable.

Maria Schaub
Winner of the 2008 WIHS Equitation Finals and 2008 North American Equitation Championship

Introduction

Over the years, numerous books have been written about training horses and riders. Although many principles remain the same, the sport of showing hunters has evolved to a performance level that requires a more classical and thorough preparation of the show hunter and the hunter seat equitation rider.

In *The Complete Guide to Hunter Seat Training, Showing, and Judging,* Ms. White-Mullin has provided a blueprint for success in today's Hunter and Hunter Seat Equitation Divisions. It is a work to be studied, and an invaluable guide to all trainers and riders. Theoretical material, which can be confusing, is presented in a clear, concise and fully understandable manner.

Historically, dressage had been regarded as a discipline that had little application to the training of show hunters. However, as outside courses began to disappear and hunters started to show in rings that required more balance and lateral bending, the use of basic dressage training became useful and necessary in order to produce winning performances. Ms. White-Mullin describes these training movements in detail, and the diagrams and photo illustrations give the reader a very clear mental picture of how to correctly perform them.

Ms. White-Mullin also provides tips that are insightful and helpful in solving training problems. Expanding one's knowledge and using a thinking approach to riding will clearly result in a better partnership with the horse. Training a horse is a great responsibility, and it is vital to know how a horse thinks and reacts to the rider's aids.

The American Forward Seat System of riding is the foundation for training and showing in the Hunter and Hunter Seat Equitation Divisions. Ms. White-Mullin presents an updated version of the essentials of horsemanship and provides a thorough analysis of all flatwork and gymnastic exercises to improve a rider's skills.

These basic skills and the dedication to working consistently in a training system are fundamental to becoming competitive in today's shows. Like pairs skaters, the horse and rider must practice together until they perform smoothly and in unison. I urge you to practice the exercises in this book and study the diagrams for executing the lateral movements in USEF Tests 1 – 19. As a judge, I often see the turn on the haunches, forehand, and the counter canter performed with an improper bend, or clashing aids.

A better comprehension of the Open Numerical Judging System, as well as what the judges are penalizing or rewarding, will make for a better informed exhibitor who knows what to improve or how to salvage a score. Learn to pay attention to the details described in this book, because during a performance the judge is evaluating every movement throughout the course. Strategies for showing in a flat class and understanding the frame of the horse required for that class can make the difference between winning and losing. You'll find Ms. White-Mullin's tips on showmanship and analysis of a week at a show are particularly enlightening and can markedly improve results.

In closing, it is important to remember that the welfare of the horse is paramount. Having greater knowledge of the classical training techniques will result in a more productive and compassionate training program. Be kind and patient, and build trust and confidence in your horse. Keep this book handy as a reference guide. It will help you attain harmony with your horse and fulfilling achievements in the show ring.

Chrystine J. Tauber
Former member of the USET Show Jumping Team, USEF Secretary and member of the Executive Committee and Board of Directors, USHJA Vice President, USEF "R" judge for hunters, hunter seat equitation, and jumpers, and FEI-approved international course designer and jumper judge

Preface

The Complete Guide to Hunter Seat Training, Showing and Judging is intended to set a national standard of practical, safe, and humane training and showing practices that will enable horse and rider to meet the established standards of judging in America. Presenting the judging standards as well, the book encompasses the full spectrum of the sport, which accounts for its title.

The first half, "Training and Showing Procedures for Hunters and Hunter Seat Riders," lays out procedures that are common among top American riders and trainers—practices that encompass sound theoretical knowledge and depend upon a good work ethic to improve the skill of horse and rider. This is not a book of "quick fixes," involving gadgets or shortcuts to achieve a goal, but rather is a step-by-step guide to success in the show ring based on proficiency. This section is addressed to the rider, but should be helpful for trainers, parents, or others interested in the sport. It goes beyond USEF Tests 1–19 to include movements such as haunches-in, haunches-out, leg-yield, and shoulder-in, which are part of the NCAA flat tests, and the half-pass and modified pirouette, which are schooling movements that help the horse and rider bridge the gap between hunter and jumper classes. The training procedures are a collection of those gained through personal instruction from such fine teachers as Gordon Wright, George Morris, and Ronnie Mutch (hunters and hunter seat equitation) and Bertalan de Nemethy (jumpers).

The second half of the book, entitled "Judging Hunters and Hunter Seat Riders," provides a detailed explanation of the judging standards in America. It is the most current version of my book Judging Hunters and Hunter Seat Equitation, which was endorsed in 1985 by the United States Equestrian Federation (then known as the American Horse Shows Association) as a guide for judges. Now in its fourth edition, it has been updated through the years to reflect changes in hunter and hunter-seat equitation rules. This section is addressed to judges, but should also be helpful for riders, trainers, parents, and others interested in the competitive aspect of the sport.

I am especially grateful to Frank and Stacia Madden, who provided demonstration riders in the midst of a very busy show schedule, and to Bill Johnson of HorsePix Photography, who took thousands of shots to capture the precise moments I wanted to show. I hope this book will be of service for years to come to all who love the sport of hunter seat riding.

Anna Jane White-Mullin
Gadsden, Alabama

Note to the Reader

The photographic examples that accompany the book are a combination of demonstration riders showing correct and incorrect aspects of riding and riders photographed by horse show photographers during public performance. These captured moments are intended for instructional use only and in no way indicate the overall ability of rider and horse.

In the training section of the book, italicized words indicate that a definition is included at that point. A glossary is also provided in the back of the book. It includes definitions of both the italicized words and any equestrian idioms that appear in quotation marks within the text.

In the judging section of the book, I will often "pin the class" by placing the errors discussed in their order of severity. In every case, I am assuming the horses being pinned are the *only* horses in the class, for many of the faults that will be placed would keep the horses that committed them out of the ribbons in most competitions.

Acknowledgments

I would like to acknowledge the many people who have helped me during the 23 years in which I've sought to chronicle American standards in equine sport. Some of them are no longer with us, but their legacy remains in the level of excellence they helped establish and pass on to future generations. My gratitude to them all:

J.A. "Bucky" Reynolds

Christina Schlusemeyer

George H. Morris

William C. Steinkraus

Kenneth M. Wheeler

Frank Madden

Chrystine J. Tauber

Joe Fargis

John Rush, III

Leo Conroy

Conrad Homfeld

Tim Kees

Michael O. Page

Stephen O. Hawkins

Daniel P. Lenehan

A. Eugene Cunningham

Earl "Red" Frazier

Charles Dennehy, Jr.

Bertalan de Nemethy

Sam Register

Gabor Foltenyi

Col. Donald W. Thackeray

Andrew B. DeSzinay

Major General J.R. Burton

Dr. M.J. Shively

Dr. Charles Crowe

Dr. Milton D. Kingsbury

Dr. Ron Blackwell

Special Thanks To

Riding Demonstrators

Carolyn Curcio

Chelsea Moss

Maria Schaub

Jessie Springsteen

Tracy Graham

Julie Cleveland

Meredith Darst

Holly Hirschman

Photographers

Bill Johnson

Randy Cutter

Dwayne Deesing

Lili Weik

Julia Borysewicz

Roy Ramsey

Conformation Drawings

Sharon Ashby

Jump Companies

Jumps West—Allyn Banalstyne

L.J. Enterprises

Owners of Photographic Locations

Beacon Hill Show Stables—Frank & Stacia Madden

Brownland Farm—Mack & Sissie Anderton

La Cresta—Shelley Wilson

Those Who Offered Additional Assistance

Judy's Tack Shop—Judy Orbesen

Fox Den Interiors—Robert Bruce & John Hinkle

Mindy Darst

Colleen Holton

Dwight Hall

Fuzzy Mayo of Jumps by Fuzzy

Jan Krisle of Windcrest Photograph

Thom A. Brede

Trafalgar Square Books Staff

Caroline Robbins

Martha Cook

Rebecca Didier

My Literary Agent

Madelyn Larsen

PART ONE

TRAINING & SHOWING PROCEDURES FOR HUNTERS & HUNTER SEAT RIDERS

The Elements of Flatwork

Flatwork: The Cutting Edge of Success

Flatwork is the adaptation of the schooling movements and principles of dressage to the needs of hunters, equitation horses, and jumpers. While dressage encompasses difficult maneuvers such as the passage and piaffe, in which the horse's steps have a tremendous amount of suspension, these movements have no reasonable application for horses being shown in the hunter, jumper, or equitation divisions. For this reason, hunter seat riders must choose the dressage exercises which are the most beneficial and disregard those that are not helpful in achieving their goals.

In the discussion of flatwork, some terminology maybe unfamiliar to you, so I will begin with a brief description of important terms. The basic elements of flatwork are pace, bending, and transitions. *Pace* is the speed at which a horse travels in each gait. *Bending* refers to the horse's body being positioned on a curve to either the left or right. *Transitions* are the brief periods of change between one gait and another and are categorized as either *upward transitions,* which are changes to a faster gait, or *downward transitions,* which are changes to a slower gait.

Advanced concepts of flatwork are impulsion, collection, and lengthening. *Impulsion* is the degree of thrust, or power, a horse has as it moves. *Collection* is the increased engagement of the horse's quarters for the benefit of lightness and mobility in the forehand. *Lengthening* is the forward swing of the horse's limbs in free and moderately extended steps, demonstrating impulsion from the hindquarters.

Although the word "flatwork" has been used in the United States for decades, prior to the 1960s it referred only to the most basic training exercises that would enable the rider to start, stop, turn, and regulate the pace of his horse. When I was a child riding in the early 1960s, only a few coaches talked about bending, and anyone who suggested the use of collection for a hunter became the center of controversy. Critics believed that collecting the animal would be detrimental to the natural beauty of its way of moving and would make the horse more excitable, while advocates of collection found that it provided greater and more subtle control of the horse. The debate finally waned when riders who practiced the more advanced concepts of flatwork were regularly winning, not only in the equitation and jumper divisions, but also in the hunter division.

By 1970, bending had become well established as a necessity in the show ring, and collection was generally recognized as part of the training regimen for equitation horses, jumpers, and hunters. When it became apparent that more collection was needed to perform precision work in the equitation division than to accomplish the basic tasks of the hunter division, some riders chose to use different horses for each. The horse that tends to be an "equitation type" has natural elevation in its forehand because of its conformation, a medium length of stride that normally covers about 12 feet but can be readily extended to 13 feet, a fairly flat jumping style, smooth-riding gaits, and an absolutely calm temperament. These elements make it easier for the rider to perform precision movements on the flat, control the horse within the lines of a complicated course, and stay in a fixed position over fences and on the flat. In contrast, an exceedingly long natural stride, a keen temperament, a powerful thrust over the fences, or gaits that are bumpy to sit on make it difficult for a rider to be competitive in the equitation division.

Of course, the ideal horse can do it all. One that has a medium-length flowing stride, good jumping form, a quiet temperament, and naturally good balance can make the adjustments necessary to be successful in both divisions. Throughout the book, however, I will refer to "hunters" and "equitation horses" separately, not only as acknowledgment that some riders continue to use different horses for each division, but also to clarify which exercises are appropriate for a horse according to the division in which it competes.

The 1980s further stressed the importance of flatwork, and this emphasis has continued to increase to the present. Now, a rider simply isn't going to get a ribbon on the flat or over fences in the equitation division at a large show unless he has a strong background on the flat. The tougher the competition, the more precise flatwork is required. Medal, Maclay, and USEF Talent Search classes all require it, and it is often the deciding factor in placing the riders.

I have heard riders say that they were not interested in the equitation division because they did not enjoy flatwork. However, when you look at who ends up each year with the Horse of the Year Awards in the various hunter divisions or examine the list of the top jumper riders in the country, it will not take long to realize that a rider who is poor in flatwork generally can't keep up in any division with those who do it well.

Work on the flat can be physically difficult, confusing, and frustrating to learn. This is because good flatwork requires precise coordination of your legs, hands, and weight. Once you are proficient on the flat, however, daily exercises will be enjoyable and fulfilling as your horse progresses. You will then view flatwork as a logical process which enhances the horse's abilities and minimizes its weaknesses, allowing your animal to be the best athlete it can be. Best of all, you will no longer consider flatwork boring, but appreciate it for what it is: the cutting edge of success that puts your horse's performance before others when the pressure is really on.

The Components of Flatwork

Frame: Collection and Lengthening

The horse's frame is the length of the animal's body as controlled by the rider. When a rider shortens his horse's body and length of step, he is collecting the horse into a "shorter frame"; when he elongates the body and length of step, he is lengthening the horse into a "longer frame."

A horse traveling on loose reins has "no frame." Its neck stretches forward to the point that its chin protrudes outward; its hocks move back and forth in sloppy movements; its topline appears flat and stiff; and it travels with most of its weight on the forehand (figs. 1.1 A & B).

Long Frame

If a rider establishes contact with the horse's mouth, but does not shorten the length of the horse's frame, hunter riders refer to the horse as being in a "long frame" (fig. 1.2). A long frame can be beneficial in certain circumstances. For example, in an under-saddle class, a horse with an excitable, "hot" temperament, may be shown to its best advantage in a long frame. Making hardly any demand on the horse to accept the weight of the hands, the rider can minimize the animal's nervous appearance.

A long frame can also be used to de-emphasize a short neck or high head carriage (fig. 1.3). By driving the horse forward with your legs, you can cause the animal to drop its head down and out (fig. 1.4).

The long frame is appropriate in beginner equitation classes and for under-saddle classes in the circumstances described above. Of course, judges realize when a rider is using a long frame to hide a problem, but the performance may beat that of someone else who has not been so clever in minimizing his horse's weaknesses.

1.1 A & B On loose reins, the horse is "strung out" with "no frame" (A). According to the USEF Rulebook, in under-saddle classes, "Light contact with the horse's mouth is required." Consequently, drooping reins are unacceptable in under-saddle, as well as equitation classes. Notice how well the same horse travels in a "medium frame" (B), with long, balanced steps and a rounded topline.

1.2 With the rider allowing the maximum length of rein that she can and still keep a steady contact with the mouth, she has the horse balanced in a "long frame." For a horse that is short-coupled—i.e., not long in the back—and is naturally well-balanced such as this animal, the long frame can show the horse to its best advantage in an under-saddle class, enabling it to travel with the longest stride possible.

1.3 This jumper reacts to contact on the reins by raising its head and traveling with a stiff, concave back and shortened steps.

1.4 The rider demonstrates how lightening contact on the reins and pressing the horse forward with her legs encourages the horse to stretch its neck down and out, minimizing the problem shown in fig. 1.3. The horse now has long steps filled with impulsion and a beautiful, relaxed arch to its neck.

Medium Frame

Many horses are shown to their best advantage in a "medium frame" in under-saddle classes. For example, a horse that is long in its body will often appear sloppy if it is allowed to travel in a long frame (figs. 1.5 A & B). The medium frame results in slightly shorter steps at each gait, but what is lost in length of step is usually outweighed by the positive results of a better balanced horse. In a medium frame, the animal's hocks lose less energy backward in the posterior phase of each step than when the horse is in a long frame. The energy that would normally be lost backward is trapped by the rider's legs and cast forward, providing greater power in the anterior phase of each step and enabling the hocks to support some of the forehand weight.

1.5 A & B There is a range of uses for the "medium frame." A "medium-long frame" (A) is appropriate for an under-saddle class and especially useful to show a long-bodied horse to its best advantage. A "medium-short frame" (B) is the norm for an equitation class.

1.6 Notice the difference between the horse in a long frame, indicated by the shaded area, and the horse in a medium frame. When collected into a medium frame, the horse's steps are shorter, its head is brought closer to the vertical, its neck is arched slightly more, and its hocks move within a more restricted area—that is, remaining engaged and not trailing as far behind the animal each step.

To collect the horse into a medium frame, you not only restrict the backward movement of the hocks with your legs, but also the forward movement of the head and neck with your hands. In response to the coordinated action of your legs and hands, the animal will raise and arch its neck slightly, making its shoulder carriage higher, lightening its forehand, and causing its head to come in closer to the vertical (fig. 1.6).

The medium frame retains much of the natural flow of horizontal energy, while channeling a portion of that energy upward, providing lightness and balance in the horse, as well as greater control and comfort for the rider. When a horse is stationary, the vertical line running through its center of gravity is located just in front of the place where a hunter rider sits. As the horse's pace increases, the center of gravity is shifted increasingly forward. Through collection, the center of gravity can be shifted backward, enabling the rider to be closer to it and producing a smoother ride (fig. 1.7).

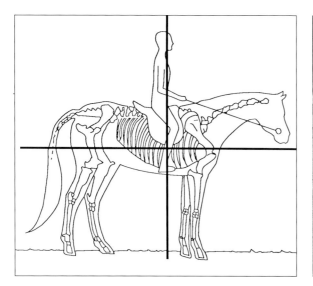

1.7 The stationary horse's center of gravity is located at the intersection of a vertical line falling just behind the withers and a horizontal line running from the point of the shoulder to the buttocks. A rider's center of gravity is located in the middle of his pelvis, so the closer you sit to the pommel, the more nearly you will be in balance with your horse. It is also important to note that the animal's center of gravity shifts forward with increased speed, but can be made to shift backward through the use of collection.

1.8 Floating across the ground, this excellent mover travels in a medium frame with a great deal of impulsion, but no sign of tension, achieving the ideal picture of relaxation and freedom of movement.

If you watch an under-saddle class, you will usually see riders on horses in a long frame rising out of the saddle at the canter. On a tense horse, a rider may be trying to avoid contact with the animal's back; but even if the horse does not have a nervous disposition, the rider will usually rise out of the saddle to avoid the bumpy motion caused by the horse's center of gravity being shifted forward. He literally cannot sit on his horse, for he is just far enough behind the center of gravity to make the ride very uncomfortable.

Not only is collecting the horse into a medium frame beneficial for making the rider more comfortable and for balancing a long, sloppy-looking animal, but it is also useful for giving an already good or excellent mover a little panache. The lighter forehand creates a slight degree of suspension in each step, making the good mover appear to be a much better mover than it really is and giving the gifted horse an even flashier, floating appearance as it moves (fig. 1.8).

The only substantial drawback of the medium frame is that nervous or sensitive horses may not appear as relaxed as when they're ridden with less pressure from the rider's hands, legs, and seat. If the horse plays with the bit a great deal, tilts its head from side to side, opens its mouth, pins its ears, or twists its tail in resistance to your signals when being collected into a medium frame, then the longer frame might be

1.9 Traveling in a short frame, the horse has its hocks engaged and its forehand light. The neck is arched higher than in the previous pictures demonstrating a long or medium frame. It is the combination of the engaged hocks carrying some of the forehand weight and the higher neck carriage lightening the weight of the forehand that results in a horse's center of gravity being shifted backward as a result of collection. This backward shift of the center of gravity and the shorter steps that accompany a short frame enable the horse to perform precise movements easier than when in a medium or long frame.

1.10 When collected from a long or medium frame into a short frame, the horse's steps become shorter, its neck arches more, and the front plane of its face draws closer to the vertical. There is less energy lost backward in the posterior phase of each step as more power is added to the anterior phase.

a preferable alternative in an under-saddle class. The medium frame is not only appropriate for under-saddle classes, but also for intermediate and advanced equitation classes.

Short Frame

The short frame substantially restricts the backward flow of energy from the horse's hocks and channels it upward, so that the motion of the hocks appears to be circular. The animal's neck rises and arches to a greater degree than at the medium frame, and the head moves to a position only a few degrees in front of the vertical (fig. 1.9). The forehand becomes quite light, and the horse's steps are

shortened as the animal's body is collected from a medium to a short frame.

The short frame is used to achieve maximum control of the horse during equitation tests of precision, such as the counter canter or changes of lead down the centerline of the arena. It is also used in training jumpers, enabling the rider to employ upper-level schooling movements on the flat to supple his horse (fig. 1.10).

Flatwork vs. Dressage

In order to understand flatwork, it is helpful to know how and why it differs from dressage. One of the main differences pertains to the categories of length of frame. In dressage, the "long frame" for hunters still would be considered "no frame"; the "medium frame" for hunters would be a "long frame"; and the "short frame" for hunters would be a "medium frame." What then is a "short frame" to a dressage rider?

A short frame in dressage refers to the utmost engagement of the hocks and elevation of the forehand. In this frame, the horse can perform such difficult movements as the passage, in which the trot has as much vertical as forward motion, and the piaffe, in which the horse maintains the sequence of the trot in place (fig. 1.11). These movements go well beyond the requirements for hunters, equitation horses, and jumpers in terms of vertical motion on the flat.

Lower-Level and Upper-Level Movements

Daily practice of lower-level dressage movements, such as the circle, half-turn, halt, and shoulder-in, promote suppleness in the horse and obedience to the rider's commands. The lower-level movements are essential to the training of all hunters, equitation horses, and jumpers.

Since a greater degree of precision is required in advanced equitation classes and jumper classes, the rider must prepare for these by incorporating upper-level dressage movements into his daily routine. Some of the movements, such as the turn on the haunches, flying change of lead, and counter canter, are included in USEF "Tests 1–19," the official tests used in hunter seat equitation classes. Other upper-level movements, such as the travers (haunches-in), renvers (haunches-out), half-pass (two-track), and pirouette (the turn on the haunches at the canter), are only used for schooling advanced equitation horses and jumpers, since the performance of these tests is not required in the show ring.

Some basic criteria for distinguishing lower-level movements from upper-level movements:

1.11 The horse is performing the "passage," an upper-level dressage movement in which the animal trots with prolonged suspension at each step while maintaining regularity in the cadence. To perform this difficult movement, the animal must be collected into a very short frame.

▶   Lower-level movements require a moderate degree of rider manipulation of the horse's horizontal energy into vertical energy, while upper-level movements demand a much greater degree of vertical thrust of the horse's momentum.

▶   Lower-level movements that require the horse to move sideways while bent to the left or right (such as the leg-yield, shoulder-in, and basic turn on the forehand) are based on the principle of the horse moving away from the direction in which it is bent; while the upper-level movements performed with the horse in a bent position (such as the haunches-in, haunches-out, advanced turn on the forehand, turn on the haunches, half-pass, and modified pirouette) require the horse to move toward the direction in which it is bent.

1.12 The rider's leg is in "at the girth" position, which enables her to bend the horse and drive it forward. It is extremely important for this position to be correct in placement and secure on the horse's side, since it places the rider's calf over the horse's stationary center of gravity and is thus closer to the horse's center of gravity in motion (which moves forward as speed increases) than is the "behind the girth" position. When viewed from the side, the front of the rider's knee and the toe of the boot should be on the same vertical line.

1.13 Approximately 4 inches behind at-the-girth position is "behind the girth" position, which controls the haunches. It signals the horse to use the proper hind leg to start the canter depart (in this example, it would signal the right hind to start the sequence for the left lead); it keeps the haunches from drifting outward on bending movements, such as circling or bending around the corners of the ring; and it initiates and maintains sideways motion during movements such as the leg-yield, half-pass, turn on the haunches, and modified pirouette.

(Note: The counter canter and flying change are two tests that do not meet both of the criteria stated above, but are considered upper-level tests because of their degree of difficulty.)

The Rider's Aids

The rider's *aids* are both his natural and artificial means of communicating with the horse. The *natural aids* are the rider's legs, hands, weight, and, on rare occasion, voice. The *artificial aids* are the spurs, stick (also called "crop" or "bat"), bit, martingale, or any other type of equipment that reinforces the rider's body commands.

The word "aid" is not only used to describe the means of communication, but also the position of the rider's body when giving a command. For example, a teacher might ask his student, "What are the aids for the canter?"

The student would reply, "The aids for the canter are the inside leg positioned at the girth, the outside leg behind the girth, and the hands positioned in an inside indirect rein."

There are two basic leg positions used in flatwork. The first, referred to as *at the girth,* is the placement of the rider's calf against the horse's flesh just behind the back edge of the girth. This position is used both to bend the horse and drive it forward (fig. 1.12). The second leg position is referred to as *behind the girth,* which is about 4 inches farther back than the first. This position affects the lateral, or sideways, movement of the horse's haunches and is also used to drive the horse forward (fig. 1.13).

The word, "lateral," defined by Webster as "pertaining to the side," has two applications in hunter seat riding. *Lateral aids* refers to the use of the rider's aids on the same side of the horse, such as the right leg and right hand. This is opposed to *diagonal aids,* which are applied on opposite sides of the horse, such as the right leg and left hand.

Lateral movements, however, refers to any suppling exercises which are used to lessen the horse's stiffness from side to side. They range from the simple circle to more difficult movements such as the modified pirouette or half-pass. Even bending a horse around the corners of a ring can be said to be a lateral exercise, for it affects the animal's suppleness from side to side.

The rider's hands complement the legs by directing the horse and controlling the amount of energy that is allowed to flow forward in horizontal motion with each step. The hands perform these tasks through the use of five reins aids and a technique called the "half-halt." The five reins aids and their functions are as follows (figs. 1.14 A–E):

1   the direct rein maintains straightness
2   the indirect rein bends the horse to the left or right
3   the leading rein (also known as an "opening rein") leads a horse to the left or right
4   the neck rein (also known as a "bearing rein") exerts pressure on one side of the horse's neck, causing the animal to move in the opposite direction
5   the pulley rein provides extreme force in an upward and backward action against the horse's mouth to stop the animal in emergency situations

1.14 A–E The "direct rein" maintains straightness in the horse's head and neck, with no evidence of bending to the right or left. It affects the horse's balance from forehand to haunches (A). The "indirect rein" causes the horse's head and neck to be bent slightly to the right or left. Pictured is a right indirect rein, in which the rider's right hand is placed above the withers and the left hand moves outward and forward to allow the horse to bend to the right. (If the right hand is placed in front of the withers, as shown, the indirect rein displaces the horse's weight from the right shoulder to the left shoulder; and if the indirect rein is placed behind the withers, the horse's weight is displaced from the right shoulder to the left haunch. The behind-the-withers position is useful in controlling the haunches in lateral movements that require the horse to move toward the direction it is bent.) The indirect rein affects the horse's balance from side to side (B). The "opening rein" and "leading rein" are different in degree, but are categorized together because they work through the same principle. Both are directional aids, which guide the horse to one side or the other. The opening rein is more subtle, with the rider's hand moving away from the horse only 5 or 6 inches; while the leading rein opens as far as 2 feet to one side to literally lead the horse in the desired direction. Pictured is the action of the leading rein (C). The "neck rein," also called the "bearing rein," requires both of the rider's hands to shift in one direction so that one rein acts as an opening rein to guide the horse, while the other presses against the horse's neck to push the animal away. In the photograph, the rider's left hand is in opening-rein position, while the right hand is over and in front of the withers, causing the right rein to make contact with the horse's neck—that is to "bear" against the neck. The neck rein enables the rider to restrict the horse's drift to the outside of a turn (D). The pulley rein is an emergency rein aid. With one hand fixed in the dip just in front of the horse's withers and the other hand pulling back and up, the rider is able to exert extreme force against the horse's mouth when the animal refuses to respond to normal hand pressure. If the pulley rein is applied while the horse is traveling near the railing, pull back with the hand nearest the rail. This way, if the horse begins to turn toward the active hand, the railing will help you stop the animal (E).

1.15 A–C The rider maintains impulsion with her legs while bracing with her back and squeezing her hands to ask the horse to half-halt, so that it becomes softer in the mouth and lighter in the forehand (A). The rider slightly eases off the rein pressure (B) and drives the horse forward with her legs so that the animal takes long, balanced, and rhythmical steps while maintaining the light forehand accomplished through the half-halt (C).

Half-Halts

The *half-halt* is a technique that consists of a sustaining leg aid and a two-phase movement of the hands. As your legs maintain the engagement of the hocks, your hands close slightly to add pressure to the horse's mouth, which is Phase One of the hand movement. The simultaneous application of the driving and restricting aids momentarily traps the horse at both ends, so that the animal seeks the logical escape route, which is upward, by raising its shoulder, neck, and head, making its forehand lighter. At the moment the horse becomes lighter in front, ease the pressure on the reins to reward the horse for the proper response. This is Phase Two of the hand movement (figs. 1.15 A–C).

The basic give-and-take motion of the hands should be instilled in a rider starting with his earliest lessons. He should not be allowed to take an unrelenting hold on a horse's mouth to slow it down, but should learn to take back slightly, then ease off as the horse slows down, so that the animal receives the reward of a giving hand. This is necessary to reinforce correct behavior. The next step of coordinating the supporting leg with the flexible hand will be much easier for the rider to learn if he is already in the habit of keeping his hand mobile, rather than fixed, during a downward transition.

The half-halt can be used for any of these three functions: (1) to balance and slow the horse while maintaining

he also uses the half-halt to alter the horse's frame when needed, for it enables him to collect the horse and lighten its forehand for precision work. To alter the frame through the use of the half-halt, you must support the horse's rhythm with your legs, so that the animal collects without slowing down and breaking into a lower gait.

Half-halts vary greatly in their length and weight. A single half-halt might last one second on a well-trained, agreeable animal or five seconds on a horse that leans against the bit. (Generally speaking, if the half-halt lasts longer than five seconds, you're not really half-halting, but have gotten into a pulling match with your horse.) The half-halt might require only a squeeze of the hands with supporting legs, or it might take a well-anchored seat to reinforce arms briefly fixed against a strong animal. The amount of pressure needed to accomplish the half-halt, then, will depend entirely upon the horse's response to the aids (fig. 1.16).

Between half-halts, maintain a light, but steady feel of the horse's mouth. If the animal tries to avoid rein contact by raising its head or bringing it in toward its chest, press the horse forward with your legs. In reaction to your driving aid, it will attempt to lengthen its stride, which will shift its center of gravity forward and cause it to stretch its head and neck outward, creating more weight on the bit.

Added weight on the bit provides a firmer feel of the horse's forward movement. Men generally feel comfortable with more weight than women do, since many women find it to be a little intimidating. Although a woman may prefer less weight in her hands, she should not be content with the feeling that she is "carrying the reins" without feeling any weight from the horse's mouth, for this means the horse is not properly moving onto the bit in response to her legs (figs. 1.17 A–H).

There should be the steady feeling of the reins lying with a slight heaviness against the base of the fingers. If the

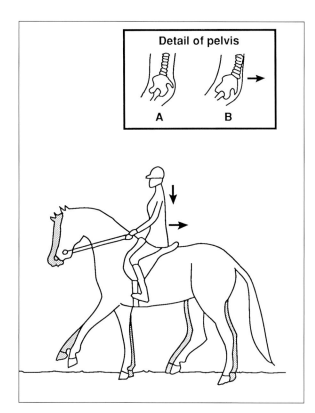

1.16 The detail of the pelvis shows the rider's lower back in normal position (A) and braced during the half-halt, when more pressure is needed on the horse's mouth than the hands alone can provide (B). Notice in the drawing of horse and rider that the rider's shoulders exert pressure downward, causing the muscles in her back to be flexed. The combination of flexed back muscles and the backward tilt of the pelvis enables the rider to use her upper-body weight to reinforce her hands during the half-halt.

the same gait; (2) to balance and slow the horse during the change from an upper gait to a lower one; or (3) to shorten the horse's frame while maintaining the same gait. At the lower levels of riding, the half-halt is used to balance the horse when going into turns, regulate the speed of the gaits, and help in accomplishing smooth transitions from upper gaits to lower ones. As the rider's education progresses,

1.17 A–H Shown on course, the rider is "carrying the reins," rather than establishing steady contact with the horse's mouth (A). When reins are held at the proper length, the rider has a light, but steady feel of the mouth, providing complete control of the horse (B). There are many variations on rein length, hand position, and the weight of the hands on the horse's mouth, including open hands, which tempt the horse to pull the reins out of them (C); low hands, which break the connection between the horse's mouth and the rider's elbow and back, which is the rider's greatest source of upper-body strength (D); wide hands that enable the horse to wander easily from side to side and overly erect hands that stiffen the rider's upper body (E); low, fixed hands that press against the sensitive bars of the horse's mouth and cause it to raise its head (F); flat hands, known as "puppy hands," that break the connection from the bit to the rider's elbow and back, leaving the rider with little power when needed in an emergency (G); and high hands that also break the direct connection from the bit to the rider's elbow and back, making the hands ineffective in controlling the horse (H).

horse is relaxed, the muscles in its neck and jaw will create this feeling of relaxed weight on the reins. To sustain this steady contact, you must be relaxed from the shoulder to the hand, so that as the horse moves, your arms follow the motion of its head and neck (fig. 1.18). You can then adjust the weight on the bit by half-halting if the horse becomes too heavy during work or by driving the horse to the bit with your legs if the contact becomes too light.

Half-halts should be used liberally throughout all of your flatwork. In the span of a 20-minute work session, a good rider uses endless numbers of them to balance the horse, regulate its pace, or change its frame. They are used in

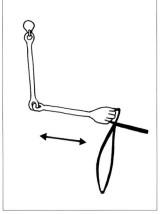

1.18 The diagram demonstrates the proper function of the rider's arm. The upper arm should move freely, as though it were loosely hung from a hook at the shoulder. The elbow should allow continuous horizontal freedom of movement as it follows the back-and-forth motion of the horse's head and neck.

closest succession during downward transitions and should be progressively lighter as the pace of the horse lessens, rewarding the animal for the proper response.

Pace

Pace is the speed at which a horse travels in each gait. The working walk, used for both equitation classes on the flat and under-saddle classes, is a four-beat gait in which the horse travels approximately 4 miles per hour, or 352 feet per minute. Since the walk involves little pace, your upper body must be only a couple of degrees in front of the vertical to be with the motion at this gait (fig. 1.19).

In all gaits, the sequence of the feet is considered to start with a hind foot because the haunches are the horse's source of power. However, the sequence at the walk actually starts with one of the horse's forefeet. If the horse were asked to walk from the halt and began with its left forefoot, the sequence of footfalls would follow as right hind, right fore, left hind, left fore, and so on.

The feet are placed in rapid succession at the walk, so that at different moments in the sequence the horse's weight is supported by a diagonal pair of legs, a lateral pair of legs, or three legs. In the moments when the horse's body is supported only by a lateral pair of legs—that is, two legs on the same side—its balance is unstable. It moves its head and neck upward and inward to maintain its balance until the other legs are placed to help support its weight, at which moment the horse's head and neck drop and move forward again. These backward and forward motions of the head should be followed by your hands when the horse is in a long or medium frame at the walk. When the animal is collected into a short frame, the elevation of its shoulders, head, and neck help it to keep its balance during the moments of potential instability, and there is very little back and forth motion of the head.

1.19 At the walk, the rider's upper body is slightly in front of the vertical, just enough to be with the motion of the horse at this relatively slow gait.

The working trot rising (also called the posting trot) is a two-beat gait, with a speed of approximately 8 miles per hour, or 704 feet per minute. The feet strike the ground in diagonal pairs at the trot, with the right hind and left fore striking together and the left hind and right fore striking together. Your hands remain steady because the alternating diagonal pairs of feet provide stability for the animal as it moves.

When the horse is moving clockwise at the posting trot, rise when its left foreleg goes forward and sit when it strikes the ground. Moving counterclockwise, rise when the horse's right foreleg goes forward and sit when it strikes the ground (figs. 1.20 A & B).

By freeing the horse's outside foreleg, posting allows the animal to remain balanced on turns. If you rise and sit in the incorrect rhythm, you are "posting on the wrong diagonal." On corners, this error causes your weight to land on the horse's back just as the animal is reaching with its outside foreleg, which must cover more ground each step than the inside foreleg does on a turn. The result is loss of balance

1.20 A & B At the posting trot, you should rise as the horse's outside foreleg moves forward (A) and sit as it strikes the ground (B). During the sitting phase, your upper body should be no more than 20 degrees in front of the vertical when the horse is in a medium frame.

for the horse, creating an awkward feeling for you and often making the horse appear lame.

At the working trot rising, close your hip angle forward to allow your torso to follow the horizontal motion of the horse. When the horse is in a medium frame, your upper body should be inclined no more than 20 degrees in front of the vertical at the posting trot. The degree of inclination will vary somewhat if you change the horse's frame. For example, if a horse is put into a shorter frame for upper-level flatwork exercises, your upper body should reflect the vertical channeling of energy by straightening to a slightly more vertical position.

The working trot sitting is performed at the same tempo as the working trot rising. During the working trot sitting, the upper body is only a couple of degrees in front of the vertical (fig. 1.21). This nearly upright position allows your weight to sink into the horse's back, so that you are firmly glued on and able to follow the motion with your seat and lower back.

The working trot with a lengthening of stride is executed at about 10 miles per hour, or 880 feet per minute. To lengthen the stride, increase the pressure of your calves until the horse begins to take longer steps. As it stretches its head and neck forward during lengthening, follow this movement with your hands; but be sure to keep a steady feel of the reins, for even a small amount of slack will encourage a break into the canter. It is very important to maintain a steady tempo during lengthening, since loss of regularity is another cause of the horse breaking into an upper gait.

When the lengthening of stride is performed at the posting trot, your upper body should be inclined no more than 10 degrees in front of the vertical. This enables you to use your weight as an additional driving aid and promotes lightness in the horse's forehand by shifting your upper-body weight more toward the haunches than at the normal working trot rising (fig. 1.22).

When the lengthening of stride is performed at the sitting trot, open your upper body to the vertical. From this upright position, you can use your weight as a driving aid; but be careful not to lean behind the vertical, for this is an unnecessarily severe position (fig. 1.23).

1.21 At the working trot sitting, your upper body should be in the same position as at the walk, just a couple of degrees in front of the vertical.

1.22 Captured during the sitting phase of the working trot rising with a lengthening of stride, the rider has opened her body to a more erect position than a rider would have at the normal posting trot (see fig. 1.20 B). This lightens the horse's forehand, and enables the rider to subtly use her seat as a driving aid.

1.23 This rider demonstrates an upper body incorrectly positioned behind the vertical during the working trot with a lengthening of stride. The combination of an overly active seat and a braced, behind-the-motion upper body forces the horse to overflex at the poll, causing its head to be pulled behind the vertical.

On the corners of the ring, you can steady the horse slightly. It is not necessary to shorten the frame, for the ends of a hunter arena are usually wide enough to accommodate a sustained lengthening. It will be helpful in competition, however, to collect the horse into a slightly shorter frame for a few steps at the end of the corner preceding the pass in front of the judge, so that the horse will be in the process of lengthening as it makes the pass, giving it a flashy appearance. This is also good insurance, for there is less chance of a horse breaking gait early in the lengthening process than when it has been moving on an extended stride for a long period of time.

The working canter is a three-beat gait ranging between 10 and 12 miles per hour, or 880 feet to 1,056 feet per minute. At the working canter, your body should be positioned just in front of the vertical, to match the upward motion of this gait.

The sequence of the horse's feet at the canter establishes what is referred to as the "lead." When starting in proper sequence moving in a counterclockwise direction, the horse's right hind leg is the first to strike. It is followed by the diagonal pair of the left hind and right fore striking together. Finally, the left fore strikes, completing the sequence of the "left lead." When moving in a clockwise direction, the sequence is reversed, beginning with the left hind leg, followed by the right hind and left fore striking together, and ending with the right foreleg. This sequence is known as the "right lead" (figs. 1.24 A–C).

1.24 A–C Traveling clockwise, the horse picks up the correct (right) lead by striking the first beat of the sequence with its outside hind foot, which lifts the other three legs (A). The second beat of the canter involves the diagonal set of legs—inside hind and outside fore—striking simultaneously. The forward thrust of the inside foreleg at this stage in the sequence makes it appear to be the leading leg. Thus, the horse is said to be on the "right lead" (B). The third and final beat is struck by the inside foreleg (C).

1.25 During a lengthening of stride at the canter, both horse and rider are beautifully balanced and relaxed. The horse is slightly behind the vertical, but does not appear to be pulling or heavy on its forehand as it exhibits tremendous impulsion during full extension.

As a point of interest, when the horse is started into the canter from a halt, it will usually put one foreleg forward to support its forehand before it starts the canter sequence with the diagonally positioned hind leg. The exception to this is when the horse is in a very collected frame, in which case it is well-balanced enough to start the canter beginning with its hind leg.

At the moments during the canter sequence in which one hind leg or one foreleg is supporting the weight of the horse, the animal is unstable. Its head and neck move back and forth during the changes from stability to instability, providing it with a means of catching its balance. Your arms should follow this movement backward slightly as the horse begins the sequence with its outside hind leg, then move forward as its leading leg strikes the ground with

each stride. Again, collection will help the horse keep its balance and minimize the back-and-forth movement of its head and neck.

The working canter with a lengthening of stride is performed at about 14 miles per hour, or 1,232 feet per minute, with the difference between this movement and the basic working canter being length of stride, rather than a change of tempo. When lengthening the stride at the canter, sit in three-point position with your two legs and seat forming three points of contact with the horse. Your upper body should be erect, so that your weight can act as an additional driving aid; but your torso should not drop behind the vertical (fig. 1.25).

Prepare for the working canter with a lengthening of stride by collecting the horse into a short frame at the canter. Then press with your legs, easing off the reins slightly as the horse responds by lengthening. The animal should be steadied in the corners of the ring, but not brought back into a shorter frame unless the size of the ring is prohibitive. Again, during competition, a slight shortening of the frame just before the pass will set up the horse so that it will be balanced and in the process of lengthening as it passes the judge, giving the performance a little flair.

Both the working trot rising with a lengthening of stride and the working canter showing a lengthening of stride are required in the flat phase of the USEF Show Jumping Talent Search Class. The lengthening of stride at the trot can be a particularly brilliant movement and give you the edge you need to win the class. As for the lengthening at the canter, it is important to make a very clear distinction between lengthening and the working canter.

The hand gallop is used for jumping fences and is also one of the USEF's Tests 1–19. It is performed at between 14 and 16 miles per hour, or 1,232 feet to 1,408 feet per minute, and should appear controlled and at a speed appropriate for the size of the arena. At the hand gallop, the horse's footfalls strike in the same three-beat sequence as at the canter. This distinguishes the hand gallop from the faster racing gallop, which through extension of the horse's limbs causes the feet to fall in four separate beats.

You should be in two-point position for the hand gallop, with only your two legs making contact with the horse, and your usual third point of contact, your seat, being raised above the animal's back. The lack of weight makes it easier for the horse to carry you at greater speed and enables it to jump less encumbered.

Your torso should be inclined forward at the hand gallop, "with the motion" of the horse. The angulation will vary somewhat as the horse's stride is shortened or lengthened. For example, when the horse is hand-galloping down the long side of the arena, your hip angle should be closed about 30 degrees in front of the vertical to be with the motion (fig. 1.26 A). Just before the short side of the arena, you should open the angle to a slightly more erect position, so that your upper-body weight can aid your arms in collecting the horse to balance it for the corner (fig. 1.26 B).

In conclusion, pace is the foundation upon which all else is built. If an animal is too slow or too fast, every other aspect of performance will be affected. In a class over fences, a horse moving too slowly may add unnecessary strides between obstacles, refuse to jump, or even plop into the middle of a fence in slow motion. Conversely, the overly fast horse may leave out a stride and dive into a fence, stop abruptly and sling the rider into an obstacle, or run out at a fence and race off. In riding, teaching, and judging, safety should be the first consideration. You must never lose sight of the importance of proper pace in achieving a safe performance that both the rider and onlookers can enjoy.

1.26 A & B Your hip angle should close to about 30 degrees in front of the vertical as your horse hand-gallops out of a corner (A) and should open to a slightly more erect position just before entering a corner, so that your upper-body weight can aid the arms in collecting the horse for the turn (B).

Evenness of pace is another important consideration, for it is the regularity of the horse's footfalls that makes the animal's performance pleasing to the observer. Whether on the flat or over fences, erratic pace robs the performance of its smoothness and points out the rider's and horse's lack of sophistication as a team.

1.27 A–D Compare the momentum of a horse with pace (A) to the more powerful stride of a horse with impulsion (B) as the two push off with the outside hind leg on the first beat of the hand-gallop. At the second beat of the hand-gallop, the difference between the horse with pace (C) and the one with the more powerful stride of impulsion (D) is also evident. Impulsion makes the horse appear round, balanced, powerful and controlled.

Impulsion

Impulsion is the power a horse has in every step. Although impulsion and pace are related, they are not one and the same. The difference is that pace equals speed, while impulsion equals thrust.

It is true that a galloping horse on light rein contact has a tremendous amount of natural impulsion, but this type of impulsion is horizontal energy, which is difficult to control on turns or within obstacles set so that they require the horse to take short strides. For beginner riders, impulsion that comes

1.28 A–C When traveling counterclockwise on a curve, bend the horse to the left with a left indirect rein, using your left leg at the girth to control the horse's left hind leg and your right leg behind the girth to control the horse's right hind leg (A). When traveling on a straightaway, the horse should be positioned straight with a direct rein and both of your legs at the girth (B). When traveling clockwise on a curve, bend the horse to the right with a right indirect rein, your right leg at the girth, and your left leg behind the girth (C).

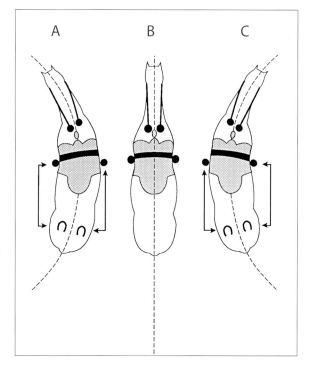

from pace will suffice for a straightforward hunter or equitation course. But when a rider progresses to more complicated courses, he must learn how to use his hands and legs properly to translate the raw energy of pace into the more sophisticated energy of impulsion (figs. 1.27 A–D).

Bending

Bending is directing the horse through the use of your hands and legs into a position in which the animal's body is curved to the left or right from head to tail. (Note: In some exercises, only the neck is bent. When applicable, this will be indicated in the text.) To position the horse in a bend, use the following aids: your hand toward the inside of the curve moves to a point just over and slightly in front of the withers; simultaneously, the outside hand moves away from the horse and forward to allow the animal to bend its neck, with the release of pressure being equal to the amount of pressure added by the inside hand; your leg toward the inside of the bend is positioned at the girth; and the outside leg is positioned behind the girth (figs. 1.28 A–D).

When viewed from above, as in figures 1.28 A–C, the horse's bend should match the curve along which the animal is traveling. According to current veterinary studies, the horse's spine is not flexible enough to adhere to an acute curve because the rib cage prevents the portion of the spine

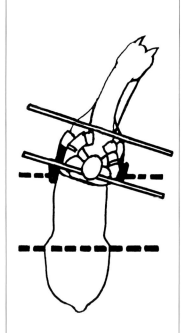

1.28 D When bending a horse, your shoulders should be parallel to the horse's shoulders (solid lines), while your hips remain parallel to the horse's haunches (broken lines). A common error committed by riders is to keep both the shoulders and hips parallel to the horse's haunches, which creates stiffness and lack of balance in the rider.

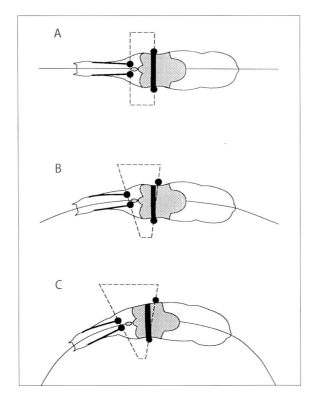

1.29 A–C The greater the degree of bend, the more your outside hand must move forward to allow the horse to bend its neck and the farther back your outside leg must be positioned to hold the horse's haunches on the curve. The dotted lines show the difference between the position of the rider's aids during straightness (A), a slight bend to the left (B), and a tight turn to the left (C).

The basic purpose of bending is to allow the horse to stay balanced on curves. Instead of letting the animal drift toward the rail or cut into the center of the ring on turns, both of which are common errors, you must use your aids to keep its weight distributed equally on both sides of its body. Bending requires the horse to yield with its inside hind leg, so that the inside hind foot is placed laterally farther underneath the animal's body on a curve than when the horse is traveling on a straight line. Consequently, bending exercises can be useful in breaking up resistances in the haunches, for the movements require the horse to submit with its inside hind leg, blocking it from rigidly resisting with that leg.

A horse may resist your inside leg, as you attempt to push its body into a bent position, and press its rib cage back against you (fig. 1.30). This is where tact comes in. The worst thing you can do is wallop the horse in the side with your heel, for the animal is responding naturally to pressure against its side. It is the horse's way of saying, "Hey, don't push me around." Instead of reacting by adding more force with your leg, try easing off the rein on the opposing side, moving your hand forward and outward in a leading-rein position. This gives the horse a sense of direction, an "open door" through which it can travel (figs. 1.31 A & B).

If you are an inexperienced rider, it will be easiest for you to learn how to bend your horse if you practice placing your aids correctly at the halt, then apply them at the walk in each direction, before you attempt bending at faster gaits. The principle of restricting pace when practicing new techniques holds true in most exercises for the horse or rider. The reason is that the greater the pace, the more the rider is at a disadvantage, since the horse can go farther astray in a shorter time, causing its mistakes to be exaggerated and the rider to become frustrated.

between the shoulder and hip from bending much at all. However, the connective tissues at the horse's shoulder and hip stretch to allow the animal's rib cage to be displaced to the outside of the curve, so that from a top view the horse appears to be evenly bent from head to tail. For practical purposes, then, the proper bend is described as being uniform from head to tail (figs. 1.29 A–C).

1.30 This is a good example of a horse leaning into the rider's leg, rather than moving away from it. As the competitor presses with his right leg to bend the horse during a dressage test, the animal resists by leaning into his leg pressure. The horse is stiff through its body, and its axis is tilted toward the right as it resists the rider's leg.

1.31 A & B In reaction to the horse being resistant to her aids for the left bend, the rider moves her right hand away from the horse a few inches in an opening rein position (A), providing an "open door" that encourages the horse to shift its shoulders slightly to the right so that the resistance is broken (B).

Once you are able to bend the horse properly each direction at the walk, attempt it at the trot, then at the canter. You should not only mold the horse's body to fit the curves at the end of the arena, but also practice circles, which require more refined coordination of your aids because you do not have the advantage of outside support from the railing.

Eventually, you can incorporate other lateral exercises into your daily work that will make flatwork sessions more interesting for you and your horse. Half-turns, half-turns in reverse, figure eights, serpentines, and changes through the circle are simple figures, which will offer variety in your basic routine (figs. 1.32 A–E). They are more effective than a circle for suppling a horse because they involve a change in the direction of the bend within the figure. This change breaks up resistances on both sides of the animal, whereas a circle encourages suppleness on the inside of the curve, but allows resistances to build on the outside of the curve, often without your realizing that the horse is becoming stiff to one side.

Your calves break up resistances by preventing the horse from bracing with its hind legs and stiffening its muscles. Think of the horse's rib cage as pliable material and your legs as the walls of a supporting corridor. Mold the horse's barrel into the desired configuration—either a left or right bend, or absolute straightness—by increasing or decreasing the pressure in each of your calves.

The hands come into play, too, as they allow or restrict lateral movement. If you increase pressure with your left leg, the horse will move to the right, unless your right hand does not relax enough and clashes with the left leg, preventing the horse from moving over (figs. 1.33 A–D). I believe the most common mistake riders make in attempting bending is not relaxing the outside aids as the inside aids are applied. A rider with a weak position or poor coordination will tend to flex all

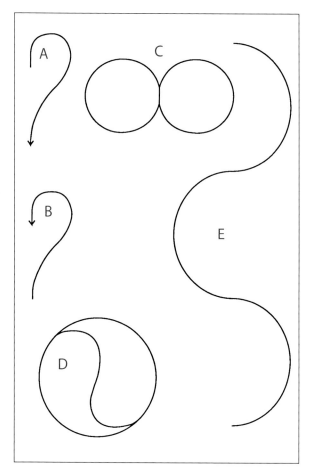

1.32 A–E Half-turn (A), half-turn in reverse (B), figure eight (C), change through the circle (D), three-loop serpentine (E).

of his muscles or relax all of them, rather than being able to flex some while relaxing others. You must be acutely aware of how your aids work independently, yet interdependently, before you can master bending or, for that matter, flatwork in general. It is the delicate coordination between your hands and legs that will allow you to mold the horse's body smoothly into a bend then back again to straight as the animal moves around the corners and straight sides of the arena (fig. 1.34).

1.33 A–D The rider is clashing her aids by pushing the horse insistently with her left leg while keeping so much tension on the right rein that the horse is prohibited from moving over (A). The horse is confused by the rider's error, as indicated by its raised head and startled expression (B). When the rider corrects the error and relaxes tension on the right rein (C), the horse obediently moves away from her left leg and assumes a calm expression (D).

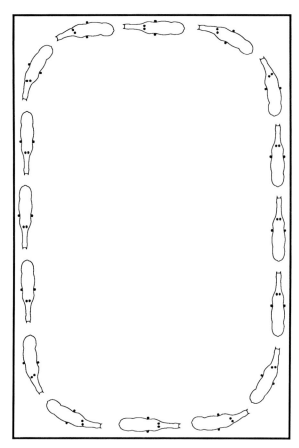

1.34 From this top view, you can see the rider's aids for traveling counterclockwise around an arena at the walk or trot. A direct rein and both legs positioned at the girth are used on the straightaways. An indirect rein, the inside leg at the girth, and the outside leg behind the girth are used on the corners of the arena. (At the canter, the hand position and inside leg aid are the same, but the outside leg remains in a behind-the-girth position even on the straightaways, poised to add pressure to maintain the canter sequence if the horse tries to break to a lower gait.)

1.35 A–C During a good transition from the canter to the halt, the horse remains collected, straight, and calm (A & B). The downward transition culminates in the animal standing squarely, ready to perform further tests (C).

1.36 A–C During a bad transition from the canter to the halt, the rider roughly pulls against the horse's mouth (A). Her upper body drops behind the vertical in a severe, braced position, and the horse is tense and pulling with an open mouth (B). At the halt, the horse fidgets and moves its haunches to one side rather than standing squarely (C).

Transitions

Transitions are the periods of change between one gait and another. For instance, when your horse is walking (four beats) and you want it to canter (three beats), you apply your aids and the horse strikes out in a new sequence of its feet as it makes a transition between the walk and canter. There are upward transitions (halt to walk, halt to trot, halt to canter, walk to trot, walk to canter, and trot to canter) and downward transitions (canter to trot, canter to walk, canter to halt, trot to walk, trot to halt, and walk to halt).

A good transition is smooth, with the horse's hocks remaining engaged, the tempo changing gradually as the animal moves into the new gait, and the frame being stable (figs. 1.35 A–C). A bad transition is abrupt, with the hocks dropping behind, the tempo changing radically from one gait to another, and the horse "falling out of frame" (figs. 1.36 A–C).

The hocks must remain engaged throughout the upward and downward transitions in order for the horse's frame to be stable. The following simulation demonstrates the way in which engagement and disengagement of the hocks affect the horse's frame. Start with your hands and knees on the floor, so that your weight is distributed on four supports, representing the stance of a horse. Then, raise your buttocks upward and stretch your head backward toward your seat. From this position, try to lower your

1.37 A & B When you begin with your spine concave, so that your buttocks and head are up (A), you will find it difficult to put your head down (B). This represents the difficulty a horse has lowering its head when its hindquarters are not engaged.

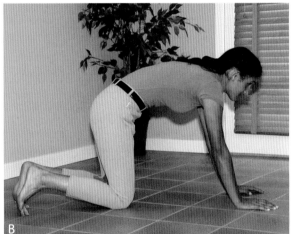

1.38 A & B If you begin with your spine convex, which represents the engagement of the horse's hocks (A), you will find it difficult to raise your head (B). This is why a horse that moves with its hocks engaged will keep its head in an acceptably low position, rather than being forced to lower its head.

1.39 A & B When the hocks are properly engaged, the horse's hips are lowered, its loins are raised, and it seeks a downward position with its head, as the head follows the arch created by the spine. This makes the topline appear rounded (A). When the hocks are not engaged, the animal's back is hollow. Its head will readily follow the concave line of the spine by rising upward (B).

head. You will find it difficult to put your head and neck down when the rest of your spine is curved upward (figs. 1.37 A & B). Now try the reverse. Curve your bottom underneath and drop your head so that your entire back is round. Then try to raise your head. You will find it equally difficult to do this (figs. 1.38 A & B).

It is the same with a horse. If you can keep the animal's hocks engaged, its hips will be lowered and its loins will be curved slightly upward, so that the horse's neck will be most comfortable following the downward curve. The horse will then remain in a stable, collected frame throughout the transitions (figs. 1.39 A & B).

Although half-halts used during downward transitions shift the center of gravity backward, causing the horse to have a lighter forehand, the lightness of the front end will not encourage the horse to raise its nose skyward. As

explained above, the curve of the spine when the hocks are properly engaged makes it uncomfortable for the horse to travel with its head up. The forehand, then, can be lightened when necessary without adversely affecting head carriage.

Transitions are important at all levels of riding, for they demonstrate the degree of the horse's obedience and, consequently, are a means of assessing the rider's safety. If the horse is not willing to slow down when you ask for a downward transition on the flat, the problem will be magnified when the animal is traveling at a much greater pace around a course of fences.

In general, problems on the flat greatly increase in severity when the horse is ridden over fences. It is essential, then, to view flatwork in relation to jumping if you are to understand the benefits of its use for hunters and equitation horses. Unlike dressage, we are not concerned with suppleness, balance, and obedience in and of themselves as an art form. Rather, our primary concern is for control of the horse on course, which is much more likely to occur when the animal has first been trained properly on the flat.

Punishment and Reward

From the horse's point of view, punishment is the application of the rider's natural and artificial aids, and reward is the lessening or absence of their use. If you want the horse to move forward a little faster, punish it with a squeeze of your legs. If this does not produce a response, use your spurs to reinforce the leg aid. If the horse is still unresponsive, apply your stick on its flank, just behind your calf, using only the degree of force necessary to motivate the animal. Once the horse is at the proper pace, relax the pressure of your calves to reward it.

Punishment from the hands depends upon the amount of pressure you have against the horse's mouth. If the horse does not slow down in response to the squeezing of your hand muscles, add weight to its mouth by pulling back slightly, until the animal does react. Once the horse acknowledges your hand aid and begins to slow down, relax the hand muscles and allow your arms to follow the motion of its head and neck, so that the animal is rewarded through lighter contact.

You should think of punishment as the active use of your aids, not as an angry or overly severe response to a horse's bad behavior. A good example of incorrect punishment is seen when a horse stops in front of a jump and is beaten severely on the head or neck. Its rider will usually try to justify his behavior by referring to it as "punishment" for the horse's disobedience. This, however, is not punishment,

but abuse, since the angry rider is trying to inflict pain, rather than correct an error with the appropriate application of his aids.

If your aids are applied too severely, the horse will become frightened and try to run, escaping in any direction available. Once a horse has decided to bolt, it is difficult to regain control and get it to concentrate on work, for it becomes solely concerned with avoiding further pain.

Timing is another factor in punishment. By promptly addressing a problem, you will let the horse know that you are alert and that you intend to be in control. If you miss the opportunity to punish for a small error, then it will gradually increase in severity and related problems will spring up. At that point, you will have to be much more forceful than if you had applied your aids sooner, when the error was small and isolated.

Punishment must therefore be: (1) applied at the proper time; (2) applied to the proper place; and (3) applied with the proper force. Reward has the same criteria, for it is just as bad to miss the timing, location, and degree of reward as of punishment. Reward, being the relaxation of your aids, is the only indication a horse has as to whether it is performing correctly or incorrectly. Humans often forget that animals do not understand most of what is said—that if an instructor tells a rider what to do, the horse has no idea what is about to be asked of it.

Imagine yourself as a deaf person in a room full of people receiving detailed instructions about an obstacle course. You cannot interpret anything being said. Everyone nods that they understand the instructions, then they leave the room to carry them out. You, however, are following the group with no idea of what is up ahead. In this situation, you are like the horse. How comforting it would be if someone took you by the hand and guided you through the obstacle course, just as a good rider gives his horse guidance with his aids; and how frightening it would be if no one helped you and, when you made mistakes, you were soundly beaten. This is the case with many horses that receive such poor guidance from their riders that they are never quite sure what they are supposed to be doing. You can imagine how frustrated and angry the horse becomes.

Riding is a partnership between man and horse. The basis of this partnership is reward and punishment, for it is man's means of communicating with his horse and the horse's means of registering whether it is performing correctly or not. The animal will learn to do exactly what you want it to do only when the incentives and restrictions of training are logical, consistent, and justly applied.

Flat Exercises for Hunters and Equitation Horses

Categorizing Your Horse

Horses, like people, change from day to day. For example, yesterday your horse might have been a placid animal when the weather was warm, but today it might be wild when a brisk breeze is blowing. For this reason, you must categorize your horse every time you ride.

Each horse will fall into one of the following three basic categories: dull, normal, or quick. You can begin studying your horse's type long before you work in the ring. For example, if a horse hangs its head low in a corner of the stall and props one hind foot up, then it would appear to be a dull horse; but if it walks around and around the stall, sticking its head out the door and whinnying every once in a while, then it would appear to be a quick horse.

Similarly, if the horse stands completely still when being mounted and is reluctant to move forward from a firm squeeze of your legs, then it would seem to be a dull horse. But if it dances around while you are trying to mount and rushes off as you swing your leg over the saddle, then it would appear to be a quick horse.

Finally, as you are walking the horse to the ring, if it plods along with its neck stretched down and out and requires a great deal of encouragement from your legs, then it would appear to be a dull horse. But if the horse carries its head high and looks quickly from one object to another, or jogs rather than walks, then it would seem to be a quick horse.

Although you have not begun to work in the arena, you already have a good idea of what to expect and, using this knowledge, can avoid certain pitfalls. For example, when anticipating a dull horse, mentally prepare yourself to be assertive, so that you will be able to enliven the plodder on the flat and not wait until you are facing a course of jumps before you deal with its slowness.

If you have mounted what seems to be a quick horse, you can anticipate that it will want to rush when working at all the gaits and will overreact to your aids. By remaining calm and applying your aids softly and slowly, you can encourage the horse to relax; but if the animal does not respond to your tactfully applied aids by settling down within a reasonable period of time, you can longe it to release its excess energy.

Longeing

Longeing is exercising the horse in a circle on a long ("longe") line held by a person on the ground. When a horse is very quick or spooky on the way to the arena, most riders will try riding it rather than longeing it first, simply because it is annoying to have to go back to the barn, dismount, search for equipment, attach it to the horse, and trudge back to the arena on foot. In my experience, however, a horse that is very tense going to the ring rarely calms down within a reasonable time.

I much prefer longeing to struggling while mounted in order to control a nervous horse. When a horse pulls while longeing, it will meet with the restriction of *side reins,* which are composed of leather and elastic connected between the horse's bit and girth. The elastic provides a little give when the horse pulls, but there is only so far that the animal can stretch its neck before it meets the fixed restriction of the leather part of the reins. In contrast, when a horse fights your hands while you are riding, it is difficult to offer as much flexibility, for most riders feel threatened by an increase in pace when they ease off the reins on a quick horse. Only a very talented and experienced rider can provide both the flexibility and restriction necessary when a horse wants to charge forward.

Longeing also offers the psychological advantage of focusing the horse's attention on the equipment as the source of its restriction; whereas, if you have been pulling on the horse's mouth for an hour on the flat, the animal associates discomfort directly with you. The situation also holds true in reverse. If your horse has been pulling against you for a long time, your arms will begin to hurt, and, if you are like most people, you will become angry with the animal in direct proportion to your degree of pain. But if you longe the horse before you try to work it, you will have a more pleasant ride afterward and not develop such ill will toward it. Even a very good rider benefits from first longeing a tense horse, for it spares him from expending unnecessary energy on horseback.

Side reins not only simulate good hands by offering some flexibility while keeping the horse in a frame, but will also help prevent the excited horse from drifting sideways and stepping on itself. They should be equal in length on both sides, since lengthening the outside rein does not create proper bending, as some people believe, but rather allows the horse to drift to the outside of the circle. If the horse is correctly fitted in side reins, the elastic in the outside rein will both accommodate the horse's bend and offer enough support to prevent the animal from becoming overly bent.

Side reins should be adjusted so that the horse can keep its head slightly in front of the vertical (figs. 2.1 A & B). Never tighten them to the point that they force the horse to bring its head behind the vertical, for this overflexed position makes it difficult for the horse to see where it is going and pulls apart the vertebrae just behind the horse's ears, inflicting pain at that point (fig. 2.2).

2.1 A & B The side reins are correctly adjusted, allowing the horse's head to be slightly in front of the vertical (A). It is important not to make the side reins too tight because they can cause

a horse to panic, particularly a young horse. The photo above (B), shows stirrups wrapped properly with the rider's reins secured beneath them so they won't get in the way during longeing.

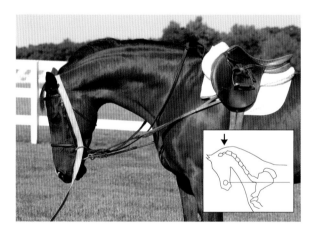

2.2 The side reins are adjusted too short, causing the horse to be overflexed at the poll. Notice the internal effect of overflexion indicated in the diagram. The arrow shows an uncomfortable stress point in the link joining the first and second cervical vertebrae, which are pulled apart as a result of overflexion. In this photograph, the reins are tied into the horse's mane. This rein position is used for a longeing session in which a rider is on top of the horse.

Boots are another important consideration when longeing. Galloping boots and ankle boots will protect the horse's legs if the animal *interferes*, striking one leg with the foot on the opposite side; and bell boots will protect the horse's heels in case the animal *overreaches*, striking the heel of a forefoot with the toe of a hind foot (fig. 2.3 A & B). (If an excited horse is allowed to run on the longe line, it will tend to bow out on the circle and interfere or overreach. For this reason, it is very important to keep the horse at a pace suitable for the size of the circle.)

I prefer a 30-foot longe line to the shorter ones. It gives the horse enough room to canter comfortably and allows you to have at least one extra loop left in your hand at all times, so that if the horse bolts, you will not be instantly pulled to the ground and dragged. Although some people slide the small loop at the end of the longe line over their hand and let it rest on their wrist, I prefer to hold the end of the line in my hand, so that I can quickly let go of it if necessary. I decided to do this after witnessing a young girl getting snared in her longe line and dragged facedown for about

2.3 A & B The horse is properly equipped with galloping boots, protecting the bones and soft tissue in the forelegs, and bell boots, protecting the coronet band in each foreleg (A), as well as ankle boots, protecting the fetlocks in the hind legs (B).

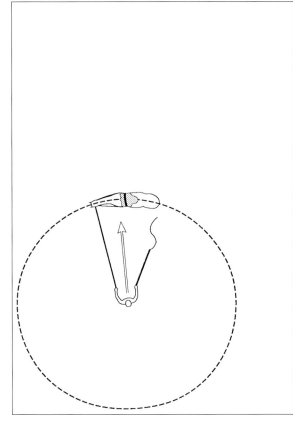

2.4 The top view of longeing shows the proper relationship of the trainer and equipment to the horse. In his left hand, the trainer holds the longe line and in his right hand he holds the whip, as the horse works counterclockwise on the circle. The trainer's chest correctly faces the horse's shoulder.

150 feet through the mud before her horse stopped. It was fortunate she was longeing inside an arena. If the horse had not been corralled by the railing, there is no telling how far it would have run before stopping.

Try to hold on to the horse if it starts to bolt, for in most cases you will be able to get it under control. But if the extra loop you have hanging from your hand is sliding rapidly through your fingers and you can see that the horse has no intention of stopping, then at the instant the line runs out, open your hand and drop the end of the line.

The longe line should be held at the level of the horse's mouth, with a steady feel all the time, just as on a normal rein. The longe line, then, represents communication with your primary restricting aid—your hands. When the horse is traveling counterclockwise, the line is held in your left hand; and when the horse is traveling clockwise, the line is held in your right hand.

A longe whip measuring 11 feet or more, including both stock and thong, should also be used. Pointed at the horse's hocks and trailing them as the animal moves around the circle, the whip is used to drive the horse forward. The whip, then, represents your primary driving aid—your legs (fig. 2.4). Hold the longe whip in the opposite hand from the one holding the longe line.

To begin longeing, choose a place that does not have slippery or deep footing, since slickness often leads to interference between the limbs, and deep footing can injure soft tissue in the legs. The longe line should be wrapped into loops, each measuring about 4 feet in circumference, with the first loop being the one on the bottom. This allows you to drop one loop at a time from the top, preventing the line from getting tangled (fig. 2.5).

Thread the snap of the line through one ring of the bit and over the horse's head, attaching it to the top of the bit ring on the other side. This enables your hand to act on both sides of the horse's mouth. While you are attaching the longe line, hold the stock of the whip under your armpit, on the side away from the horse. This is the method used to carry the whip whenever you are working with a standing horse or are walking from one site to another. The thong should be wrapped around the stock and tied, so that the horse cannot get its feet caught in it (fig. 2.6).

Once the longe line has been threaded through the bit and attached on the opposite side, untie the thong of the whip and twist the stock until the thong is completely unwound. Then, drop a couple of loops of the longe line and quietly back away from the horse, moving toward its haunches, with the whip held perpendicular to the longe line. This makes the horse aware of the whip without having it in such close proximity that the animal dashes off.

The horse will usually begin to move forward when it sees the whip, at which point you let a few more loops drop by allowing them to slide through your hand. If the horse has not begun to move, slowly bring the whip toward its hocks until it responds by walking forward. Allow the horse to travel on a large circle, with about 18 feet of line at the walk and up to 26 feet of line at the trot and canter.

When starting the horse on the circle, move the whip toward the hocks as soon as possible without spooking the

2.5 The longe line is wrapped properly in preparation for work, with the handle on the bottom loop and the snap on the top.

animal. The whip should form one leg of a triangular shape made up of the horse's body, the longe line, and the longe whip (fig. 2.7). If the horse runs wildly from the whip, drop it on the ground until the animal has worked off some of its energy. Then, pick it up again.

On the other hand, if the horse ignores the whip and plods forward, move to a position in line with its rear end and motivate the animal by flicking the whip toward its hocks. By moving toward the rear of the horse, you give the animal an open door through which its forehand can travel (fig. 2.8).

If it ignores your movement toward its haunches and the motions of the whip, tighten the circle by slowly taking up a loop or two, until the horse is close enough to the thong to respect it. Once the animal is working in a good rhythm, drop the loop or loops slowly to allow it to move back onto a wider, more comfortable circle. If it begins to ignore the

2.6 The trainer holds the whip under her armpit, on the side away from the horse, to prevent frightening the animal. The thong is wrapped around the whip and tied with a half knot prior to work so that the horse will not get its feet tangled in it while walking to the arena.

2.7 The trainer begins by letting two loops of the longe line slide through her hand and drop, while holding the whip perpendicular to the horse to prevent spooking it in the initial stage of work. Since the horse was going to be longed, but not ridden afterward, the reins and stirrups were removed to keep it simple.

whip again, bring it back onto a smaller circle. You can hit the horse lightly on the hocks with the whip to encourage it forward, but be prepared to get out of the way when you do, since a horse will sometimes kick out at the whip. Be persistent in your encouragement with the whip if necessary, but make sure the animal realizes when you are moving toward its hocks. (Remember that a horse's natural reaction is to kick anything that surprises it from behind.) By watching the horse's expression, you can tell if the animal is aware of your movements or is ignoring you.

Correct longeing requires your complete concentration. You must watch the horse's expression and monitor its rhythm incessantly, so that you will know what adjustments are necessary at each moment. For example, if the

horse slides its haunches to the outside of the circle in an attempt to stop and face you, it is important to move to its rear end quickly. If you haven't been paying attention, you won't notice the problem developing and will not be able to react in time to keep the horse moving around the circle. You will then have to take up all of the loops in the line and start again.

Although you monitor the rhythm of the horse's haunches when longeing, your body should not be turned toward the haunches, but toward the horse's shoulder. This position enables your leg toward the rear of the horse to step around your other leg as you turn. For example, when longeing the horse counterclockwise, your right leg steps around your pivotal left leg (fig. 2.9). When longeing a well-trained

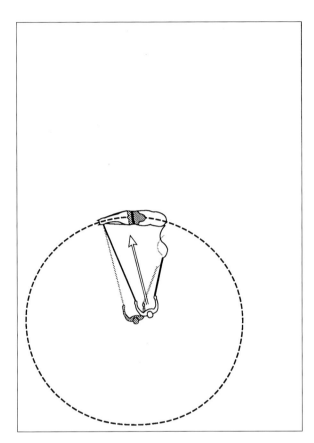

2.9 The trainer's foot toward the direction in which the horse is traveling is the pivotal foot, and the opposite foot steps around it. In this case, the trainer's left foot is the pivotal foot and her right foot steps around it as the horse moves counterclockwise. This helps the trainer keep her balance, which is especially important if the horse bolts.

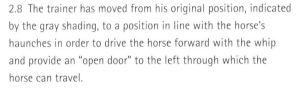

2.8 The trainer has moved from his original position, indicated by the gray shading, to a position in line with the horse's haunches in order to drive the horse forward with the whip and provide an "open door" to the left through which the horse can travel.

horse, your pivotal foot will step in approximately the same place each time, for the horse will respond properly to the longe line and whip; but when longeing a horse that is inexperienced, you usually will not be able to remain in the center of the circle at all times. Instead you must move toward the haunches when necessary to motivate the horse, then move toward the shoulder when the horse is going forward properly. (Theoretically, by moving in front of the shoulder, you should be able to slow your horse. But in practice, if you place yourself too far to the front of the horse, it will stop, then turn and move in the other direction, getting the line wrapped around its head.)

The direction of longeing should be changed about every five minutes, so that the animal will not have stress on its body in one direction for too long. To change direction, place the whip under your arm or drop it on the ground, so that it won't spook the horse as you rewind the loops. Then, say "whoa" until the animal stops and rewind the line, placing each loop over the preceding one. Once you have gathered the loops all the way to the horse, unhook the line from the far side of its head, making sure you keep a hand on the reins once the longe line has been removed. Thread the line again, starting from the far side. After hooking the snap onto the bit ring, pick up the whip and begin to longe the horse in the new direction.

Longeing is not a cure-all, but it can be helpful in releasing some of the excess energy of a tense horse. However, the original use for longeing was not as a means of tiring the animal, but of training it. Traditionally, longeing has been used to accustom young horses to working under tack and to improve the balance and rhythm of horses of all ages. If the longe line is gradually shortened so that the horse is brought onto a smaller circle, the exercise will teach the horse to collect itself. The smaller circle is more stressful on the horse's body, however, and should only be maintained for one or two revolutions before the animal can return to the original track.

When the horse's equipment is adjusted properly and the person longeing the animal keeps it going forward in a steady rhythm at each gait, longeing correctly develops the horse's haunches and topline. Four five-minute sessions, with a change of direction between each, is plenty of work on the longe line for normal training. With a tense horse, it may take another 10 minutes, but if you longe longer than this you are risking lameness. Longeing is confining, and the same physical stress that quiets the tense horse can break it down if used to excess.

When you have finished longeing, take up the line by wrapping it in loops, with each new loop being placed on top of the preceding one. Tie off the line by wrapping the end of the last loop around the other loops, then sliding the snap hook through the small hole left at the top. You can then store the longe line by hanging it from the snap hook (figs. 2.10 A–G).

Unsnap both side reins from the bit, then take them off the girth. To prevent the horse from spooking from the dangling side reins, cross the ends with the snaps over the horse's withers until you are able to remove the other ends from the girth (fig. 2.11). Make all adjustments to side reins outside the barn, both when connecting the reins before work and when taking them off afterward. A horse fidgeting in side reins may rear and fall backward, which is particularly dangerous in a busy, paved barn aisle.

Wind the thong around the stock of the whip and tie half a knot to hold it in place (fig. 2.12). The whip can be hung on a wall or stored in a corner of your tackroom.

Devising a Work Plan

A good rider evaluates the animal's strengths and weaknesses in the first few minutes of work, then spends the rest of the session practicing specific exercises to improve the trouble spots. This is the only way you can get the most out of your riding time, for each day you should seek to improve the horse at least slightly in one of its weak areas. If all goes well, the flat session lasts about 20 to 30 minutes, including several two-minute breaks, which should be interspersed evenly throughout the session. If you are having difficulty, you can continue working the horse for up to another half hour, again including several breaks. Working longer than this becomes less and less productive. A horse that will not respond positively within an hour is either being ridden very poorly or is so excited and distracted that you should have taken the edge off by longeing beforehand.

Although you may have a specific exercise or two that

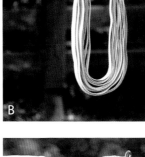

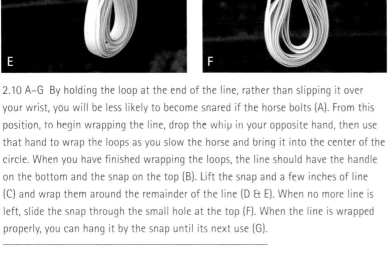

2.10 A–G By holding the loop at the end of the line, rather than slipping it over your wrist, you will be less likely to become snared if the horse bolts (A). From this position, to begin wrapping the line, drop the whip in your opposite hand, then use that hand to wrap the loops as you slow the horse and bring it into the center of the circle. When you have finished wrapping the loops, the line should have the handle on the bottom and the snap on the top (B). Lift the snap and a few inches of line (C) and wrap them around the remainder of the line (D & E). When no more line is left, slide the snap through the small hole at the top (F). When the line is wrapped properly, you can hang it by the snap until its next use (G).

2.11 To prevent the side reins from dangling against the horse's legs and spooking it while you are removing the equipment, unsnap each rein from the bit and cross it over the withers before you remove the other end from the girth. The photograph shows the trainer removing a side rein from the girth, after the snap ends have been crossed over the withers.

2.12 A half knot holds the thong around the stock of the longe whip. This makes the whip neat for storage.

you would like to practice that day, your general work plan should be formulated according to your horse's response in the first few minutes of work. For example, if the horse is a little dull that day, choose lively exercises, such as lengthening at the gaits, or practice upward transitions to promote obedience to your legs. The basic problem of lack of pace needs to be solved before you attempt any lateral exercises, since lateral movements tend to slow the horse down.

When you finally achieve the forward momentum you want, it might be so late in the training session that the horse is very tired. In this case, it would be better to end on a good note, having been successful in increasing the horse's sensitivity to the leg, than to attempt a more difficult movement on a tired horse.

Occasionally, the reverse situation occurs, in which your horse starts out working much better than expected and you find you can introduce a more difficult movement earlier than you had planned. The work plan, then, should be devised each day as you ride, for if you have a preconceived plan and are inflexible, you will not get the best results from your horse.

The Walk

Establishing Pace

When you enter an arena, allow the animal to stretch and relax at the walk on loose reins for a couple of minutes before you begin work. This gives the horse a good feeling about the ring, rather than making the animal think of it only as a workplace.

Then, take up the slack in the reins until you have a soft, but steady, contact on the horse's mouth, with the animal traveling in a long frame at the walk. Think of the ideal tempo for your particular horse and, through the use of your aids, ask the animal to stick to it. (If the tempo you are dictating turns out to be slightly slow or fast when the horse reaches it, you can make the necessary adjustments.) On a dull horse, dictate a marching rhythm that makes the horse's hind end work, but not a tempo so fast that the animal is encouraged to break into a trot. On a quick horse, dictate a steady rhythm that is slower than that at which the horse wants to travel, so that it encourages it to calm down and stretch for longer, more relaxed steps.

Mark the rhythm of the walk by silently counting 1,2; 1,2; 1,2; etc., as you mentally track the footfalls of the hind feet each time they strike underneath your seat. Although the walk is a four-beat gait, the feet fall too quickly to reasonably count them in fours, so only concern yourself with the footfalls of the hind two feet. (The front feet can only go where the hind feet push them, so if you control the hind feet, you control the horse.)

Motivating the Dull Horse

If the dull horse will not keep the proper tempo without being nagged by your legs, then supplement your leg aid with spurs or a stick. The horse should think: "If I do not move forward from leg pressure, then the rider will spur me; and if I do not move forward from the spur, then he will punish me with the stick." Finally, the horse concludes that it would be better to respond to the leg and avoid the spur and stick altogether.

I often see riders jabbing their horses every step with the spur. In this case, the rider is not using his reinforcements properly. If the horse doesn't respond to the spur, then punish the animal with the stick. If the stick seems to fall on lifeless flesh, then punish the horse more forcefully. You know you've accurately gauged the strength of the stick when the horse reacts with respect for it. If the horse ignores it, you have not hit the animal hard enough; and if it reacts to the stick with fear, then your punishment has been too harsh. Apply the stick with just enough force to get the performance you desire, for excess use of force creates new problems, such as anxiety and too much pace.

Controlling the Quick Horse

Quickness of movement is not only a by-product of nervousness, but also a perpetuator of it. If you can persuade the horse to physically slow down, the animal will usually become more mentally relaxed. This takes your complete concentration, for you must dictate every step on a quick horse, or else the animal will immediately resume a fast walk.

As discussed earlier, half-halts can be used to establish and maintain the proper rhythm at the walk, or they can be used during a downward transition to slow the horse gradually until it halts. Half-halts reprimand the quick horse, but halting is even more effective, because it requires the horse not only to slow down, but to obey to the point of immobility. Therefore, when you ask the horse to halt, you further promote obedience to your aids.

In changing from a walk to a halt on a long frame, emphasis is on the horse's willingness to respond to your restrictive aids and stand still at the halt. Although engagement of the hocks is not an issue when the horse is asked to halt while in a long frame, the horse should nevertheless stand squarely and not stop with its hocks trailing behind.

Walking and halting several times teaches the horse to wait for you to dictate the rhythm. At the halt, require the horse to stand immobile for four to six seconds, the same period of time used in competition. When schooling, if the horse is jittery and wants to move, you can say "whoa" in a low, calm voice, or reach down with one hand and pat the animal near its withers. This action does not solve the horse's nervous problem, but it does reassure the animal—particularly a young horse—and can calm it down a little.

If the horse wants to lurch forward into the walk again, or if it has pulled during the downward transition, the halt can be followed by backing. To back, apply leg pressure, but completely restrict any forward movement with your hands, so that the horse moves into the bit and, finding no forward escape, moves backward. At that instant, ease the pressure of your legs to allow the horse to step backward. On a very sensitive horse, you may not need to use your legs to motivate the animal, but may get the proper response from adding pressure in your hands alone. In this case, your legs simply maintain straightness of the hindquarters.

Backing requires the quick horse to submit completely, not only by prohibiting it from rushing forward, but also by making it concentrate on moving in the opposite direction from the one in which it would rather go. It works well in correcting horses that pull because it makes them activate their haunches in upward and backward steps, rather than allowing them to use their haunches in low, forward, bracing steps to exert more pressure on the bit.

On jittery horses that do not want to stand, backing may elicit the frightening response of rearing. A horse that is nervously dancing around, champing at the bit, or looking anxiously from one object to another should be longed to release some of its energy before it is restricted with halting or backing, both of which make it too easy for the animal to channel all of its energy upward.

The Importance of the Walk

The walk comes into your work plan time and again when, for example, you practice a lateral movement at the walk before attempting it at the upper gaits; when you give your horse a break on a free rein; or when you collect the reins after a break and walk for a short while before picking up another gait. You do not have to walk the horse for long periods of time, but do practice the walk a little each day, so that your horse considers it to be a working gait and does not anticipate the trot by jogging whenever you pick up the reins.

Intersperse free walks into your work frequently, so that the horse can stretch and relax. If you do not do this about every five minutes, then its muscles will become so cramped that it will begin to fight you.

The Trot

The Upward Transition to the Trot

Once you have established the proper pace at the walk, pick up the trot by squeezing with your legs and slightly easing off the pressure on the reins, so that as you ask the horse to go forward, you give it a comfortable place to go. The transition should be smooth, with the horse's head remaining steady, rather than bobbing upward as the horse takes the first step of the trot. Smoothness results when you use only the amount of leg pressure needed to reach the trot and when you maintain a light feel of the reins, rather than abruptly releasing all the pressure on them during the upward transition.

The trot is the most useful gait in flatwork for a number of reasons. First, many exercises can be performed at this gait. Second, it is faster than the walk, so it is not as boring; and it is slower than the canter, so it is not as intimidating to the rider. Third, it enables you to prepare the horse for the canter and jumping. Finally, it can be used for longer periods of time than the canter without exhausting the horse.

Establishing Pace

Begin your work at the trot by dictating a rhythm with your legs. If the horse does not move at the proper pace, but is quick or dull, correct it the same way as you did at the walk: half-halting the quick horse until it responds to your restrictive aids and slows down; or pressing the dull horse forward with your legs (accompanied by spurs or stick, if necessary) until it reaches the proper pace (fig. 2.13).

At the posting trot, coordinate the squeezing of your calves against the horse's sides with the sitting phase of each step, so that your two legs and seat act together as driving aids. Once the horse is moving in a nice rhythm at the trot for a few minutes in a long frame, collect it into a medium frame through the use of half-halts.

As the horse's body becomes shorter, it will be necessary to shorten your reins. If you do not, you will find your hands coming back toward your stomach to take up the slack, resulting in their being in an ineffective position (figs. 2.14 A & B).

2.13 When applying the stick at the posting trot, strike the horse during the sitting phase. This enables your weight to work with your legs, spurs, and crop as a driving aid and is less awkward than applying it while rising. It is best to switch the stick to the outside each direction if you must use it on the flat in competition, since its application will be more discreet.

2.14 A & B The rider's hands are correctly positioned just over and slightly in front of the withers, in a direct line between the rider's elbow and the horse's mouth. The hands should be 2 to 3 inches apart, with the thumbs tilted just inside the vertical (A). When the reins are too long, the hands become ineffective.

It takes longer for the rider to add pressure to the mouth, since slack must be taken up first. The rider cannot use upper-body weight to reinforce the hands because there is no longer a direct line between the horse's mouth and the portion of the rider's back that is used as a brace during half-halts (B).

2.15 A & B With her upper body on the same axis as that of the horse, the rider is aligned with the animal's center of gravity. (Notice that the buttons on her shirt are lined up with the center of the horse.) She is in balance with her mount as it travels around the curve (A). When the rider tilts the axis of her upper body inward, her weight negates the pressure of her inside leg so that the horse is stiff, rather than softly bent on the curve (B).

Adding Bending and Transitions

Now you must choose between working on bending or transitions. If the horse is a normal type and willingly moves forward at a suitable pace for the trot when collected into a medium frame, you should choose bending as the next exercise, to test the horse's lateral suppleness. If the horse is a dull type and must be driven forward in order to maintain the correct pace in a medium frame at the trot, you should also choose bending movements as the next exercise, but only large, sweeping figures that encourage the horse to maintain impulsion. On a normal or dull horse, then, the routine up to this point is the establishment of the proper pace at a walk and trot on a long frame; the collection of the horse into a medium frame at the trot while maintaining a suitable pace; then the incorporation of bending movements into the horse's work to test its lateral suppleness.

Care must be taken to make all bending movements large enough for the horse to maintain its balance on the curves. A small curving figure will usually cause the horse to lessen its pace, lean to the inside of the figure, and shorten its steps as it tries to catch its balance.

You should also be aware of the influence of your upper-body weight as the horse moves around a curving figure. You will find it particularly difficult to bend your horse if you lean toward the inside of the curve, for even though your inside leg may be firmly pushing the horse away, its effect will be canceled by your weight, as it forces the horse to lean to the inside of the figure in order to catch its balance (figs. 2.15 A & B).

Some horses will lean to the inside of a curve without any encouragement from the rider's upper body. For example, a typical "school horse" will often be in the habit of cutting corners. To counteract a horse's tendency to lean inward,

2.16 When a horse tries to cut the corner of the ring, apply your inside leg at the girth, shift both hands slightly toward the outside of the turn, put more weight in your outside hip, and subtly tilt the axis of your upper body toward the outside of the curve, as shown. These aids bring the axis of the horse closer to the vertical, prohibiting the animal from leaning inward and cutting the corner.

shift the weight of your outside hip and upper body toward the outside of the curve, so that your weight acts as an aid and gives your inside leg added strength (fig. 2.16).

Finally, add transitions to your work to test the normal or dull horse's willingness to obey your driving and restricting aids. If you are on a quick horse, you will usually benefit more from proceeding directly to transitions after establishing the pace at the trot, since transitions are generally a stronger deterrent to excess speed than bending exercises.

Although your initial concentration is on downward transitions on the quick horse, you can soon combine bending exercises with transitions, such as performing a downward transition each time you cross the centerline during a serpentine. The combination of bending movements and frequent transitions is particularly effective in controlling a quick horse because: (1) a horse naturally slows down a little on a turn in order to keep its balance; (2) the horse's inside hind leg moves slightly to the side—farther underneath the horse—on a turn, causing the horse to take a split-second longer to place its foot than when it is traveling on a straightaway; (3) the slight lateral displacement of the horse's inside hind leg prevents the animal from using its haunches to brace against your hands; and (4) the transitions not only require the horse to submit to your aids by

2.17 A & B During the leg-yield, the horse travels on a diagonal line that is at a 45-degree angle from the railing. The animal's head and neck should be slightly bent away from the direction of travel, while its body from withers to tail remains almost parallel to the rail. (The forehand should slightly precede the haunches.) The horse maintains the two-beat sequence of the trot, with the left foreleg and right hind leg striking together (A), followed by the right foreleg and left hind leg (B).

slowing down in reaction to the half-halts, but also to submit to the point that it changes to a lower gait.

Lateral Exercises at the Walk and Trot

Leg-Yield

To increase the suppleness of the horse, you can add other lateral exercises to your work program. The leg-yield is an elementary lateral exercise, which can be performed at either the walk or sitting trot along the long side of the arena or across the diagonal of the ring, with the horse positioned at no more than a 45-degree angle from the direction in which it is moving.

If the horse begins by traveling counterclockwise, then performs a leg-yield across the diagonal of the arena, your aids would be as follows (figs. 2.17 A & B):

- right indirect rein
- right leg behind the girth
- left leg at the girth

The horse's body remains straight during this movement, except for a slight bend at the poll away from the direction of travel. Your right hand bends the horse only to where the bulge of its right eye can be seen, while your left hand restricts the animal from rushing. Both hands are shifted slightly to the left to reinforce the right leg as it drives the horse toward the proper direction of travel.

To keep the animal's body from becoming bent from withers to tail, your right leg must be positioned behind the girth. Pressure exerted by the right leg creates the lateral movement in the haunches, while the at-the-girth position of the left leg prevents the horse from bowing its barrel toward the direction of travel and helps to maintain impulsion. As in all lateral movements, pressure from each of your legs changes as necessary to maintain the proper position and impulsion.

If the horse begins by traveling counterclockwise, then performs a leg-yield along the railing on the long side of the arena, your aids are as follows:

- left indirect rein
- left leg behind the girth
- right leg at the girth

To initiate the movement, bring the horse's forehand off the track by moving both hands slightly toward the inside of the ring, while slipping your left leg back into a behind-the-girth position and applying enough pressure to make the horse take the first step sideways. The animal should continue traveling down the long side of the arena with its body at a 45-degree angle from the railing and its left legs crossing in front of its right legs.

The function of the hands is critical at the start of the movement. In the span of a few seconds; they must: (1) half-

2.18 The horse is resisting slightly in its head and neck as the rider initiates the leg-yield on a line running parallel to the railing.

halt the horse to balance it in preparation for the movement; (2) create a slight left bend at the horse's poll through a left indirect rein; (3) bring the horse's forehand off the track by moving together to the left; then (4) change the direction of travel by shifting to the right, creating lateral motion in conjunction with the left leg aid. Thus, there is a shift of the hands to the left, immediately followed by a shift to the right. This must be done subtly, or the horse's impulsion will be interrupted by the roughness of your hands.

If the horse tries to leave the track, your outside hand can be used as both a restricting aid and an opening rein for a moment or two, correcting the error by prohibiting forward movement while guiding the horse toward the proper direction. Your hands, then, change both their strength and position to make the adjustments necessary to maintain the leg-yield (fig. 2.18).

2.19 In the left shoulder-in, the horse's left foreleg travels on one track, its right foreleg and left hind leg follow the second track, and its right hind leg is on the third track. The horse is properly bent to the left from head to tail.

You may find it easier to perform this movement across the diagonal, as in figs. 2.17 A & B, since your legs remain in the same position as when you were traveling around the preceding corner of the ring; whereas if you choose to perform the leg-yield on the rail, you must change the position of both of your legs to initiate the movement.

Shoulder-In

The *shoulder-in* promotes control of the horse's inside hind leg, which is critical to the correct execution of a number of upper-level movements. I often refer to the shoulder-in as "more than a bend," since the horse stretches its inside hind leg a little farther sideways than the normal bend requires in order to sustain the correct position during each step of the shoulder-in. This causes it to lower its inside hip in collection, which can be very useful on a strong, stiff horse because it prevents the animal from bracing with this foot, using it as a base from which to pull against the reins.

The shoulder-in is executed at the walk or sitting trot on the long side of the arena. In a left shoulder-in position, the horse is moving on three tracks, with its left fore on one track, its left hind and right fore on a second track, and its right hind on a third track. You should concentrate on the centerline, formed by the left hind and right fore, and drive the horse's feet forward along that line to maintain the correct position. You can best do this by looking down the line and feeling the horse's left hind leg reach under your seat with each step (fig. 2.19).

To perform the left shoulder-in when moving counterclockwise, first balance the horse with half-halts, then bring both of your hands slightly to the left, moving the horse's forehand in that direction until the animal is at a 30-degree angle from the rail. The moment you displace the shoulders, press with your left leg in an at-the-girth position to begin lateral movement. (The at-the-girth position of your inside leg, coordinated with an inside indirect rein, causes the horse to be bent uniformly from head to tail. Note the difference between this and the behind-the-girth position of the inside leg during the leg-yield, which causes the horse to remain straight from withers to tail.)

Throughout the movement, the driving aid is predominantly your left leg, although the right leg helps in maintaining impulsion. Your left leg and hand sustain a slight bend to the left throughout the movement; your right hand controls the pace and prevents the horse from "popping its shoulder" to the right; and your right leg prevents the haunches from swinging toward the rail, an error which would result in the horse's body becoming too straight from withers to tail so that the animal's feet would be tracking a leg-yield pattern.

For the left shoulder-in, then, move the forehand away from the track by bringing both hands slightly to the left, then sustain the movement with the following aids:

- left indirect rein
- left leg at the girth
- right leg behind the girth

Since all lateral movements tend to slow down a horse, you should follow them with straightforward work that encourages long steps and an energetic tempo.

Turn on the Forehand (Basic and Advanced)

The usefulness of the *turn on the forehand* is controversial. It was deleted from the USEF Dressage Division rules in 1990 because many riders feel that it encourages the horse to lean on its forehand and lose impulsion in its haunches and therefore is a deterrent to collection. This opinion is not shared by all, however. Those who disagree feel that the turn on the forehand encourages the horse to remain active in its haunches, even when the animal's forward movement is very restricted, and thus promotes collection.

Although the turn on the forehand has been deleted in the Dressage Division rules, it has not been deleted from the USEF Equitation Tests 1–19. Therefore, you will find specific information about both the basic and advanced executions of this movement in the explanation of USEF Test 12 in chapter 3.

The basic turn on the forehand, shoulder-in, and leg-yield are relatively simple to perform and are beneficial in the training of all hunters, equitation horses, and jumpers.

2.20 The horse is correctly bent around the rider's inside leg and traveling on four separate tracks while performing the haunches-in along the railing.

Although more difficult movements such as the advanced turn on the forehand, travers, renvers, turn on the haunches, half-pass, and modified pirouette might be useful for training a hunter, they are usually reserved for horses that will also be performing tests of greater precision in equitation competition, or for jumpers whose courses demand concentrated power in the haunches.

Travers (Haunches–In)

When the *travers (haunches-in)* is performed at the walk or trot along the railing of the arena, the horse's haunches are pressed toward the inside of the ring by your outside leg (fig. 2.20).

2.21 The haunches-out is the inverse position of the haunches-in. The horse moves along the railing on four separate tracks, bent around the rider's outside leg.

When traveling counterclockwise, the aids for the travers are:

• left indirect rein

• left leg at the girth

• right leg behind the girth

To move into a left haunches-in from a straightaway, your right leg slides back into position and presses the horse's haunches off the track, while your hands move into a left indirect rein position, bending the horse toward the direction in which it is traveling. (If the horse resists the left indirect rein by stiffening its shoulders, use an outside opening rein to guide the shoulders toward the right, into the correct position.) Your left leg complements the left rein in sustaining a uniform bend

throughout the animal's body and drives the horse forward in the movement. Your right leg holds the haunches off the track, while your right hand prevents the horse from rushing and works with the left hand to control the degree of bending.

In the haunches-in, the horse's body is approximately at a 30-degree angle from the wall, but the haunches are bent slightly more around the rider's leg than when performing the shoulder-in, so that the animal's feet travel on four tracks, instead of three. (Originally, the haunches-in was a three-track movement, but because of the difficulty of judging the less obvious degree of bending, the movement was changed to four tracks for dressage competition.)

Renvers (Haunches-Out)

The *renvers (haunches-out)* is the inverse position of the haunches-in, with the horse's tail turned toward the wall, instead of toward the inside of the arena (fig. 2.21). When this movement is performed along the rail, the horse's shoulders must be brought off the track as the movement begins, so that the haunches will not bump into the railing.

To perform the haunches-out at the walk or trot while moving counterclockwise on the long side of the arena, bring the horse's shoulders off the track into a left shoulder-in position. Then create a right bend with a right indirect rein while simultaneously sliding your left leg back to keep the haunches on the track. Sustain the bend and impulsion by firmly pressing with your right leg at an at-the-girth position, for it is difficult to bend the horse outward when it has just been bent inward on the preceding corner of the arena.

The aids, then, for the haunches-out while moving counterclockwise around the ring are:

• right indirect rein

• left leg behind the girth

• right leg at the girth

The travers and renvers are particularly beneficial for schooling a tense horse. Animals that have a keen temperament are often distracted by the smallest movement in or around the arena. The upper-level lateral movements, which encourage the horse's concentration, can work wonders in making a high-strung animal pay attention to its work. They also are physically demanding and rid the horse of excess energy sooner than less difficult movements.

Turn on the Haunches

Specific information about the *turn on the haunches* can be found in USEF Test 18 in chapter 3.

Half-Pass (Two-Track)

Another useful upper-level movement is the *half-pass*. The half-pass receives its name from being a half-forward and half-sideways movement—that is, the horse travels on a diagonal line that is at a 45-degree angle from the long side of the arena. The combination of the forward track and sideways track is the reason this movement is also commonly referred to as the "two-track."

The half-pass can be performed at the walk, trot, or canter, although it would be unusual to incorporate it at the canter into the schooling routine of an equitation horse or jumper. When moving counterclockwise, in order to perform the half-pass across the diagonal, your aids are as follows:

- left indirect rein
- left leg at the girth
- right leg behind the girth

The left indirect rein creates a slight bend in the horse's neck. The left leg at the girth drives the horse forward during the half-pass; and the right leg in a behind-the-girth position initiates and sustains the lateral motion. To begin the half-pass, move both hands to the left to bring the horse's

2.22 A & B The horse travels along a diagonal line at a 45-degree angle from the railing during the half-pass, the same as for the leg-yield across the diagonal. However, the horse is bent toward the direction of travel for this movement, rather than away from it as in the leg-yield. Again, the trot sequence is maintained, with the right fore and left hind striking together (A), followed by the left fore and right hind (B). The horse's legs should cross freely during the half-pass, exhibiting impulsion and steadiness of cadence.

inside shoulder slightly off the track, just as in the shoulder-in. Then, when you immediately apply your right leg to begin the lateral movement, the horse's shoulders will be correctly preceding the haunches. The animal's body should be almost parallel to the long sides of the arena during the movement, with the forehand preceding the rest of the body only slightly.

The horse's right foreleg crosses in front of its left foreleg, and its right hind leg crosses in front of its left hind leg (figs. 2.22 A & B). Since it is difficult for most riders to position the horse properly and initiate the crossing of the legs when they first try this movement, it is best to begin at the walk, rather than at a faster gait, so that you have time to think about what you are doing and correct your errors.

Once you can perform the movement at the walk, try it at the sitting trot, encouraging your horse not only to cross the outside legs over the inside ones, but also to have a swinging, athletic motion during the crosses. By concentrating on an imaginary line from your left seat bone to a point at the end of the diagonal line on the other side of the arena, you will naturally shift your aids to move the horse laterally. You may, however, have trouble maintaining the slight bend in the neck and keeping the horse's shoulders in front of its haunches, since these are typical problems during the half-pass. If the horse starts to invert its bend or catch up to its shoulders with its haunches, use a left opening rein to correct these errors. As always, if impulsion drops radically during the movement, straighten the animal and drive it forward until the desired impulsion is regained, then attempt the movement again.

Although the half-pass can be beneficial in training a horse, it is a difficult movement that is performed badly by many riders and, for this reason, may hinder more than help a horse.

Teaching the movement to an equitation rider is more for the sake of rounding out his education than necessary for improving his horse, since there are other, easier movements that can teach the horse the basic concept of moving toward the bend, such as the advanced turn on the forehand, turn on the haunches, or travers.

If you believe the difficulty of the half-pass outweighs its benefits, do not hesitate to discard it from your schooling routine, since it is not included in any equitation tests and therefore is not mandatory for a hunter seat equitation rider to perform. However, if you find it useful in training your equitation horse or jumper, then incorporate the movement into your work.

Choosing Lateral Exercises

When working a horse, it is not necessary to practice all of the lateral movements in each flatwork session. Instead, you should choose the ones that seem to address the horse's particular problems. For example, if an animal does not want to move away from the leg, practice the leg-yield or turn on the forehand. If the horse is quick or a little stiff to the inside, the shoulder-in will be helpful. To develop strength and suppleness in the haunches and increase your control over them, practice the turn on the haunches, travers, or renvers; or to test the horse's obedience and balance, perform the half-pass (figs. 2.23 A–F).

The Canter

The Canter Depart

Following the use of lateral exercises and transitions between the lower gaits, your horse's resistances should have been resolved to the point that you can try a *canter depart,* which is an upward transition into the canter from the walk or trot. A basic way to make a horse take the correct lead is to turn its head toward the outside of the arena, then apply pressure with your outside leg in a behind-the-girth position. This causes the horse to strike with its inside foreleg in order to catch its balance. The easiest aids, then, for the canter depart when traveling counterclockwise are:

- right indirect rein
- left leg at the girth
- right leg behind the girth

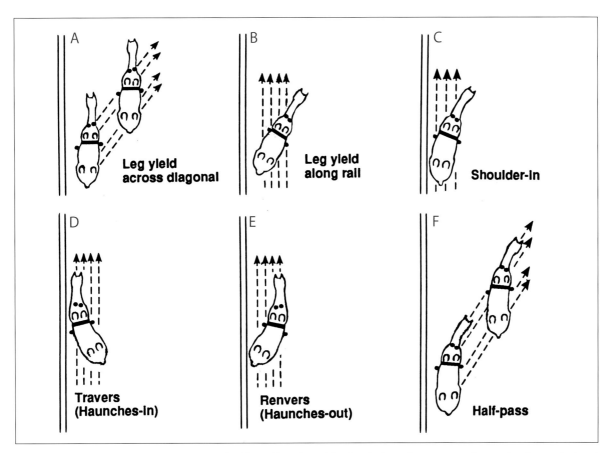

2.23 A–F For the sake of comparison, the rider's aids and horse's position for the lateral movements discussed so far are depicted from a top view.

These aids are effective for getting the left lead, but they lack the subtlety that is desired for show riding. A horse that has its head turned toward the outside of the arena during the canter depart usually looks as though it is falling onto the lead. To avoid this unbalanced appearance, use the following, more sophisticated aids for the left lead:

- left indirect rein
- left leg at the girth
- right leg behind the girth

Using this second set of aids, when you apply your right leg for the canter depart, the horse will not drift toward the inside of the arena, since the left indirect rein holds its shoulders toward the rail. When using either set of aids listed above, be careful not to let the horse gain speed and "run into the canter" from the trot. If it speeds up and becomes strung out, steady it to a slow, even trot, then ask for the canter.

A young horse or inexperienced rider will find it easier to pick up the canter from a slow sitting trot than from the walk. Once you have become proficient at the canter depart from the trot, attempt it directly from the walk, using the same aids as the second set listed om p. 59. The indirect rein should be applied only slightly, so that it does not noticeably turn the horse's head toward the inside of the arena, but simply prevents the inside shoulder from bulging inward. The application of your outside leg should also be subtle, providing enough pressure to create the canter sequence, but not so much that the horse moves through the canter depart with its haunches thrust toward the inside of the ring.

To prepare for the canter from the walk, collect your horse slightly. Collection accomplishes three things: (1) it increases the horse's vertical thrust; (2) it shifts the horse's center of gravity backward, lightening the forehand; and (3) it causes the horse's feet to strike closer together. Just as it is easier for a human to lift a heavy object when he is holding it close to his body than when he has to reach outward and lift it, it is easier for the horse to lift three legs during the canter depart when they are positioned close to the lifting hind leg than when they are far from it.

When you apply your aids for the canter—an inside indirect rein followed by an outside leg behind the girth—the horse may react to the pressure from your leg by throwing its head upward, rather than staying in a frame. To counteract its tendency to escape upward during the transition, I have found it beneficial to place the horse's nose lower than normal just prior to the canter depart, so that if the head rises a little too much, it will still be within an acceptable range. To position the nose lower, collect the horse and, two or three steps before the canter depart, squeeze a little harder with both legs and close your fingers, so that the horse puts more weight on the bit and tries to put its head down a little. When you feel that it is steadily on the bit with its head in a fairly low position, ask for the canter depart.

As the horse lifts into the canter sequence, it will move its head upward into a normal head carriage, or, at worst, only slightly higher than desired.

Pace is an important consideration during and immediately following the transition into the canter. If you let your horse become too quick during the depart, either by running into the canter from the trot or by lunging into it from the walk, it will be much more difficult to prevent the animal from gaining speed at the canter than if you had controlled the pace more effectively during the upward transition. By imagining in advance the tempo you desire and concentrating on gradually building through the upward transition to that tempo, you can control the initial steps of the canter. If a horse disregards your effort to control the pace and runs into the canter, practice a series of closely scheduled downward and upward transitions, so that by isolating the problem, you can train your horse to perform the upward transition properly.

On a horse that has a serious problem with lurching into the canter, allow it to travel only six or eight cantering steps before asking it to perform a downward transition to the walk. Maintain the walk until the horse is calm and moving in a steady tempo, then attempt the transition into the canter again. On a horse that is a little quick or slightly heavy on the forehand during the upward transition, but does not have a major problem, allow more room between one transition and the other (fig. 2.24).

At a prolonged canter, you must rely on half-halts to deal with an excitable or heavy horse. If you have done your homework well, no matter how tense your horse gets, it will not ignore the half-halts completely. Force of habit works for you. When a horse has practiced downward transitions at every quarter of the ring, it is accustomed to collecting itself frequently during the canter. The horse may be stronger on

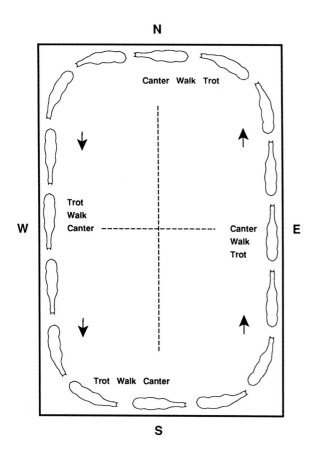

N

Canter Walk Trot

W

Trot
Walk
Canter

Canter
Walk
Trot

E

Trot Walk Canter

S

2.24 To practice upward and downward transitions, you can divide the ring into fourths and perform the transitions at each quarter mark. For example, when traveling counterclockwise, begin by picking up the left lead at the south end of the arena, then continue cantering until just before you reach the easterly quarter mark. Perform the downward transition through the trot, leaving enough room for all of the trotting and walking steps before you reach the middle of the long side of the arena. At the easterly quarter mark, pick up the canter again. You should go directly into the canter from the walk on an experienced horse, but can use a few preliminary trotting steps during the upward transition on an inexperienced animal. Perform the same sequence at each quarter mark for an entire circuit of the ring, then reverse direction and practice the exercise traveling clockwise.

the bit than you would like, but it is a rare occasion when the well-schooled horse suddenly turns into a runaway.

The exercise requiring four downward and upward transitions for every revolution of the ring is as useful for training dull horses as quick ones. While the goal on the quick horse is to teach submission during the downward transitions and a relaxed, steady pace during the upward transitions, the goal on the dull horse is to make the upward and downward transitions prompt. You begin by collecting your horse, then asking for the upward transition with your outside leg. If the horse does not willingly respond, punish it with the spur or stick on the same side as your initial leg aid, using only the degree of punishment necessary to make the horse canter promptly.

Just before you reach the end of the first quarter of the ring, use half-halts to perform a downward transition, supporting the sides of the horse with your legs to keep the hocks engaged, rather than letting the animal brake sharply in front and drop its hocks out behind. Establish a marching rhythm at the walk for a few steps, then collect your horse in preparation for the upcoming gait and ask again for a canter depart. Each time you ask for the upward transition, encourage the dull horse to be prompt by immediately using a spur or stick if it lags; but be careful not to apply the aids with more force than necessary, or the horse will soon develop the opposite problem of rushing through the canter depart.

Designating certain points in the arena for the performance of specific movements allows you to test the effectiveness of your aids and teaches the horse obedience. If you never make restrictions for yourself during schooling, you may be very surprised and embarrassed to find out in the show ring that your flatwork is not accurate. It is better to address a given problem at home, where you have the time to solve it.

Schooling Exercises Performed at the Canter

Flying Change of Lead

The *flying change of lead*, in which the horse changes from one lead to another while maintaining the canter, is difficult for many riders because it requires excellent coordination of aids, a good feel for the horse's balance and sequence of footfalls, and sensitivity to the animal's emotional state. A good flying change that is smooth and accomplishes a total change of the sequence of footfalls, known as a "complete switch," will occur only when the horse remains balanced approaching and during the change, when you apply your aids at the proper instant, and when the horse reacts willingly.

The flying change should not be introduced until the horse can perform the following exercises well: upward and downward transitions between the walk and the canter, the shoulder-in at the trot, and the turn on the haunches. Downward transitions prepare the horse to collect itself leading into the flying change; upward transitions prepare the horse to remain steady in its frame and tempo during and following the change of leads; the shoulder-in encourages collection of the haunches and lateral suppleness, which is especially important when the flying change of lead is performed between a bend in one direction and then another, as in the figure eight; and the turn on the haunches promotes control of the horse's rear end, which is essential to the successful change of lead in the horse's hind feet, as well as its front feet.

During the flying change, the horse switches the sequence of its footfalls in a moment of suspension following the placement of the leading leg. For example, if the horse changes from the right lead to the left lead, the moment of suspension follows the placement of the horse's right forefoot. For a split second, all of the horse's feet are off

the ground, at which time you apply your aids, causing the horse to adjust the sequence of its footfalls so that its right hind leg begins the new sequence, rather than its left hind leg. Approaching the point at which the change occurs, the sequence of the horse's feet is left hind, right hind and left fore together, then right fore. Leaving the point at which the change occurs, the sequence of the footfalls is right hind, left hind and right fore together, then left fore (figs. 2.25 A–C).

It is easiest to teach the flying change on a half-turn. Canter the horse down the long side of the arena on the inside lead, perform a half circle to the middle of the arena, then follow a diagonal line back to the rail, asking for the flying change just as the horse returns to the track. The oblique angle on the approach to the rail will help you, since it encourages the horse to collect itself slightly and to change leads in order to keep its balance. This does not mean that the horse will automatically change, for many animals are content to remain on the former lead (counter canter) or alter the sequence of feet in front, but not behind (cross canter). (Following an attempt to change from the left lead to the right lead, the cross canter sequence of the horse's footfalls would be: right hind, left hind and left fore together, then right fore.)

You must apply your aids firmly, but not harshly, in order to make both an accurate and smooth flying change of lead. When changing from the left to the right lead, approach the change with your hands in a direct rein position, your left leg at the girth, and your right leg behind the girth. Both hands should be shifted slightly to the left so that the right rein acts as a neck rein, working in conjunction with the right leg to hold the horse on the left lead until the exact moment for the switch. Your right leg in a behind-the-girth position monitors the horse's right hind leg, guaranteeing the maintenance of the correct sequence of footfalls. It is particularly

2.27 A–F The rider half-halts the horse to slow and balance it in the stride preceding the modified pirouette (A). Her aids are applied to initiate the turn, and the horse responds properly with a light forehand and a slight shift of its axis toward the inside of the turn (B & C). The rider is properly in the center of her horse (D) as the animal continues around the turn with a light forehand and steady cadence (E & F). Notice that the reins are a little long and the hands slightly low during this movement. A shorter rein would allow her to be more subtle, as well as effective, with her aids.

foot should fall in exactly the same spot each time, or ever so slightly in front of that spot. This movement is unneccesarily restrictive for training equitation horses and jumpers and for this reason is modified so that the turning radius of the pivotal foot can be as much as 15 feet. Technically, this is no longer a pirouette, but should be called a *modified pirouette.*

As in the turn on the haunches to the left, the aids for the modified pirouette to the left are:

• left indirect rein

• left leg at the girth

• right leg behind the girth

The modified pirouette is preceded by a series of half-halts to shorten the stride of the horse and shift its center of gravity backward. As you begin the turn, look toward the direction in which you are turning and keep your shoulders back and hands up. You want as much lightness in the horse's front end as possible, for the lighter the forehand, the more precise the turn will be (figs. 2.27 A–F).

If you can perform the turn on the haunches well at the walk, then the modified pirouette at the canter will not be very difficult for you to learn. This movement is extremely beneficial for jumpers, providing excellent preparation for classes with tight turns. Although the modified pirouette is useful in training an equitation horse, I am reluctant to suggest that a rider use it when warming up before most equitation classes, since a horse's temperament usually gets keener and its stride shorter when it is required to perform abrupt turns. However, if I feel that a turn required in an equitation class is so tight that the horse might overshoot it without special preparation just prior to going into the ring, then I would use the modified pirouette in warm-up. Basically, you should try to prepare the horse with the more strenuous exercises at home, so that you can ease off a little at the show and have the ideal combination of accuracy and relaxation in the horse's performance.

General Suggestions

The Horse's Good and Bad Sides

Just as humans are right-handed or left-handed, horses are usually better coordinated and more supple on one side than the other. Use a horse's good side to help its bad side improve. For example, if a horse's bad side is the left and the horse is very stiff moving around the corners of the ring when traveling counterclockwise, first work on a suppling movement such as a left shoulder-in to address this stiffness, then change direction and perform the same movement on the horse's good side. The animal may not be very responsive to the aids when applied to the left side, but will respond better when asked to do the same movement the other direction. Using the good side has two functions: (1) it helps you to teach the horse the

proper execution of the movement; and (2) it enables you to reward your horse by using your aids more softly than when you were correcting stiffness on its bad side.

Drilling the horse only on its bad side is a mistake. Since the animal's lack of coordination makes it difficult to perform the movement, you may find yourself in the position of applying all punishment and no reward. In this case, the horse will become more anxious and perform the movement worse, instead of better.

Let the Slower Gaits Help You

When you are having difficulty controlling your horse, drop to a slower gait and work there for awhile. For instance, if your horse is tense when you are working on flying changes, do not repeatedly force the animal to attempt the change of lead, for it will only become more upset. Go back to the trot or walk and work on some suppling exercises at these slower gaits. Then, when the horse is more relaxed and obedient, try the difficult movement again.

Variety Prevents Boredom

A variety of exercises keeps the horse from getting bored, so be creative when you work on the flat, blending one movement into the other rather than going around the arena several times between one exercise and the next. Change direction frequently to check the horse's lateral resistances on each side, and perform many downward and upward transitions to test your horse's obedience and teach the basic idea of collection (figs. 2.28 A & B).

Forming a Well-Rounded Schooling Program

Although I suggest specific exercises for both quick and dull horses, they are intended only as a general guide. For example, downward transitions are extremely helpful in regulat-

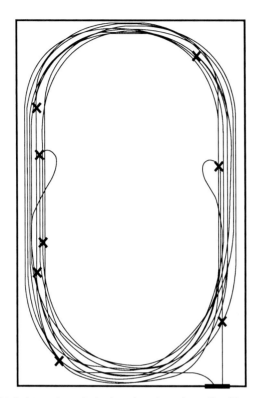

2.28 A A top view of a bad work pattern shows the rider going around and around the arena performing few transitions (indicated by the symbol "X") and rarely changing the direction of travel.

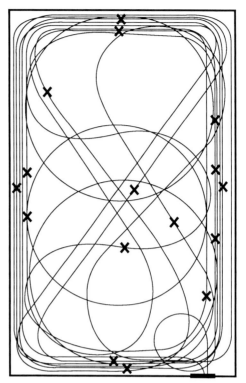

2.28 B A good work pattern shows the rider using the inside of the arena as well as the track. Changes of direction are numerous and are accomplished through patterns such as the half-turn in reverse, the change across the diagonal, and the serpentine, as well as the typical half-turn. Transitions are also frequently practiced.

ing the pace of a quick horse, but this does not mean that you must never practice lengthening the horse's stride. The preponderance of your work should address the horse's particular problems, but you do not want your horse to go into competition without a well-rounded education on the flat. By practicing movements that expose the horse's weaknesses, you obtain a clearer picture of the animal's development, which will help you determine how far you are off the mark in your competitive aspirations.

Altering Your Plan

Never hesitate to go back to easier movements when you find the tougher ones are beyond the present capabilities of your horse. By going back to something the horse knows well, you reassure the animal. An easier movement can regain confidence and relieve tension in both you and your horse. To press ahead at all costs is never the answer. This is particularly true if you or the animal is very tired.

USEF Tests 1–19:
Tips for Training and Showing

Test 1
Halt (4 to 6 seconds) and/or back.

During the test of the halt, the judge is as concerned with the downward transition as with the halt itself. When a horse correctly performs this test, its hocks stay engaged throughout the downward transition, until the halt is completed with the horse standing squarely on all four legs. In order to keep the hocks engaged, you must maintain pressure with your calves against the horse's sides and may even have to increase that pressure if the horse begins to pull on the reins and drop its haunches out behind. The combination of a supporting leg and multiple half-halts encourages the horse to stay in the proper frame and not elongate its body.

When the downward transition is correctly performed, you feel the horse's hind feet "dance" beneath your seat.

This lilting feeling is caused by the hocks' circular movement as they remain engaged. If you do not experience this, but instead feel that the horse's back is flat and its hind feet are striking behind your seat, then you know the horse has lost the engagement of its hocks. This incorrect position of the animal's hind legs compromises your ability to perform specific movements accurately, since your control over the horse decreases as the hocks lose their engagement.

The degree of collection necessary at the halt depends upon the difficulty of the segment of the test immediately following the halt. For example, if the end of a test calls for the rider to halt and then exit the arena at a sitting trot, the horse could successfully perform the final segment while collected into a medium frame. However, if a test asks the rider to halt and then pick up the counter canter, a short

3.1 A & B The horse is resisting the rider's aids to back up by raising its head and reluctantly dragging its feet (A). Another way a horse can evade is to bury its head in its chest and back crookedly (B).

frame would be necessary at the halt, in preparation for the difficult movement that follows.

The main points judged during the test of the halt are: (1) smoothness and straightness during the downward transition; (2) accuracy of the halt—that is, halting at a designated place; (3) a square stance; and (4) immobility for 4 to 6 seconds. Owing to its usefulness as a test of obedience, the halt is frequently asked for by judges in gauging all levels of riders.

The second portion of Test 1 is backing. Horses have a natural distaste for moving backward because they don't like to step into an area they cannot see. You may notice this if, when dismounted, you try to make a horse step backward. The animal's initial reaction will often be to raise its head and plant its hind feet firmly in objection.

When mounted, if you simply pull on the reins to make your horse back up, you probably will get the same reaction of head raised and feet stuck (figs. 3.1 A & B). To overcome this problem, you must think of backing as another aspect of

the impulsion you have been creating in all of your forward work. The only difference is that the impulsion is now being channeled in the opposite direction.

To prepare to back, take a steady hold on a short rein. Then, applying leg pressure to press the horse into the bit, keep a firm feel on the reins so that the horse cannot take even a single step forward. Motivated by your leg, but unable to escape forward, the horse will attempt the backward route, at which moment you should ease the pressure of your legs (and hands, if possible) to reward the horse. From that point on, use only enough leg and hand pressure to continue the backward movement for the required number of steps in a steady tempo.

In response to the aids, the horse's steps should be deliberate, with the feet moving backward in diagonal pairs. The hooves should not drag, nor hurry backward; rather each step should be in a definite rhythm that demonstrates your complete control of the horse (fig. 3.2).

3.2 The horse is backing properly by moving its feet in diagonal pairs, staying straight throughout its body, and steadily remaining in a frame.

When backing is not followed by another test, you must count the number of steps the horse takes going backward and be sure it walks forward the same number of steps to resume its starting position. When backing is used within a series of tests—for example, "Jump fences 1, 2, and 3, halt, back four steps, trot fence 4, then return to the lineup at a sitting trot"—the horse is not required to take the same number of forward as backward steps, but instead assumes the next gait immediately after the backward steps.

In this typical multiple test, if your horse becomes anxious at the halt preceding backing, try not to become panicked yourself. A tense horse requires a very calm rider, one whose apparent lack of anxiety assures the animal that there is no reason to worry. Never rush from one movement to the next. Instead, take time to calm the horse and prepare for the next part of the test.

If your horse is so excited at the halt that there is no way you can stop its squirming for a full four seconds, at least make sure the animal goes in the right direction for the next movement—backward, not forward or sideways. This way, you will only be faulted for a brief halt, rather than for incorrect steps during the backing test, which is a greater error.

Most horses naturally slow down as they back, due to their concern about moving into a space they can't see. This gives you the opportunity to settle into a slower tempo if you are on a quick horse. Following the backing steps, try to maintain this relaxed tempo when forward motion is resumed. By establishing a slower tempo and dictating it with your aids—that is, through half-halts and applying your aids softly and slowly—you can consciously restrict the speed of each step.

It is important to realize that the speed at which your aids are applied is as important to the horse's reaction as the force of the aids. Especially on a tense horse, if your aids are applied too quickly, the animal will overreact and instantly go above a suitable rhythm. You will get the best results only when you feel confident enough to use time liberally, in both training and showing.

Nervousness often causes riders to react too quickly or too forcefully with their aids, resulting in rough or imprecise performances. Backing is a very precise movement, usually requiring the horse to take a specific number of steps designated by the judge. The rider who uses his time wisely to think through and monitor this process will surpass the anxious competitor who is too hurried to think clearly or apply his aids tactfully.

TEST 2
Hand gallop.

The *hand gallop* is a three-beat gait that is faster than the canter. The horse should move with bold, flowing strides

3.3 The rider has opened her upper body angle on the approach to the short side of the arena so that her shoulder lies about halfway between her knee and hip joints. This enables her to use the weight of her torso to reinforce her hands as she collects the animal, lightening its forehand and subtly shortening its stride going into the turn.

during the hand gallop, but the pace should not be so fast as to appear unsafe for the size of the arena. As the horse changes from the canter to the hand gallop, you should rise into two-point position to free its back at the increased speed.

At the hand gallop, just as at the canter, the horse's body is straight on the straight sides of the ring and bent on the corners. When traveling on straightaways, you can extend your horse's stride at the hand gallop to between 12 and 13 feet; but on the corners of the ring, you should collect the horse to a slightly shorter stride to help it maintain its balance.

Shorten your horse's stride by opening your hip angle slightly as you approach a corner, so that the weight of your upper body helps your hands and arms restrict the horse's horizontal motion. As the horse's hocks become more engaged and the forehand rises slightly in response to the your restricting hand, arm, and upper-body weight, the distance between the footfalls of the horse's hind and front feet will be shortened, enabling the horse to be balanced on the corner while maintaining the same tempo (fig. 3.3). As the horse starts to move out of the corner toward the

3.4 As the horse departs the end of the ring and hand-gallops down the long side of the arena, the rider closes her hip angle forward to match her center of gravity as closely as possible to that of her horse. Her shoulder is correctly aligned directly over her knee and toe.

long side of the arena, relax the pressure on its mouth by moving your hands slightly forward, easing the restriction of the forehand and allowing the animal to strike farther forward with its front feet. As the horse's frame lengthens, close your hip angle forward to follow the more horizontal motion (fig. 3.4). The collecting and lengthening of the horse's frame should not be obvious, but only used as subtle, balancing techniques.

The main problem riders have during the hand gallop is the horse getting too "strong" by pulling and going faster. If you feel this problem coming on, open your hip angle slightly when going down the long side of the arena, so that you can subtly use your upper-body weight to brace against the strong horse. Performing a series of half-halts on the approach to the corner will help you bring the horse back to the proper pace. This is particularly effective if the arena is rectangular rather than oval. If worse comes to worst, you can circle the animal to slow it down, but this is usually obvious to the judge.

If your horse tends to get excited around other galloping animals, don't start out at peak pace. As you pass in front of the judge on a straightaway, increase your horse's pace, then settle back to a speed that is below normal as you move into the corner. Better to be slow and controlled than to start at the normal pace for the hand gallop and increase to a speed out of control.

Again, the use of downward transitions as a training technique at home is invaluable. If your horse has been taught daily to collect itself in reaction to your half-halts, it is much less likely to ignore your aids and run off in the show ring.

TEST 3

Figure eight at trot, demonstrating change of diagonals. At left diagonal, rider should be sitting the saddle when left front leg is on the ground; at right diagonal, rider should be sitting the saddle when right front leg is on the ground; when circling clockwise at a trot, rider should be on left diagonal; when circling counterclockwise, rider should be on right diagonal.

The figure eight is made up of two circles of equal size, joined by a short, straight juncture. The middle of this juncture is known as the "center point" of the figure. You should initially establish the center point by approaching it at the sitting trot, then posting as your shoulder crosses it.

The most important aspect of performing the figure eight is having a plan. An unthinking rider will start toward the figure with no idea where he is going, other than that he will first turn in one direction, then another. In contrast, a smart rider figures out exactly where he will go beforehand. He selects markers throughout the ring, such as a patch of dirt or the wing of a fence, to help him remember where his center point will be and where each quarter of each circle is. When it is his turn to perform the test, he simply rides according to his plan and does

not have to worry that his pattern might be inaccurate.

When planning a figure eight, you must consider where you would like to go and what obstacles might be in the way of achieving two identical circles, each approximately 50 to 60 feet in diameter. A judge has already figured this out when he calls for the test, for he would not ask for the figure eight unless the competitors had enough room and a reasonable path on which to perform it. A judge will usually say where he would like the test performed, but will not provide detailed instructions about the pattern. The center point of the figure should be in line with the judge as he stands in the ring or sits in the judge's box, so that he can see you head-on when you change the horse's bend and switch diagonals.

Start collecting and straightening your horse during the last quarter of the circle before the center point. Once you hit the center point, at which time your horse should be straight from head to tail, start bending and gradually lengthening your horse's stride until you reach the end of the first quarter of the new circle. At this point, you should be on the proper length of stride and in the correct bend for the remainder of the circle.

Your eyes are extremely important in Test 3, for if you aren't looking ahead, you won't be able to sight your predetermined markers. Look to the center point when you are halfway around each circle, keeping your eyes riveted there so that you can make the necessary adjustments each step to put your horse on target. Although you are looking directly at the center point, you will be able to spot your marker for the beginning of the fourth quadrant by using your peripheral vision. Being deadly accurate to the center point is important (fig. 3.5).

You should change from one diagonal to the other as your shoulders cross the center point at the end of the first circle. If you sit for one extra step at the center point instead of rising in the usual rhythm, you will automatically be on the proper diagonal. Although you should be able to check your diagonal in each direction through feeling, it is acceptable to check it with a glance while keeping your head up. It is incorrect to drop your head or lean over the horse's shoulder to look.

TEST 4

Figure eight at canter on correct lead, demonstrating simple change of lead. This is a change whereby the horse is brought back into a walk or trot (either is acceptable unless a judge specifies) and restarted into a canter on the opposite lead. Figures to be commenced in center of two circles so that one change of lead is shown.

To establish the center point of the figure eight when it is to be performed at the canter, approach the figure at the sitting trot, then pick up the canter as your shoulder crosses the center point. The change of lead following the first circle should occur as your shoulder crosses the center point again. This means that all walking or trotting steps must take place before that point. From practicing downward transitions, you'll know approximately how many feet it takes your horse to move downward from one gait to another. From practicing upward transitions, you'll know how many feet it takes to get the horse into the canter after the aids are applied. Add these two pieces of information together to determine how long it will take you to prepare your horse for the new lead at the center point.

If the judge has not designated in which direction to begin the figure eight, you have the advantage of choosing the lead change according to how well your horse takes a particular lead. For instance, a horse might readily pick up its right lead, but might not be as reliable in taking the left. In

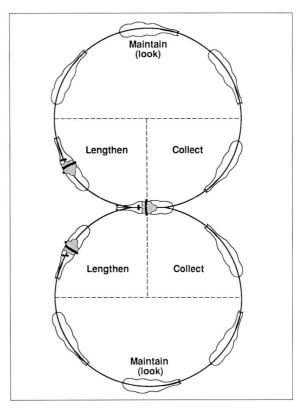

3.5 From a top view, you can see the proper placement of the rider's aids for the figure eight. In each direction, use an inside indirect rein and an inside leg at the girth to bend the horse, while keeping the outside leg in a behind-the-girth position to prevent the animal from shifting its haunches to the outside of the figure. The horse's body should be bent to match the curve of each circle, except when the horse crosses the centerline of the figure, at which point the horse should be held straight with a direct rein and both legs positioned at the girth. (If you change to your new leg position a moment before you change your hand position as you leave the center point, you will prevent your horse from anticipating the upcoming direction of travel and falling toward the inside of the circle.) It is important to collect the horse in the quadrant preceding the center point, to balance it for the change of bend. Once the animal has changed its bend, press it forward to resume the original length of stride. The horse should be traveling with the correct length of stride by the time it completes the first quadrant and should maintain this length of stride for the following half of the circle. Be sure to look toward the center point when you are half of the circle away from it, so that you will have plenty of time to make the necessary adjustments to be precise and balanced as you meet the centerline.

this case, you should start the figure eight with a circle to the left, since you would have a long initial approach to the center point in which to prepare the horse for the more difficult lead. Then, when the horse comes around the circle and has only a few steps in which to change leads, you will be more confident about picking up the easier lead.

Your eyes are very important during this test, even more so than in Test 3, because everything happens much quicker at the canter than at the trot. You may glance to check your lead, but it is preferable to know the leads through feel, so that your eyes are free to sight each predetermined marker without interruption.

The size of each circle in the figure eight at the canter should be about 50 to 60 feet. If the judge calls for a figure eight at the trot to be followed by a figure eight at the canter, the path of travel should be identical for both tests.

TEST 5
Work collectively or individually at a walk, trot, and/or canter.

Test 5 reveals the quality of your position, use of aids, and knowledge of the principles of flatwork at the three basic gaits. The most important feature of the rider's position is his leg, since this is the foundation upon which all else depends. The ball of the foot should be placed on the stirrup iron and the heel pressed down and in, just behind the girth.

The stirrup leather falls vertically and the stirrup iron rests perpendicular to the girth when the leg is positioned properly. When viewed from the side, there is a direct line from the rider's knee to the toe of the boot. The toe is turned out slightly in keeping with the rider's conformation, but it should not be turned so far that it causes the back of the calf to come into contact with the horse.

Contact is distributed evenly between the inside of the rider's calf, the inner knee bone, and the inside of the thigh. The calf rests against the flesh of the horse, just behind the back edge of the girth. The rider's base of support, the thighs and seat, should be securely forked just behind the pommel.

The torso is carried erect with the shoulders dropped and the collarbone raised. The rider's eyes look on a line parallel to the ground and are focused in the upcoming direction of travel. The hands and arms follow the motion of the animal's head and neck, giving a flexible, elastic appearance. There should be a direct line from the rider's elbow to the horse's mouth.

The judging standards for Test 5 depend upon the sophistication of the riders on hand. For example, emphasis for young or inexperienced riders is on basic position and use of the aids to accomplish an even rhythm in the gaits, smooth transitions, bending, and most importantly, sufficient control of the horse. For more advanced riders, the elements of impulsion, collection, and precision also come into play.

We have already dealt with these principles of flatwork, so let's turn to the element of showmanship. At the walk, many riders allow their horses to drag along in a dull rhythm, as though the horse were taking a break. The rider who maintains impulsion will not only stand out in this crowd of sleepers, but will also have an edge on his competitors because his horse will be prepared for anything the judge might suddenly request.

You should make good passes in front of the judge at all of the gaits, for no matter how well you ride, if the judge doesn't see you, you will not get a ribbon. Plan your passes ahead of time so that you do not find yourself blocked from the judge's view by other competitors. In fact, in top competition, when the flat classes are crowded, one competitor will often try to block another during a pass, so that someone

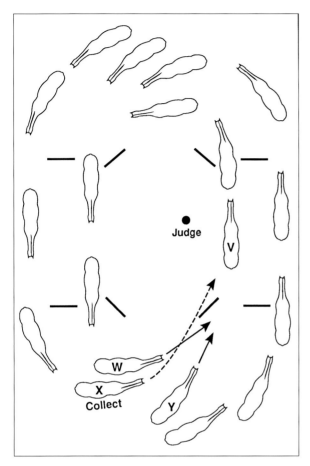

3.6 A Collection can be used to advantage in a crowded arena. Rider X foresees a collision between himself and riders W and Y as they all try to pass through the narrow gap between two fences. To avoid the problem, rider X collects his horse, allows rider W to pass him, then turns to the left of the fence on the diagonal line and works his way to an open spot behind horse V.

3.6 B Lengthening the stride is another technique that is useful in a crowded arena. Rider X realizes that if he does not make a move, he will be crowded out of the judge's line of sight by rider W. To prevent this, rider X lengthens his horse's stride and passes rider W, arriving at a clear spot behind rider V in time to be seen by the judge.

who might have had a chance at a ribbon will go unseen. It is not necessary to take on an overly assertive attitude by trying to block out other competitors, but neither should you be so naive as to end up being the one who gets blocked.

If you are smart, you will collect or lengthen your horse's strides when necessary to put yourself into a clear spot (figs. 3.6 A & B). If your horse begins to act badly, you can circle to avoid passing the judge, or can duck behind another competitor to hide your problem, as well as your number, until the horse settles down (figs. 3.7 A & B).

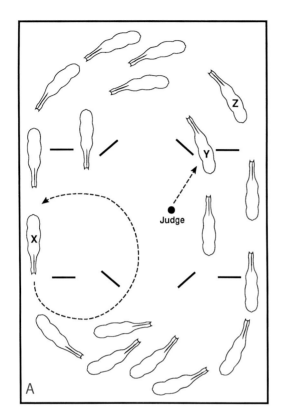
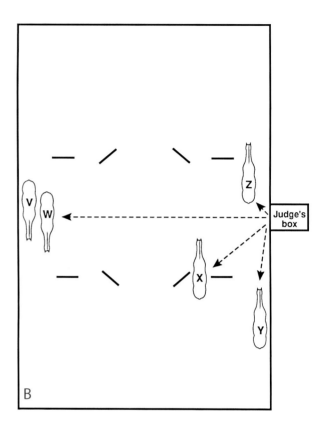

3.7 A & B Rider X circles his uncooperative horse to avoid passing in front of the judge until he can correct the problem. Rider Z has hidden his misbehaving horse behind rider Y's animal so the judge cannot see his horse or his number (A). When your horse is performing well, make sure the judge can see you. Riders Z, W, and X are in good positions to be seen by the judge (B). It is often difficult for a judge to see the horse, rider, or number from a judge's box outside the ring when the competitor is directly against the rail, as in the case of rider Y; and it is impossible to see a competitor when he is blocked by another, as in the case of rider V. Many judges prefer judging flat classes from outside the arena because they can see everything going on in the ring at once, so be sure to stay off the rail enough that the judge can catch your number as you pass.

Be aware of what is going on with other competitors in the ring—for example, a horse that is pinning its ears back as though it wants to kick, or one that seems about to run off with its rider. By choosing a different path, such as circling, or taking the path on the inside, instead of the outside of a jump, you can move away from problems that are coming up fast on your horse's tail (fig. 3.8).

TEST 6

Jump low obstacles at a trot as well as at a canter. The maximum height and spread for a trot jump is 3' for horses, 2' for ponies.

Test 6 is frequently seen in work-offs over fences. The instructions are often something like, "Without stirrups,

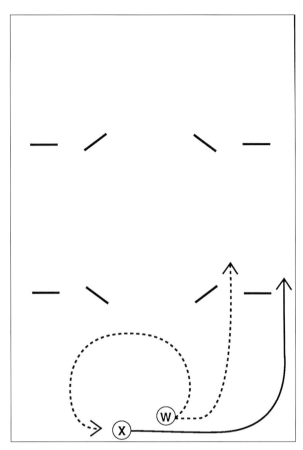

3.8 To avoid the misbehaving horse symbolized by X, the rider on horse W can either circle behind it as he hears it approaching or can take a different path, allowing the horse to pass at a distance.

3.9 The pulley rein can be used to stop a horse quickly; but too often the animal gapes its mouth, advertising the severity of the rider's hands. For this reason, you should only use a pulley rein if you cannot stop the horse on time with a direct rein.

horse to break into the canter and even leave out a stride, which may result in your "getting left," with your upper body being so far behind the horse's motion at takeoff that you hit the animal in the mouth and/or back in midair.

To avoid problems at a trot fence, leave plenty of room on the approach so that you will have time to get the horse into a steady tempo. Ideally, you'd like to leave 20 feet or more between the point of the halt and the upcoming jump. One aid that will make this possible on a strong horse is a pulley rein (fig. 3.9). Although a horse should be obedient enough to stop in response to a direct rein aid, when the closeness of the fences (three or four strides) demands an immediate halt, you may have to use a pulley rein to ensure that your horse will stop. It is better to be a little rough and get the job done than to let the horse pull you too close to the upcoming trot fence. The pulley rein should be applied firmly and close to the horse's neck. Though severe, this rein aid is preferable to the high, sawing hands that you often see during work-offs (fig. 3.10).

jump fences 1, 2, 3, and 4. Halt. Back four steps, then trot fence 5."

The difficulty of Test 6 is maintaining the trot all the way to the obstacle. Too little leg can result in "chipping in," whereby the horse adds an unnecessary step at the base of the fence. The passive leg can even result in the competitive disaster of stopping in front of the fence. On the other hand, if you are too assertive with your legs, you can cause the

3.10 The pulley rein is a preferable alternative to rough, "sawing hands," in which the rider alternately pulls hard on one side of the mouth, then the other as shown in this demonstration. While the pulley rein creates a fixed stopping-point with pressure added as needed, sawing hands alternately pull on the mouth and release pressure, being much less effective in stopping the animal.

Count slowly to five at the halt, then calmly signal the horse to resume the trot. A nervous, hurried rider doesn't give himself time to think, so he often makes a stupid mistake that could easily have been avoided if he'd only taken a little more time. A hurried rider also creates anxiety in his horse. Overly quick aids prevent the horse from concentrating on the fence and often cause the animal to commit an error. You should approach precision work methodically and give your horse calm, firm, second-to-second communication.

Once you have eased your horse into the trot from the halt, try to maintain a distinct rhythm all the way to the fence. I've found that posting is preferable to sitting to

a fence for two reasons. First, posting helps you dictate a clear rhythm to the horse. Second, and most importantly, the horse associates the up and down motion of posting only with the trot, so the gait you desire is quite clear. The sitting trot is easily confused with the preparation for a canter depart. A horse may break into the canter, not because it is trying to rush the fence, but because it actually believes you want it to canter. By posting, you make your intention much clearer.

Some riders claim that sitting to the fence helps them feel when the horse is leaving the ground and, thus, prevents them from getting left. I find it easier, however, to follow the motion of the horse when posting approximately 20 degrees in front of the vertical than when sitting just a couple of degrees in front of the vertical. If a horse begins to jump earlier than expected, you can simply keep your seat out of the saddle, rather than sitting that step. Both sitting and posting are acceptable in the show ring. It's a matter of personal preference.

As for controlling the last steps before takeoff, it is important to make the horse trot all the way to the fence. The animal can canter the very last step and not be too heavily faulted; but there is a serious penalty if any of the preceding steps are cantered. The reason for this is that a horse may canter the very last step because it is adjusting its feet for takeoff in the pattern it is accustomed to using at the canter, an error which is considered to be a horse's bad habit, rather than a major riding mistake. (If your horse consistently canters the last stride to a trot fence, you may be able to remedy this problem by working through cavalletti and an X fence, which encourage the horse to maintain the trot sequence until takeoff—see chapter 4). If the horse canters the last two or three steps, however, it shows that the rider is not in control. As always, lack of control is heavily penalized.

TEST 7

Jump obstacles on figure-eight course.

A figure-eight course requires a horse to change leads either on the ground or in the air, according to how the fences are set (figs. 3.11 A & B). When the horse must switch leads on the ground with a flying change at the center of the figure eight, prepare through collection. Use half-halts to lighten the forehand and shorten the horse's stride, balancing the animal for the switch. If you hold your outside leg back and both your hands away from the direction of the upcoming lead on the approach to the center point, you will discourage your horse from changing too early or switching in front but not behind (figs. 3.12 A–C).

If the horse does cross canter, immediately half-halt and apply your outside leg again, giving the animal a second chance to switch behind. This, however, interrupts the stride once more, making it increasingly difficult for the animal to meet a suitable takeoff spot to the upcoming fence. It will also be harder for you to see a good distance to the fence if you are preoccupied with correcting the awkward-feeling cross canter. It is much better to get the job done the first time and allow plenty of time to calculate the approach to the upcoming obstacle.

To make the horse land on a specific lead, use an outside leg aid, the same as for the canter depart. Pressure from your left leg causes the horse to land on the right lead, and vice versa. By shifting both hands in the air slightly toward the direction of the upcoming turn, you can increase the intensity of the signal to land on the desired lead. Outside rein pressure acts as a neck rein, while the inside rein's movement toward the turn acts as an opening rein (fig. 3.13).

Look for the upcoming turn while you are in the air, over the fence. If you have an exceptionally good eye, you can look in the direction of the upcoming turn before you jump the obstacle. Although this will give you extra time to concentrate on the turn to the next fence, it does involve some risk. Horses usually go where the rider is looking, since most people subconsciously shift their bodies toward their focal point. If a horse is very sensitive, it will pick up on your early preoccupation with the upcoming turn and drift in that direction, possibly running out at the fence. If you realize the potential for this, you can make sure you control how much weight you cast toward the direction of the turn and receive the benefit of looking as early as possible, without encouraging a runout.

TEST 8

Question(s) regarding basic horsemanship, tack and equipment, and conformation.

A good study guide for this test is *The United States Pony Club Manual of Horsemanship: Basics for Beginners through D Level*. You can acquire this and other study materials from: United States Pony Clubs, Inc., 4041 Iron Works Parkway, Lexington, KY 40511. Phone: (859) 254.7669. Fax: (859) 233.4652. Web site: www.ponyclub.org.

TEST 9

Ride without stirrups. Riders must be allowed option to cross stirrups.

Riding without stirrups requires a sound position and physical fitness. To be secure enough on your horse to perform this test well, you must practice regularly without stirrups at the posting trot and sitting trot.

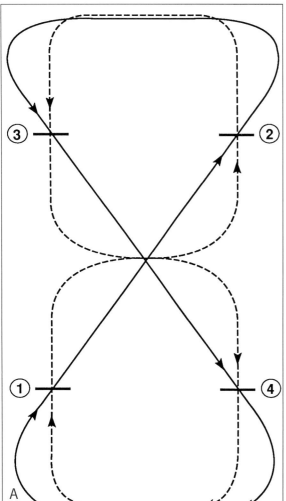

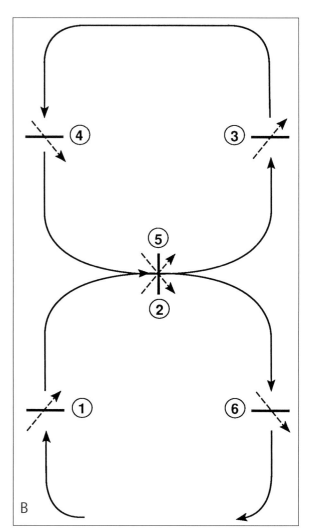

3.11 A The arrangement of the fences requires the horse to either perform a flying change of lead in the middle of the ring (dotted line) or jump the fences at an angle and travel across the diagonal lines on whatever lead the horse lands on following the first fence on each line (solid line). Both are difficult tests of precision, but jumping fences at an angle is generally considered the more difficult of the two. In order to take the difficult option, you must make sure the fences are far enough off the rail to allow you to travel on a direct line both approaching and following each fence.

3.11 B This arrangement of fences requires the horse to either change leads in the air over the middle fence (with the path indicated by the solid lines) or to jump the fences at an angle across the two diagonal lines (as indicated by the dotted lines). Again, in order to successfully ride the diagonal path across the arena, you must be sure that the fences are set far enough from the railing to allow a straight approach to and from each fence. There must be enough space between the fences and the railing to assure the horse that it will not bump into the long side of the arena.

3.12 A–C The rider has shifted her hands away from the upcoming left lead and is keeping her left leg in behind-the-girth position to hold the horse onto the right lead until the exact moment for the flying change. Notice that her weight is shifted to the right to reinforce her other aids (A). The horse successfully switches the sequence of its feet (B), making a "clean change" to the left lead, so that the footfalls occur in the proper order (C).

3.13 The top view shows the rider's aids used in midair to make the horse land on the right lead. The predominant aid is the rider's left leg, which signals the horse for the right lead, the same as during the canter depart. The hands reinforce the left leg by shifting slightly to the right, so that the left hand acts as a bearing rein, while the right hand functions as an opening rein. The bearing action of the left rein against the horse's neck tips the axis of the horse slightly to the right, making it nearly impossible for the horse to land on the left lead.

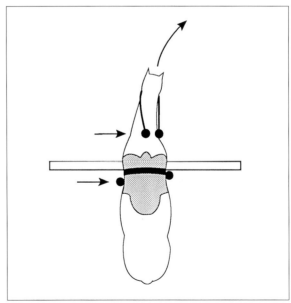

THE BIG PICTURE
Here's Looking at You, Kid!

"...the horse is actually in the air with its head pulled back, looking at me in the judge's stand!"

In some ways I feel responsible for the fault I'm about to discuss, which is throwing the horse onto the upcoming lead while in the air. I've seen it done by riders hurling their bodies toward the direction of the lead, by riders kicking their horses in the air, and by others who yank the animal's head away from the upcoming lead—in some cases done so severely that the horse is actually in the air with its head pulled back, looking at me in the judge's stand!

In previous books, I've described the aids that can be given in the air to encourage the horse to land on the inside lead just before a turn. They don't involve the rider throwing his weight around in the air; they don't involve kicking the horse with the leg toward the railing; and they don't involve yanking the horse's head in the air so that it no longer can see the ground on which it is about to land!

Any aid given to a horse in midair must be very subtle. If the horse lands on the proper lead, but the rider is accomplishing this through rough or dangerous aids, a judge is still going to penalize the horse's performance. Think about it this way: If a horse has a dangerous takeoff and flails its legs in the air to clear a fence, the judge's penalty is great, even though the rails weren't touched. If a horse lands on the proper lead, but the judge can see that the rider is jeopardizing a safe landing by shifting his balance radically in the air or kicking and yanking the horse while airborne, the judge is still going to severely penalize the performance, whether it is in an equitation class or a hunter class.

What every judge desires is for the rider to have "invisible aids." The animal should go around the ring as though it is traveling of its own volition, even though every great rider knows that it is a thousand subtle adjustments that create this illusion. When I first mentioned asking the horse for the lead in the air, I assumed people would realize that rough aids were dangerous; but apparently everyone did not get the memo! So here I am many years later asking you to subtly apply your aids in the air so that I won't feel the pangs of guilt associated with a horse looking back at me at the end of a line.

In keeping with this, it is important to remember that the rider should be as still as possible at takeoff, in the air, and on landing so as not to jeopardize the balance of the horse. It is the horse, not the rider, who should be jumping the fence, yet I often see very assertive riders pumping up and down on the horse's back the last few strides before the fence, then leaping forward onto the neck at takeoff. An overly active body distracts the horse at best and causes the horse to rush and hit the fences at worst. Don't forget the horse is entirely dependent upon your aids for guidance, so everything you do must be calm and precise.

While you've been talking to your coach and getting a clear idea of what you're trying to accomplish on course, unfortunately the horse has been standing there listening to "blah, blah, blah, blah, blah...." Horses don't understand our language. They are entirely dependent upon your aids to guide them from fence to fence on course, so be sure the commands you're giving are not rough and demanding, causing the animal to be confused and excited, but are compassionately decisive, instilling trust and calmness in your horse.

When performing Test 9, keep your lower legs positioned as though your feet were in the stirrups. The only allowable modification is that when posting or jumping a course of fences, you can hold your knees slightly higher than usual to give your torso the extra support your stirrups would normally provide. This change in the knee position should be slight, so your legs do not appear to be cramped.

On the flat, your upper-body position is the same as for the walk, trot, and canter with stirrups; but on course, the upper-body angulation is a little different. Instead of approaching the fences in two-point position, with no contact between your seat and the horse, use a *modified three-point position,* in which your crotch touches the saddle to give added support in compensation for the absence of stirrups. In modified three-point position, your upper body angulation should be about 10 degrees in front of the vertical, just enough to take some of your weight off the horse's back.

The rougher the horse's gaits on the flat or the greater the horse's thrust over fences, the more difficult Test 9 will be. It takes strength, balance, coordination, and concentration to ride well over fences without stirrup support. Although jumping without stirrups will familiarize you with this test and give you self-confidence, the most beneficial preparation comes from daily work on the flat without stirrups.

TEST 10
Jump low obstacles at a walk as well as at a canter. The maximum height and spread for a walk jump is 2'.

In Test 10, the horse should march in a solid rhythm at the walk to the fence and hop over it. If the tempo of the horse is slow at the walk, the animal will usually stop at the obstacle, not realizing it is supposed to jump. The horse must be guided absolutely straight to the fence in a brisk, but steady-cadenced walk, so that it will walk every step to the fence and not break into a trot before jumping.

You can encourage the horse at takeoff with a "cluck," which is a clicking sound made with your mouth. The cluck, if applied each time you use your stick in schooling, will become linked with the stick in the horse's mind, so that when you need an additional aid in competition, but don't want to use the overt action of your crop, you can cluck to your horse and initiate a forward response from the association of the two aids.

On landing after a walk or trot fence, the horse should be cantering. If you've ever seen a horse land trotting after a fence, you'll know why this is not correct. It looks very disjointed and, lacking the rolling motion that serves as a shock absorber, is extremely uncomfortable for the rider.

TEST 11
Dismount and mount individually.

Test 11 is fairly simple for riders who regularly mount from the ground. It may prove to be an embarrassment, however, for those who think that a leg-up from a groom is the only way to get on a horse.

To dismount, put both reins in your left hand and get down in either of two ways: drop your right stirrup and swing your right leg over the horse's croup to the near side, then drop the left stirrup and slide down; or drop both feet out of your stirrups and vault to the ground on the near side. Either way is acceptable, but sliding down is preferable on a young or spooky horse.

To mount, turn to face the horse's rear end, holding the reins in your left hand. Grab some mane in your left hand,

3.14 A & B With many horses being large today, especially imported ones, riders often find it difficult to mount from the ground. When the rider attempts to mount with her normal stirrup length, she finds that she cannot reach the stirrup with her foot (A). She properly handles this problem by dropping the stirrup—i.e., going down a few holes in the stirrup leathers—then attempts to mount again, correctly placing the toe of her boot in the girth to prevent poking the horse (B). In these photos, the excess part of the reins, or "bight," is incorrectly lying across the saddle flap. It should be lying along the horse's shoulder, out of the way of the rider.

3.15 Although the rider is facing the proper direction, her toe is in the flesh, which is likely to cause the horse to move forward as she mounts. Her right hand is incorrectly grasping the saddle flap and pad, which will only help her rise halfway up the horse, as opposed to properly reaching for the back of the seat of the saddle, known as the "cantle," which will enable her to rise above the animal.

3.16 This rider is jeopardizing her safety in many ways. By facing the horse's head, she immediately will be behind the animal if it moves forward during mounting. Maintaining overly long reins, she won't be able to stop the horse. Having no grip on the mane, she could fall to the ground if the horse moves suddenly; and poking the horse with her toe, she is signaling it to move. This is a recipe for being dragged.

also, to avoid pulling on the horse's mouth when mounting. Grasp the back of the stirrup iron with your right hand and turn it toward yourself, inserting your left foot in the iron and turning the toe of your boot into the girth, so that your toe won't poke the horse's flesh as you mount (figs. 3.14 A & B). Then grasp the cantle of the saddle with your right hand and, aided by one or two bounces on your right foot, pull yourself up above the saddle and swing your right leg over the horse. Do not land heavily on the horse's back, but gradually sink into the saddle; then separate your reins into their proper position for riding. Find the other stirrup iron by

feel, rather than looking for it or reaching down to position it on the foot. As mentioned earlier, you can locate your stirrup by lightly tapping the inside of your foot against the iron. This will let you know how high you must raise your foot to reach the iron.

Horses that are not usually mounted from the ground may not want to stand still during this test. Even if your horse is mounted from the ground regularly, it may try to move around, particularly if you habitually mount incorrectly, poking the horse's flesh with your toe (fig. 3.15). In either case, you must keep a short rein while mounting so that the horse will have contact against its mouth and not be free to roam forward.

You must also consider your horse's back when mounting. A horse with a sensitive back may try to move forward as you mount, or may sink down several inches to avoid your weight. To minimize these reactions, whenever you mount you should keep your weight on your knees for a second or two before settling into the saddle. This way, the horse won't associate mounting with pain.

It is important to mount properly, not only for competition purposes, but also to avoid an accident at home. If your horse is anxious about being mounted from the ground, use a mounting block until the animal becomes more relaxed. For safety reasons, this is preferable to having someone hold the horse while you are trying to mount it from the ground, since a nervous animal is likely to panic if firmly restrained.

Under no circumstances should you face the front of the horse when mounting. This position is dangerous because it makes it impossible for you to catch up to your horse if the animal moves forward. As a result, you could easily be dragged (fig. 3.16).

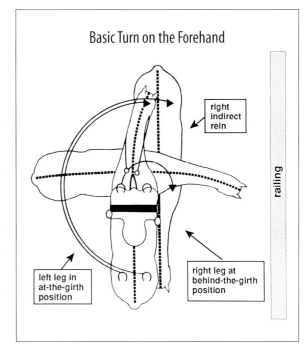

Basic Turn on the Forehand

right indirect rein

railing

left leg in at-the-girth position

right leg at behind-the-girth position

3.17 The aids for the basic turn on the forehand are described in the boxes. The movements of the horse's feet are indicated by the solid lines connected to the hoof prints. The neck remains bent throughout the movement, until the animal is straightened as it meets the rail.

TEST 12

Turn on the forehand.

The turn on the forehand is a lateral exercise in which the horse's hindquarters circle around the forehand in a steady cadence through 90, 180, or 360 degrees. Initiated from the halt, the turn on the forehand can be performed in either of two ways: the horse moving away from the direction it is bent (basic) or the horse moving into the direction it is bent (advanced). A competitor is correct whether he bends his horse outward or inward; but whichever way he

chooses, he must stick to that method throughout the turn and not let the horse slip from being bent in one direction to the other.

Whether performing the basic or the advanced method, if the railing were on the horse's right side, the animal would move its haunches to the left to complete a 180-degree half-turn on the forehand. The horse's neck in the basic turn is bent slightly toward the rail with a right indirect rein (fig. 3.17). Your right leg should be drawn back about 4 inches behind the normal left leg position in order to activate the haunches into sideways movement.

The aids for the basic turn on the forehand to the left are as follows:

- right indirect rein
- right leg behind the girth
- left leg at the girth

If you maintain a behind-the-girth position with your right leg throughout the movement, your horse's body will remain basically straight from withers to tail during the turn, rather than being bent around your right leg. However, the bending in the horse's neck and the motion of the animal's legs during the turn will make the horse appear slightly bent from head to tail.

While your right hand maintains the bend in the neck and your right leg pushes the haunches to the left, your left hand and leg restrict the horse from stepping forward or backward, respectively, or from moving hurriedly to the left. The horse's steps should be in a steady rhythm, with the right foreleg turning and stepping in place (not stuck to the ground and twisting), the left foreleg stepping around the right foreleg, and the right hind leg crossing the left hind throughout the turn. It usually takes about four steps to make a half-turn on the forehand on a willing horse, but the number will vary somewhat with each animal. Therefore, don't be concerned with the specific number of steps as much as with the maintenance of a steady tempo throughout the test and the successful completion of the turn.

For the advanced turn on the forehand, the horse's neck is slightly bent to the left as the animal stands with the railing on its right side (fig. 3.18). Use a left indirect rein, which is the opposite direction from the previous rein aid, but position your legs the same as before.

The aids for the advanced turn on the forehand to the left, then, are as follows:

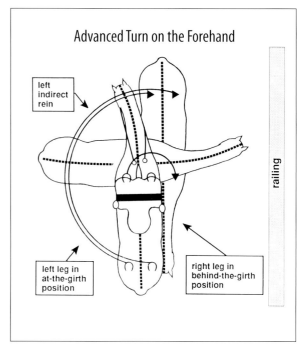

Advanced Turn on the Forehand

left indirect rein

left leg in at-the-girth position

right leg in behind-the-girth position

railing

3.18 During the advanced turn on the forehand, the rider's legs remain in the same position as for the basic turn; but the direction of the indirect rein is changed, so that the horse's neck becomes bent toward the direction of travel. The animal's feet track the same pattern as during the basic turn.

- left indirect rein
- right leg behind the girth
- left leg at the girth

When you press with your right leg, the horse's body will bend slightly around your left leg as the animal moves to the left, into the bend. The horse's feet step in the same pattern as described earlier. This method of turning on the forehand is more difficult than the first because it requires the horse to move into, instead of away from, the direction in which it is bent.

Although the horse should not walk forward as an evasion of your aids during the basic or advanced turn on the forehand, the pivotal forefoot may move slightly to the side during the turn so that the horse is tracking a small half-circle with the pivotal foot, rather than stepping in place. There is no rule as to the size of this half-circle, but, generally speaking, a turn in which the pivotal foot remains within a 9-inch radius is acceptable.

Throughout the turn, the horse's neck should remain in a steady, slightly flexed position—that is, the neck should be slightly arched as a result of the head being positioned just in front of the vertical, with the poll being the highest point on the curve of the neck. If you keep constant pressure with your calves throughout the turn, you will be able to maintain the horse's proper head carriage; but if your leg pressure is intermittent, the horse will stop moving fluidly through the turn and will usually begin to raise its head obstinately. A constant rhythm is your best friend through any lateral movement. It prevents many problems and minimizes the ones that do arise.

TEST 13
Figure eight at canter on correct lead demonstrating flying change of lead.

When changing from the left to the right lead with a flying change at the center point of a figure eight, you should begin with a left indirect rein, left leg at the girth, and right leg behind the girth as you approach the center point. Just before you reach the center of the figure, straighten the horse by adding pressure on the right side of the horse's neck with a neck rein, while easing the tension of the left rein. When the neck rein on the horse's right side is used in conjunction with your right leg at a behind-the-girth position, the pressure of the aids will keep the animal from anticipating the lead change and falling prematurely into the new lead or into a cross canter. At the instant the horse has completed the third beat of the canter sequence with its leading leg and is in a moment of suspension, position your aids as you would for an upward transition into the right lead, moving your hands into a right indirect rein position, moving your right leg forward to an at-the-girth position, and moving your left leg back to a behind-the-girth position. The left leg is the active aid, giving the animal the signal to switch leads the moment that it reaches the behind-the-girth position.

If your horse does not change leads properly the first time, try the exercise again, making sure you are pressing firmly with your left leg. The emphasis should be on your outside leg, not your hands, during the flying change. The hands help collect and balance the horse, but it is the leg that motivates the animal to switch leads.

The timing of your outside leg is very important. Remember, it must press against the horse the split second the animal completes the three-beat sequence of its feet, which is the exact instant when the horse's four feet are suspended above the ground. This is the only moment in which the horse can change to the new lead.

It helps if you silently count the footfalls a few strides before the change: "one, two, three...one, two, three...one, two, three...." This will make you acutely aware of the sequence and help you apply the outside leg aid at the proper moment. Your timing will be correct if you leave the leg that will be giving the signal in an at-the-girth position as you think "one, two, three" several times, then move this leg to a behind-the-girth position between the count of "three" and "one." If you are either too late or too early, the horse will stay on the first lead.

If you think you are using your legs strongly enough and at the proper time, but are still not getting the change of leads, check to see if you are riding the proper figure-eight pattern of two circles joined by a straight section at their juncture. If you are riding across the center of the figure obliquely, the lack of an acute turn will make it easy for the horse to stay on the wrong lead (figs. 3.19 A & B).

It is essential that you not let the horse anticipate the upcoming turn that follows the change of leads and thrust its weight toward the new lead. When the horse shifts its weight inward just prior to or during the switch, it often ends up in a cross canter. A second more of straightness and balance will allow the horse to switch the sequence of all four feet.

The flying change is difficult for both horse and rider. To perform it correctly, the horse must be well-coordinated, balanced, and obedient. To achieve the change of lead in all four of the horse's feet, the rider must have good timing, a sensitive feel for his horse, and an educated approach to the application of his aids. For this reason, the easier test of the simple change is used by judges much more often than the flying change, which is generally reserved for testing top-level riders.

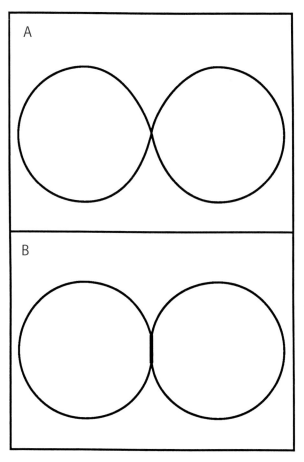

3.19 A & B When you cross the center point on an oblique line, it is easy for the horse to avoid the flying change and begin the second circle on the counter lead (A). By traveling straight down the centerline a step or two before the center point, you create a more acute curve at the beginning of the second circle and encourage the horse to change leads (B).

TEST 14

Execute serpentine at a trot and/or canter on correct lead demonstrating simple or flying changes of lead.

The serpentine is not used as a test as often as the figure eight, since it requires more space and can be hard to perform in a show ring filled with jumps. However, it is an excellent movement to incorporate into daily work because, like the figure eight, it alternately supples each side of the horse. Also, when performed with an even number of loops, it provides an interesting way of changing direction.

As in planning any figure, mentally divide the ring so that each section of the figure will be equal. A serpentine usually consists of three or four loops. The figure begins and ends as the rider's shoulder crosses the centerline, and any change of diagonals or leads should occur on the centerline. As with the figure eight, all transitional steps preceding a new lead during a simple change occur before the cen-

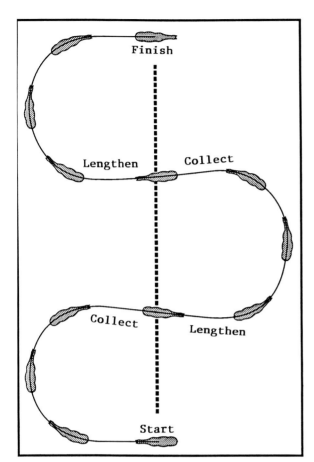

Finish

Lengthen   Collect

Collect   Lengthen

Start

3.20 Collect the horse slightly as you approach the centerline to balance it for the upcoming change of bend; then press it forward as you depart the centerline, to regain the initial length of step. These alterations must be very subtle, with the tempo remaining the same as the length of stride changes. Otherwise, the pace will appear erratic.

terline, so that the new lead is taken as the rider's shoulder crosses it.

To keep the horse balanced through each change in the direction of bending, collect it by half-halting the last few steps before the centerline. As you move away from the centerline, press the horse forward with your legs to regain the original length of step (fig. 3.20).

TEST 15

Change leads on a line demonstrating a simple or flying change of lead.

Changing leads on a straight line is difficult because the horse must respond solely to your aids, without any indication of direction that would cause it to take a particular lead. You will see simple changes performed through both the walk and trot at horse shows, but the classically correct simple change is only through the walk. The trot is reserved for inexperienced horses and riders.

Usually two changes of lead are required, which means the animal actually canters on three leads. If the test is to be performed down the centerline and you are allowed to choose the beginning lead, plan for the first change of lead to be the easiest. For example, if your horse switches more easily from the left to the right lead than vice versa, then start on the left lead. The reason is that a horse is more likely to be lacking in impulsion and a little sleepy in its responses during the first switch than during the second. However, if the test is to be performed next to the railing on the long side of the arena, start off on the inside lead as usual.

If the test is to do flying changes, use the "one, two, three" silent counting sequence discussed under Test 13 to help find the proper moment for the switch. I also find that slightly raising the hand on the side of the upcoming lead, just as the horse is switching, helps to keep the animal straight down the line, counteracting its tendency to fall toward the new lead.

All precision work demands that your eyes be active. You must find a focal point and ride straight to it, not letting anything distract you from that line. By fixing your eyes steadily on the focal point, you will immediately notice if your horse is drifting in one direction or the other. If you look

3.21 Two changes of lead on a line are indicated by the symbol "X." When beginning on the left lead at "start," the horse canters directly to the first X and performs a flying change at that point. If simple changes are required, all steps at the walk or trot should occur before X, as indicated by the dotted lines. At the completion of the test, the horse should halt squarely on the line and stand immobile for 4 to 6 seconds. As in all precision work, collection will not only provide greater control of the horse, but also offer more time to make corrections during the test. The horse's steps are shortened through collection, giving the competitor on a horse in a short frame more steps to work with than one on a horse in a medium or long frame.

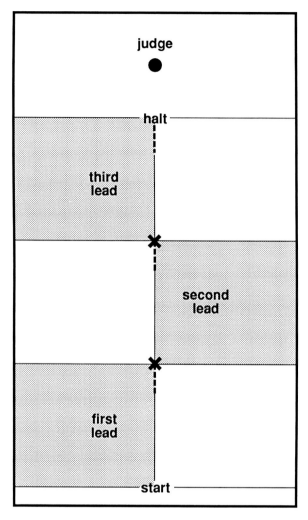

somewhere else, you won't notice how far you have gone off the line until it's too late to make the necessary corrections.

When planning simple or flying changes on a line, divide the ring into sections, starting with the place at which you will pick up the canter and ending at about 20 feet before the last possible place you can halt. Divide the line equally and make mental notes of objects in or around the arena that will let you know exactly where the changes should occur. As in all figure work, the steps performed at the lower gait during a simple change should precede the points you have designated in dividing the arena—that is, the horse should begin a new lead at each designated point (fig. 3.21).

The extra 20 feet at the end of the ring allows you a margin for error. If your horse is slow in taking the leads and overshoots the designated points, or if it is strong and pulls you past the markers, you will still have enough room to fit in all of the lead changes, provided the horse's dullness or pulling are not so severe as to negate a 20-foot margin.

On the other hand, if your horse performs well and you are able to do the upward transitions at exactly the designated points, then halt at the place you had planned. Leaving an extra 20 feet will be viewed by the judge as a sign of the horse's obedience, since it is always more impressive to see an animal halt in the open than stop simply because it has run up against the railing. If the judge happens to be standing at the end of the line during your test, it would be wise to allow a little more than 20 feet between yourself and him. The worst scenario would be trampling the judge with your disobedient horse.

TEST 16

Change horses. (Note: this test is the equivalent of two tests).

Test 16 is considered to be the most difficult of Tests 1–19. For this reason, when it is used in classes that require "two or more tests of the top four competitors," such as the USEF Hunter Seat Medal Class and USEF Adult Equitation Class, it is counted as two tests.

When performing Test 16, ignore your instincts to correct the horse and instead concentrate on getting along with it. If the strange horse is not well trained, try to get the most out of it that you can without irritating the animal. Sometimes the results of this strategy are very good; but other times they are not good at all, since chance plays such a large part in this test.

Many riders feel disoriented by a strange horse's gaits, size, responses to the aids, or, in the case of a class involving fences, the jumping style of the animal. The more experience you have on a variety of horses, the less intimidated you will be by these differences. In time, you will learn to put horses into categories—such as a puller, a quick horse, a short-strided horse, and so forth—and will be able to ride the unfamiliar animal based on your general knowledge of its type.

If the judge will allow it, use your own saddle on the new horse, so that you'll be comfortable and correctly fitted. Don't let the owner of the strange horse adjust any of the animal's equipment for you. Although my competitive experiences in the Equitation Division were generally good, I nevertheless found that people were sometimes not honest when handing an unfamiliar horse to me.

Be wary of competitors who try to tell you about their horses. Let it go in one ear and out the other. All that matters is your ability to get along with the new horse for a limited amount of time. Common sense and concentration will be your best guides.

TEST 17

Canter on counter lead. (Note: no more than 12 horses may counter canter at one time).

At the counter canter, instead of traveling around the arena on the inside lead as usual, the horse will travel on the outside (counter) lead. The movement is difficult, not only because it demands good balance and coordination in the horse, but also because it is opposed to what the horse has previously been trained to do. Force of habit, as well as uncertainty about its balance, makes the horse want to switch back to the inside lead, particularly on the corners of the ring.

The horse starts the counter canter sequence by pushing off with the hind leg toward the inside of the ring. When traveling counterclockwise, the horse starts with its left hind leg, followed by the right hind and left fore striking together, then the right fore (the leading leg) striking alone. The horse is bent slightly from head to tail toward the leading leg (figs. 3.22 A & B).

The aids for the counter canter when traveling counterclockwise are as follows:

- right indirect rein
- right leg at the girth
- left leg behind the girth

Your hands, in a right indirect rein position, bend the horse slightly to the right; your right leg at the girth aids your hands in maintaining the bend toward the rail; and your left leg, in a behind-the-girth position, starts and maintains the sequence of footfalls. The left leg presses the horse's

3.22 A & B The horse is correctly bent to the outside at the counter canter. It is collected into a short frame that enables it to remain balanced on curves during this difficult movement (A). When performing the counter canter in a group of competitors, it is wise to shift the horse's haunches far enough to the outside of the arena that the horse will not be able to place the hind leg that is nearest the rail underneath its body and switch leads (B).

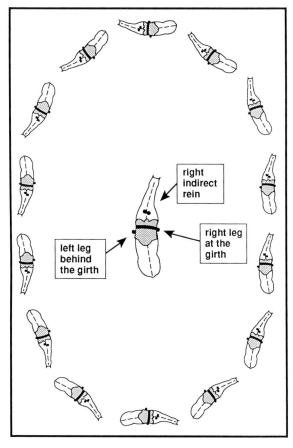

3.23 The diagram shows a top view of the horse's position and rider's aids during the counter canter in a counterclockwise direction.

haunches toward the railing at the start of each stride, so that the horse will not be able to move its right hind leg underneath itself far enough to change the sequence of its feet to the opposite lead. If you move both your hands slightly toward the rail as you approach the ends of the arena, the left rein will act as a neck rein to reinforce the pressure of your left leg and hold the horse on the counter lead.

You should feel the horse's left hind foot beneath your seat each time it strikes the ground. By monitoring this foot, you can control the sequence of the footfalls, both on the straight sides of the arena and the corners, so that the horse remains on the counter canter in a clear, three-beat sequence. When traveling counterclockwise, the animal should be slightly bent toward the right on the straight sides of the arena and wrapped around your right leg a little tighter on the turns to prevent switching leads (fig. 3.23).

Collection is necessary to sustain the counter canter, since a horse in a long frame will lose its balance and switch leads on the corners. However, take care not to let the horse's shoulders, neck, and head become too light through collection, since lightness in the forehand makes it easy for the horse to switch from one lead to another. If you sense that the animal is preparing to change leads, press it forward and toward the rail with your leg that is toward the inside of the arena. As the horse responds by stretching its head and neck out and down, follow this movement with your hands. Allow the horse to shift its center of gravity forward enough to add a little weight to the forehand, making it less tempting to switch leads. However, do not allow the horse to add so much weight to its forehand that it loses its balance and is forced to switch.

When first training a horse to perform the counter canter, begin on the inside lead, then make a half-turn back to the track and continue cantering in the new direction on what has become the counter lead (figs. 3.24 A–D). Pull the horse up before the corner and reward it for remaining on the counter lead with a one-minute break. Next, begin the same way, but ask the horse to perform the counter canter around the first corner you meet, making sure that you do not ride so deeply into the corner that the horse is inclined to switch leads. From this you can progress to riding the horse around both corners of the short side of the arena. Finally, teach your horse to pick up the counter canter to

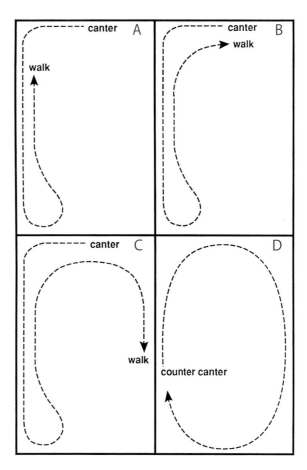

3.24 A–D The counter canter should be introduced in stages. First, canter down the long side of the arena on the inside lead, then perform a half-turn and counter canter back down the long side (A). Next, perform the half turn, then counter canter around one corner (B). Finally, perform the half-turn, then counter canter around the two corners of the short side of the arena (C). Once you are able to counter canter around an entire short side, you will be prepared to go around the whole arena (D).

begin with and continue cantering around the entire arena on the counter lead.

There are performance techniques that will help you attain and maintain the counter lead in competition. If you

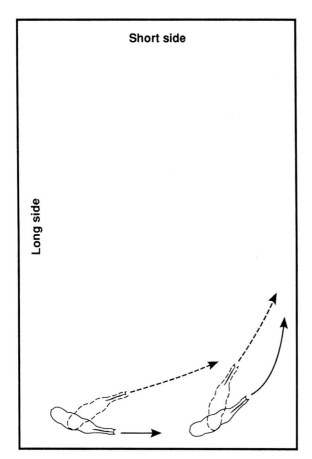

3.25 If you are on the short side of the arena when the judge calls for the counter canter, make it easier for the horse to pick up the lead by angling it toward the long side. Your angle will not have to be as acute when you are traveling on the last half of the short side (the horse to the right) as when you are on the first half (the horse to the left).

find yourself on the short side of the arena when the judge calls for this test, turn your horse toward the upcoming long side as subtly as possible before you ask it to canter (fig. 3.25). The reason you should do this is that it can be mentally confusing and physically difficult for the horse to pick up the outside lead when the track around the short side of the arena so clearly dictates the need for the inside

lead. By steering your horse onto a straighter path, you will not only make it easier for the animal to initially pick up the counter lead, but also to maintain it through the remainder of the short side.

It is very important to know exactly what is going on around you during the counter canter. If someone is having trouble with a horse ahead, note this and immediately try to steer clear of the problem. For example, a bad-tempered rider in front of you may abruptly jerk his horse to a halt if the animal switches off the counter lead. If you are oblivious to this situation, you may end up cantering into the rump of the competitor's horse.

It is also important to sense trouble approaching your horse's tail and get out of the way as it comes by. This is not as easy at the counter canter as when your horse is on the regular lead, since it is next to impossible to circle back and allow the other competitor to pass without your horse switching to the inside lead. However, you can carefully steer your horse away from the approaching problem, so that the competitor with the misbehaving horse will have a wider path in which to pass.

Ride around a rectangular arena as though it were an oval, so that the horse can ease along the soft turns of the egg-shaped pattern, rather than be encouraged to switch on the acute corners of the rectangular ring (figs. 3.26 A & B). It also helps to start the counter canter away from other horses and to try to maintain as great a distance as possible between your horse and others throughout the test, so that your animal won't be distracted and switch leads.

Since a horse's main defense is its ability to kick with its hind feet, it will often move its rump slightly toward another horse that is coming up from behind, about to pass. If you are on the rail on the counter lead and your horse moves inward toward a passing horse, your animal may

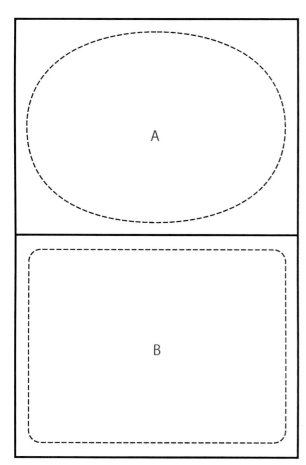

3.26 A & B It is much easier to maintain the counter canter when traveling on an oval path (A) than when going deeper into the corners on a rectangular pattern (B).

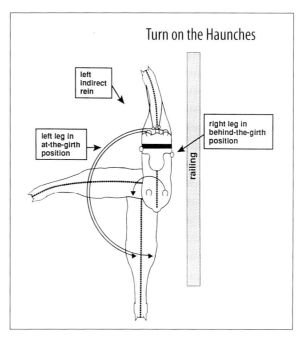

3.27 During a turn on the haunches, the horse moves toward the direction it is bent. The diagram shows the aids of the rider and the movement of the horse's legs during a turn on the haunches moving counterclockwise. When performing the turn in a clockwise direction, the rider's aids and horse's bend would be reversed.

switch leads in order to catch its balance. To counteract this tendency, keep firm pressure against the horse with your leg that is toward the inside of the ring. By pushing the horse's haunches in the direction of the rail with each step and positioning both your hands slightly toward the rail so that they aid your leg in prohibiting a drift toward the inside of the ring, you can generally prevent the horse from switching.

The counter canter is a difficult test of obedience and should be ridden with great care, since a moment's slip in your concentration or in the horse's balance will result in a change of leads.

TEST 18
Turn on the haunches from the walk.

The turn on the haunches can be executed through 90, 180, or 360 degrees, but is usually tested as a 180-degree half-turn on the haunches (fig. 3.27). During this movement, the horse's forehand should move in a steady cadence around the horse's inner hind leg, which is the pivotal foot.

The aids for the turn on the haunches performed in a counterclockwise direction are as follows:

- left indirect rein
- left leg at the girth
- right leg behind the girth

The pivotal foot (left hind) is not required to step in the same spot each time it leaves the ground, but may move slightly forward, so that it forms a small half-circle having a radius of no more than 9 inches. The right hind foot steps around the pivotal left hind, while the right foreleg crosses over the left foreleg.

Both of your hands should be shifted slightly to the left, so that the left hand can act as a subtle opening rein, while the right hand works as a neck rein. The left hand aids the left leg in creating and maintaining a bend to the left. The left leg not only maintains the bend, but also prevents the horse from slowing down or stepping backward during the movement. The right rein, acting as a neck rein, helps push the horse sideways toward the bend, as well as restricting the animal from stepping forward; and the right leg pushes the horse sideways and, along with the left leg, prevents the horse from stopping or stepping backward.

Requiring the horse to move toward the direction it is bent, the turn on the haunches is an excellent preparatory exercise for horses that must perform tight turns on courses. The same aids as those used for the turn on the haunches are applied to equitation horses and jumpers when neat turns are required: the outside leg and hand prevent the horse from bulging around the turn, the inside leg and hand maintain the bend to the inside of the turn, and both hands work together to guide the horse around the turn. (The inside hand can also be used in a more overt leading-rein position if you need to execute a very tight turn in a jumper class.) The turn on the haunches is a preparatory

movement for the modified pirouette, which more closely resembles a tight turn on course because it is performed at the canter.

The turn on the haunches is a good test of your coordination. If your inside leg becomes predominant, the horse will not move toward the bend; and if your outside leg completely overrides your inside aids, the horse will change its bend to the outside during the movement. If your hands do not restrict the forward movement and channel it sideways, the horse will simply walk forward; and if the hands are applied too harshly, the animal will stop or back up.

Since you are primarily being tested on your ability to smoothly change straightforward energy into sideways energy, the regularity of the horse's steps throughout the turn is more important than anything else. You should concentrate on maintaining an even rhythm throughout the turn. If you must choose between the two, it is better to let the horse swing wide on the turn to maintain a constant rhythm than to restrict the horse to a tight radius and lose the rhythm.

The horse's bend to the inside of the turn must be maintained throughout the entire exercise. It is a major fault for the animal to switch its bend from one direction to the other during the movement. If the horse tries to change, move your left hand farther to the left to lead the horse around the turn, preventing it from moving its head and neck to the right and popping its shoulder to the left (figs. 3.28 A–E).

A teacher can help a rider learn the correct feeling of the outside aids by simulating their pressure and effect as follows:

Standing on the side of the horse that is away from the direction of the turn, the teacher places one hand on the rider's calf and the other on the horse's neck. Then, the teacher asks the rider to apply the aids for the turn on the

3.28 A–E The rider is using a left opening rein to guide the horse through the turn on the haunches, which is a difficult movement because it requires the horse to move toward the bend in its body. The horse begins with tentative steps in the first crossing of the forelegs (A & B), but moves more freely as it progresses (C & D), with its best step being toward the end of the 180-degree turn (E). The hind feet should be more active throughout the turn, with the right hind stepping around the pivotal left hind foot in a marching rhythm. The rider is properly maintaining the bend toward the direction of travel, but her eyes are down, rather than looking slightly ahead throughout the turn.

3.29 By pressing against the rider's outside leg and the horse's neck, a teacher can help a student learn the correct feeling of the turn on the haunches.

haunches and pushes with both hands to increase the pressure of the rider's aids (fig. 3.29).

In response, the horse will move properly through the turn, and the rider can get the correct feel of the shoulders preceding the haunches in a steady tempo around the turn. This teaching tool demonstrates how much leg pressure is needed, for if the teacher must press hard against the rider's calf to push the horse through the movement, then it is apparent that the leg is not active enough.

TEST 19

Demonstration ride of approximately one minute. Rider must advise judge beforehand what ride he plans to demonstrate.

Prepare for this test by thinking up an innovative arrangement of movements that will blend together well and highlight your skills. You might do something like this:

Without stirrups, pick up the posting trot. Halt halfway down the long side of the arena. Back four steps. Pick up the counter canter. On the far side of the ring, perform two simple changes of lead. Halt. Pick up the canter on the inside lead and perform a four-loop serpentine, with flying changes of lead. At the end of the serpentine, perform a downward transition to the working trot sitting. Lengthen the horse's stride at a posting trot down the long side of the arena. Perform a downward transition to the halt at the end of the long side, then return to the outgate at a sitting trot.

This test could be made harder by adding flying changes on the line or simpler by using the inside lead instead of the counter canter around the corner. Of course, there are many other movements that could add interest to the test. The reason I find the demonstration ride appealing is that it allows you to use additional movements, such as a half-pass, that you never see in the normal course of a show.

I think Test 19 would be an excellent choice as the last test in the Medal or Maclay Finals. It would allow top-level riders to demonstrate their particular strengths and would be more interesting to watch than normal tests, in which all of the riders are required to perform the same movements.

Basic Courses for Hunters and Equitation

A Systematic Approach to Jumping

A training program incorporating flatwork, cavalletti, gymnastic exercises, and practice over single lines, as well as entire courses, is the tried-and-true method that has produced many of the finest horses and horsemen in America. Although the initial element in your training program is flatwork, this does not mean that the horse must be performing upper-level movements before it is introduced to jumping. It is not even necessary to teach it flying changes before you start jumping gymnastics or single lines of fences, since the horse should always be halted on a straight line after these exercises to convey the principle of collecting at the end of a line. The horse should, however, be correctly performing basic exercises on the flat before it is asked to jump. It should be able to keep a steady pace at each gait, perform lower-

level bending exercises, and perform upward and downward transitions properly.

Overly ambitious riders and trainers introduce jumping too early, before the horse is either mentally or physically prepared to carry the rider's weight over obstacles. This often results in the horse developing an unorthodox style of jumping that departs from the classical ideal of a rounded back, outstretched neck, and tightly folded legs with the forearms held parallel to the ground or higher (fig. 4.1).

When people speak of a horse having "bad form" over fences, they are referring to a contortion of its body to clear the rails. Even a very nice horse can be made to look bad if it is placed at a spot so far from or so close to the fence that it cannot clear the rails without diving or twisting in the air. Your skill in placing the horse at a suitable spot is the most critical factor affecting the horse's form in the air. Therefore,

4.1 This animal demonstrates good jumping form, with knees held high, hooves tucked, and the topline forming a convex arch as the neck stretches out and down to counterbalance the hindquarters.

if you are not accurate in your placement of the horse, you should not blame the animal for poor form, but should work on improving your timing—that is, your ability to adjust the horse's stride to meet the proper takeoff spot—so that you will give the horse a reasonable opportunity to jump well. (See "Developing a Better Eye," in chapter 6 for a full discussion of learning to find a suitable spot.)

There are times, however, when a rider places his horse at a suitable point for takeoff, but the animal still does not jump well. This would truly be considered "bad form," since the animal could not jump well from a reasonable spot. Although form faults are difficult to correct, this type of horse can usually benefit from being worked over gymnastic exercises, which are designed to teach the horse to use its body properly at takeoff and in the air.

Some horses, like some people, are just not good athletes and will show little improvement when regularly schooled over gymnastics. But most horses respond posi-

tively to this training, not only because the series of fences improves the horse's form and fitness, but also because the cavalletti that precede them help to teach the horse evenness of pace.

If you start with flatwork, then progress to cavalletti, gymnastics, and lines, you will have prepared your horse well for the challenges of a full course. I am not saying that every horse will have a wonderful jumping style if it is brought along this way, but each horse will develop the best jumping style that it possibly can within its natural limitations.

Cavalletti

When starting an inexperienced horse over fences, let the animal become comfortable first with a single pole on the ground. There are four options for introducing the pole: (1) walk a large circle and cross the pole once each circuit; (2) walk a figure eight, using the pole as the center point of the figure; (3) cross the pole at a walk and quietly pull up on a line, then reverse with a small turn and cross the pole again; or (4) walk the pole and make a series of sweeping half-turns back to it, uninterrupted by the halt (figs. 4.2 A–D).

Walking over the pole on a continuous circle breaks up lateral resistance on the side of the horse toward the inside of the turn (fig. 4.2 A). The figure eight offers the additional benefit of resolving resistances on both sides of the horse (fig. 4.2 B). These exercises are useful for introducing nervous or strong horses to the pole.

Pulling up at the end of the line simulates collection following a line of fences and is also useful for settling a tense horse. The small turn that follows breaks up lateral resistance on the inside of the turn and further stresses collection (fig. 4.2 C).

Sweeping half-turns encourage the horse to go forward and maintain impulsion, while gently promoting lateral suppleness around the broad turns. This is a good exercise for a normal or dull horse (fig. 4.2 D).

At the walk, the horse should have a steady, marching rhythm. It is not necessary to rise into two-point position as your horse crosses the rail at a walk, but you should close your hip slightly forward two or three steps before the pole to lighten the weight of your seat on the horse's back as the animal approaches and crosses the rail (fig. 4.3). Follow the motion of the head and neck with your hands when the horse stretches down and out to observe and cross the rail, so that it learns to expect a sensitive, following hand, rather than a hard, restricting hand that interferes with its balance over a jump.

Once the horse is relaxed walking over the pole, pick up the trot and perform one or more of the same exercises. They may be performed at either the sitting or posting trot, although I prefer the posting trot for all pole exercises. On a horse that is inclined to be dull, the posting trot allows you to squeeze with your calves at the same moment your seat touches the saddle, so that your legs and weight work together as driving aids. Do not pump up and down, driving the horse predominantly with your seat, but rather apply your weight subtly as a secondary aid, coordinating it with the primary driving aid of the legs.

The posting trot is also beneficial on a tense horse. When you are in the rising phase, all of your weight will be removed from the nervous horse's stiff back; and, during the moments in which you sit, if you support your upper-body weight on your crotch and touch the saddle lightly, you can minimize your weight upon the horse's back.

Posting can also help you slow the pace of a quick horse. By posting slightly slower than the actual tempo,

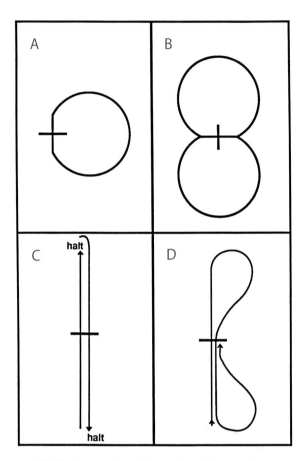

4.2 A–D The diagram shows four options for introducing a ground pole to a horse: circle (A); figure eight (B); halting at the end of each line (C); and continuous half-turns (D).

you will encourage the horse to lessen its pace to match the tempo you are dictating. You cannot completely fall behind the beat of the horse, or your weight will suddenly land hard on the animal's back, becoming a rough, driving aid. You can, however, post on the slow side of the tempo to regulate the pace subtly.

When the rail is approached at the trot, rise out of the saddle in two-point position two or three steps before the pole and maintain this position until all of the horse's feet

4.3 As the horse crosses the pole at the walk, the rider maintains three-point position, but inclines her upper body forward to relieve some of her weight from the horse's back.

4.4 The rider rises into two-point position several steps before the rail and holds this position until all four feet have crossed the rail at the trot.

have crossed the rail. This will prevent your seat from pounding on the horse's back when each of the feet lands with a small jolt after the rail (fig. 4.4).

Poles in a Series

Once the horse is relaxed crossing a single pole, place several rails at random sites in the arena and incorporate them into your flatwork to further accustom the animal to them. The next step is to place three poles close enough to one another for the horse to put one forefoot between each two poles. When the poles are set in a series, they are referred to as *cavalletti*. Measuring from the inside of one pole to the inside of the next, the distances will be approximately 4'6" to 4'9" for horses, 4'3" for large ponies, 3'9" for medium ponies, and 3'3" for small ponies.

Trot through the cavalletti poles, then adjust the distances if necessary to comfortably fit your animal's length of step, making sure that the measurements are the same for each space. For example, all of the spaces could be adjusted from a measurement of 4'6" to 4'8", but it is wrong to leave the first space measuring 4'6" and change the remaining spaces to 4'8". (If you have an inexperienced, tense, or bold horse, it is possible that the animal may try to jump all three poles, rather than step between them. In this case, add two more poles to discourage the error.)

Keep adding poles the same distance apart until you are able to trot over six poles in succession, with the horse moving in comfortable steps in a steady rhythm. To begin with, you simply want the horse to place one front leg anywhere between each pair of poles. But as your horse begins to understand the exercise and gain confidence, ask for more precision, adjusting the animal's steps on the approach so that its feet will land exactly halfway between the first pair of rails and continue to land in this position throughout the

4.5 A & B The horse stretches its neck downward to focus on the cavalletti poles (A) and enters the exercise with a rounded topline and balanced steps (B). Roundness throughout the

cavalletti promotes a proper "bascule," in which the horse counterbalances its hindquarters by stretching its neck out and down while in the air over a fence.

remaining poles. This placement of the feet creates the ideal setup for the gymnastic exercises that will follow.

If the horse lengthens or shortens its steps within the cavalletti, it will inevitably bump into the rails or add an extra step between the poles, signaling you that it is out of rhythm. If the distances between the poles are set too short or too long, the horse will commit the same errors, in which case you must adjust the poles to your particular horse's needs.

One of the most important features of cavalletti is that they encourage the animal to "seek the ground" with its head and neck, for the horse becomes focused on the poles as it tries to place its feet between them. This aspect of cavalletti training promotes the development of the proper *bascule*, which is the horse's use of its outstretched head and neck to counterbalance its hindquarters in the air (figs. 4.5 A & B).

Cavalletti are additionally effective in developing the horse's athletic ability because the increased action, as the horse raises its feet over the poles, develops strength in the muscles, flexibility in the joints, and elasticity in the horse's back, all of which are essential to an athletic jumping effort. The horse can be made to work harder if you use elevated cavalletti that measure 6 to 8 inches from the top of each pole to the ground. Most people, however, lay jump poles on the ground, since this requires no special construction. When using jump poles, be sure to check their alignment before the horse approaches them each time, making sure that one or more has not been kicked away from its original position.

Adding Crossed Rails

Once a horse is working well through the series of six poles, set a pair of standards at each side of the final pole. Then, using the final and next-to-last pole, make an obstacle between the standards by crossing the poles. This construction is commonly referred to as *crossed rails* or an *X* (fig. 4.6). For horses,

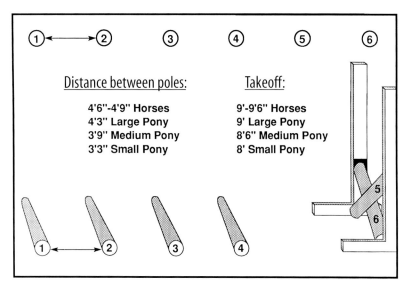

Distance between poles:

4'6"-4'9" Horses
4'3" Large Pony
3'9" Medium Pony
3'3" Small Pony

Takeoff:

9'-9'6" Horses
9' Large Pony
8'6" Medium Pony
8' Small Pony

4.6 The diagram shows how six cavalletti poles (indicated by the numbered circles at the top) are rearranged to make four cavalletti poles and an X-fence. Measurements between the elements are given for both horses and ponies.

the space between the last (fourth) pole in the series and the obstacle should be double the distance between any two cavalletti poles. This does not hold true for pony distances, however. (See fig. 4.6 for pony measurements.)

Initially, set the X at 1' height in the middle for inexperienced horses and 6" for inexperienced ponies to invite them to jump. The X can be raised incrementally as the animal gains confidence. The maximum height of the center of the X for the following exercises should be 1' for small ponies, 1'3" for medium ponies, 1'6" for large ponies, and 2' for horses.

After moving several times across the poles and over the X fence, the animal will be accustomed to trotting the cavalletti and immediately setting itself up to jump. Following each time it crosses the last pole, sit lightly in the saddle, with your upper body inclined forward so that you can stay with the motion as the horse leaves the ground. If you close your upper body too far forward, ahead of the motion at takeoff, you will burden the forehand with your weight and make it much more difficult for the animal to

jump. On landing, your hips should stay with the motion, rather than the hip angle opening up and your seat dropping back into the saddle before the horse's feet have touched ground (figs. 4.7 A–J).

The X fence sets the animal up for gymnastic exercises. Its construction holds the horse to the middle, starting it on the proper line toward each successive obstacle. It also puts the horse into the canter sequence on landing, so that it can jump any upcoming, larger obstacles more easily.

The cavalletti poles and X fence are beneficial to the horse and rider in many ways. By creating a perfect takeoff spot each time to the X, the cavalletti rails increase the horse's confidence and promote good jumping form. For the rider, cavalletti provide timing practice, requiring adjustment of the horse's trotting strides about 20 to 30 feet away from the initial rail in order to position the horse correctly for its first step over a pole. Since you must approach the poles at the proper speed in order to place the horse's feet correctly between them with each step, the spacing between

4.7 A–J The rider helps her horse maintain its balance by staying with its motion on the approach to the fence (A), at takeoff (B), and in the air (C). In contrast, this rider demonstrates how being ahead of the motion overloads the horse's forehand on the approach to the fence (D), at takeoff (E), and in the air, where the horse's leg position suffers from the rider's error (F). Compare the rider's hips that are with the motion on landing, so that her seat feels the saddle, but does not land heavily on the horse's back (G) with the rider whose hips have fallen behind the motion, and error known as "dropping back" (H). The first step after landing, this rider is correctly in balance with her horse (I), in contrast to the rider who is too far forward after landing (J).

the poles allows you to evaluate your sense of pace. If your horse is too slow or too fast on the approach, you can detect the mistake immediately after entering the cavalletti as the animal fumbles through the poles.

The cavalletti and X also enable you to practice the *mechanics* of riding over fences—that is, heels down and lower legs held snugly in place; knees aiding the lower leg in supporting the upper body weight; seat being held out of the saddle from takeoff until landing; upper body staying with the motion of the horse; hands following the horse's neck as it stretches forward; and eyes maintaining a straightforward line. Through such a simple and controlled exercise, you can practice the style you will need to be successful over more difficult obstacles.

Gymnastics

Gymnastics are exercises performed over a series of fences for the purpose of increasing the strength and agility of the horse. In the following exercises, the gymnastic routine is preceded by cavalletti poles and approached from a trot. Gymnastic exercises can also be set up without the cavalletti and approached at a steady canter, with the distances between the elements lengthened at least a foot more than when they are approached from the trot. Gymnastics are not only useful for teaching the horse and rider the mechanics of jumping, but can also be helpful in proving to a rider that he needs to do very little to help the horse jump.

Horse Exercises

It is best to start with a simple one-stride distance from the X to a narrow ascending oxer. This gives the horse the least opportunity in which to develop balance problems, such as

falling on the forehand, or rhythm problems such as rushing (fig. 4.8). Your initial objective is to make the horse as comfortable as possible through the exercise. The distances provided in fig. 4.8 are suitable for starting most horses and ponies in gymnastic training. However, since each animal has a slightly different length of stride, these distances must be adjusted to suit a particular animal's stride perfectly.

Use only poles when setting gymnastic fences, rather than solid elements such as a brush box, coop, wall, or gate. Poles are not only easy to adjust, but also will readily fall to the ground if a horse crashes into them (fig. 4.9).

The starting height for the rear rail of the oxer depends upon the animal's size and level of experience. In general, if you begin 6 inches lower than the maximum height over which you school your hunter, you will have a safe starting point. In the beginning, keep the front rail of the oxer 6 inches lower than the rear. The slope of the rails will encourage the animal to come forward to the fence and clearly show it that the obstacle has width. The width of the oxer should be very narrow for an inexperienced rider or animal—about 2' wide for horses and 1' wide for ponies. This discourages the animal from diving between the rails.

So far, we have made the necessary preparation for gymnastic work: adjusting the cavalletti to the horse's natural length of step; setting an X as the regulating fence for the horse's initial takeoff; and adjusting the distance between the X and oxer to comfortably fit the natural stride of the horse. Once the animal is moving confidently through the exercise, you can increase the difficulty by shortening the distance between the X and oxer in increments no greater than 6 inches at a time. Make sure that both the front and back rails of the oxer are moved closer to the X, so that only the distance between the X and the oxer has been changed, not the width of the oxer.

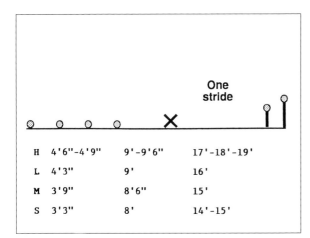

H	4'6"–4'9"	9'–9'6"	17'–18'–19'
L	4'3"	9'	16'
M	3'9"	8'6"	15'
S	3'3"	8'	14'–15'

4.8 Four cavalletti poles and an X-fence set the horse up for the one-stride distance to an ascending oxer. Measurements between elements are provided for horse (H), large ponies (L), medium ponies (M), and small ponies (S). To the left are distances between the cavalletti poles; in the middle are distances for the takeoff to the X; and to the right are measurements for the one-stride distance. (Note: When there is a range of measurement in the diagrams—as in the horse distances above—the measurements accommodate animals with a short, medium, or long natural stride.)

4.9 Four cavalletti poles lead to an X-fence, followed by a one-stride distance to an ascending oxer. These gymnastic obstacles by Jumps West are painted to aid in teaching. The stripe in the middle of each pole helps the rider focus on the center of the fences, which is where the obstacles should normally be jumped. The stripes to each side of center are useful when teaching riders to approach an obstacle off center, which is sometimes necessary in negotiating difficult bending lines and turns. No element of a gymnastic exercise should be set higher than 4', even for jumpers. Remember that the momentum of the horse is naturally restricted through the trot poles and the animal will lose momentum over each successive jump. Concentrate on shaping the horse's topline by using fences of a moderate height and make every effort to avoid straining the animal.

Shortening the distance between obstacles forces the horse to make a more powerful vertical thrust at takeoff and/or shorten its stride between fences. You must be careful, however, not to close the distance so much that it becomes an impossible trap, causing the horse to crash or jump oddly to clear the rails. Although 6-inch adjustments seem to be small, it usually takes only three or four of them before the horse begins to have difficulty with the shorter distance. If the animal does get into trouble, adjust the distance back to the original, comfortable striding so that confidence can be regained (figs. 4.10 A–C).

Having jumped the narrow oxer several times as the distance between fences was gradually shortened, the animal should be comfortable jumping a fence with width. Now

4.10 A–D The diagrams in figure 4.10 A through H show how altering the distance between fences or changing the height or width of fences affects the horses jumping style. The X-fence remains 2' high at its center and stationary throughout this exercise, while the oxer's dimensions and position are changed. The initial one-stride gymnastic is set to allow a horse with a medium-length stride to take one comfortable 11-foot stride between the X-fence and ascending oxer, when the gymnastic is approached at a trot. (A 12-foot stride would be normal if the exercise were approached at a canter.) The small symbol "X" above the oxer marks the peak of the horse's arc in the air (A). If the exercise is shortened to 17 feet, the horse must either take one 11-foot stride and take off closer to the oxer or shorten its stride to 10 feet to leave the ground the same distance from the oxer as before. The arrows show that when the stride is shortened to 10 feet, the horse's jumping effort is more horizontal than when the horse stays on an 11-foot stride and must use a vertical thrust to clear the front rail (B). If the exercise is shortened to 16 feet between the fences, the horse is forced to shorten its stride to 10 feet to be able to jump the oxer without knocking down the front rail. The shortened distance results in the horse having to both shorten its stride to 10 feet and thrust vertically off the ground (C). By moving the back rail 6" inches away from the front rail of the oxer, you can encourage the horse to stretch its body horizontally in the air, as indicated by the arrow above the fence. This promotes the proper bascule, as the horse stretches its neck down and out to counterbalance its hindquarters. You should always widen a gymnastic oxer while the fence is in ascending structure, so that the horse can clearly determine the new width on the initial approach (D).

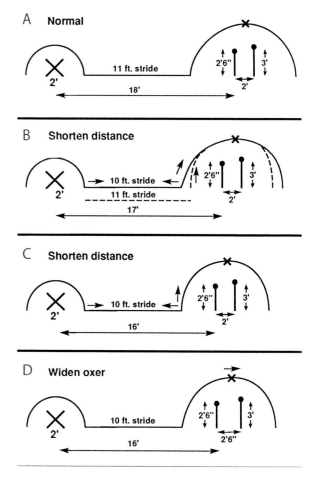

you can begin to widen and raise the oxer to influence the development of the horse's power and form. First, move the back rail away from the front rail. (This and all other adjustments in the following discussion, both horizontal and vertical, will involve 3-inch adjustments for ponies and 3- to 6-inch adjustments for horses. Your choice between a 3-inch or 6-inch adjustment for a horse will depend upon the animal's athletic ability and level of confidence.) Pulling the back rail away from the front one forces the animal to use a greater horizontal thrust to clear the fence (fig. 4.10 D).

Once the animal is jumping the wider oxer with confidence, raise the front rail of the obstacle step-by-step until it is level with the back rail, forming a square oxer. This will require either two 3-inch adjustments, with the animal jumping over both heights, or one 6-inch adjustment (fig. 4.10 E). If the horse or pony jumps the square oxer in

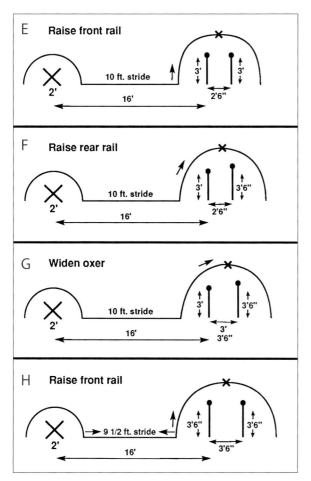

4.10 E–H Once the new width has been established, you can raise the front rail of the oxer until it is even with the back rail, forming a square oxer. The arrow indicates the increased vertical thrust that is necessary to clear the front rail when the oxer is squared (E). The height of the rear rail can be raised, requiring more power from the horse, but allowing the animal to use an easier, more horizontal thrust than if the oxer were squared (F). The oxer can be widened to encourage the proper bascule over this larger fence (G). By raising the front rail, you will require the horse to demonstrate power in its vertical thrust at this fairly large obstacle. Notice that the horse's length of stride between the fences has shortened once more to enable the animal to leave the ground at a reasonable takeoff spot in front of the oxer (H). Generally speaking, a horse must leave the ground at least as far from the obstacle as the height of the front rail in order to avoid knocking that rail down. A horse will rarely leave the ground closer than 3 feet from any fence, even a very small obstacle, such as the X-fence.

good form and with complete confidence, the back rail can be raised. This will force the animal to have a stronger vertical thrust off the ground to surmount the greater height, but will also allow the motion to be directed somewhat horizontally—that is, the animal's motion will not have to be as vertical to clear the first rail as it would have to be if the oxer were square (fig. 4.10 F).

Once the animal has gone through the exercise with the back rail raised, you can pull the back rail away from the front rail again. Let's imagine that at this point you decide you do not want to raise the fence to a height any

greater than that of the back rail. To adjust the fence to the maximum level of difficulty while maintaining this height, keep widening the obstacle step-by-step, until the fence is as wide as the back rail is high (fig. 4.10 G). Once the animal has jumped the fence at its maximum width, the front rail can be raised step-by-step until the oxer becomes square again, causing the animal to work harder to clear the first rail by demanding a stronger vertical thrust (fig. 4.10 H).

In short, the fence adjustments should be made by raising the rear rail, widening the obstacle, then raising the front rail, in that order, until you arrive at the desired height and width. By raising the rear rail first, you allow the horse to gauge the new height of the obstacle, while taking an easy path that is a blend of horizontal and vertical motion. In spreading the fence, as the second step, you use the far rail to define the width of the obstacle. Finally, by raising the front rail until it is even with the rear one, you test the horse's power and agility over the now familiar dimensions.

Generally speaking, both the height and width of an obstacle in a gymnastic setup should not exceed the measurement of the maximum height of the fences in the hunter division in which the animal shows:

Small Ponies 2'3"

Medium Ponies 2'6"

Large Ponies 3'

Children's Hunter Horses 3'

Adult Amateur Hunters 3'

Junior Hunters 3'6"

First Year Green 3'6"

Second Year Green 3'9"

The exception applies to horses that are shown in classes with fences set higher than 4'. Although a Regular Working Hunter may be required to jump fences up to 4'6" in competition, the maximum height for a gymnastic exercise for a Regular Working Hunter should be 4'. (Gymnastic fences for jumpers should also be set no higher than 4'.) If you normally show your horse in equitation classes, but not in one of the hunter divisions, use the height limit in your most demanding equitation class as your maximum height and width for the gymnastics. The maximum dimensions stated above are only guidelines. If you have set a fence well under these, but your animal appears to have reached its athletic or emotional limits, do not raise or widen the fence any further.

The goal of the exercise described on the pages prior is to teach the horse the proper mechanics of jumping. The cavalletti encourage the horse to maintain a steady rhythm when approaching an obstacle and force the horse to adjust its center of gravity backward quickly at a fixed takeoff point, which has been determined by the placement of the X fence. Through this restrictive approach, the horse learns to combine quick reflexes and power at takeoff, as opposed to increasing its pace to a fence and using speed to hurl itself over the initial obstacle.

Numerous adjustments can be made to gymnastic exercises according to what you are trying to accomplish. For example, if the animal jumps poorly from a normal takeoff spot and is only comfortable jumping from a long spot, your main concerns would be to teach the horse to engage its hocks and shift its center of gravity backward at takeoff and to use its hocks powerfully to thrust its body upward. This would involve shortening the distance and raising the rails, to create a more vertical thrust.

If a horse does not follow through properly in its arc— that is, does not keep its knees high, legs tightly folded, back rounded, and head and neck stretched down and out—then widen the obstacle to encourage the horse to stretch in the air. If you reach the width limits listed above, but the horse is still not using itself, you can widen the fence a little more; but be careful not to make the fence too wide for its height, since this will encourage the horse to dive between the rails. As a rule of thumb, the width should not exceed the height by more than 1' for horses or more than 6" for large ponies. I would not suggest widening a fence beyond the height of the obstacle when working with a small or medium pony.

Lengthening exercises can also be used to encourage the horse to take longer strides rather than adding an extra stride at the base of an obstacle. To make the horse lengthen

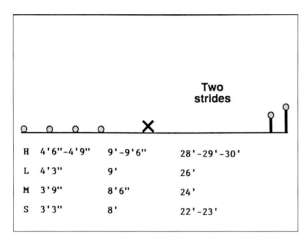

H	4'6"-4'9"	9'-9'6"	28'-29'-30'
L	4'3"	9'	26'
M	3'9"	8'6"	24'
S	3'3"	8'	22'-23'

4.11 The distances for a two-stride gymnastic are shown for horses (H) and large (L), medium (M), and small (S) ponies.

	1st distance	**2nd distance**	**3rd distance**
✕	One Stride	One Stride	One Stride
H	17-18-19	18-19-20	19-20-21
L	16	17	18
M	15	16	17
S	14-15	15-16	16-17
✕	Two Strides	Two Strides	Two Strides
H	28-29-30	29-30-31	30-31-32
L	26	27	28
M	24	25	26
S	22-23	23-24	24-25
✕	Three Strides	Three Strides	Three Strides
H	41-42-43	42-43-44	43-44-45
L	38	39	40
M	35	36	37
S	32-33	33-34	34-35

4.12 The distances listed are a "mix and match" chart for any combination of one-stride, two-stride, and three-stride gymnastic distances between an X-fence and three oxers. For example, to set a one-stride, two-stride, one-stride combination for a large pony (L), use the one-stride measurement of 16 feet from the column marked "1st distance," the two-stride measurement of 27 feet from the column marked "2nd distance," and the one-stride measurement of 18 feet from the column marked "3rd distance." These distances are intended to be used as a starting point. Adjust them as necessary.

its stride, set the distance between the X and oxer so that the horse must extend its stride a little to reach the takeoff spot, but not so long that the animal will find it easier to add a step. In this case, you must press the horse forward with your legs between fences to encourage it to lengthen to the proper spot, making it very difficult to shorten and add a stride.

After the horse is jumping well over a one-stride distance, introduce two strides between the X and oxer (fig. 4.11). From these early lessons with one-stride or two-stride distances, you can build a variety of combinations, using several oxers and even extending the distances to three strides or more (fig. 4.12). Notice in fig. 4.12 that for each successive position, you must add 1 foot in length. This accommodates a slight increase in impulsion that occurs throughout a gymnastic exercise, resulting in a natural lengthening of stride.

By setting short-to-long distances or long-to-short distances, you can teach the horse to make instantaneous stride adjustments. As a rule of thumb, your alterations from the normal gymnastic distances should not be greater than 1 foot per stride when either shortening or lengthening. However, you should not just subtract 1 foot per stride to make a short distance, then add 1 foot per stride to the following distance to make it long, since shortening or lengthening one distance will change the way the following distance rides, even if you don't change the footage in the following distance.

For example, suppose you initially set four cavalletti poles and an X followed by three oxers, with the distances between the jumps being 18 feet, 19 feet, and 20 feet to accommodate the horse's natural lengthening of stride (fig. 4.13 A). If you decided to change the last two distances to a short-to-long arrangement, then you would only have to change the measurement of the middle distance, since the final distance would ride longer than before as a result of the decreased momentum the horse would have from shortening its stride.

On the other hand, if you started with the same initial setup and wanted to change the last two distances to a long-to-short arrangement, once again you would only have to change the measurement of the middle distance, since the increased momentum needed to negotiate this longer distance would make the final distance ride shorter (fig. 4.13 B). (Although the measurement between the last two oxers would remain constant, the position of both fences would change, since if you only moved the second oxer, the distance between it and the third oxer would not remain the same as before.) You could change the distance between the last two oxers if you wanted to make the final distance ride a little longer or shorter; but it is wise not to adjust this distance until you see how difficult the change in the preceding distance has caused the final distance to ride when the final distance is set according to the normal measurement.

The exercises that I use the most involve the cavalletti and X followed by three oxers. I always use a one-stride distance between the X and first oxer when other oxers are to follow because I think it offers the most stabilizing setup for gymnastic training. If the animal is fairly inexperienced or tends to have a dull pace, set one stride between the first and second oxer then two strides between the second and third oxer to encourage the horse to continue its forward movement through the exercise (fig. 4.14 A).

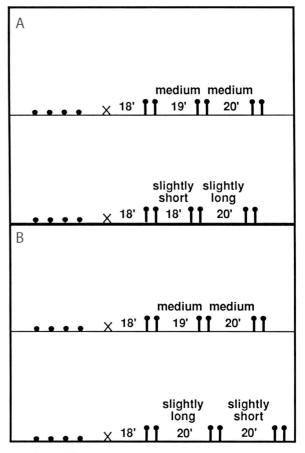

4.13 A & B Whenever you change one distance within a combination, it will affect the way the other distance or distances ride. For example, if you began with the combination set at 18 feet, 19 feet, and 20 feet, then reduced the middle distance to 18 feet, you would not only cause that distance to ride shorter than before, but would also cause the following distance to ride longer, since the horse would be approaching it with less momentum (A). Conversely, if you lengthened the middle distance from 19 feet to 20 feet, you would not only cause it to ride longer, but would also cause the following distance to ride shorter, since the horse would be approaching it with more momentum than before (B).

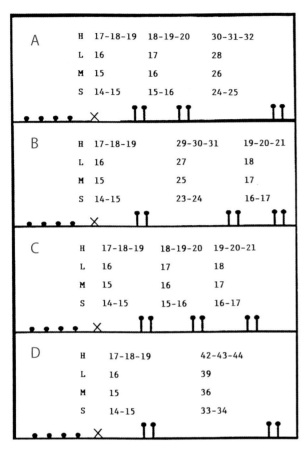

A	H	17-18-19	18-19-20	30-31-32
	L	16	17	28
	M	15	16	26
	S	14-15	15-16	24-25

B	H	17-18-19	29-30-31	19-20-21
	L	16	27	18
	M	15	25	17
	S	14-15	23-24	16-17

C	H	17-18-19	18-19-20	19-20-21
	L	16	17	18
	M	15	16	17
	S	14-15	15-16	16-17

D	H	17-18-19		42-43-44
	L	16		39
	M	15		36
	S	14-15		33-34

4.14 A–D The measurements are for the gymnastic exercises I find to be most useful: one-stride, one-stride, two-stride combination (A); one-stride, two-stride, one-stride combination (B); one-stride, one-stride, one-stride combination (C); and one-stride to three-stride combination (D).

———

To test a horse's coordination and concentration and to encourage it to balance itself at the end of a line of obstacles, use a two-stride to one-stride distance between the first and third oxer. This creates the alternation of a one-stride distance following the X, then a two-stride distance, and back to a one- stride distance, requiring the horse to quickly perceive the shorter distance between the last two obstacles

(fig. 4.14 B). It is important for a horse and rider to feel comfortable through combinations using one stride followed by two strides and vice versa, since these are commonly used in equitation and jumper courses.

To tighten a horse's form and sharpen its reflexes, use all one-stride distances. Be very careful not to set the fences too close or too high, for the horse will really be in trouble if it is overfaced within such a quick succession of fences (fig. 4.14 C).

Occasionally, you can use a three-stride distance following the initial one stride between the X and first oxer (fig. 4.14 D). This will gauge your horse's willingness to sustain a steady pace when it has more time to gain speed. This setup is particularly beneficial when working with quick horses, as a test following the preceding exercises. It will show you whether or not your horse has learned that it can approach the fences in a steady tempo and clear them. If the horse tries to run, return to one of the earlier exercises in which it has less time to gain momentum.

Rider Exercises

Most "rushers"—that is, horses that run to fences—are topped by a nervous rider who panics when the horse grows tense and who increases the problem by reacting too quickly and strongly with the aids. The rider usually pulls hard on the mouth of the animal to restrain it, while leaning too far forward to the fences to make sure he will not get left behind on takeoff. The unsympathetic hands cause sheer panic in the horse, while the inclined body encourages the horse to run. In fact, it is common to see a nervous rider drive his horse to a fence by pressing his upper body forward to the quick tempo of the horse's last steps before takeoff. It's as though the rider is so nervous he can no longer concentrate on anything other than getting from one side of the fence to the other.

4.15 A–D The reins have been tied into the mane prior to this exercise. The rider holds them long enough to steer straight toward the cavalletti, then drops the reins as she enters the poles (A). She successfully remains with the motion of her horse throughout the poles (B), at takeoff (C), and during landing (D). Her foot is a little flat in the landing phase, but she still has enough weight in the heel to support her upper body so that she doesn't lose her balance on landing.

If this description fits you and your horse, try to find a placid animal on which you can practice low gymnastic exercises, set no higher than 3'. First, knot the end of the reins around a clump of mane, so that when you drop them as you cross the second pole, they will not sag so far downward that they get caught in the horse's feet as it jumps. When your reins are absent, you will probably fear that if you cannot pull on the horse's mouth, the animal will tear through the fences in a mad gallop, even though you know you are now riding a calm horse. To reassure yourself, remember that the

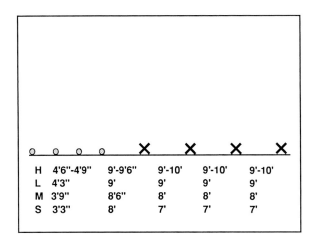

H	4'6"-4'9"	9'-9'6"	9'-10'	9'-10'	9'-10'
L	4'3"	9'	9'	9'	9'
M	3'9"	8'6"	8'	8'	8'
S	3'3"	8'	7'	7'	7'

4.16 Distances for four cavalletti poles and a series of four bounces are listed for horses (H) and large (L), medium (M), and small (S) ponies.

reins are only a few inches away and can be easily retrieved if anything goes wrong during the exercise; but try not to use them at all if possible.

Unable to slow the horse with your hands, you will become acutely aware of the effect of your upper body on the horse's pace. You will notice as you approach the exercise that if you lean forward, the horse will become quicker. You will then react naturally by opening your hip angle, so that your upper body goes back to its correct, original position. In most cases, this will immediately result in the horse slowing its pace. Through repetition of this exercise, you can learn to resist inclining too far forward on the approach to fences, inadvertently using your upper body as a driving aid.

I have found it interesting that asking a rider to pull back on imaginary reins further slows the horse in the gymnastic exercise. As you draw your hands backward, you will naturally open your hip angle and shift your weight to the horse's rear, causing the animal to shift its weight that direction, too, and not run on its forehand (figs. 4.15 A–D).

Another gymnastic exercise that will teach you to use minimal movement with your upper body over fences is a series of *bounces,* which are fences with no strides between them. Bounces are best set as a series of small X fences, rather than oxers, since the shape of the X holds the horse straight down the line, enabling you to concentrate on matters other than steering. The bounces can be set alone or following cavalletti (fig. 4.16).

When approached from the trot, the distances between the Xs should be approximately 9 to 10 feet for horses, 9 feet for large ponies, 8 feet for medium ponies, and 7 feet for small ponies. Set the center of each X 1' off the ground for a horse or large pony, 9" for a medium pony, and 6" for a small pony. As the animal rocks back and forth during the multiple jumping effort, you must adjust your center of gravity to match your animal's. These adjustments occur quickly, but subtly; and if you are not synchronized properly, the exercise feels very awkward. Through practice, you will eventually learn to keep your balance in the air, much as a person on roller skates learns how to adjust his balance so that he won't fall down.

Bounces can be negotiated with the rider holding the reins or with the reins knotted around a clump of mane. When the reins are taken away, you can keep your hands in normal position, or you can practice jumping with your arms extended outward (figs. 4.17 A–D) or with both hands on top of your hunt cap (fig. 4.18) to accentuate the feeling of seeking your center of gravity in the air .

Conclusion

Gymnastics can be fun if they are introduced properly. They offer a means of focusing on a particular fault, rather than having to deal with many problems at the same time. For example, if you have trouble keeping your heels down over fences, you can concentrate on doing only this within the

4.17 A–D Practicing over bounces with your arms extended will help you discover the correct placement of your upper body above the horse at takeoff (A), in the air (B), and on landing (C). This rider's leg remains steady and her upper body balanced throughout the exercise (D).

gymnastic setup, since the fences are set in such a way that the horse's straightness, tempo, and takeoff point are predetermined by the cavalletti and X, before you reach the first of the gymnastic fences.

Gymnastic exercises are also a nice change for the horse. They break up the monotony of galloping down lines with many strides between the fences and make the animal think harder about what it is doing. On a dull horse, this will result in quicker reflexes as it wakes up a bit to negotiate the closely set fences; while on a quick horse, the result is often a slower animal because it concentrates on the multiple fences, rather than just thinking of running.

4.18 Another method of finding your balance is to perform the exercise with your hands on your hunt cap.

There is the odd horse that is unnerved by gymnastics. Typically, this is the animal that has been overfaced in competition, particularly horses that have been shown in the jumper division without being properly prepared. In this case, progress may be slow, but gymnastic exercises are perfectly suited for rebuilding the confidence of a ruined animal.

A weekly routine for most horses includes a day of gymnastics, a day of schooling lines and/or courses, four days of flatwork (one of these days can be hacking in the woods), and one day of rest. Brief sessions of flatwork—about 10 minutes of work interspersed with one or two breaks lasting about a minute each—should always precede the jumping activities.

Striding between Fences

In the early 1960s, hunter courses were frequently set in a field with the fences so far apart that the number of strides between them was of no concern. You simply maintained a steady hunting pace around the course, often built on uneven terrain, and tried to find a bold, but safe, takeoff spot to each fence. The open field allowed a horse to reach a true hunting pace. Riders who rode too slowly were strongly penalized, based on the idea that an overly slow pace during a hunt would cause you to fall behind the field of horses and get lost in the countryside.

All of this began to change in the latter half of the decade. More and more hunter classes were held in arenas, which required less land, allowed the classes to run in a shorter time, provided level and more controllable footing, and gave the rider a greater advantage over his horse, since a railing aids steering and pace control. This containment, however, necessitated the measurement of strides between fences, for it soon became apparent that poorly set fences resulted in bad performances and accidents.

Today, the correct measurement and setting of courses is one of the most important and complicated elements in putting on a successful horse show. Any serious rider or coach should understand the basic principles of course designing, so that he can set good practice courses at home and correctly analyze courses at shows.

Course measurements for horses are based on a 12-foot stride as the standard. When jumping a line of two fences, a horse will generally land about 6 feet from the first obstacle, take 12-foot strides between the fences, then take off 6 feet before the second obstacle. Therefore, the combination of the landing and takeoff distances gives you an extra 12 feet that must be added to the total footage of the strides.

Distances between Fences for Horses			
Strides	3' Children's Hunter	3'6" Jr/Am. Hunter	4' Regular Working
1	25	26	27
2	36	37	38
3	48	49'6"	51
4	60	62	64
5	72	74'6"	77
6	84	87	90

4.19 The standard footage between fences is given for horses competing in the Children's, Junior, Amateur, and Regular Working Hunter divisions in a level ring with good footing. Adjustments to these distances should be made when the lay of the terrain, quality of footing, size of the arena, or other elements affect the horses' ability to perform in the standard striding.

For example, if a horse takes four 12-foot strides between the fences and has a 6-foot landing and 6-foot takeoff, the measurement for the line would be 48 feet plus 12 feet, or 60 feet in all for the four-stride line.

From this standard measurement, the lines in hunter courses are lengthened 6 inches to a foot per stride when the height of the fences or the level of the horses' ability warrants it (fig. 4.19). For example, a children's hunter, which is restricted by the USEF from jumping higher than 3', would not need as much momentum on course as a regular working hunter, which is required to jump at least 4' in A-rated sections. The children's hunter would comfortably move between the fences in the standard 12-foot striding; while the regular working hunter would naturally take longer strides between the fences—about 1 foot longer each stride—in keeping with the momentum necessary to jump the bigger fences. The junior working hunter would jump fences halfway between the heights of the children's and regular working hunters and would travel about 6 inches farther each stride than the chil-

Distances between Fences Previously Used for Ponies			
Strides	Small Ponies	Medium Ponies	Large Ponies
1	20	22	24
2	30	32	34
3	39	42	46'6"
4	48	52	58
5	57	62	69'6"
6	66	72	81

New Distances between Fences for Ponies			
Strides	Small Ponies	Medium Ponies	Large Ponies
1	20	22	24
2	30	32	34
3	41	43'6"	46
4	51	54	57
5	61	65	69
6	72	75'6"	80'6"
7	83	87	92

4.20 A & B Prior to 1990, the distances for three or more strides for ponies were based on a 9-foot stride for small ponies, a 10-foot stride for medium ponies, and an 11½-foot stride for large ponies, as shown in the diagram (A). The newer distances for ponies are based on averages of a compilation of several course designers' figures. You can see that in some cases the footage varies greatly from that used in previous years. There continues to be so much debate on appropriate pony distances that the USEF no longer provides specific recommendations, except for "suggested distances" for one-stride in-and-outs, which are the same measurements in both charts (B).

dren's hunter. A horse's takeoff and landing spots will actually be slightly farther from the fence as the height of the obstacle is raised; however, when figuring distances for horses, you use a 6-foot landing and takeoff and alter the length of the strides to accommodate the height of the fences.

The addition of 6 inches to a foot per stride is also appropriate for upper-level equitation riders. However, in equitation classes the courses are not set entirely with the longer distances as in the hunter classes, but rather alternate the long distances with some normal and some short ones to test the rider's ability to adjust the horse's length of stride promptly, yet smoothly.

Pony distances have been controversial for years. In the past, many horse shows have not altered the distances between the horse and pony classes, except for in-and-outs, which must be adjusted to meet USEF requirements. This generally resulted in the large ponies having to gallop too fast to make the horse strides, the medium ponies being at about the right pace when adding one extra stride each line, and the small ponies having to race around the course even with the addition of an extra stride each line.

To deal with this problem, course designers sought a formula to use for calculating pony distances. Until 1990, this formula was based on a 9-foot stride for small ponies, a 10-foot stride for medium ponies, and a 11 ½-foot stride for large ponies. These calculations applied to the number of strides only, not to the takeoff and landing, which were still calculated at 6 feet each. For example, when figuring four strides between fences for a medium pony, you calculated a 6-foot landing from the first fence, four strides at 10 feet each, and a takeoff spot 6 feet from the second obstacle, totaling 52 feet (fig. 4.20 A).

In October, 1990, *Horse Show Magazine,* the official publication of the USEF, published a list of suggested distances for ponies. These distances were based on a compilation of information provided by notable course designers for pony competitions. In some cases, the distances vary greatly from those that would be derived through the older method of calculation. There continues to be so much debate on the correct distances for ponies that the USEF no longer advocates specific distances, but leaves it to course designers (fig. 4.20 B).

Analyzing Distances

When analyzing distances, there are many important considerations besides the measurements between the fences. They include the size of the arena, the quality of the footing, the lay of the land, the position of objects in and around the arena, and the types of fences used at each location.

A suitable size for an arena for hunters and equitation horses is at least 240 feet long and 120 feet wide. If the arena is smaller than this, it will be difficult for the horse to travel down the lines in the standard striding, since it would be hard to gain enough momentum out of the corners to the first fence in each line. If the competition area is much larger than these measurements, such as on an outside course, the standard striding will ride a little cramped.

Footing is always an important consideration, not only in determining how the lines will ride, but also in regard to your horse's soundness. Deep footing bogs a horse down and makes it difficult for the animal to travel between the fences in the standard striding. It can cause pulled muscles, tendons, and ligaments and be a threat to your horse's soundness not only at the show, but permanently, if the injury is serious enough. Course designers usually shorten the distances between fences when the footing becomes overly deep either from sand that has loosened under impact during the show or from deep mud caused by relentless rain.

Muddy footing not only presents the problem of pulling on the horse's legs, but also of being slick, which makes jumping fences and turning corners quite difficult. Slippery footing intimidates the animal, causing it to shorten its stride and tempting it to stop at the fences. If the horse tries to stop at the last moment, it can skid into the fence, cutting or puncturing itself or, in rare cases, damaging its bones.

Ice is another dangerous condition, combining slickness and hardness and causing accidents involving both soft tissue and concussion to bones in the foot and leg. In short, don't jump a horse on ice. Even if the temperature isn't as low as the freezing point, the horse's performance can be drastically affected by cold weather. A chilly breeze makes most horses "feel good" and sometimes elicits a buck and a squeal of delight as the animal releases some of its excess energy. In cold weather, it usually takes much longer to work a horse down to the quiet emotional level you would like, particularly if the weather has just turned cold. A horse will want to "gain down the lines," progressively lengthening its stride between the fences, rather than maintaining even strides between obstacles. The lines, then, will ride shorter than normal unless you open your body angle and steady the horse with your hands, restricting it from lengthening. Even then, the horse may get the best of you. In this case, longeing or a controlled hand gallop will be your quickest and most effective solution.

The slope of the terrain is another consideration. Traveling uphill drains impulsion, while traveling downhill makes it easy for the horse to lengthen its stride. The exception to this is very hard or slick footing on a downward sloping terrain. If the footing is so hard as to be uncomfortable (such as red clay in the summer) or slick (such as short, dry grass), the horse will protect itself from the concussion or slipperiness by taking shorter strides. In these cases, a line will ride longer than normal, even though it is being jumped downhill.

The position of other horses or of objects in or around the ring may also affect the way a line rides. Generally, a horse will want to take longer steps traveling toward other horses at the in-gate than when traveling away from them. A horse may also react to sounds or moving objects and change its length of stride. A few things that typically distract a horse are the movements of people near the ring, particularly noisy children; a loudspeaker set close to the arena; decorative flags used to mark off areas such as the concession stand and secretary's booth; or a judge's umbrella, particularly if a strong wind causes it to billow. A horse show photographer may even spook a horse and capture the animal's horrified expression for posterity! The horse's normal reaction is to shorten its stride as it ducks away from these distractions; but if the horse is terrified, it may lengthen its stride and try to run away.

The type of fence used at each location is a very important consideration when determining the difficulty of the lines. For example, a 48-foot distance between two vertical fences would ride as three medium strides on a horse with a 12-foot stride (fig. 4.21 A). If the last fence on the line were an oxer instead, the line would ride a little longer, since the center of the horse's arc would not be over the first rail of the oxer, but between the first and second rail (fig. 4.21 B). If both fences on the line were oxers, then the distance would ride even longer, with the horse's arc coming earlier on the first fence and later on the last (fig. 4.21 C).

In general, verticals encourage a horse to go forward and oxers slow a horse down. On course, two oxers in a row will rob a horse of impulsion and make the line ride longer than if the horse's arc peaked at the same two places over verticals. Also, a square oxer will tend to slow a horse down more than an ascending oxer, particularly when the fences are big.

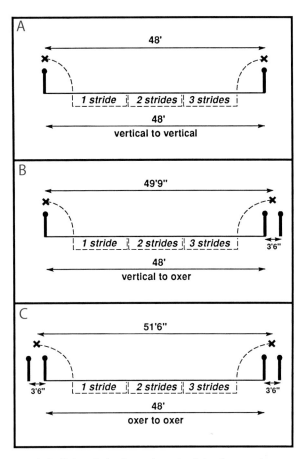

4.21 A–C Although the fences in each of the diagrams have a distance of 48 feet between them when measured from the base on the landing side of the first fence to the base on the takeoff side to the second fence, each of the lines rides differently because of the construction of the fences. In the first diagram, the peak of the horse's arc (indicated by the symbol "X") occurs directly over each vertical fence (A). When the second fence is changed to an oxer, the peak of the arc occurs between the two rails, making the 48-foot distance ride the same as a 49 3/4-foot distance between two vertical fences (B). If both fences were oxers, the 48-foot distance would ride the same as a 51 1/2-foot distance between two vertical fences (C).

A triple bar, which is sometimes used in equitation classes as well as jumper classes, encourages the horse to lengthen its body in the air, so that the animal lands in a long frame, on a long stride. It is more difficult to collect the horse when moving from a triple bar to a vertical fence than when moving from an oxer or from a vertical to a vertical fence.

An oxer can be helpful when placed at the end of a normal or short line. The width of the fence slows the horse in the air, making it easier for you to collect in preparation for the upcoming corner. Also, the horse can be a little deep to an oxer and usually maintain the correct form. However, oxers can present a problem when they are placed at the end of a long line, for the horse may not be able to meet the takeoff spot accurately and may dive through the rails from an overly long spot.

Vertical fences are easy to negotiate when the horse can leave from a normal or long spot; but many horses hang their forelegs, knock the top rail down, or even stop when placed too deep to a vertical fence. You can see, then, that you approach different fences in different ways. You would like to meet an oxer, either square or ascending, from a normal to slightly deep takeoff spot; on the other hand, it is preferable to meet a vertical from a normal to slightly long spot. When approaching a triple bar, try to find a slightly deep spot, since this will discourage the horse from becoming too long and flat in the air.

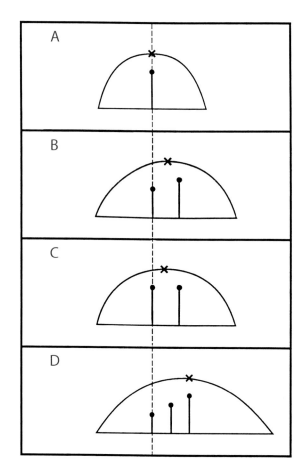

4.22 A–D The peak of a horse's arc occurs directly above a vertical (A), approximately two-thirds the distance from the front to the back rail of an ascending oxer (B), halfway between both parts of a square oxer (C), above the last rail in a triple bar (D).

Walking Courses

Before you ride over a course, walk the distances on the lines to determine how each line will ride. In order to do this correctly, you must be able to walk a 3-foot step and know by feel that it is accurate. Practice beforehand by stretching a measuring tape on a floor and walking beside it with your eyes focused straight ahead. Count your steps as you walk, then stop after several steps and see how many feet you have covered according to the tape measure. The footage on the tape should measure three times the number of steps you took. For example, 12 feet would equal four steps at 3 feet each.

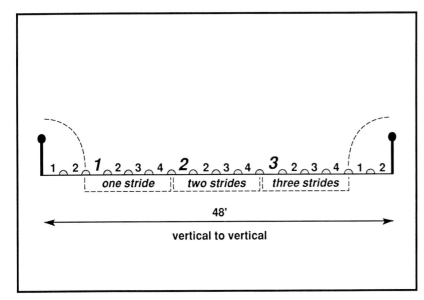

4.23 To accurately walk distances between fences, you must know how a 3-foot step feels. When walking from vertical to vertical, as in the diagram, you would begin by taking two 3-foot steps from the first vertical fence to mark the landing point. (Each step is represented by gray half-circles.) Then, count the strides as follows: "One... two, three, four" to mark the first stride; "Two... two, three, four" to mark the second stride; "Three... two, three, four" to mark the third stride. At that point, when you walk the final two steps to the fence, you will realize that the takeoff is exactly 6 feet, which means that the line is a normal three-stride distance for a horse.

To figure how a distance will ride, walk the distance from where the center of the horse's arc will occur on one fence to where the center of its arc will occur on the next. Over a vertical fence, the center of the horse's arc is directly above the fence; over an ascending oxer, in which the first rail is 3 to 6 inches lower than the second, it is about two-thirds the distance from the first rail to the second rail; over a square oxer, it is halfway between the two parts of the obstacle; and over a triple bar, in which three ascending rails form the fence, it is over the last rail (figs. 4.22 A–D).

To walk distances to determine horse strides, begin by standing on the landing side of the first fence in the line. Note where the center of the horse's arc will be according to the type of fence, then walk two 3-foot steps to establish the approximate landing point. When calculating from a vertical fence or triple bar, you can back against the fence, then walk

forward two steps to find the landing point. When an oxer is used, you must visually estimate a 6-foot distance from where the center of the horse's arc will be.

Mentally designate the landing spot by counting "one, two" for your initial 3-foot steps. Then begin counting the actual strides, thinking, "*one*...two, three, four" for the first 12-foot stride, "*two*...two, three, four" for the second 12-foot stride, "*three*. . .two, three, four" for the third 12-foot stride, and so on, until you are within takeoff range for the upcoming fence. Finally, count the last steps to see if the takeoff is set normally, which would be two steps (6 feet) to the center of the horse's arc (fig. 4.23).

When analyzing distances of three strides or longer, if you are only able to take one 3-foot step before reaching the center of the second fence, then the line will "ride short"—that is, the horse will have to travel on strides shorter than 12 feet

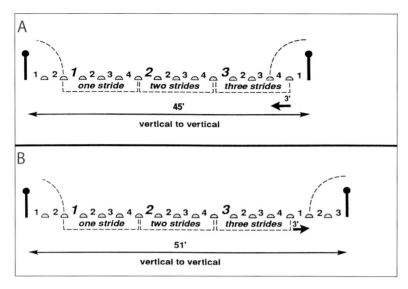

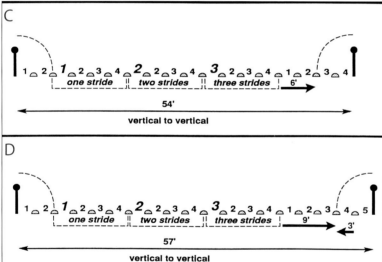

4.24 A–D When walking a line, if you have only one step left for takeoff instead of two, then you know the line will ride short. In this example of a three-stride distance, you would have to collect the horse to an 11-foot stride to ride the line properly. The horse would then be able to accommodate the 3-foot less than normal footage by deducting 1 foot for each of the three strides (A). If you had an extra step left before takeoff, then you would have to gallop the horse on a 13-foot stride down the line, covering the extra 3 feet by adding a foot per stride (B). If there were two extra steps left before takeoff you would have to increase the horse's stride to 14 feet to make the distance, with the extra 6 feet being covered by the horse extending 2 feet per stride (C). Finally, if there were three extra steps left before takeoff the horse would have to travel on 15-foot strides to make the distance, or add one stride and cover the distance in 11' 3" strides. To make the 15-foot strides, most horses would have to run. The better option is to collect the horse 9 inches per stride and ride the distance in four moderately collected strides (D).

to end up at the correct takeoff spot (fig. 4.24 A). If you count two steps and still have room for one more step before reaching the center of the horse's arc, the distance will "ride long," and you must lengthen each of your horse's strides beyond 12 feet to reach the proper takeoff spot (fig. 4.24 B). If you have two extra steps left, then you must choose between riding a very long line or adding an extra stride and riding a very short line, with the decision depending upon the horse's length of stride and jumping ability (fig. 4.24 C). Finally, if you have three extra steps left, you must either ride a tremendously long line, or add a stride and ride a slightly short line. The latter is usually the better decision even when there are five or six strides on a line, since you don't want your horse to run to the fences (fig. 4.24 D).

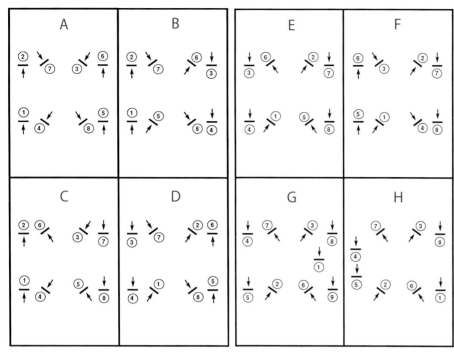

4.25 A–H Most horse shows use the same basic pattern for every hunter section, varying the course for each class by merely changing the order in which the lines are ridden (A–F). The course can be made more interesting through the use of a single fence on a line (fence 1 in diagram G); starting between two fences in a line (fence 1 in diagram H); or using an in-and-out on course (fences 4 and 5 in diagram H). (The more typical setting of an in-and-out is as part of a three-fence line, in which the in-and-out is used at the end of the line.)

The degree to which the horse's strides must be adjusted depends on how many strides there are between the fences. For instance, if you have only three strides between fences, then shortening or lengthening the takeoff spot by 3 feet will force the horse to collect or extend its stride 1 foot per stride; whereas if there are six strides between the fences, the horse would need to alter its steps only 1/2 foot per stride to reach the correct spot.

Once you have analyzed the course according to 12-foot increments, adapt your plan to the length of stride your horse actually takes. If the animal has a stride longer than 12 feet, long lines will ride normally, medium lines will ride a little short, and short lines will ride very short. Conversely, if your horse is short-strided, short lines will ride normally, medium lines will ride long, and long lines will ride very long.

Setting Fences

Most hunter courses consist of two outside lines and two inside (diagonal) lines. Occasionally you will see a variation on these patterns through the addition of a single fence or the starting of the course over the second fence in a line (figs. 4.25 A–H).

To set a typical course of two outside and two inside lines, consider the length of the ring and plan for at least three straight strides to the first fence and following the last fence on each long side of a rectangular arena. In an oval ring, plan at least two straight strides preceding the first fence and two straight strides following the last fence on each long side of the arena (figs. 4.26 A & B). These arrangements give you time to adjust your horse's stride if you are

4.26 A & B When setting hunter fences in a rectangular ring, allow for at least three straight strides preceding and following each outside line (A). In an oval arena, allow for at least two straight strides preceding and following each outside line (B).

and at least three straight strides in an oval arena, since the horse will have to regain more impulsion after the acute turn to a diagonal line than when approaching an outside line. (Nothing is psychologically worse for a rider than seeing that a striding adjustment is necessary and not having the time to make it!)

For horses, there are usually four or five strides between fences on an outside line in a hunter course set in an arena, unless an in-and-out is used, in which case the most typical striding is four strides to a one-stride in-and-out. Remember to account for the 6-foot landing and 6-foot takeoff within the line when you are figuring the striding. For example, if you want the horse to take five strides between fences, measure six multiples of 12 feet, or 72 feet (fig. 4.27).

If the arena is at least half as wide as it is long, you can center the fences of each diagonal line on the imaginary lines from corner to corner. If the width is less than half of the length of the ring, it will be difficult, if not impossible, to set the diagonal lines, since they will crowd the outside lines (figs. 4.28 A–D).

When using an in-and-out, place it toward the end of the course, as the last segment in a line of fences. It will ride best if the "in" is a vertical and the "out" is an oxer. The vertical fence will invite the horse into the combination, and the oxer will help the horse maintain good form as it leaves the combination.

As for choosing types of fences for various locations, you can't go wrong with a brush box as your first fence. Generally, horses are most comfortable with substantially built obstacles in natural colors, such as brown or green. Busy patterns tend to confuse horses visually, as do fences that allow daylight to poke through; and objects that move, such as a bucket in the pillar of a wishing well, will spook many horses.

Fences with shadowy places also make a horse hesi-

approaching a bad takeoff spot. (I prefer a rectangular arena to an oval one, not only because it is more useful for training horses and riders, but also because it gives the person setting the course more options and makes it easier to measure the arena.) When setting a diagonal line, leave at least four straight strides before the first fence in a rectangular arena

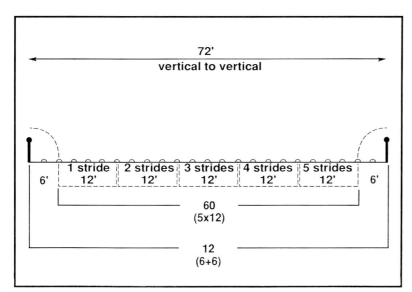

4.27 Remember to count the 6-foot landing and 6-foot takeoff when figuring the distance between fences. For example, a five-stride distance for a horse would be five strides multiplied by 12 feet per stride (60 feet) plus a 6-foot landing and 6-foot takeoff (12 feet), totaling 72 feet.

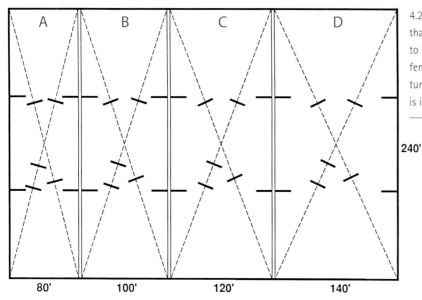

4.28 A–D If the width of the ring is less than half the length, it will be difficult to set a good course. Notice how the fences become less crowded and the turns less acute as the width of the ring is increased.

tant to jump. I think this must be a combination of the visual problem that shadows present (since a horse's eye does not rapidly adjust to a decrease in light) and a natural instinct to avoid any shady crevice where an aggressive "critter" could be hiding.

The way you decide to place your fences, then, depends upon how difficult you want to make your schooling course. If you want a simple, inviting course, use quiet colors, solid construction, and definite ground lines to establish the bases of the fences. Place more challenging obstacles, such as the wishing well, at the end rather than the beginning of a line. Use the more difficult fences on lines coming toward the in-gate or out-gate, rather than going away from them. When setting fences for a hunter try to make the course appealing to the horse so that the animal will be encouraged to perform its best (figs. 4.29 A–H).

When setting a practice equitation course, you can increase the difficulty of the fences by adding brightly colored rails, standards, or panels; by placing decorative objects around the fences; by setting spooky fences at the beginning of lines or on lines going away from the in-gate; by altering the distances between fences so that they are slightly longer or shorter than usual; or by lessening the number of poles on the face of an obstacle, making it airier and less inviting (figs. 4.30 A–F).

The point of practicing over equitation-type courses is to test your ability to apply your knowledge and physical skill to achieve a desired result. You don't want to overface yourself by setting a course that is too difficult any more than you want to overface your horse by setting jumps that are too wide or high or that require impossible striding adjustments. However, you do want to challenge yourself to think, just as a good course designer at a horse show would do. Take time, then, in working out your course plan, concentrating on testing the specific skills that will be required of you in the show ring. Nothing will give you more confidence at a horse show than having prepared yourself well at home.

We have looked at courses largely from the course designer's point of view so far, considering the elements that go into making a safe, yet challenging course. Now we will analyze courses from the rider's point of view, starting with the simplest course for a beginner equitation rider and moving on to the most advanced concepts tested in the

Medal, Maclay, and USEF Talent Search Finals. Although I am not dealing specifically with jumpers in this book, I will discuss the major elements of course analysis and execution that pertain to jumpers, since the jumper division is really an extension of the equitation division.

Basic Goals on Course

When your horse or pony is comfortable over cavalletti and gymnastics, you can move on to jumping segments of a basic hunter course. Break down the course into several elements: the initial circle, the first line, the second line, the third line, the fourth line, and the ending circle.

First, let's consider the purpose of the initial circle, how it should be performed in competition, and errors commonly made at this stage in the course. The purpose of the initial circle is to establish the proper pace for the entire course. When the circle is properly performed, you enter the ring and complete the first quarter of the circle at the posting trot. Then, you sit for a few steps to feel the sequence of your horse's footfalls and, once you sense that the horse is balanced and attentive, ask for the canter. Immediately after the horse has taken the proper lead, rise into two-point position. For the remainder of the circle, attempt to establish the proper pace. By the end of the circle, the horse should have the same pace it will have at the end of the course—no slower, no faster (fig. 4.31).

The circle gives you a chance to know your horse. A perceptive rider can sense a tense or tired animal and compensate for these problems on the approach to the first fence. As when working on the flat, you must be adaptable and deal with each problem as it arises, rather than permanently tagging your horse with a certain label, such as quick

4.29 A–H Although these hunter fences appear different (A–D), their basic construction is the same, with a flower box at the base, followed by a small wall, then a small gate that is hung so that the bottom of it is just below the top of the wall, and finally poles set as a vertical fence or oxer. This is a popular combination of elements, enabling course designers to set fences quickly for everything from a small pony to a regular working hunter. The next four fences were made by Jumps West, which manufactures both wooden and PVC fences. Some of the traditional-style fences shown are a brush box and rails (E), gate and rail with a flower box as a ground line (F), aqueduct with rails (G), and rolltop with rails (H).

4.30 A–F These equitation fences by L.J. Enterprises are composed of poles and a sectional picket fence (A), poles and a hanging gate (B), planks and poles (C), and a small aqueduct and poles (D). The combination is composed of three color-coordinated fences, made up of two walls, a hanging gate, and poles (E). The tan-and-green gate-and-rail fence was set for an equitation course, but could also serve as a hunter fence because of its natural colors and lack of stripes on the poles (F). These photographs were taken while the course was in the process of being set the day before the Wachovia Jumper Classic at Beacon Hill Show Stables, so all of the elements were not yet in place.

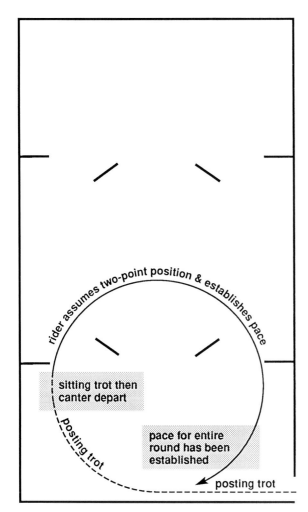

rider assumes two-point position & establishes pace

sitting trot then canter depart

posting trot

pace for entire round has been established

posting trot

4.31 The initial circle on course should give you enough space to reach the proper pace prior to the first line of fences. Begin with a posting trot the first quarter of the circle, then perform a sitting trot a few steps and ask for the canter depart. Immediately rise into two-point position and increase the horse's length of stride. By the end of the circle, you should have established the correct pace for the course. By performing the canter depart at the same place each time and striving to achieve the correct pace by the end of the circle, you give yourself restrictions, which enable you to notice changes in the horse from one class to another.

or dull, thinking that the horse never changes. The horse that was quick while schooling the course yesterday might now be tired and move reluctantly toward the fences. In contrast, the horse that is usually dull might react keenly to a billowing spectators' tent and suddenly be more alert in the show ring than it has ever been in its life!

The circle foretells much that will happen on course. For example, a horse that dwells as it passes the gate toward the end of the circle is an animal that is "herdbound," preoccupied with staying near other horses. A herdbound animal works against the rider's efforts by concentrating on other horses rather than on the fences. It will usually be very bad down the first line of the course, either chipping in at the first fence or refusing to jump altogether. A horse that timidly shies from objects during the circle will often shorten its strides to each fence, run out, or stop at a fence. This is often the green horse, requiring a firm, but tactful, rider to get it through the course.

The overly bold animal that progressively lengthens its steps during the circle is the potential runaway. If you have not attended to this problem by bringing the horse down to a suitable pace before the circle ends, it is likely to leave out a stride within a line and jump dangerously.

The circle is important, then, not only because it provides room to get the horse to its proper pace, but also because it allows time to evaluate your horse's general behavior and make the necessary adjustments to minimize potential problems. If your horse is dull, use the circle as a runway to lengthen the animal's stride and increase its pace. If it is quick, use the railing to slow the horse down, rather than rushing toward the first fence (fig. 4.32). You will find that the circle is often a more reliable indicator of how the horse will behave on a course than the earlier warm-up session in the schooling area, for an animal can be relaxed

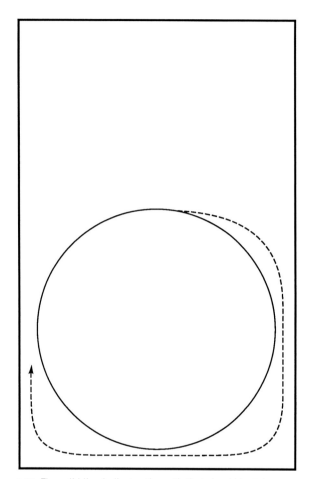

4.32 The solid line indicates the path that should be taken during the initial circle on a normal or dull horse. This path allows you to steadily increase the pace until the desired speed and length of stride have been reached. The dotted line indicates an alternate route that is useful for horses that start out too fast. Having completed the first half of the circle, you should realize if you are in trouble and steer the horse on a fairly square pattern, using the railing to confront the animal and help you slow it down.

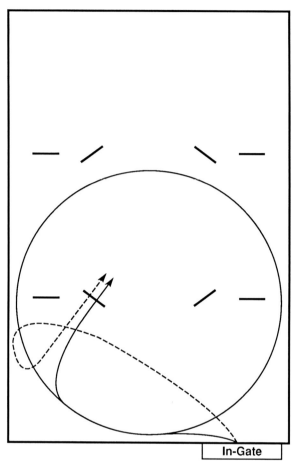

In-Gate

4.33 The solid line shows the correct path to the first fence, which is a full circle followed by the approach to the fence. The dotted line shows a path that is used only by the most poorly educated rider.

working alongside other horses when schooling, yet be panicked when asked to jump fences by itself.

It is the circle that frequently reveals a poor rider. He will often run his horse into the canter from the trot and pick up the wrong lead. If he is really bad, he won't realize his mistake and will approach the first fence on the incorrect lead rather than immediately bringing the horse back to the trot and correcting his error. A poor rider may also make

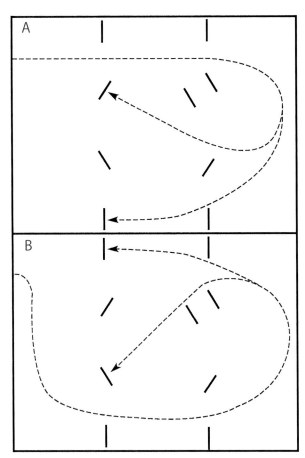

4.34 A & B If the approach to the first fence allows plenty of room to establish pace, you do not need to circle. For example, starting between two fences on a line coming home, you could use a long clockwise (A) or counterclockwise (B) approach and leave the circle out altogether.

a circle that is too small, preventing the horse from reaching the proper pace or length of stride; or he may circle in the wrong direction to the first fence, which though completely illogical happens from time to time (fig. 4.33).

Since the main purpose of the circle is to set the proper pace for a course, you should not only use it when showing, but also when schooling your horse at home. The exception

is when the approach to the first fence is so long that you can establish the correct pace without riding a circle (figs. 4.34 A & B).

Once the pace is set, concentrate on the first line of fences. In a typical hunter course, the first line starts as the horse crosses the centerline of the ring at the end of the circle and ends when the horse crosses the centerline on the opposite end of the ring (fig. 4.35). As a general principle, you should move the horse forward coming out of a turn, since a curve will tend to decrease the horse's pace, and should collect a horse going into a turn to balance it for the upcoming curve. From the centerline of the ring to the first fence, then, encourage the horse to move forward so that it can as closely as possible maintain the pace and length of stride established in the initial circle. After the last fence on the line, collect the horse in preparation for the upcoming corner (fig. 4.36).

Look at the first line of fences all the way from the centerline. This will give you plenty of time to decide what adjustment to the horse's stride is necessary to reach the proper spot to the first fence and will enable you to make the adjustment subtly. If you concentrate on the upcoming fence and don't allow your eyes to wander, you'll find a suitable takeoff most of the time.

You should visually line up the middle of the fences and keep your eyes riveted on that line no matter what happens. A bucking horse, an animal that is threatening to stop at a fence, or one that is "drifting" to the left or right on the approach to an obstacle are typical situations that can cause you to lose your focal point. If the horse is successful in distracting your attention either downward or to the side, you will not realize how far it is moving off the proper line. When you finally look up, you might be unable to steer it over the fence (figs. 4.37 A & B). The proper response to a horse's bad behavior is to stare down the line of fences and drive your

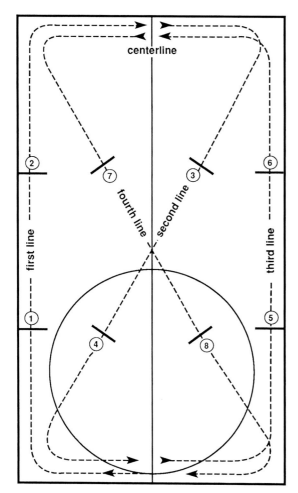

4.35 Think of a hunter course as four lines, with each beginning and ending at the centerline. (Note: When asked to "pull up on a line" following a fence, halt while in a straight line with the obstacle, rather than turning the corner.)

4.36 Press the horse forward from the centerline to prevent it from shortening its stride radically in the corner; maintain even strides between the fences; then collect the horse to shorten its stride, balancing it for the upcoming corner and, possibly, a change of lead.

horse as straight as possible from the center of one obstacle to the center of the next, figuring out at each instant how to make corrections that will keep your horse straight and get it to a good takeoff spot (fig. 4.38).

For the first line of fences, most people have to ride forward, pressing their horses into long strides not only to the

first obstacle, but also between the first two fences. (The exception, of course, is when you are on a very long-strided horse.) Even if the first line is based on the same length of stride as the other lines, it will usually ride longer. There are two reasons for this. First, the initial fence is often set going away from both the in-gate and out-gate, so that the horse

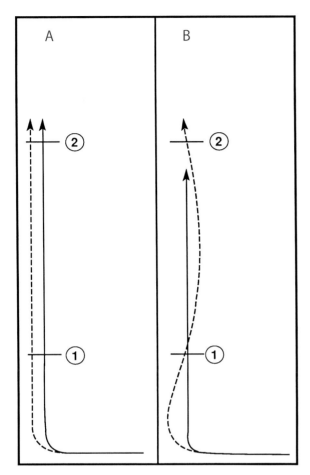

4.37 A & B A rider distracted from focusing on the fences may slightly overshoot a line, so that he jumps it off center (A), or may overshoot the line so far that he ends up wavering between the fences (B).

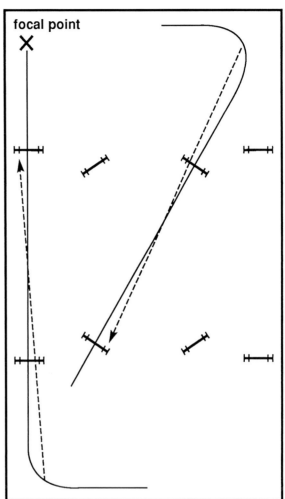

4.38 To ride a line of fences properly, turn onto the line just as you see the far standard of the last fence on line come into view between the standards of the first fence on line. As you turn, look to the far end of the ring to sight a focal point that will help you steer the horse down the middle of the line of fences. Although the use of a focal point is demonstrated in the example of the outside line, it is even more important to have a focal point at the end of a diagonal line. A diagonal line, being off the rail and at the end of a more acute turn, is easier to overshoot.

is not being drawn "home" toward the gates, which represent access to the companionship of other horses, as well as to a bath, food, and the comfort of a stall. Second, a horse is usually calmer prior to the first fence than it is after jumping several fences on the course. This holds true for even the most placid animal.

Knowing this, you should approach the first line by increasing the horse's length of stride out of the corner, seeking a bold, but reasonable, takeoff spot to the first fence; then expect to ride strongly to the next fence, since in most cases this is necessary in order to reach the proper spot to the second fence on the first line. Once the horse has landed over the second fence, collect it, shortening its strides and balancing it for the upcoming turn.

A horse will land after the second fence with a great deal of impulsion and a stride that is longer than that established in the circle. Unchecked, it will become faster and longer in stride throughout the course, "running under the fence" at the end of each line or leaving out a stride and "diving" over the obstacles. Both of these are terrible errors, the second being very dangerous.

It is important, then, for you to collect the horse back to its initial length of stride at the end of each line. Teach the horse to expect collection at this point by schooling courses one line at a time and halting just before the turn at the end of each line (fig. 4.39). Once your horse understands that it must submit to your restricting aids, you can attempt to jump a line of fences and continue around the corner. If the horse lands on the counter lead after the last fence on the line, ask it to perform a flying change just before the upcoming turn.

Several exercises discussed earlier have prepared your horse for the flying change at the end of a line. First were the downward transitions on the flat. Later, flying changes were introduced during flatwork. Now, repeated halting serves to

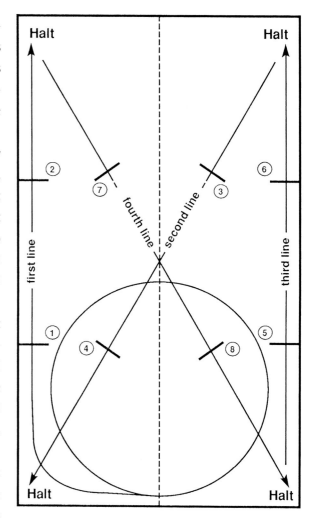

4.39 Halting at the end of each line promotes obedience in the horse. Approach the first line by circling, to reach a jumping pace. For the following lines, on a normal or dull animal you can circle at the ends of the ring preceding the approach to each line. If your horse is quick, pick up the canter at the place you halted and go directly to the next line, denying it the opportunity to gain too much speed.

THE BIG PICTURE
Using the Whole Ring

"More footage means more time to think through problems and more room to correct them."

While judging a horse show, I may see as many as a third of the competitors not fully utilizing the space within the arena. By allowing the horse to stay away from the railing on the ends of the ring, the rider can lose a great deal of footage. This loss is important because more footage means more time to think through problems and more room to correct them.

To understand the importance of extra footage, it helps to stand at the center of the short side of an arena and walk a direct line to the upcoming fence, counting your steps along the way. Then, start at the same place and stay along the rail as long as possible before turning onto the line to the upcoming fence. You will find that there is a great deal of difference between the footage of the first and second paths. You can easily lose three strides or more, according to how early the horse leaves the railing at the end of the arena. If the animal cuts the entire end of the ring and never travels along the rail, the amount of footage lost is simply astounding.

If you already have difficulty finding the correct takeoff spot, then cutting the corners will only add to the problem. To get the greatest advantage from the arena, ride directly to the rail at the end of a line, then bend your horse along the turn, traveling close enough to the railing that it will serve as a barrier to keep the horse from drifting, but not so close as to catch any part of your leg on the rail. Stay along the rail as long as you can without overshooting the turn to the upcoming fence. This path will give you extra time to think and act, which is a tremendous advantage in any endeavor, equestrian or otherwise.

In keeping with this, be sure to make your initial circle big enough—about half the size of the arena. The beginning circle is the runway that enables you to reach the proper pace before the first fence. I've seen tiny circles that don't allow the pace to be achieved, and I've seen circles that were big enough, but performed by a rider who doesn't seem to realize that the size of the circle relates to pace on course. To use the whole ring to your best advantage, you must not only take a generous path, but also be smart in your use of that space.

mark the place where the flying change should occur. If all of these exercises can be performed well by your horse, the flying change at the end of a line should be no problem.

The main error riders commit in attempting the flying change on course is turning the corner too soon, tracking a sloping turn that makes it very easy for the horse to remain on the counter lead. In contrast, a horse that is ridden directly toward the rail until the last couple of strides will be confronted by the rail and encouraged to make a decision about its lead (fig. 4.40). The deeper path to the rail also provides an extra stride or two during which you can think about the next line and correct any problems that might have arisen. For instance, if the horse is playing around or pulling a little, the extra strides make it easier to regain control before going forward to the next line.

I must stress again the importance of your eyes on course. If you will look in the direction of the upcoming turn while applying your outside leg for the flying change, the horse will clearly sense the direction you intend to go at the moment of the switch—that is, around the turn, not over the railing! The principle is similar to the situation of an automobile running off the road because the driver is sightseeing. When the driver looks to the right, everything in his body is subtly drawn in that direction. If he doesn't realize that the car is "following his eyes," he will inadvertently steer the vehicle off the road. While this works against a driver, it can work for a rider. A horse is not only affected by your intended aids, but also by delicate shifts in your weight. Therefore, when you look in the direction you are about to turn, the subtle movements of your body that occur at the same time will signal the horse that you want it to go in that direction. This does not mean that you should throw your weight to the inside of the turn, for this makes it more difficult for the horse to perform the flying change; but you should allow

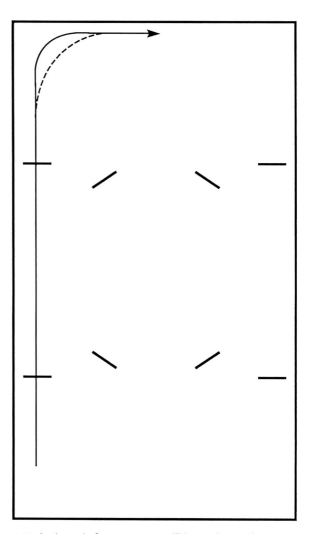

4.40 At the end of an arena, you will have a better chance of getting the flying change if you steer the horse on a fairly deep path through the corner (indicated by the solid line), rather than steering it on a path with a less acute curve (indicated by the dotted line). On the deeper path, the horse is confronted by the railing and must collect itself and make a decision about its lead. In contrast, the shallow path makes it just as convenient for the horse to remain on the counter lead as to perform a flying change.

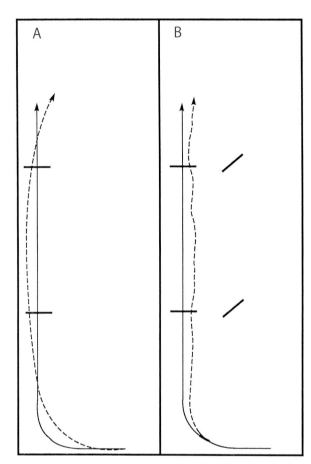

4.41 A & B If you allow your horse to bulge (A) or waver (B) down a line, you will have to drive it between the fences at an overly fast pace to make up for the lost footage.

horse is in a line of fences, the less footage the animal loses to sideways motion. Straightness, then, makes it possible for the horse to travel down the line in the proper striding without having excessive pace. In contrast, a horse that wanders off the correct line must increase its speed to lengthen its stride, so that it can make up for the footage lost in sideways motion (figs. 4.41 A & B).

A rider's eyes will often indicate his potential for success. If he homes in on the fences and doesn't let his horse or the surroundings distract him from his plan, he has a great chance for success. But if his eyes show no concentration, no sense of purpose, you can tell he is not going to do well.

The first line in the course ends as the horse crosses the centerline (see earlier fig. 4.35). From the last fence on the line until this point, collect the animal to control its pace and length of stride; make sure it is on the inside lead going into the turn; and bend it around the corner so that it will be balanced on the curve. When a horse is collected enough to go into a turn safely, it will be slightly below the length of stride appropriate between the fences. To get back to the desired length of stride, you must gradually increase the horse's impulsion as the animal comes out of the turn, so that it lengthens its stride incrementally. This is commonly referred to as "flowing out of the turn."

If you desperately drive your horse forward during the last two or three steps before the jumps, rather than encouraging it to lengthen gradually to the correct takeoff spots, then your animal will become anxious. It may turn into a chronic rusher and dash to every fence, or it may begin to add an extra stride at the base of the fences rather than making the extraordinary effort to lengthen its stride within the short space. In fact, some horses will combine these errors of rushing to the fences, then adding an extra stride before takeoff, when they don't trust their riders' commands.

your natural reflexes to provide an additional aid as your body follows the direction in which you are looking.

Using your eyes well is critical when you are approaching a line of fences. By focusing down the entire line, rather than from one fence to another, you encourage straightness in your horse and make it much easier for the animal to get down the line *in the numbers*—that is, in the number of strides intended by the course designer. The straighter a

To give your horse the best opportunity to jump safely and confidently, do not make radical adjustments to its stride, particularly just in front of the fences. Encourage it to maintain a steady tempo around the course, rather than allowing it to shorten its stride and slow down too much on the corners of the ring. Going into the corners, the horse should be collected just enough to ensure the change of leads and a safe turn. Any more collection than this works against the performance (fig. 4.42).

When spectators describe a horse on course as looking like a "machine," what they are noticing is the rider's ability to subtly collect and lengthen the stride, maintaining a steady tempo with little variation in pace. Everything looks smooth and flowing when the tempo is regular; and, when the pace is even, the takeoff spots are more likely to be the same than when the horse is approaching certain obstacles slowly and others much faster.

For the second, third, and fourth lines, press the horse forward out of the corners, maintain a steady rhythm and length of stride between the fences, and collect when going into the corners. Usually, it will be easier to make the horse go forward to these lines than to the first line because it is more alert after jumping a couple of fences and has more natural impulsion, particularly when traveling toward the in-gate or out-gate. In fact, you may have to open your body angle a little and steady the horse as it travels home, in order to keep it from extending its stride too much.

When approaching a line that is set across the diagonal of the ring, you should look toward the first fence on the line earlier than when approaching a line set on the long side of the arena. The reason for this is that diagonal lines are set closer to the centerline than are the outside lines, so that if you wait until you reach the centerline to look, you will tend to overshoot the diagonal. You should also increase the

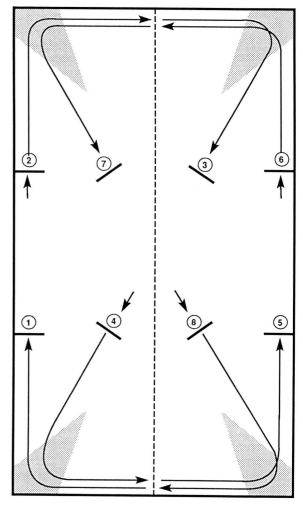

4.42 Horses lose impulsion in the corners of the arena (indicated by the gray-shaded areas). This is helpful when you are trying to collect an animal at the end of a line, but is a drawback when you try to increase impulsion on the approach to a new line. By pressing the horse forward from the centerline, you can prevent its impulsion from "dying." This will make it easier for you to find a good distance to the fences, as well as make the performance smoother.

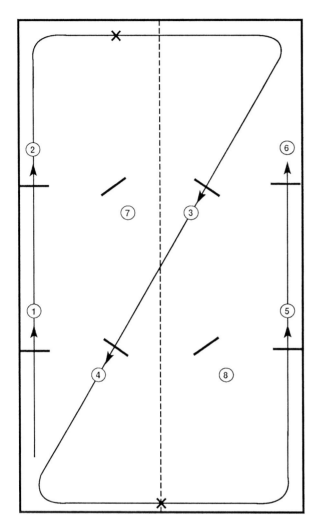

4.43 When approaching a diagonal line of fences, look toward the line when the horse is about two strides before the centerline of the ring. When approaching an outside line, look as the horse crosses the centerline. The point at which you should look at the upcoming line is indicated by the symbol "X."

horse's impulsion sooner to a diagonal line because the turn to it is more acute than to an outside line, making it more difficult for the horse to reach the proper pace and length of stride before the first fence in the line. Look for the upcoming fence and begin to move your horse forward approximately two strides (24 feet) before the centerline, when approaching a diagonal line of fences (fig. 4.43).

Following the final line on course, make another large circle before you exit the arena. Use this circle to subtly correct your horse, so that it will be schooled for the next round. If the animal was a little quick on course, collect it and slow its rhythm during the final circle. If the horse was dull on course, firmly squeeze it forward with your legs to send a clear message that lagging is unacceptable. Either correction should be discreet. There is no point in jerking your horse or kicking it in the side out of anger. This behavior only demonstrates that abuse begins where talent and education end.

The final moments in the ring are very important. They give you the opportunity to show off, if, for example, you are riding a horse that moves very well in the hunter division or if you are a beautifully proportioned, correctly positioned rider in an equitation class. Nothing makes a judge feel better than to glance at a competitor on the final circle and think, "What a nice trip. That will be hard to beat." The judge is hoping for a clear winner, and it is up to you to prove that you are just that.

5

Intermediate and Advanced Equitation Courses

You can change a basic hunter or equitation course into an intermediate or advanced equitation course through one or more of the following additions: (1) a line of fences that measures shorter or longer than the standard striding; (2) a combination, composed of two or more fences with only one or two strides between them; (3) a turn between fences (either a bending line or a rollback turn); (4) a fence which must be jumped at an angle; (5) a narrow fence; (6) an end fence; (7) a long approach to a single fence; or (8) a novelty fence.

Isolated and Related Distances

By changing a course from measurements based solely on a 12-foot stride to measurements based on some 11-foot strides and some 13-foot strides, you can make a straightforward course very tough (fig. 5.1). For instance, in fig. 5.1, you could make four simply-arranged fences very difficult by alternating long and short strides. The setting of the first line of fences on 13-foot strides would require a tremendous amount of initial impulsion, not only because the distance is set long, but also because this is the first line on course, which typically rides longer, and the line is jumped traveling away from home. The distance between the first two fences on the second line, based on 11-foot strides, would require the horse to be collected, which would be especially difficult because the line is ridden coming toward home. The one-stride in-and-out, set at the end of the second line, measures 25 feet and is composed of two oxers. The wide structure of the fences and the slightly long distance between them demands increased impulsion in a very short time to

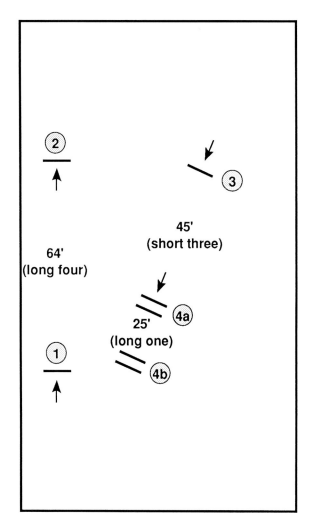

5.1 A change of only a few inches per stride can affect the way a course rides. For example, by combining short and long lines that have been altered from the standard striding by only 1 foot per stride, you could make a very simple course quite difficult. To negotiate the fences on the course in the diagram, a horse would have to have a tremendous amount of impulsion for the first line, collect greatly for the distance between fences 3 and 4a, then travel the one stride between fences 4a and 4b on a very long stride.

make the one stride following the collected strides preceding fence 4a. I am not suggesting that you actually set fences this way, for this is a radical example of changing measurements to increase the difficulty of a course. I am only using the example to show how changing just 1 foot in length per stride can greatly increase the difficulty of a course.

Usually at a horse show the course designer makes the first line of fences on an equitation course fairly easy by keeping it on a 12-foot stride, then varies the subsequent measurements according to the level of difficulty appropriate for the particular class. To make a course slightly difficult, he could change the footage about 6 inches to 1 foot per stride within a line that consists of only two fences. The distance between fences on a two-fence line is referred to as an *isolated distance*. If the riders are more advanced, the course designer might construct three fences on a line and use long-to-short distances or short-to-long distances to test the rider's ability to immediately adjust the animal's length of stride. These are referred to as *related distances*, since the distance between the first and second fences on the line affects the way the distance between the second and third fences can be ridden.

When riding through an *isolated long distance* —that is, a distance that measures longer than normal on a two-fence line—if you wait until you have jumped the first fence before lengthening the horse's stride, you will find it much more difficult to reach the proper takeoff spot to the second fence than if you had prepared by lengthening before the first fence. For example, if there are three long strides between two fences, you should lengthen your horse's stride a little each step for about four to six strides before the first fence. This will set the horse on a sufficient length of step for it to make the long distance without having to run for it (fig. 5.2).

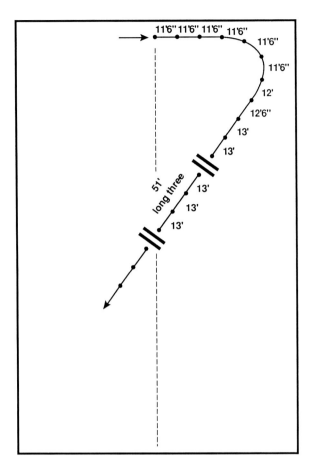

5.2 When approaching an isolated long distance, press the horse forward with your legs to prevent it from shortening its stride too much in the corner on the short side of the arena. Increase the length of stride until it is appropriate for the distance between the fences. Ideally, you should have the horse on the correct length of stride at least two strides before takeoff. Once you have achieved the correct length of stride, maintain it each stride between the fences so that the line rides smoothly.

When approaching a long distance, don't wait to see a spot to the first fence before you make your move, but rather build impulsion early out of the corner so that the horse's

lengthening of stride will help you find the long spot. I refer to this as "galloping into a spot," for when you keep increasing the impulsion and length of stride to a fence, an appropriately long takeoff spot usually presents itself.

As the horse lengthens its stride, its energy flows more horizontally, requiring you to close your upper body forward in order to continue to be with the motion of the horse. It is important that you react to the lengthening with your upper body, rather than precede the lengthening by shifting your torso forward. If you lean ahead of the motion, trying to use your upper body as a driving aid, you will think your horse has begun to extend its stride, even if it has not. This is because you have moved your eyes forward, producing the same optical effect of covering more ground in a stride that would occur if you kept your upper body still and let your horse lengthen in response to your legs.

So don't be fooled into thinking your horse has lengthened, when all that has really happened is that you have moved your eyes forward. By staying with the motion and driving the animal with your legs, you can feel whether the horse surges forward in a true lengthening of stride, or ignores your legs and stays the same.

Your hands should maintain a sensitive feel of the reins, so that as the horse begins to lengthen its stride and elongate its neck, you follow the motion of its head by moving your hands forward. If you try to lengthen the stride by suddenly offering slack in the reins, your horse will feel abandoned and may stop at the fence. On the other hand, if you do not ease off the horse's mouth at all, the animal won't be able to lengthen its stride sufficiently to cover the long distance and may have to add an extra step at the base of the fence in order to meet a safe takeoff. The horse may even react to rigid hands by refusing to jump, fearing that it cannot keep its balance in the air without having the freedom of its neck. The hands, then, must provide enough contact to reassure the horse, but not so much as to restrict the motion of its head as it tries to lengthen its frame and use its neck to balance itself in the air.

More difficult than an isolated long distance is a line in which the long distance is followed by a short distance. To ride related distances well, you must consider how the approach you make to the first distance in the line will affect the way the second distance rides. For example, if a line is composed of three long strides preceding three short strides—that is, the related distances form a *long-to-short line*—you should plan to lengthen the horse's stride and increase its impulsion more than normal on the approach to the first fence. This approach allows the horse to take strides decreasing in length on the approach to the second fence (fig. 5.3).

By slightly collecting during the first three strides, you will be able to find a medium spot to the second fence and not land too far into the next, short line. Although you should not "drop back" in the air over the second fence by letting your seat hit the saddle before landing, you can open your upper body angle a little sooner than normal so that it subtly aids in restricting the length of the horse's landing. A slightly open upper-body angle between the second and third fences will also aid you in collecting the horse for the three short strides.

To understand how important it is to lengthen the stride before the first fence in a long-to-short line, consider what happens when you do not. If you find a medium spot to the first fence and have a medium length of stride, you must then drive the horse forward to the second fence in order to make up the footage of the long line. This causes the horse to land over the second fence with the impulsion building, rather than diminishing, making the follow-

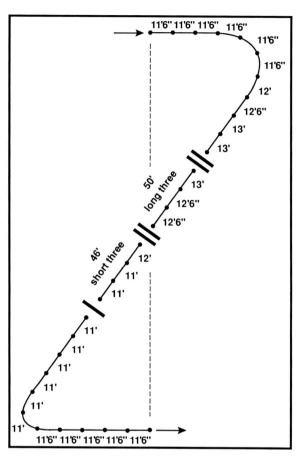

5.3 When approaching a long-to-short line, you must increase the horse's length of stride until you have slightly more than you need for the first distance. This way, you can collect the horse throughout the line.

ing three short strides very difficult. In other words, instead of the horse smoothly collecting throughout the line, it goes from a medium stride on the approach, to a quick, lengthening stride between the first two fences, to an abrupt, collected stride between the second and third fence.

Now let's examine the opposite exercises from those discussed above. To ride an *isolated short distance*—that is, a

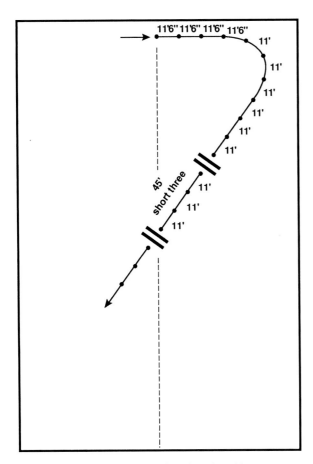

5.4 Let the natural shortening of the horse's stride on a corner help you set up the horse for an isolated short distance. Be sure that the horse's stride is shortened through collection, rather than slowness, for the animal must have impulsion to make a good jumping effort.

distance that measures shorter than normal on a two-fence line—maintain a slightly collected stride on the approach to the first fence with a restricting hand and a strong degree of impulsion with a supporting leg. Open your upper-body angle slightly from its normal two-point angulation so that it can subtly reinforce your hands. The more vertical upper body is in keeping with the increased vertical motion of

the horse when it is traveling in a shorter frame and offers a position of readiness so that you can add the weight of your torso as a subtle restraining aid, in case you need a little more strength to collect your horse than your hands and arms alone can provide (fig. 5.4).

To ride a *short-to-long line* correctly, you must increase impulsion gradually through the line. It is important, then, to start with the horse collected on the approach to the first obstacle. The horse's natural inclination to "die in the corners" before approaching the lines will make it easy to shorten the stride; but you must make sure you maintain plenty of impulsion, rather than simply allowing the animal to slow down to decrease the length of stride. Otherwise, you will have to abruptly increase the pace, rather than smoothly extending the stride to successfully ride the line (fig. 5.5).

On the approach to the first fence, your upper-body angle should be open slightly more than the normal two-point position in order to reinforce your restricting aids. Then, in keeping with the forward shift of the horse's center of gravity as the animal changes from short to long strides, your upper body should close slightly forward between the second and third fences. To facilitate the horse's jumping effort, close your hip angle only enough to balance your upper body over your legs when the horse is in the longer frame—not so far forward that you add unnecessary weight to the horse's forehand.

Within a short-to-long line, many riders will land over the second fence, wait one stride to get reorganized, then desperately push the horse forward for the remaining strides before the third fence. This often results in the horse being unwilling to leave the ground from an overly long spot and adding an extra stride at the base of the third fence. If you press the horse forward every stride, you can make the long

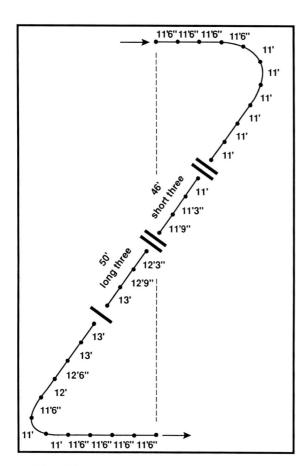

5.5 When riding a short-to-long line, keep a slightly open body angle and a restrictive hand to prevent the horse from overextending its stride in the short distance. Then, press with your legs and ease the tension on the reins for three long strides, closing your body angle forward as the horse incrementally lengthens its steps. Be prepared to collect your horse immediately upon landing, since the animal will be on a very long stride as it approaches the corner.

segment of the test both easier for the horse and smoother in overall appearance.

To be on the safe side in setting long-to-short or short-to-long practice exercises, lengthen or shorten the normal distance by 6 inches per stride for horses and 3 inches per stride

for ponies. Remember that the 12-foot total of the takeoff and landing distances should not be counted as a stride. For example, a long-to-short exercise for a horse, involving three long strides followed by three short strides, would measure 49 1/2 feet to 46 1/2 feet in a line of three vertical fences.

For horses only, you can increase the difficulty of the exercise by adding or deducting up to another 6 inches for every stride—that is, making the long three strides to short three strides measure a maximum of 51 feet to 45 feet. However, this may be dangerous for lower-level riders or unathletic horses. In fact, I wouldn't practice distance alterations with anyone who was not already riding very well over basic hunter and equitation courses.

Combinations

The addition of a combination is another means of making a course more difficult. Since the fences are placed so close to each other—only one or two strides apart—the horse must have quick reflexes and the rider must be able to adjust to the rapid shifting of the horse's center of gravity during the multiple jumping efforts. A talented, intermediate-level rider mounted on a horse of average ability should be able to stay with his horse's motion in a combination when the distances are set normally (for example, a 24-foot one-stride distance followed by a 36-foot two-stride distance for a horse). However, when a combination is set up to present a short-to-long distance (for example, a 23-foot one-stride distance followed by a 38-foot two-stride distance) or vice versa, the difficulty is greatly increased.

The principles of riding short-to-long or long-to-short distances in combinations are the same as for riding related distances with more strides between the fences. The only dif-

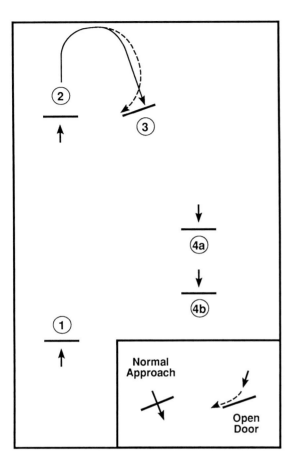

5.6 The solid line between fences 2 and 3 shows the correct path between the fences. The dotted line indicates the path of a horse that has swung too wide on the turn, so that as it approaches the fence, an "open door" is created. From the diagram in the box, you can see how much more tempting it is for the horse to run out at the fence when there is an open door created by an oblique approach than when a fence is approached head on.

ference is that you have less time to correct an error. The placement of your horse at the proper takeoff spots and your feel for the horse's impulsion and length of stride are critical when the fences are as close together as they are in combinations.

Turns

Hunter courses provide long, straight approaches to fences so that the horse has plenty of time to see an obstacle, reach the proper impulsion and length of stride, and balance itself for takeoff. However, in equitation or jumper classes, turns often present problems for both horse and rider. It is sometimes unclear to the horse where the upcoming fence is, since the fences are not necessarily placed on the long sides of the arena or across the diagonals, but may be at other less familiar locations.

You must use your aids successfully to guide and balance the horse so that it will be both psychologically and physically prepared to jump. This will be difficult if you are weak in your position, since you will find it hard to keep your balance when turning the horse. If loss of balance results in your leaning on the hand toward the outside of the turn while you attempt to turn the horse with your inside hand, you will lose one side of your steering mechanism. When your outside hand becomes inactive, the horse drifts to the outside of the turn and overshoots the proper line to the upcoming fence. This usually results in a refusal, a run-out, or too deep a spot to the fence as the unbalanced animal adds an extra stride at takeoff (fig. 5.6). To correct an outward drift, apply a strong outside leg and move both hands a little toward the inside of the turn, so that your inside hand is in a slight opening-rein position and your outside hand creates a neck rein. The pressure of the outside leg and neck rein "walls up," or contains, the energy that is escaping to the outside of the turn (figs. 5.7 A–C).

Another error that may occur during turns is the horse "cutting in" by leaning toward the inside of the turn and making a tighter turn than you desire, rather than fully using the available space. Cutting in causes loss of impulsion, pro-

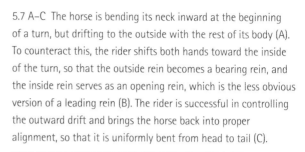

5.7 A–C The horse is bending its neck inward at the beginning of a turn, but drifting to the outside with the rest of its body (A). To counteract this, the rider shifts both hands toward the inside of the turn, so that the outside rein becomes a bearing rein, and the inside rein serves as an opening rein, which is the less obvious version of a leading rein (B). The rider is successful in controlling the outward drift and brings the horse back into proper alignment, so that it is uniformly bent from head to tail (C).

5.8 The rider is preventing the horse from cutting in on a turn by applying her inside leg at the girth and shifting both of her hands slightly toward the outside of the turn. She has also shifted the axis of her upper body slightly to the outside in order to use her weight as an aid.

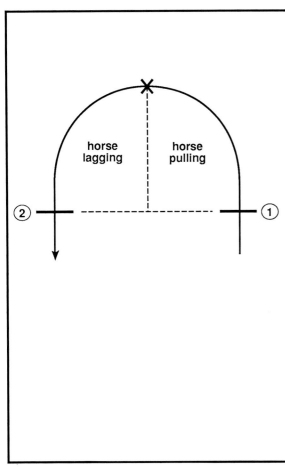

5.9 When turning between fences, a horse will generally pull against the reins the first half of the turn, then lag the remaining half, reluctant to move forward from the rider's legs. This is most evident when the turn is very tight. To counteract this tendency, you must open your upper-body angle and collect the horse to the point marked "X"; then drive the horse forward with your legs to increase its impulsion and length of stride, closing your body angle again and easing the pressure of your hands as the horse's momentum becomes more horizontal.

vides less room for you to look for a takeoff spot, and makes the horse unbalanced since most of its weight becomes tilted to the inside of the turn. To correct this problem, apply more inside leg to maintain the bend and restrict the horse

from popping its shoulder inward. Also, move both hands slightly toward the outside of the turn, so that the outside hand acts as an opening rein to guide the horse and the inside hand works as a neck rein to push it away from the direction in which it wants to lean (fig. 5.8).

Horses tend to have too much impulsion going into a turn and too little coming out of one (fig. 5.9). To counteract these tendencies, land over the fence preceding the turn with your hands up and your body angle open slightly more than normal, rather than leaning forward onto your hands for support. This will enable you to begin collecting the horse on the first stride after landing. Once you reach the center of the turn, add leg pressure and drive the horse forward, increasing its impulsion and length of stride in time to have a good jumping effort over the second fence. You must be insistent in lengthening the stride, since it is hard to press an animal forward coming out of a turn, particularly if the turn is short and acute (fig. 5.10).

The biggest mistake riders make on turns is not looking soon enough. On sweeping turns, look for the next fence as soon as you possibly can without having to look completely backward over your shoulder. On tight turns, look for the upcoming fence while you are in the air over the fence preceding the turn (figs. 5.11 A–C).

Once you have looked for the upcoming fence, do not look away from it. Keeping your eyes fixed on the obstacle will allow you to see a takeoff spot while you are turning (figs. 5.12 A–C). The curve presents not only the options of collection or extension, but also of cutting or widening the turn in order to reach a good takeoff spot, actually making it easier to see a spot from a turn than when approaching from a straightaway. If you keep your eyes fixed on the upcoming fence, you can make the necessary adjustments to the horse's length of stride and path to the fence to meet a perfect spot (fig. 5.13).

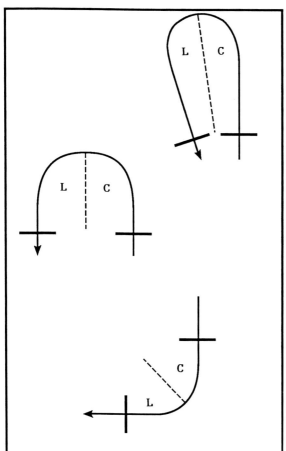

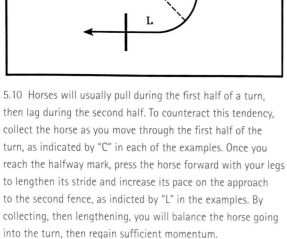

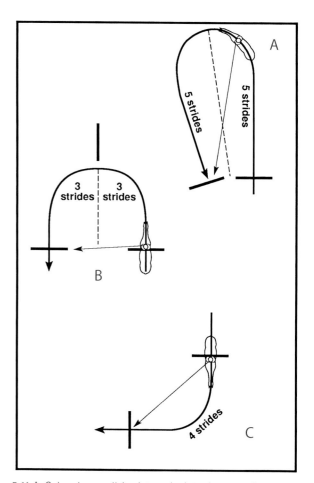

5.10 Horses will usually pull during the first half of a turn, then lag during the second half. To counteract this tendency, collect the horse as you move through the first half of the turn, as indicated by "C" in each of the examples. Once you reach the halfway mark, press the horse forward with your legs to lengthen its stride and increase its pace on the approach to the second fence, as indicted by "L" in the examples. By collecting, then lengthening, you will balance the horse going into the turn, then regain sufficient momentum.

5.11 A–C In a long, roll-back turn, look to the upcoming fence as soon as you start to turn the corner. In the diagram, the rider is correctly looking sideways over his shoulder at the earliest point he can reasonably see the fence (A). On a tight roll-back turn, you cannot afford to lose sight of the second fence for even a moment. In the diagram, the rider is correctly spotting the second fence while he is in midair over the first fence. He should maintain this focal point throughout the turn to make sure he does not overshoot the fence (B). A right-angle turn is less difficult than a roll-back turn, but still requires concentration on your focal point, especially when the turn consists of only a few strides, as in the diagram (C).

5.12 A–C The rider has found a takeoff spot (A), and begins to look for the upcoming fence, which is located next to the one the horse is jumping and is only six strides away on a tight roll-back turn. By applying pressure with her left leg and shifting both hands slightly to the right (B), she signals the horse to take the right lead. The horse responds in the air by stretching its right foreleg forward, in preparation for landing on the right lead (C).

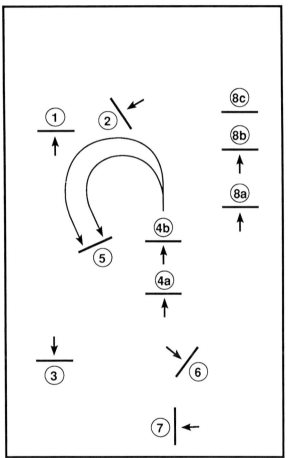

5.13 The solid lines between fences 4b and 5 indicate the shortest and longest paths you could reasonably take in an equitation class. By turning on these lines or anywhere between them, you can use the path of the turn, as well as adjustments to the horse length of stride, to help you meet a suitable takeoff spot to fence 5.

Your Eyes on the Prize

"You can't make a sound decision if you don't see there's a problem."

The importance of a rider's eyes cannot be stressed enough. During a course of fences, they enable you to plan ahead and help you stay balanced in the air while the horse is jumping. On the flat, they help you find the best path in front of the judge and alert you to the dangerous behavior of other horses in the ring.

By the time you start showing a horse in public, you should be able to ride with your eyes up all of the time, except for a quick glance to check a diagonal or lead. Yet when I started to choose a cover shot for my last book, I found it difficult to locate pictures of riders with their eyes looking forward over a fence—even among photographs of professionals. In picture after picture, riders were ducking in the air, looking at the ground instead of through the ears of the horse.

Good use of the eyes is what separates someone who rides with purpose from someone who depends on luck. You should have a plan going into the show ring, and that plan should be written all over your face. Your eyes should be steadily looking ahead, checking out everything as you travel around the course, both when the horse's feet are on the ground and when they are in the air jumping a fence.

It doesn't matter how good your "eye for a distance" is if you aren't looking at the fence soon enough—you'll look just in time to see you're in trouble, but not in time to do anything about it . The eyes are an extremely important tool, which should never be underestimated.

Jumping on an Angle

When you are jumping a fence on an angle, your hands and legs should form a narrow corridor that prevents the horse from drifting on the approach to the fence or in midair. Form this corridor by maintaining pressure against the horse with both legs and placing your hands a little closer to each other than normal as you approach the fence (fig. 5.14).

Eyes are essential to your success in jumping fences at an angle. If you find a focal point on the far side of the obstacle and ride straight toward it, your horse will have a clear sense of direction. But if your eyes wander, the horse will begin to wander also, unsure of where it is meant to go (figs. 5.15 A & B).

Jumping on an angle is usually reserved for advanced equitation courses and jumper classes (often as an option in "jump-off" rounds in which the speed with which the course is negotiated is a deciding factor for final placement). It is a test of your control of the horse and requires you to have a keen sense of the animal's balance as you approach the fence. You must maintain steady contact with the horse's mouth on the approach, during takeoff, and in the air. Otherwise, the animal will find it easy to run out at the obstacle.

It's best to find a medium takeoff spot to a fence that will be jumped at an angle because a deep spot can easily cause a knockdown, while a long spot encourages a run-out. The balance of the horse on the approach is just as important as the takeoff spot. Horses tend to shift their weight away from a fence when approaching it at an angle, probably due to their confusion about whether they are being asked to jump it or simply gallop past it. When this happens, you must counteract the tendency by using a firm hand and leg on the side of the horse that is away from the fence and, if needed, using an opening rein on the side nearest the fence (fig. 5.16).

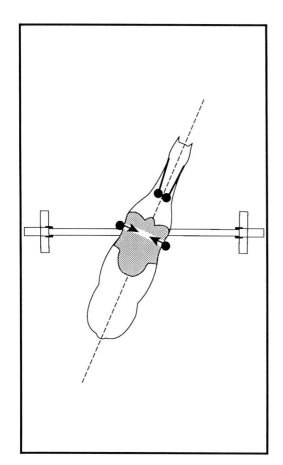

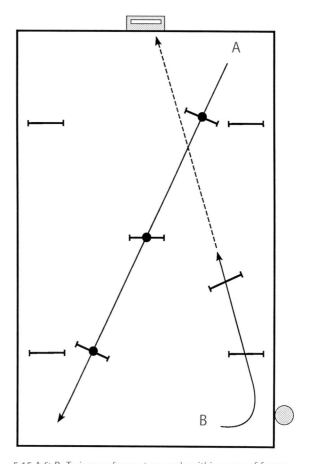

5.14 The diagram shows the horse jumping a fence on an angle. When approaching the fence, concentrate on a focal point on the far side of the obstacle, as indicated by the dotted line. Use supporting legs and closely positioned hands to form a narrow corridor that holds the horse in a straight line on the approach to the fence, in midair, and all the way to your focal point.

5.15 A & B To jump a fence at an angle within a row of fences, line up the obstacles and ride straight between them (A). Be sure to let your focal point extend far enough that the line you plan to ride will not cause you to run into other fences after you have jumped the difficult angle fence (B). Notice in figure B that the rider has used some markers to help him stay on a good line to the angle fence. When walking the course, he planned to turn onto the line at the trash can (indicated by the circle outside the ring) and to focus on the concession booth (indicated by the rectangle at the top of the diagram). These mental notes about the path he needed to take helped him to correctly jump line B and avoid running into the first fence on line A.

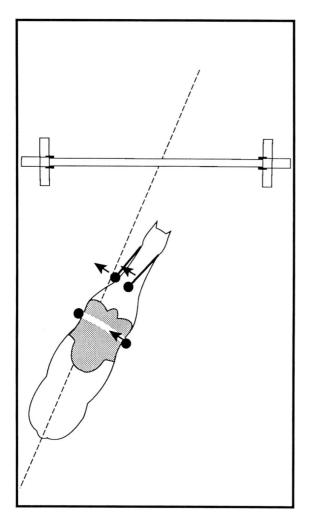

5.16 If your horse begins to drift away from an angle fence, shift both hands toward the fence and press with your leg that is away from the fence, to hold the horse onto the proper line.

5.17 This gate is 6 feet wide, the minimum width for a "narrow fence" in equitation classes. Be sure to have a narrow fence for practice purposes, since one always seems to find its way into important equitation competitions.

Narrow Fence and End Fence

The narrow fence, with its face measuring between 6 and 8 feet in width, is commonly used in equitation finals (fig. 5.17). To ride well over a narrow obstacle, you must be able to steer your horse perfectly straight through the center. If the animal drifts to either side, a run-out can easily occur.

The most difficult setting of a narrow obstacle is as an *end fence*—that is, a fence at one end of the ring that is set perpendicular to the short side of the arena. Typically, it is placed away from the railing to present a steering problem. This requires you to collect your horse after the preceding obstacle and turn toward the upcoming narrow fence without falling on your hands for support, for if your hands drop, you are sure to overshoot the curving line. Your eyes must be active in locating and maintaining the bending line so that you will realize immediately if your horse is cutting inward or drifting outward on the curve. Many refusals in the equitation finals have occurred at a narrow fence set at the end of the arena, since the fence is placed where a horse least expects to find it and the tight turn that precedes it doesn't allow a margin for error (figs. 5.18 A & B).

A Long Gallop to a Single Fence

A long gallop to a single fence may also present a problem. Often, the rider lengthens the stride correctly coming out of the corner, but rather than maintaining the proper length of stride once the horse reaches it, he allows the animal to keep on extending. As a result, the rider sees a takeoff spot that is much too long and places the horse so far from the obstacle that it either dives over the fence or loses heart at the last moment and chips in.

To prevent this mistake, lengthen the stride as usual coming out of the corner of the ring, but concentrate on maintaining the length of stride you have achieved after the first four straight strides, rather than letting the horse lengthen for the next five or six strides before the fence (fig. 5.19).

Novelty Fences

Novelty fences are obstacles that look strange because they are made of unusual materials or are oddly shaped. For example, if a soft drink company is sponsoring a Grand Prix at a horse show, one of the fences you might see in the equitation as well as jumper classes is a large rubber soft drink bottle, lying on its side to form the length of the fence. Technically, this is not a difficult fence; but it

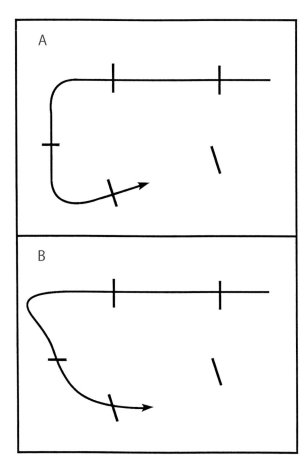

5.18 A & B A narrow fence set at the end of the arena and away from the rail presents a steering problem for the rider. You can avoid overshooting the line by looking for the fence while in midair over the preceding obstacle. You must also keep your hands up as you land, so that you will be able to turn the horse immediately and accurately toward the narrow fence (A). By overshooting the line to an end fence, you create problems at the next set of fences. Although the rider has been able to jump the narrow fence and the one that follows, his horse is not lined up to jump the second fence on the diagonal line and is headed for a run-out (B).

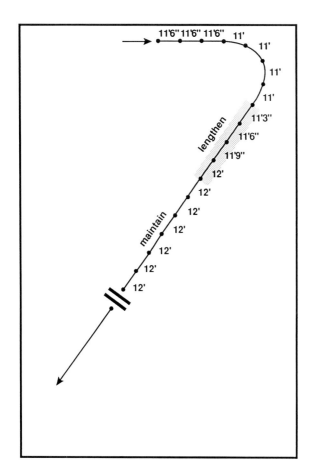

5.19 On a long approach to a fence, you should incrementally lengthen the horse's stride for about four strides out of the corner, as normal; but do not allow the horse to continue to extend its stride beyond that point. Instead, maintain a medium length of stride for the remainder of the approach to the fence. This will help you find a medium takeoff spot.

may present a psychological problem for the horse or rider because it looks odd.

Sometimes a novelty fence has moving parts that will spook an animal, such as objects that move in the wind. Others may be designed in such a way that the horse has

to jump through an arch, which more often than not is ignored by the horse and intimidates the rider. You should be aware of potential problems when approaching a fence that is out of the horse's realm of experience; but don't become so preoccupied with a novelty fence that you have a hang-up about it, for this will prevent you from concentrating on other important elements while on course.

Summary

You can be successful in low-level hunter and equitation competition, where the distances are conservative and the fences low, by maintaining a steady pace throughout the course and finding good spots to all your fences. As you progress competitively, however, you will find it necessary to be able to alter your horse's length of stride through changing its frame during the course. This allows you to negotiate more difficult distances while maintaining a steady tempo that makes your round beautiful both visually and audibly.

When faced with the most difficult equitation or jumper courses, you must be capable of analyzing the technical difficulties of the course, not only as singular problems, but also as interrelated tests. By analyzing how preceding or following lines affect the way a particular fence should be ridden, you can devise an overall plan that will work smoothly, rather than one that will result in riding from one fence to another with no apparent continuity. It is the rider who has the mental capacity to devise a good plan, the technical ability to ride out that plan, and the artistry to perform difficult tests with fluidity that will rise above the others in paramount competitions.

6

Solving Typical Problems

Rider Problems

Developing a Better Eye

Difficulty in determining what adjustments must be made to place the horse properly for takeoff is known as a *bad eye*. Two things have struck me about riders with this problem. First, they usually look too late at the upcoming fence, leaving themselves little time to make a decision and adjust the horse's stride. Second, they usually have a poor sense of rhythm, which is evident not only as they approach the fences, but also when they work on the flat. They find it difficult to feel the tempo of the horse's footfalls at the different gaits, even at the slowest gait, the walk. (Not surprisingly, they usually have little, if any, musical ability.)

As discussed earlier, on course the rider's eyes should: (1) look toward an outside line of fences as the horse crosses the centerline; and (2) look toward a diagonal line of fences about two strides before the centerline. Your eyes should never lose sight of the focal point at the end of a line of fences. When you look to determine what adjustments must be made to meet a good takeoff spot, you should still be aware of your focal point through use of your peripheral vision. By looking soon enough and not allowing your eyes to wander for even a moment, you will notice that your success rate in meeting good spots will greatly increase.

The reason for maintaining a steady tempo on course is to prevent the horse from having to change its pace drastically at the last moment to reach the correct takeoff spot. Typically, the problem of erratic pace arises when a rider allows his horse to slow down when passing the in-gate. He must then drive the animal forward too forcefully a few strides before the upcoming fence to have enough momentum and length of stride to travel between the fences in the correct number of strides. To prevent this error, concentrate on maintaining even strides throughout the course, particularly when you are traveling past the in-gate or out-gate. This will make it much easier for the horse to meet the fences properly.

Some riders have trouble finding a good distance because their horses are moving slightly slower than the appropriate pace throughout the entire course. If your stirrups are too long, you will be particularly prone to this problem. I think the reason is that long stirrups cause your seat to be closer to the saddle, so you subconsciously slow the horse down to create a smoother ride. If the stirrups are the correct length for jumping (resting at the middle of your ankle bones when your feet are dropped out of the stirrups and your legs are relaxed) then you will not be uncomfortable at a hand-gallop and will therefore be more likely to maintain the proper pace (figs. 6.1 A & B). (When I'm very tired and start missing spots to fences, I take my stirrups up an extra notch to further distance myself from the horse's motion, so that I will be encouraged to hand-gallop rather than drop to a slower canter tempo to the obstacles.)

The following ground-pole exercise, which represents one line of fences, will help you learn to sustain the correct pace on course and develop a better eye. It allows you to simulate jumping a line of fences without having to stress the horse physically with the much greater effort of taking off and landing over larger obstacles. In a rectangular arena, measure 24 feet from the railing at the end of the line and place a ground pole there; this will be pole number 4 and will represent the place at which the horse should change leads after it jumps a line of fences. Then place three more poles in line with pole 4, leaving spaces of 57 feet, 60 feet, and 57 feet between them for horses; 54 feet, 57 feet, and 54 feet for large ponies; 51 feet, 54 feet, and 51 feet for medium

ponies; and 48 feet, 51 feet, and 48 feet for small ponies. These are all four-stride distances between poles.

The distance between the first and second pole represents the approach to a line of fences; the distance between the second and third pole represents the footage between a line of two fences; and the distance between the third and fourth pole represents the space in which you must collect your horse, balancing it for the upcoming turn (figs. 6.2 A–C).

To practice establishing and maintaining the proper pace on course, build the horse's impulsion and increase its length of stride around the end of the ring, approaching the line of poles at a pace you believe to be correct. Try to negotiate the space between poles 1 and 2 and between poles 2 and 3 in four strides each. On most horses, you will have to progressively lengthen the horse's steps between poles 1 and 2 to cover this distance in four strides, since the horse is coming out of a corner, which restricts not only its pace, but also its length of stride. However, you should be able to cover the distance between poles 2 and 3 in four even strides, since the horse should have reached the proper length of stride just before jumping pole 2. Following pole 3, perform a downward transition, halting in front of pole 4. After halting for 4 to 6 seconds, walk the horse over the pole.

Now analyze each segment of your performance. If your horse added a stride between the first and second pole, the pace to the first obstacle (represented by pole 2) was too slow. If the horse left out a stride between the first and second pole, or took half a step on the near side of the second pole and half a step on the far side (representing a crash), then the pace to the first obstacle (pole 2) was too fast.

The same holds true for the distance between poles 2 and 3. If the horse added a stride, it did not have enough pace; and if the horse left out a stride or straddled the rail, then the pace was too great. Finally, consider the

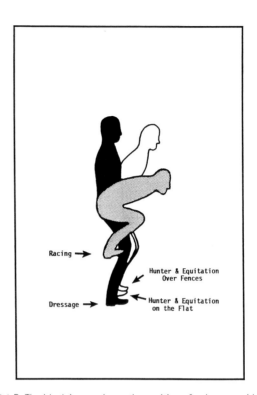

6.1 A When the stirrup is at the correct length for jumping, the bottom of the iron hits the middle of the rider's anklebone as the leg hangs relaxed along the horse's side.

6.1 B The black image shows the position of a dressage rider. His stirrup rests just below the anklebone, but his leg falls far down the side of the horse because the front of the flap of a dressage saddle is shaped more vertically than the flap of a hunter seat saddle. The dressage saddle is cut to promote deepness of the rider's seat and to enable the rider to keep his upper body balanced as precisely as possible over the horse's center of gravity. As pace increases, it is necessary for the stirrup iron to be raised, as indicated by the white and gray images. The white image shows the leg position of a hunter seat rider, whose knee rests farther forward than the dressage rider and whose stirrup length is shorter for jumping fences than for working on the flat. The shortest length of stirrup is used for racing, which is indicated by the gray image. The shorter the stirrup, the less the rider's weight encumbers the horse.

horse's willingness to stop at the fourth pole. If the horse pulled on the reins and crossed the pole, then you know it would be unwilling to collect its frame and lighten its forehand for a change of lead.

Practice smoothly negotiating the three poles and halting before the fourth. When you are able to do this exercise well, continue galloping over the fourth pole, asking the horse to switch leads as it crosses this pole, if it is traveling on the counter lead. Use an outside leg at a behind-the-girth position to signal the horse to change leads while in the moment of suspension above the pole.

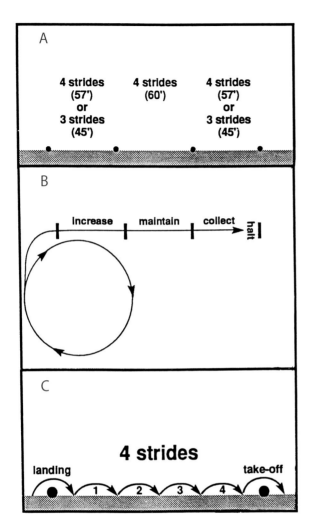

6.2 A–C You can simulate a line of fences by setting four poles on the ground, with the space between the first and second pole representing the approach to the first fence, the space between the second and third pole representing the distance between two fences, and the space between the third and fourth pole representing the area in which you must collect your horse before the corner. The diagram shows the distances for horses, using either four strides between each set of poles in a large ring, or three strides for the first and third distance in a smaller ring (A). To practice riding a line, start with a large circle that will enable you to reach the correct pace for the course. Increase the horse's length of stride between the first and second pole to make up for the natural shortening of stride that takes place as the horse goes around the corner following the circle. You should achieve the correct length of stride before you jump the second pole, then maintain it between poles 2 and 3. Following pole 3, collect the horse and halt for 4 to 6 seconds in front of pole 4. Finally, walk the horse over pole 4. If the animal is slow to respond in the downward transition and ends up straddling the fourth pole at the halt, do not back up over the pole, since this could damage the fetlocks. Instead, halt the proper length of time, then walk the horse forward (B). The horse should take four even strides between the poles which represent the fences (C). However, if your horse is consistently too strong to the fourth pole, you can approach the second pole with more momentum so that you can collect between poles 2 and 3, making the halt in front of pole 4 easier.

If your ring is too short to set the poles four strides apart, delete one stride between poles 1 and 2 and poles 3 and 4, so that the approach and departure will call for three strides, instead of four. The measurements would then be 45 feet, 60 feet, and 45 feet for horses; 43 feet, 57 feet, and 43 feet for large ponies; 40 ½ feet, 54 feet, and 40 ½ feet for medium ponies; and 38 feet, 51 feet, and 38 feet for small ponies. This tighter setting of the distances is harder to negotiate because it requires abrupt adjustments of the horse's stride, particularly during the last strides before the halt. It also causes more trauma to the horse's legs leading into the halt, which is the main reason that I prefer the four-stride setting.

The next step is to raise poles 2 and 3 so that you can practice seeing distances to actual fences, with the approach and departure still marked by poles 1 and 4. (Set the fences 3' high for horses and 6 inches below the normal fence heights for ponies. Use additional poles to fill in the spaces underneath poles 2 and 3 so that these fences are not too airy.) During this exercise, the horse's arc should be even—that is, the animal should leave the ground and land equidistant from the center of each obstacle—and the strides between the fences should be of equal length. If you have difficulty finding a good takeoff to the two fences, draw lines in the dirt 6 feet away from the near side of them to help you concentrate on placing your horse's front feet on these lines. Of course, white lines made with lime would be even easier for you to see, but sometimes a horse will spook at something unfamiliar on the ground, which can be dangerous at the point of takeoff. If you decide to mark the takeoff with a bright substance, practice over very small obstacles first.

When training your eye, it is beneficial to set three separate lines of fences—normal, short, and long—with the same number of strides between them, so that they can be used for comparison (fig. 6.3). To set the short and long lines, subtract 6 inches to 1 foot per stride for the short line and add 6 inches to 1 foot per stride for the long line, still allowing for a 6-foot landing and takeoff at each obstacle. Concentrate on pace and evenness of stride, rather than worry about the takeoff spot. By keeping the horse collected on the approaching strides to the short-distance line, and by galloping forward on lengthened strides to the long-distance line, you can greatly increase your chances of finding a suitable takeoff spot to the first fences in each line.

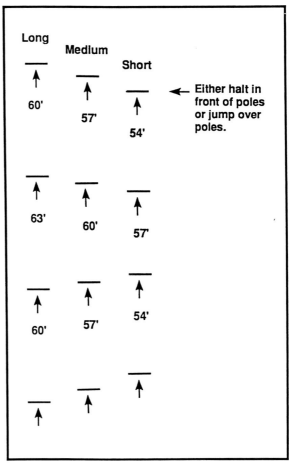

6.3 By setting three lines of varying lengths side by side, you can compare the feeling of riding to long, medium, and short lines. The distances listed are for horses, with the striding between each set of poles being four strides.

Finding the Right Spot to the First Fence

A common problem among hunter seat riders is finding a bad spot to the first fence in a class. It usually results from the rider coming out of his initial circle at too dull a pace, so that he looks at the first fence only to see a deep distance or a distance that is much too long for the amount of impulsion his horse has. This leaves him with two choices: (1) place the horse at the deep spot, then struggle to lengthen the horse's strides to the second fence; or (2) try to jump from the long spot out of too little impulsion, in which case the horse will either make a dangerously weak attempt or will chip in, adding an extra stride at the base of the fence.

Often, when a rider meets a bad spot to the first fence in a couple of classes, he becomes so preoccupied with that fence that he spends the rest of the show worrying about it. If you have this problem, concentrate on using the time you have during the initial circle to steadily increase the horse's pace. Look at the first line as you cross the centerline of the ring and keep your eyes riveted on it while driving the horse forward through the corner, preventing it from shortening its stride. Try to "override" the approach to the first line a little by having more impulsion than you think you need. By doing this, you will have about the right amount to the first fence and will find a better spot.

Strengthening the Rider's Position

You must be physically fit in order to remain glued to your horse at all times. Fitness can prevent such accidents as being slung into the fence if your horse stops, or sliding off if it spooks to one side. Ideally, you would like to be so fit and well-coordinated that the only way you would hit the ground is if your horse fell, too.

To help reach this level of fitness, you should practice the following exercises: (1) maintaining two-point position at the trot with stirrups; (2) sitting the trot without stirrups; and (3) posting the trot without stirrups.

Work done in two-point position strengthens the front and inner part of your thighs, so that you'll soon become fit enough to hold yourself out of the saddle over a fence, rather than weakly dropping your seat onto the horse's back. Two-point work also strengthens your lower leg, making your calves steadier against the horse's sides and creating more weight in your heels.

To perform this exercise, first shorten the stirrups to your jumping length. Then pick up the trot and work around the ring in two-point position, with your heels pressed downward, your calves snugly held on the horse's sides, and your knees and thighs supporting the weight of your upper

6.4 The rider is practicing in two-point position at the trot to improve her strength and balance. She holds a bit of mane in her inside hand to stabilize her upper body, while using her outside hand to steer the horse. (Normally, holding the horse to the rail with the outside hand, instead of an inside indirect rein, is incorrect; but in this particular exercise, it is acceptable because it enables the rider to maintain her balance at this bumpy gait so that she can concentrate on improving her leg.) The horse is a little keyed up in the windy weather, making it necessary for the rider to maintain pressure on its mouth. If the horse were calmer, the rider could have a little slack in the reins for this exercise, which doesn't require the horse to be in a frame. Notice the steady leg position and excellent depth in this rider's heels, the mark of a diligent student.

body. You can grab a bit of mane in one hand to stabilize your upper body, but do not lean on your hands (fig. 6.4).

It is essential for beginning riders to practice two-point position daily, since this will provide the security they need to jump safely. It is also a good exercise for an intermediate or advanced rider, particularly one who has just one horse a day to ride. Two-point position will help upper-level riders achieve and retain the degree of fitness they need to ride over complicated courses.

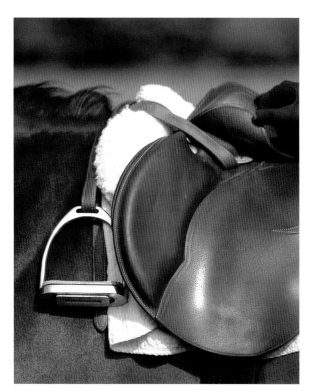

6.5 To cross your stirrups correctly, pull each buckle down about 8 inches, turn the top leather upside down to prevent a lump beneath your thigh, then turn the bottom leather upside down and drop the stirrup over the other side of the horse. Both stirrups are crossed in this photograph. The buckles should rest on the saddle pad (as shown) or lie along the side of the horse's withers, but should never be placed so that they dig into the top of the withers.

The second strengthening exercise is sitting the trot without stirrups. It helps you learn to sit comfortably and securely and to remain in the center of the horse. To prepare, drop your stirrups, pull the buckle on each stirrup down about 6 or 8 inches, then cross the stirrup leathers over the horse's withers. If you turn the top strap of the leather upside down before you cross it, your inner thigh won't be resting on a lump that could bruise you (fig. 6.5).

Your crotch should stay as close to the pommel as possible during this exercise, so that you are forked into the saddle with a secure thigh and knee position. (If you begin to slip backward, grasp the pommel with one hand and adjust your position by pulling yourself forward.) Your calves should rest snugly against the animal's sides, and the toes of your boots should be tipped upward as though you still had your feet in the stirrups. When working without stirrups at the sitting trot, then, your leg position should be exactly the same as it was when you had stirrups.

The third exercise, which is more strenuous than sitting the trot without stirrups, is posting without them. This strengthens your thighs and calves, stabilizes your knee position, and helps your upper body find its center of gravity over your legs. As discussed earlier in the description of USEF Test 9, your leg position at the posting trot without stirrups should be the same as with stirrups, except that you can carry your knee slightly higher to make up for the lack of support from your irons.

Between every three- to five-minute session of work without stirrups, you can take a break, walking the horse on a long rein and hanging your legs loosely along the horse's sides to stretch and relax the muscles so that they will not cramp. It is virtually impossible for most riders to keep posting without stirrups for even three minutes when they first begin this exercise. In fact, many cannot make more than one circuit of the arena before they feel exhausted. This exercise is very taxing; it is best practiced correctly for short intervals, rather than incorrectly for extended periods of time.

At this point a fourth set of exercises should be mentioned. Although they do not increase your strength, they help you learn how to stay on the horse through balance rather than through gripping. These exercises entail your being longed without stirrups or reins by an instructor, so that you can concentrate on your body rather than on controlling the horse. To prepare, set the horse up as described in the longeing section in chapter 2, except for the stirrups and reins. Remove the stirrups entirely and knot the reins around a clump of mane or around the part of a martingale that rests just in front of the withers.

When being longed, try to feel your center of gravity at the various gaits and keep it as closely aligned to the horse's center of gravity as possible. If you slip backward in the saddle, grab the pommel with your outside hand and the cantle with your inside hand and adjust your seat to the front of the saddle. By remaining close to the pommel and keeping your weight equally distributed on each side of the animal's body, you will be able to sit comfortably at every gait.

Your leg should remain in a normal riding position while you perform the various suppling exercises with your upper body. The exercises are designed to reduce tension in your body, help you develop better balance, and raise your level of confidence (figs. 6.6 A–H).

Memorizing a Course

For many riders, it is easier to remember shapes than numbers. For this reason, they don't think of a course as fence 1, fence 2, fence 3, etc., but memorize the shapes of the lines.

To do this, separate the segments into outside lines, inside lines, half-turns, half-turns in reverse, circles, figure eights, and so on. For instance, think about the course in fig. 6.7 A as an outside line, a path describing the number eight, and an outside line. In fig. 6.7 B, memorize a circle (once around) and an eight. For the course in fig. 6.7 C, visualize a single fence, then a half-turn to a half-turn. In equitation classes, it is particularly helpful to think of the segments as shapes, since the courses are usually more complicated than the those found in hunter classes. For example,

fig. 6.7 D would be a half-turn to a half-turn in reverse.

Memorize your course as early as you can and be sure to walk it before you ride it. When walking between the fences, pay attention to your approaches to the lines and decide at what point you should look at the upcoming line. Work this strategy into your plan, so that your eyes will automatically turn toward the line when you get to certain points on course.

Discuss the course with your coach or, if he is not available, go over it several times in your mind, until you are sure you know where to go. Finally, think about your plan just before you enter the ring, so that it is fresh in your mind.

Sitting the Trot Comfortably

A major area of tension in many riders is the stomach. If you hold your stomach in, you will find it impossible to sit on the horse comfortably, since your contracted abdominal muscles will pull you upward, away from the horse's back. Even worse is a tense stomach combined with tense thighs, because the pinching of the thighs makes the upward pull even greater (fig. 6.8).

If you are unable to sit a trot comfortably, most likely your stomach and thighs are tense. To solve this problem, take a deep breath and let the air out slowly, allowing your abdominal muscles to relax. Don't try to hold your stomach in when you ride, but let it hang out in front of you. Let your buttocks and thighs relax also, so that they sink into the saddle. If you cannot feel your seat bones resting on the saddle, you know the muscles in your buttocks are tense.

Now check your calves to make sure you didn't relax these muscles when you relaxed the muscles just above. Every part of your body from the waist down should be exerting downward pressure, with the stomach, buttocks, and thighs providing passive weight and the calves and heels provid-

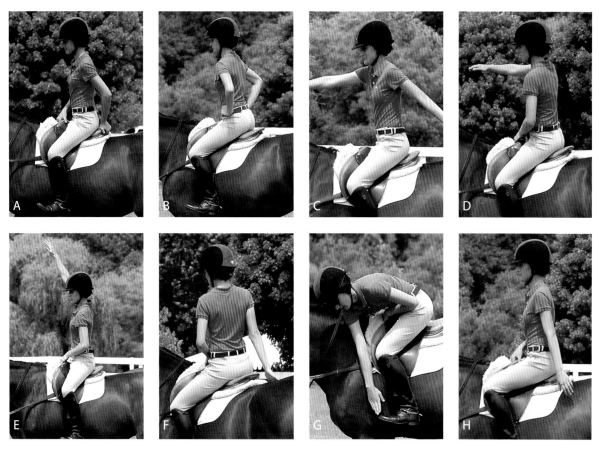

6.6 A–H Grasping the pommel with her outside hand and the cantle with her inside hand, the rider adjusts her seat by pulling herself to the front of the saddle (A). Longeing with hands on the hips helps the rider feel her center of gravity and prevents her from hanging on the horse's mouth for support, as riders holding reins sometimes do (B). The rider raises her arms to shoulder level and turns her torso to the left (C), then to the right. This exercise helps to reduce upper-body stiffness and increases a rider's confidence on horseback. In the next exercise, while rotating her arm in a clockwise motion (D & E), the rider feels her weight sink deeply into the horse as the arm moves back and downward (F). This exercise shows the rider how a relaxed, deep seat feels. You can rotate one arm, then the other, using the hand on the opposing arm to grasp the pommel and hold you steadily near the front of the saddle. Touching the toe with the opposing hand (G) is another exercise that reduces upper-body tension. Although this is intended to be performed on both sides of the horse, you will find it much easier to do it to the inside of the circle than the outside, since centrifugal force pulls you toward the outside of the figure. As you bend in each direction, you will feel yourself moving away from the horse's center of gravity, then back over it again as you rise to the original, erect position. This rider is in the process of raising her knees above the pommel (H), which will encourage her to find the horse's center of gravity and stay on through balance, since she is no longer able to hold on by gripping with her legs. When doing this exercise, hold the pommel with your outside hand.

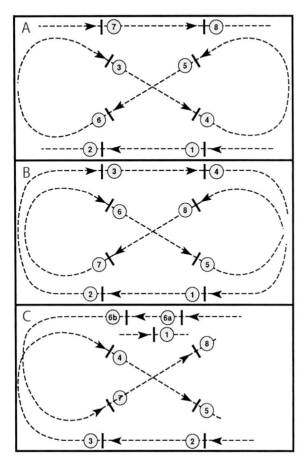

6.7 A–C Memorize the first course as an outside line, the pattern of the number "8," and another outside line (A). The second course is once around, followed by an 8 (B). The third course is a single fence and two half-turns (C).

6.7 D This equitation course can be easily memorized as a half-turn followed by a half-turn in reverse.

ing active weight. The knee simply acts as a hinge, remaining close to the saddle to offer stability, but not pinching to hold you on.

If you're still having difficulty sitting the trot, try the same exercise without stirrups. The lack of stirrup support will make it easier for you to sink your hips deeper into the saddle. Once you are comfortable riding the sitting trot without stirrups, try it with stirrups once again.

Straighten your back so that your spine, working as a solid unit rather than a series of flexible discs, can be used to reinforce your hands and arms. In trying to keep the back straight, you may tend to get stiff. To counteract this, concentrate on relaxing the muscles in the back, allowing them to drop downward. The straightness of your spine, then, enables you to be effective and elegant, while relaxed back muscles allow you to follow the horse's motion and not look stiff (fig. 6.9).

Your shoulders should be spread and dropped downward, anchoring your arms at the widest part of your back, so that the shoulders offer a strong link between your back and hands. Nervous riders often draw their shoulders upward toward their necks. If this happens, try to relax the muscles leading from your neck to your shoulders by dropping and separating your shoulders. The shoulders should maintain this position, or even a lower one if the horse begins to pull, since by pressing downward with your shoulders and flexing the muscles in your back you can put yourself in a position of greater power. Draw your head and neck upward, following the line of the spine, so that they work in concert with your back.

The divisions of the body, then, are: everything below the waist dropped downward; the spinal column stacked upward with the surrounding muscles relaxed; the shoulders spread wide and dropped downward; and the head and neck following the upward line of the spine.

If you feel yourself getting nervous, check for tension points and try to relax the muscles that are taut. Applying the techniques described above will alleviate the detrimental responses of your body to anxiety and give you a sense of control of the situation.

6.8 A tense stomach and pinched thighs cause the rider's seat to be drawn out of the saddle at the sitting trot.

6.9 At the sitting trot, the rider's upper body is correct, with the back stretched upward, but the shoulders dropped low rather than held up tensely near her neck. Her stomach and thighs are relaxed, enabling her seat to follow the motion of the horse.

Horse Problems

Teaching Flying Changes

As discussed earlier, you can set a series of four poles on the ground to simulate a line of fences, with the fourth pole representing the point at which the horse should change leads (see figs. 6.2 A–C). As the horse's legs cross over the fourth pole, they will be approximately 4 inches farther off the ground than when galloping between the poles. This additional elevation gives the animal more time to switch the sequence of its feet than when you ask for a change of leads without using the pole.

Ask for a change of leads by applying pressure with your outside leg over the fourth pole, but only if the horse is on the counter (outside) lead following the third pole. It is very important to feel which lead the horse is on, for the animal will react angrily if you keep asking for a change of lead when it is already on the correct one. On course, there are usually not many strides between the final fence on a line and the corner, so you must make an immediate decision concerning the necessity of a lead change. Being able to feel the lead your horse is on is just a matter of practice: try to feel which you are on, then glance to see if you are right. After awhile, you will feel whether you are right or wrong and will not have to look anymore.

If applying your outside leg over the fourth pole does not produce the correct lead, the next time you go through the exercise, circle the horse toward the inside of the arena as you cross the fourth pole. The turn will encourage the horse to change leads in order to catch its balance. You may have to practice turning over the final pole several times to teach the horse the correct response to your outside leg aid (fig. 6.10).

You can set an entire course of poles on the ground until

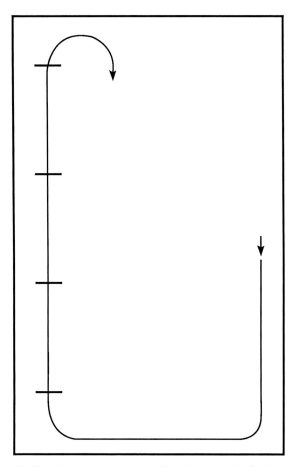

6.10 If the horse is reluctant to switch leads over the fourth pole, turn the animal toward the desired lead as you jump the pole. This will not only reinforce your aids, but also encourage the horse to switch leads to catch its balance.

you and the horse have mastered stride regulation and flying changes of lead in both directions, switching from the left to the right lead and vice versa. Then, build obstacles at the second and third poles on each line, still using the introductory pole to help rate the horse and the final pole to aid with the flying changes. Make sure the arena is big enough so that you don't run into a pole from one line while approaching a pole on another line (figs. 6.11 & 6.12).

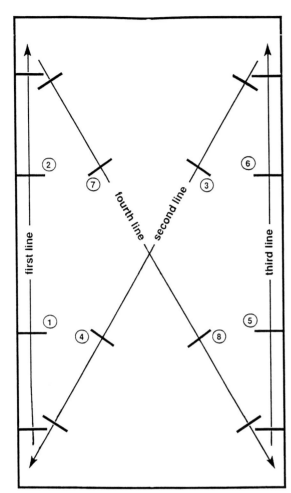

6.11 If you are not careful, the ground poles you set will interfere with the approach to or departure from other lines.

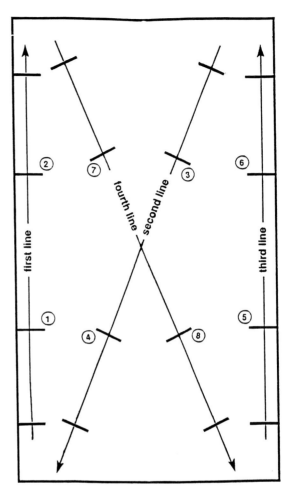

6.12 If your ring is wide enough, you will be able to angle the diagonal lines toward the short side of the arena. This will prevent the ground poles from obstructing the paths to other lines.

The horse may begin to anticipate your leg aid by becoming too quick to the poles used for lead changes. In this case, go back to the original exercise of halting before the fourth pole on each line. After the halt, ask the horse to walk across the pole, pick up the canter, and proceed to the next line.

If you have a horse that anticipates the lead change by diving toward the turn, striped poles will help you solve the problem. Paint your schooling poles so that approximately a 2-foot band of white is in the center of each pole. After you line up the poles for this exercise, make sure you ride to the center of each pole. This will make it obvious to you if the horse is beginning to drift while moving down the line. Halt the horse in front of the center of the last pole on each line until the animal realizes it won't be allowed to anticipate the direction of the turn. Once the horse is obediently following a straight path to the final pole, start the exercise from the beginning and jump the fourth pole, switching leads while in the air.

By encouraging elevation through collection and balance through straightness, you will find that most horses respond positively to the aid for the flying change. Of course, your outside leg must be applied at the appropriate time, as the horse's feet are coming off the ground for the split second of suspension that occurs just after the leading leg strikes. If your leg is applied at the wrong moment, the horse will not switch leads.

When the horse is comfortable changing leads over poles in both directions, remove the lead-change poles one by one, starting with the pole over which the horse is the most confident. (You can leave the ground poles leading into each line to help you practice placing your horse correctly at the first fence on a line; or you can remove these poles, too, and practice riding a normal course.) If the lead-change problem crops up again, reset the final pole on the lines where needed.

Preventing the Horse from Rushing Fences

A horse that rushes fences is not an animal that "loves to jump," as uneducated riders often remark, but rather is the horse that is anxious about jumping. Once a horse has learned to rush, it is difficult to break the habit. It may take many hours and much patience to develop trust between the horse and rider again. In fact, it is best to remove an inexperienced rider from a rusher and place him on a horse that is very dull, requiring little hand pressure and steady leg pressure, so that the rider can learn the correct use of his aids. Conversely, it is wise to put a well-educated, patient rider on the rusher, so that the horse can be properly retrained.

There are several exercises used to teach a horse not to rush, all of them based on the idea of denying it the chance to run to the fences. In the first exercise, approach a fence at a trot or canter and pull up in front of the obstacle, making the horse stand for a few seconds. The downward transition should be as smooth as possible; but if the horse is running to the fence, use a pulley rein rather than let it ignore the aids and jump the obstacle.

If the horse is frantic and cannot approach the jump at the canter without wanting to accelerate tremendously, try approaching the obstacle at a posting trot. You may even have to approach it at the walk if the rushing is completely beyond control. A walk fence should be set quite low to make the jumping effort easy from the slow pace—about 1' for horses and 9" or less for ponies. The idea is to regulate pace on the approach, promote discipline through denial (that is, make the horse stop, rather than allow it to run at the fence), and develop trust, so that the animal will confidently obey your commands.

It is interesting to watch different riders attempt to retrain horses that rush. The impatient, uneducated rider will pull the horse up harshly before the fences and back it up rapidly, using only his hands. All this does is make the horse more anxious. In contrast, a good rider will take care to quell the animal's fear. He will be firm, but not abrupt, in using his aids. If he backs the horse, he will be tactful with his hands and legs, using only the amount of pressure necessary. He will also be very careful in applying his aids after the halt, using minimum leg pressure to resume forward motion. At first his horse may overreact even to the slightest use of the aids; but after a few times the animal will learn there is nothing to fear and may even heave a large sigh of relief as it realizes the rider is not its foe.

Backing is useful in retraining a rusher because it requires greater obedience in the horse than the halt alone. An anxious horse is still thinking "forward," and only a mental change in direction will enable it to move backward. After you halt, ease the pressure on the reins to reward the horse for stopping. Then, add enough pressure on the reins to restrict the horse from moving forward as you apply your leg aid for backing up.

You may experience a brief deadlock in which the horse does not respond at all to your legs when you try to back. Attuned to the idea of running forward, it may refuse to think about moving in the other direction. The lack of response to the leg requires the slight persuasion of a spur or stick to reinforce the initial leg aid. You may ask, "Why would you use a spur or a stick on a rusher?" The answer is that you are seeking obedience in the horse. In the correct sequence of aids, the leg is followed by the spur, then the stick (it is leg, then stick, if you are not wearing spurs). It doesn't matter in which direction you are going, if the horse doesn't respond to your legs, reinforce them with the use of a spur or stick. The message to the horse is that you are willing to increase your aids until it reacts in the manner you desire.

Besides restricting a rusher by halting or backing, you can use a circle to teach obedience. As you approach the fence, try to regulate the pace of the horse. If it begins to speed up, circle before the obstacle, denying it the opportunity to rush toward the fence. Complete the circle and make a second approach, again trying to regulate the pace. If the horse tries to rush a second time, circle once again. Continue this pattern until it responds by sustaining an even pace all the way to the fence.

Personally, I prefer halting at an obstacle, or halting and backing, rather than circling on the approach. While circling is a means of disciplining the horse and regulating its pace, I would rather stop in front of the fence and literally show the animal there is nothing to fear. I want the horse to put its head down and sniff the obstacle. This gives me the opportunity to reassure it with a pat on the neck.

The nonchalance of the rider should calm the horse and help it begin to look at the obstacles. A scared horse never really looks at the fences. It doesn't try to gauge itself for a safe, comfortable jumping effort, but flies over the obstacles as though its tail were on fire. For this reason, I think it is important for a rusher to learn to look and be rewarded for doing so with a calming and reassuring pat.

In general, when dealing with a nervous horse, try to instill a sense of calmness in the animal by emphasizing the relaxation of your aids, especially your hands. Instead of grabbing at the horse's mouth when the animal gets quick, maintain rein contact as lightly as possible. This sends the subtle message, "I am not afraid, so there is no reason for you to be afraid." You can halt, back, or circle the horse to control it if it continues to rush; but it is never appropriate to incessantly hang on its mouth, since this perpetuates the animal's hysteria and deadens the feeling in its mouth.

It is difficult to maintain leg pressure on a tense horse without the horse interpreting it as a driving aid. To develop a steady, yet sensitive leg, think of your calves as a clamp with a slight but consistent pressure. If you concentrate on hugging the horse's sides lightly with your legs and never succumb to removing them entirely when the horse is tense, it will learn not only to accept the legs, but also to expect their support. The steadiness of the legs will then be comforting to the animal, and the horse will worry when this security blanket is taken away, rather than when it is on. As the horse increasingly accepts the pressure of the legs, you will be able to add more pressure, until you reach the point where you can manipulate your horse mainly through your legs, with the hands acting only to balance the animal and help the legs in steering.

Correcting Disobediences (Refusals)

A horse usually stops at fences for one of the following reasons: (1) the rider places the horse too deep to or too far from the obstacle for the horse to jump it comfortably; (2) the footing is slippery or deep, making the horse doubt that it can clear the obstacle; (3) the horse is steered to the fence poorly, so that it sees the obstacle too late to set itself up properly or is so off-balance that it is unable to jump; (4) the horse is frightened by a fence that has patterns on it that are visually confusing; (5) parts of the obstacle or of nearby objects or surroundings are mobile or noisy; (6) the fence is too big for the horse to believe it can jump it; or (7) the pain of an unsoundness overrides the horse's fear of being punished for refusing.

You can control many of a horse's reasons for stopping at a fence. Practicing over ground poles and obstacles will help you develop better pace regulation, placement of the horse, and steering. Exposing the horse to many show grounds will decrease the animal's chances of overreacting to spooky fences or surroundings. (Some riders pay stabling fees for their green horses and ride them around several different show grounds to familiarize them with the atmosphere before the animals are ever entered in competition.) Placing the horse in the proper division for its abilities will preclude it from being overfaced by large fences; and proper veterinary treatment and rest will solve many kinds of unsoundness.

Bad footing continues to be a problem at some shows. You must use good judgment in determining when the poor quality of the footing is affecting your horse's performance, for you cannot develop absolute obedience in a horse if your demands are unreasonable. By asking the horse to jump in threatening conditions, you may cause a crash and undo the many hours you have spent building its trust.

It's a long road to accurate riding, and on the way you'll make some mistakes that will leave you sitting on a horse on the near side of an obstacle wondering what to do now that it has refused the fence. First of all, think of the correction for a refusal as a matter of opposites. You want to do exactly the opposite of what the horse wants to do. For instance, if the horse refuses the fence by running out to the left, turn it back to the right as a correction. Then, make the animal stand in front of the fence to receive its punishment. Conversely, if the horse tries to run out to the right, turn it back to the left, again making it stand in front of the fence to be punished.

Whether the horse tries to run out at the fence or simply stops directly in front of it, the issue is the animal's lack of obedience in going forward over the obstacle. For this reason, once you have the horse standing squarely in front of the fence, punish its source of forward momentum, which is the rear part of its body, with your stick in the area just behind your calf (fig. 6.13). If the horse stopped straight, you can punish it on either side; but if it veered when stopping, apply the stick on the side to which the animal tried to escape.

By being prompt with your correction, you won't have to exert a tremendous amount of physical force. You are not trying to inflict pain, but rather just enough discomfort so that the horse would rather jump the obstacle on the next approach than be punished again with the stick.

6.13 The correct punishment for a run-out is applied on the side to which the horse tried to escape. For example, this horse would be receiving punishment for having run out toward its right side. Before you apply the stick on the horse's barrel, make sure the animal is facing the fence so that it clearly connects the punishment to lack of forward movement over a particular obstacle.

You should always carry a stick when jumping, so that it can be used immediately. If you have to hunt for one when a problem arises, the horse may have forgotten what it did wrong by the time you apply it, so that the punishment is seemingly unrelated to the initial problem.

Riders will sometimes say, "I don't carry a stick because my horse is scared of it." The solution is to always carry a stick, so that the animal learns to regard it as standard equipment. Carry it on the flat, as well as over fences, until the horse is comfortable with its presence. Any horse that convinces you that you shouldn't carry a stick is controlling you. Remember, you are the brains, the horse is the brawn. Any other relationship is dangerous.

Always remember to ease off the mouth when the horse leaves the ground to jump, for if your hands are hard and restricting, you will encourage it to refuse fences. Especially when it has stopped and you are approaching the obstacle

for the second time, emphasize your driving aids—legs and seat, too, if necessary—and relax your hands as much as possible, keeping just enough tension on the reins to steer the horse. Your objective is to make going forward much easier than stopping.

You may not be able to keep a very light hand on a horse that wants to run out. In fact, you may have to use a great deal of hand pressure to hold it into the fence as it tries to veer in one direction. If this is the case, be sure to release as it leaves the ground, offering more than enough slack in the reins over the fence so that it will realize that forward is the most comfortable direction.

If you ride the horse accurately to take-off spots, but it tries to refuse fences, ask a veterinarian to check for unsoundness. Lameness in a leg or foot, sore back muscles, or a spinal problem are typical unsoundnesses that will cause a horse to stop.

Preventing the Horse from Cutting Corners

Several problems are created when a horse cuts the corners of the ring on course. First, the horse's weight is distributed too heavily toward the inside of the turn, so that the animal is unbalanced on its approach to the upcoming line. Second, this habit is usually accompanied by the horse being bent in the wrong direction, so that its vision is jeopardized. Third, by cutting corners, the horse leaves the rider with fewer strides in which to make adjustments following and leading into lines of fences.

The main thing to remember in solving this problem is to push the horse to the rail with an inside leg and an inside indirect rein, rather than pulling it to the rail with an outside hand. The following exercises will help you correct a horse that cuts corners. First, pick up a canter and rise into two-point position, then try to canter the correct path around the short side of the arena. Concentrate on keeping the horse bent correctly. If it tries to throw its shoulder to the inside of the ring, sit and perform a downward transition to the walk; then push the animal away from the center of the ring with pressure from your inside leg. Your hands, which should maintain an inside indirect rein, can aid your inside leg by shifting slightly toward the outside of the ring. This causes the inside rein to act as a neck rein and the outside rein as an opening rein.

If the horse still tries to lean to the inside, practice a leg-yield, requiring it to cross its inside feet over its outside feet, so that it displaces its weight to the outside of the figure. You can use an opening outside rein to give the animal a clearer sense of the direction in which you want it to move. If the horse does not respond sufficiently, switch both reins to your outside hand and use your stick behind your inside leg to reinforce your leg aid. When the horse responds correctly by displacing its body toward the outside of the figure,

reward it with a long rein and a one-minute free walk to let the exercise sink in.

Then gather your reins and pick up a posting trot. Try to keep the animal bent in the proper direction around the short side of the arena. If it attempts to throw its shoulder to the inside, walk again and go through the procedure just described. When the horse is trotting around the end of the ring without trying to lean inward, pick up a canter and practice going around the short side with your body in three-point position. If the horse throws its shoulder to the inside again, walk and go through the procedure suggested earlier. Once the canter work in three-point position is correct, rise into two-point position and approach the short side of the arena, going back to the procedure at the walk if necessary.

Finally, try galloping around the ring in two-point position, keeping the horse to the rail with an inside indirect rein and inside leg. (Your outside leg should be supportive enough to prevent the horse from switching to the counter lead.) You can also attempt a course of fences to see if your flatwork has solved the problem. Remember that the greater the pace, the more the horse will be at the advantage. Therefore, if the problem starts again, go back to the walk and perform the necessary exercises to correct the horse at the point at which it begins to cut the corner.

Calming the Anxious Horse at Shows

There is no quick way to cure a horse's anxiety, but there are methods to minimize the problem. It helps to ship the horse to shows early, so that the animal has at least a full day in the new surroundings prior to competition. Take it out to graze near the show rings and familiarize it with any objects that might later present a problem, such as a barrier made of plastic string lined with hanging flags. Let the horse look, listen, and smell its environment.

If your animal is very nervous at the new location, don't try to walk it by hand. First, longe it on a large circle for about 20 minutes, changing direction every five minutes. After longeing, give the horse a bath (provided the weather is warm) and let it cool out and calm down. Once it is dry, return it to the stall so that it can drink water and urinate. Remember, it is easy to become so obsessed with working a horse down that you don't allow for its basic physical needs.

Give the horse about an hour's break. (This might be a good time for you to get a bite to eat so that hunger won't affect your mental attitude toward the horse. It is vital that you approach the nervous horse patiently if you are to improve its state of mind.) Then, tack up and ride for about 30 minutes. If the horse still seems tense, you can ride for up to another 30 minutes; but do not ride longer than an hour during any single session.

Avoid movements that are not easily within the horse's level of education. By sticking to familiar tasks, you will promote confidence and relaxation. Also, take frequent breaks and try to let the horse move on a long rein at the walk, showing that you are relaxed in the new surroundings. Of course, you don't want to take this so far that your horse catches you napping and suddenly dashes off to the hinterlands, leaving you behind on the ground! But trust your horse as much as you reasonably can.

If the animal is still nervous after an hour of riding, cool it down again and let it rest in the stall awhile. Then do another session later in the day. Be sure to provide plenty of water and hay between these sessions.

Next morning, take the horse out of the stall, and if it seems reasonably relaxed ride it a while. (If, however, the animal is still very tense, longe it first.) Do about 10 minutes of flatwork, then gallop the horse for about three minutes to see if it becomes excited from the increased pace. Testing the

horse at pace is the best way of determining its anxiety level. If the animal is quiet, cool it down and put it in the stall until you need to prepare for the first class. If the horse becomes keyed up during the gallop, continue to gallop in three-minute sessions, with a few minutes of break time between, until the horse becomes more relaxed. (If you cannot control the animal at the gallop, return it to the longe line, again alternating directions every few minutes.)

You must find that fine line between reducing the horse's anxiety and working the animal to the bone. If your horse calms down, but in the process becomes lame, colicky, or tied up, then the work obviously hasn't done much good. Short, multiple riding sessions will give you the opportunity to gauge its energy level correctly, whereas the flow of adrenalin caused by a lengthy, emotional work session will often disguise an animal's exhaustion. Through regular breaks, you give the horse a chance to realize how tired it is, as well as give yourself the chance to evaluate precisely when the horse's spent energy has produced the calmness you desire. Following the correct preparation for the first day of showing, the anxiety level of the horse will remain the same or decrease throughout the show as it becomes tired and more familiar with the surroundings.

Warming Up for a Class

When you're warming up for a class, you want to simulate the upcoming conditions as much as possible. If you are going to ride in an under-saddle class, then you should walk, trot, and canter your horse in the schooling arena in the same frame and with the same pace at each gait that you will be using in the class.

If you find your horse is too strong or too dull, now

is the time to correct these errors, while you are still out of the judge's view. You may want to switch bits—say, from a snaffle to a pelham—if your horse is too strong, or add spurs if an additional driving aid is needed. The time you spend in warm-up, then, should not be just to loosen the horse up for the class, but to correct any last-minute problems.

When you're going to show over fences, begin by warming up on the flat for a short time—less than 10 minutes, unless the animal is excited and needs to be worked longer. Start the jumping portion of your warm-up by trotting the horse over a small X (about a foot off the ground at the center for horses and even lower for ponies), then halt at the end of the line.

After trotting back and forth over the X two or three times, change its construction to a vertical fence, set about 6 inches lower than the height of the fences in the upcoming hunter or equitation class. Hand gallop the horse around the schooling arena once to wake it up a bit, then approach the fence, seeking a medium takeoff spot from a medium pace. After the jump, halt at the end of the line. If your horse is excited and wants to rush the fence, turn the animal around and jump the fence off a short approach. If the horse is dull and doesn't want to reach the proper pace, make a large circle at the hand gallop and approach the fence again, being prepared to use your stick if the animal tries to slow down.

Once the horse is jumping the vertical well at the low height, raise the fence 3 inches and jump it once or twice at the new height. Then raise it another 3 inches, so that it is at the height at which the horse will be shown. When you have jumped the vertical one or two times at this height, you can change the fence to an oxer to encourage good form in the air. You may even want to raise the uppermost poles of each element of the oxer one notch higher than the height

of the fences in the class to make the horse pay attention. (Although a square oxer will not be found in hunter classes, you can use it for warming up both hunters and equitation horses. It makes a horse try harder to clear the fence than does an ascending oxer and thus "tunes" the horse.)

Consider the type of course you'll be jumping and prepare during your warm-up for the specific tests on course. For example, if a hunter course is set with long strides between the fences, practice riding up to pace by galloping around the arena then approaching the warm-up fence with long, bold strides. If an equitation course contains a tight turn, a fence to be jumped at an angle, or some other test that is difficult, then simulate it in your warm-up. (Difficult tests should be practiced over fences set no higher than the normal height for the class, since a higher fence will encourage the horse to stop.)

If your horse tends to spook at colorful or unusual objects in a ring, you can prepare by placing a wool cooler over a vertical fence to make the animal hesitant to approach it in practice. If the horse tries to slow down or stop at the fence, punish it with the stick so that it knows it must go forward. Once you have cleared the obstacle, take the cooler away and jump the fence again. In this way, the horse will not end the practice being anxious, but will clearly get the message that it must go forward.

When you have finished schooling, you should feel completely prepared to ride the course ahead. The schooling area is not a place for you to try new tests that you haven't taken the time to practice at home. Instead, it should be used as a last-minute preparation, to ready yourself and your horse to perform well in the upcoming class.

Make sure you have enough time to think about the course before you enter the ring. Mount early enough so that you can school and still have one or two horses waiting ahead of you when you get to the in-gate. If there is a delay and you cannot compete soon after warming up, take the horse to an area where you can gallop just before you go in, so that it won't be dull from waiting.

Monitoring Horse and Rider

A horse show should not be viewed as a single competition spanning several days, but rather as a number of different competitive situations. Typically, horse and rider begin with a high level of excitement caused by the new surroundings, the bustle of people and animals, and the anticipation of winning a ribbon. This usually lasts throughout the first day of a multi-day show and may even extend into the second day, if the number of classes ridden the first day were few.

By the third day, however, the horse and rider are tired. Gone is the earlier elation, replaced either by a nice sense of "things are going well" or the opposite feeling that "my horse is going terribly; I can't see my spots to the fences; the judge doesn't place me even when I think my horse has gone well," and so forth.

Going into the final days of the show, everyone is really tired. The riders who continue to win are those who are able to stay mentally sharp for each class, even though they are physically tired.

The changes in the horse and rider that occur from day to day are the result of many subtle changes that take place from class to class. Generally, in the first class the horses are "backed off" at the fences, warily approaching the unfamiliar obstacles. Frequently riders do not compensate for this, and they "under-ride" to the fences, not using enough leg to create sufficient pace and impulsion for the course.

By the second class, everyone is awake. Those who

didn't ride well in the first class are kicking themselves and closely watching the round of the horse that won class one. In general, it will take a better performance to win the second class than it did the first, for everyone's competitive spirits have been aroused. The next few classes will be very competitive, particularly if they come before lunch. By noontime, the heat and the lure of food distract many competitors. After lunch, there is usually a post-meal lag as riders struggle to fight the drowsiness brought on by digestion. As for those who skipped lunch, they are feeling the effects of the lack of food.

By the end of day one, both horse and rider are tired, as well as the grooms and coaches who are just coming down from the emotional high of setting up their stable area and schooling for the first day of the show. As day two starts, the horses will be calmer, as will the riders. This is usually a good competitive day, but riders will begin to notice that it takes more leg to get their horses up to pace than it did the day before. From day three on, it is a matter of maintenance of the horse's and rider's energy levels, as well as of the horse's soundness. The big winners are the competitors who best minimize the aspects of nervousness leading into the show and who sustain an appropriate level of energy throughout the final days.

At a one- or two-day show, you and your horse will experience the same changes mentioned above, but they will occur in a much shorter time frame. If you're smart, you will be aware of the pitfalls of showing and will avoid becoming overly tired, hungry, cold, wet, or sunburned. You'll protect yourself so that your mind and body can produce peak performances for as long as possible.

Each time you mount for a class, think about the changes that have occurred in the horse since the previous performance. For example, if your horse was taken back to the barn for a break between classes, what went on during the break? Even if you have a groom, you should know the answer to this question, not only from asking the groom, but also from checking on the horse periodically. Did the horse have plenty of water and hay during the break? Was there enough ventilation in the stall to be comfortable on a hot day, or was there sufficient protection from the wind on a cold day? Breaks between classes are opportunities for the animal to relax. If your horse is so uncomfortable that it is denied this respite, there is a good chance it will not be willing or able to perform its best in the next class.

If the time between classes is so short that the horse must be kept near the ring, make sure its needs are not neglected. On a hot day, keep the animal in the shade whenever possible and have water available in a nearby bucket. On a cold day, keep a wool cooler at ringside. It will allow perspiration to pass through the fabric and bead up on top of the blanket, while the fibers next to the horse remain relatively dry, keeping the animal warm.

As for maintaining your own energy level, on hot days it helps to have something to drink in an ice chest at ringside, saving numerous trips to the concession stand. A folding chair to rest on between classes is also helpful. The ultimate energy-saver is a small motor scooter or a golf cart to spare you from endless walks to and from the barn. In general, avoid fatigue as much as possible throughout the show. The most important classes are usually held toward the end, and you don't want to run out of steam then.

Setting an Attainable Goal

Besides evaluating yourself and your horse on a daily basis, try to formulate some long-term goals. Of course, they cannot be determined until you have had a certain amount of experience. Your basics must be strong—that is, heels down, lower legs secure, your upper body balanced over your legs, and your hands sensitive to the horse's mouth. You must also be jumping small courses, demonstrating your ability to determine the proper takeoff spot to the fences. Once you have reached this point, you are ready to sit down with your coach—and, in the case of a junior rider, your parents—to discuss long-term goals.

If a child is well-proportioned for riding, has several years still ahead in the junior division, and shows a good eye for fences, then the coach should be thinking about the Medal, Maclay, and USEF Talent Search Finals. The family's finances will come into play as a show schedule is devised. Although you can save money by stabling your horse at home, shipping the animal yourself, and doing your own grooming at shows, it is difficult to be highly competitive if you are exhausted from doing the chores as well as the riding. You'll have a better chance if you have a loyal relative or friend who is willing to get up before dawn to feed and braid your horse, as well as help out in other ways for the duration the show.

It is important to set attainable goals. Riders who do not have a good physique for the sport, those who are mounted on inadequate horses, or those who can't afford to show regularly are setting themselves up for disappointment if they set goals that are too high, such as winning one of the Finals. Parents can get caught up in a bad situation as well by making financial commitments they cannot reasonably meet. You must be realistic about the rider's and horse's ability and about the available financial backing. Otherwise, what was intended to be a fun and exciting experience will be tainted by frustration and financial woes.

THE BIG PICTURE
New Kids on the Block
"Currently, 40 colleges and universities offer Equestrian as a varsity sport,
and more continue to add the program each year."

Some exciting new opportunities have arisen for young riders in the past few years, most notably, the emergence of "Equestrian" as an NCAA sport, offering college scholarships for top female riders. There has also been a move to include equestrian competitions in high school athletic programs, with some scholarship opportunity there, too. Below is information about these and other relatively new programs:

National Collegiate Athletic Association (NCAA)

The National Collegiate Athletic Association is a voluntary association of 1,281 institutions, conferences, and organizations. The mission of the NCAA includes governing intercollegiate athletics competition in a fair, safe, equitable, and sportsman-like manner and integrating athletics into higher education so that the educational experience of the student-athlete is paramount. Its headquarters are currently located in Indianapolis, Indiana.

In 1998, "Equestrian" was classified as an NCAA emerging sport. Many people within the horse industry have united in an attempt to advance the sport to full NCAA championship status. In order to attain this goal and hold an NCAA Equestrian Championship, there must be 50 Division I/II/III schools that sponsor Equestrian as a varsity-level program.

Currently, 40 NCAA colleges and universities offer Equestrian as a varsity sport, and more continue to add the program each year. The NCAA has allowed the sport of Equestrian to have 15 full scholarships per school. (Equestrian is considered by the NCAA to be an equivalency sport, which means one scholarship may be divided among more than one student-athlete.) Availability of and requirements for scholarships vary for each university. To see the list of colleges that have NCAA Equestrian programs, go to: **www.varsityequestrian.com/universities.html.**

Interscholastic Equestrian Association (IEA)

The Interscholastic Equestrian Association was founded in 2002. The mission of the IEA includes introducing students in both private and public middle and secondary schools to equestrian sports and providing them with organized competitive events. In 2007, the IEA Founders College Scholarship Awards were initiated, offering scholarship money for the winners of each championship class.

The IEA has grown from approximately 120 members in its first year to nearly 1,300 by its fifth year. The IEA is an affiliate of the United States Equestrian Federation (www.usef.org) and the Intercollegiate Horse Show Association (www.ihsainc.com).

IEA competitions involve jumping over fences no greater that 2'6" and competing on the flat. Both at the local and national level, none of the riders supply their own horses or tack. Instead, the horses, saddles, and other tack are provided to

THE BIG PICTURE cont.

the students at the show, with the host school arranging for those horses and equipment. The riders and horses have only a short orientation period before performing in the ring. The scores during competition are based solely upon horsemanship, not upon the quality of the horse.

For more information on the IEA, visit the following website: **www.rideiea.com.**

United States Equestrian Federation Youth Council (USEF Youth Council)

The United States Equestrian Federation Youth Council had its inaugural meeting in January, 2007, in Louisville, Kentucky, and its first Youth Convention at the 2008 USEF annual meeting. One of the goals of the USEF Youth Council is to cultivate interest in equestrian sports at the high school level by encouraging schools to create riding teams or clubs. The Youth Council is in the process of creating materials that can be shown to school administrators to inform them about the benefits of riding and let them know how to start an equestrian club or team. For more information on the USEF Youth Council, go to: **www.usef.org**.

United States Hunter Jumper Association (USHJA)

The United States Hunter Jumper Association was formed to represent all levels of hunter and jumper participants under the umbrella of the USEF. The first national convention of the USHJA was held in November, 2004, in Tucson, Arizona. Since then, many programs have been developed to help association members, such as the USHJA Junior Career Development Program, which was created to allow youth to apprentice for a day with a judge, show manager, show secretary, steward, course designer, vet, or farrier. The program provides junior riders with the opportunity to have a better understanding of what goes on in these areas at a horse show and to determine if they would like to pursue a career in these positions.

The USHJA has also initiated many other programs, such as the Trainer's Symposium, the Mentor Program, the Trainer's Certification Program, and the International Hunter Style Challenge. For more information on the USHJA and its programs, go to: **www.ushja.org.**

Winning

Riders who have the best competitive records over long periods of time rely on hard work and serious analysis of their riding experiences to keep them ahead of other competitors. If you devote your time to practice as you should, then your confidence level will rise along with your skill. Instead of looking at a test and thinking, "Can I do this?" you will be so well prepared that your only concern will be to ride to the best of your ability and excel at that which you have practiced many times before.

A systematic approach to riding will help you most when you are under the stress of an unusual situation, such as competing in bad weather, riding an unfamiliar horse, or showing indoors, where schooling is often limited in both time and space. These are the kinds of situations that end in defeat for the seat-of-the-pants rider, for difficult situations demand more technical skill, which is gained only through a dedicated approach to the sport.

If possible, surround yourself with people who are committed to your success—an attentive coach, a reliable groom, and even supportive friends or relatives. Your dedication should inspire the people you work with and fuel their desire for your success. When a rider wins at the highest levels of competition, you will usually find he or she has a wonderful support team.

Concentrate on excellence in your daily work, rather than focusing mainly upon the goal of winning. Continuous progress means you have the possibility of being truly great in your sport, while ribbons and trophies can be gained simply when you are better than the rest of your local competitors, who may not ride particularly well. Of course, we're all happy when we get a ribbon, but the thrill of winning may cloud the priority of improving your skill.

Most importantly, put winning in perspective, not only for the sense of fulfillment that a sound personal philosophy can provide, but also for the betterment of the sport. Too often we focus solely on talent and ambition while overlooking other important aspects of people's characters. If we as a society turn away from the concept of good sportsmanship and place all our emphasis on winning, we will demean the most important and inspiring qualities of mankind. Talent and ambition are an exciting combination, no doubt; but it is dedication, emotional stability, and a gracious acceptance of defeat, as well as victory, that are the marks of a true winner.

PART TWO

JUDGING HUNTERS
& HUNTER SEAT EQUITATION

7

Under-Saddle Classes

The Ideal Horse

The *USEF Rule Book* states that horses being shown in under-saddle classes "should be obedient, alert, responsive, and move freely." Let's begin by examining the ideal horse, one that exhibits all of these qualities.

The ideal horse moves freely, stretching for long, athletic steps instead of taking short, high steps. Viewed from the side, it will be seen to swing its legs close to the ground and reach to the full length of its stride at all gaits (figs. 7.1 A–D). Observed from the front or hind perspective, it travels squarely.

This ideal animal is "on the bit" and in a balanced frame at all gaits. It is neither "overflexed," with its head forced behind the vertical, nor is it strung out on loose reins with no frame at all; rather, it is positioned between these two extremes. The ideal frame for each horse depends on its particular conformation, disposition, and locomotion (figs. 7.2 A–C). For safety reasons, "light contact with the horse's mouth" is required by the *Rule Book*, so any horse being shown on reins so loose that they compromise the rider's control must be penalized.

Our ideal horse keeps a constant rhythm at each gait and maintains appropriate forward momentum into downward transitions, making them smooth rather than abrupt. Its hindquarters, well under it, demonstrate continuous forward impulsion. On the corners of the ring the horse is bent from head to tail in the direction of travel, and on the straight sides of the ring, its body is straight (figs. 7.3 A & B).

This ideal animal is prompt, yet smooth, in both upward and downward transitions. It is relaxed, but not dull, and is willing to go forward. Attentive, but calm, it doesn't become

7.1 A–D This pony is an "excellent mover," skimming its toe across the ground at the walk (A & B), then sweeping its leg forward with a low, long step to reach the full extension of its stride (C & D).

7.2 A–C "On the bit," with impulsion at the trot, the pony strides forward with a sense of purpose (A). The side view (B) shows the floating appearance and very long stride that are indicative of an "excellent mover." From the rear view (C), the pony's impulsion and balance are still obvious. This animal has wonderful natural carriage, staying well-balanced even when its young rider loses steady rein contact in frames B and C.

7.3 A & B Although these horses are pictured in a class over fences, they provide a good comparison of a horse that is not bent on the corner (A) to one that is correctly bent in the direction of travel (B). Notice the difference in balance and field of vision.

excited or buck and play if you call for a hand gallop. A pleasant expression and ears pointed forward indicate the animal's cooperative attitude.

Now the ideal is established, let's look at a variety of performance faults you may see while judging and consider their relative penalties.

Unsafe Performance

Unsafe behavior receives the heaviest penalties in this as in every phase of hunter seat riding that is judged on quality of performance. The horse that bolts (runs off) with its rider and the horse that rears are most dangerous. Less serious offenders, but still receiving heavy penalties, are the horse that bucks

and the animal that shies. These forms of bad behavior are severely penalized because they endanger the rider and can cause harm to other competitors in the class.

The only exception you might consider in this area would be a horse that bucks or shies mildly under "extenuating circumstances." For instance, if an otherwise well-behaved horse gives a little buck when another competitor's horse runs into it from behind, you might forgive this behavioral fault; but you should penalize severely a horse that lets out a walloping buck with no apparent provocation. Similarly, you should penalize heavily a tense horse that goes around the ring looking for trouble, shying in response to every sound and movement, or even shying at inanimate objects. However, you can be lenient with an animal that shies slightly when someone parked by the railing inconsiderately starts a noisy engine just as the horse is passing by.

In judging performance, everything is relative. The little buck or small shy might end up being a deciding factor in top company, but a horse's normal reaction to an unusual situation should not necessarily exclude the animal from the ribbons.

Length of Stride

Less heavily penalized than the serious behavioral problems, but still considered major faults, are flaws in the animal's locomotion. A horse with short, high-action steps lacks the athletic appearance we desire in a hunter and is often a bumpy, unpleasant ride. This "poor mover" should place only when a small number of entries or a lack of quality competition leaves you no choice (fig. 7.4).

Preferable to this is a "fair mover," a horse that has either a long stride and high action or a short stride and low action—that is, its way of moving is good in some respects, but it still has a major locomotion flaw (figs. 7.5 A & B).

Surpassing the fair mover in quality is the "good mover." This horse displays a long enough, low enough stride to be in the ribbons in moderately stiff competition, or to place in higher competition if the better movers commit major faults, but it lacks the exceptionally long, flowing stride that marks a top-quality horse. A "good mover" and an "excellent mover" are virtually indistinguishable in photographs, since the main difference between the two is the extra flowing motion the "excellent mover" has, which cannot be captured when you stop the action, even in sequential photographs. However, when judging a class, it will be obvious to you which are the "good movers" that travel long and low, and which are the "excellent movers" that travel long, low, and with such ease that they seem to float across the footing.

7.4 This "poor mover" has mostly upward motion at the trot, with its hocks and knees displaying excess vertical action and its upright neck adding to the impression of extreme vertical motion.

An "excellent mover" is the picture of elegance as it swings its limbs forward with each step and stretches for the ground. This high-quality animal has minimal upward action and maximum forward thrust of the limbs (figs. 7.6 A–C). In the forelegs, the knee and fetlock joints hardly bend, so that in all gaits the hooves travel close to the ground; the animal is said to move with a "daisy-cutting" motion. The hind legs stretch forward with each step, maintaining solid impulsion at each gait and throughout the transitions. The hock joints open and close with a fluid movement that allows the horse to reach forward with its hind legs in flowing, athletic steps. Lesser movers may appear stiff in the hocks, take short steps with the hind legs, and trail their rear ends; in contrast, an excellent mover shows smooth, low, long, and powerful steps in its hind end, "engaging" its hocks while working at each gait.

7.5 A & B Seen at both the stretch phase (A) and the raised-joint phase (B) of the trot, this horse appears to be a "fair mover." Although the horse has a long neck, its high head carriage restricts the length of stride, making the stride shorter than if the horse stretched its neck down and out as it traveled.

7.6 A–C In this sequence of an "excellent mover" at the canter, the animal's long stride consistently reaches the full extension of its limbs. The pony has lots of impulsion, but remains relaxed and balanced—a winning combination.

7.7 A–C A horse can resist the rider's hands by pulling (A), or can evade contact by raising its head (B) or drawing its head toward its chest (C).

Appropriate Frame

Besides noting length of stride, consider the horse's general carriage or "frame." A strung-out horse that moves with its head poking out at the end of a loose rein is most unattractive when compared to a horse that has been put on the bit and is carrying itself in a balanced frame, with hocks well under its body at each step. You are not looking for a horse to be so collected that it could perform a piaffe, but neither do you want to pin a horse that hacks quietly only on a loose rein, for the rider's avoidance of putting the horse on the bit suggests that the animal becomes excited, resistant, or evasive when contact is established with its mouth (figs. 7.7 A–C). A horse in under-saddle classes should accept the bit and go to it willingly, rather than hang on the rider's hands or duck behind the bit to escape pressure (fig. 7.8).

7.8 This horse accepts the bit and travels in a long, relaxed frame appropriate for an under-saddle class.

Body Straightness

An animal that doesn't move straight should be penalized, since lack of straightness limits the horse as an athlete and often leads to unsoundness. However, a horse that doesn't move straight should be penalized less severely than a short-strided animal. The reason for this is that a horse with a long, smooth stride may not move completely straight, but as long as its lack of straightness doesn't cause lameness, the animal will have an adequate stride to make a smooth round over fences. The choppy, short-strided horse, on the other hand, may move straight, but it will never have the athletic ability to turn in a smooth, flowing trip, and its short, uncomfortable gait will make it unpleasant to ride.

Common Locomotion Faults

Any deviation from straightforward locomotion should be penalized. For instance, some horses move crookedly throughout their bodies, with their hind feet and their forefeet traveling on separate tracks (fig. 7.9). Since this crookedness pervades the horse's every effort on the flat and over fences, you should penalize it severely.

Horses that do not move crookedly throughout their bodies may still have a locomotion problem because of the turn of their legs—either the entire leg or the leg from the knee or fetlock down. The worst fault resulting from these structural problems is "plaiting": the animal places one foot in front of the other so that the hooves on opposite sides of the body track the same path, instead of the right feet tracking one path and the left feet tracking another (fig. 7.10). Most often found in horses with base-narrow, toe-out conformation, plaiting is heavily penal-

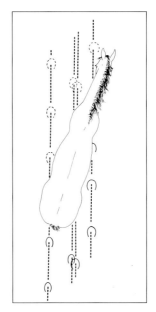

7.9 A horse that moves crooked ("dog-style") is often a sufferer from trochanteric bursitis. The animal shifts toward the sound side since the stride on the affected side is shortened.

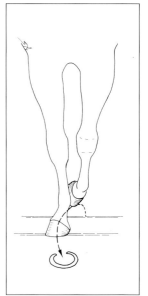

7.10 In plaiting ("single-tracking"), the horse's front feet are placed directly, or almost directly, in front of each other. Plaiting often causes stumbling and is heavily penalized in under-saddle classes.

ized because it can cause stumbling and result in injury to the horse and/or rider.

A lesser fault in locomotion is "winging," in which the horse brushes past the inside of one leg with the hoof of the opposite leg and places the foot outside the imaginary line from shoulder to ground on which the hoof should land during travel (fig. 7.11). Associated with toe-out conformation, winging is penalized because it can cause trauma in one or both of the legs involved, first from the brushing of the hoof against the opposite leg, and second from the excess pres-

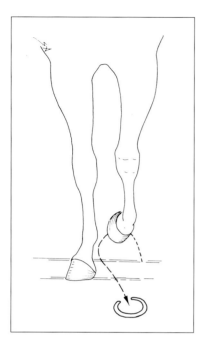

7.11 (left) Winging ("wing-in") is penalized for the excess pressure it puts on the inside of the leg as the hoof is placed to the outside of the proper track and for the interference to the opposite leg, which often results from moving in this manner.

7.12 (right) Paddling ("wing-out") causes unequal weight distribution on the leg as the foot is placed to the inside of the proper track. However, it is not as heavily penalized as winging or plaiting because paddling does not cause interference.

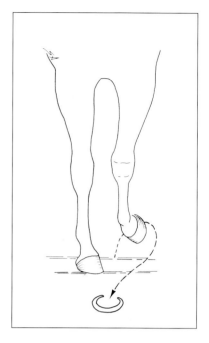

sure the horse places on the inside of one leg as it sets the hoof down too far to the outside of the correct path.

"Paddling" is another locomotion fault seen in under-saddle classes. Here the horse swings its foot to the outside of the imaginary line from shoulder to ground on which the hoof should be traveling and places the hoof to the inside of that line, causing excess weight to be thrust upon the outside of the foot (fig. 7.12). Associated with toe-in conformation, paddling shows a lack of proper weight distribution on the leg and a lack of straightforward thrust of the horse's legs. However, paddling poses no danger of one leg interfering with another, so you should penalize it less severely than plaiting or winging.

Rhythm, Transitions, and Bending

Rhythm is another aspect of performance to consider in judging under-saddle classes. The animal that maintains a constant rhythm at its gaits is more attractive than one that looks as though it will "die out" and break gait or one that seems to be "on the muscle," gaining momentum with every stride. You should notice a horse's rhythm in all gaits, including the walk, for too often judges as well as riders regard the walk as a "time out." It is important that competitors who do try to show their mounts in a solid cadence at the walk receive credit for the quality of their performance at this often "forgotten gait."

The rhythm of the gaits should not be broken abruptly by downward transitions that look as though the horse is "slamming on the brakes." Both upward and downward transitions should be as smooth as possible, with a prompt and fluid transition being preferable to a prompt but abrupt one.

Besides maintaining steady rhythm in the gaits and performing smooth transitions, a horse in under-saddle classes should be bent in the direction of travel around the corners of the ring and move straight on the straight sides. A horse that negotiates corners improperly—with its head turned to the outside—should be penalized heavily, for its lack of correct bending jeopardizes its balance, limits its field of vision, and in most cases causes the animal to shorten its stride because it loses some of its forward momentum as it leans to the inside of the ring.

Summary

After you have weeded out any horses that display behavioral problems (bolting, rearing, bucking, for example), or commit major performance errors (breaking gait or picking up the wrong lead), consider each remaining animal's action of the limbs, length of stride, and frame. Then look for alignment problems, such as crooked movement throughout the body, plaiting, winging, or paddling. After you have used the criteria detailed above to select the horses of the best quality in the class, consider each animal's overall performance: its willingness to go forward in a definite cadence at all gaits, whether or not it was bent properly on the corners of the ring, the smoothness of its upward and downward transitions, and the general presentation its rider has made of it during the class. Next, pin the class accordingly.

Although you may call for a hand gallop in under-saddle classes (unless the class specifications do not allow it), this test often does more harm than good, for it only takes one uncontrollable animal to ruin the performances of a number of other competitors. In calling for the hand gallop, you risk losing your top horses and may find yourself in the embarrassing position of pinning several "clunkers." I believe this is the reason the hand gallop is being seen less

7.13 At the hand gallop, the rider is in two-point position: legs are on the horse's sides while the seat is held out of the saddle. By adding leg pressure, the rider causes the horse to lengthen its stride and increase its pace to a controlled, three-beat "gallop in hand" at 14 to 16 mph.

and less each year at major shows; many judges have found that the risk of the test outweighs any benefit it may provide in determining the best horse.

However, if you do decide to hand-gallop the horses, ask no more than eight at a time to perform the test. Look for animals that increase their pace beyond a canter (10 to 12 mph) to a controlled gallop (14 to 16 mph), while demonstrating the features desired during the other gaits—especially long, low strides and relaxed obedience. If a horse becomes dangerously fast or switches leads during this test, it should be dropped to the bottom of the class. Consider the condition and size of the arena before calling for this test; slippery footing or an overly small ring can threaten the safety of horse and rider at the increased pace of a hand gallop.

When properly performing this test, the horse calmly increases its pace, lengthens its stride, and remains on the bit without fighting the rider's hands (fig. 7.13). Horses that "suck back" and refuse to increase pace in resistance to the rider's legs should be penalized heavily for not performing the test. Animals that become excited and pull against their riders or that buck and play rather than remain calm are also heavily penalized. Although the *Rule Book* requires rein contact during all under-saddle tests, following the hand gallop the rider may allow the horse to move back into line on loose reins to demonstrate the horse's relaxation following this test.

THE BIG PICTURE
Warmblood Influence in the Hunter Ring

By Randy Roy

It's the way it is and the way it's going to be—Thoroughbreds are a rarity in the hunter ring today. With the increase in the number of American racetracks, more race dates are provided than ever before. Horses that don't make it at the big tracks can win at smaller tracks, so the large number of Thoroughbreds that used to go to sale directly from the big tracks are no longer available.

Consequently, Warmbloods are now probably 95 percent of the hunter divisions and are what we are all shopping for. It started in 1965 when A.A. Steiert of Skyline Farm imported a Hanoverian weanling called "Abundance," which became the sire of Ruxton, five-time USEF Regular Working Hunter Horse of the Year. This was our introduction to Warmbloods.

The time period following this I call the "Warmblood invasion," as they have all but replaced the Thoroughbreds. As trainers and buyers, we now repeatedly go to Europe to find our prospects and "made" horses for clients. There are so many breeding farms in Europe and so much to choose from.

When we first started importing Warmbloods, they were a lot like our draft horses—heavy, big-boned, large-footed, and not so attractive. The Europeans have since introduced a lot of Thoroughbred blood into their breeding, resulting in a more refined horse. Most of the Warmbloods today are of much better quality—attractive and closer to the Thoroughbreds we were accustomed to for so long. The best of the Warmbloods have good bone and substance, but still are attractive and appealing. They have the impulsion behind that is associated with top European horses, but are now being bred to have the flowing motion in front that has long been the signature of an excellent Thoroughbred. Plus, durability is most important in a jumping horse, and Warmbloods are physically strong.

As judges, we have become less picky about bits as Warmbloods have a tendency to pull more and are not as light in the bridle as Thoroughbreds; therefore, you see pelhams more frequently in the equitation division than in years past. In fact, we have accepted a lot of things that arrived with the Warmblood invasion:

- brands—often on both sides of the horse's body
- height—taller horses than what we are accustomed to
- heavy build—more bone, bigger legs and feet, less elegance than Thoroughbreds
- more contact and flexion—we often see a different sort of ride than that used for the light, sensitive mouths of the Thoroughbred
- scope—more capable of jumping higher, wider, trickier fences
- speed—slower movers than most Thoroughbreds

Warmbloods now dominate the hunter and equitation divisions, and they are here to stay. When I think about their influence, I look at it in a very positive way. I like their strength, stride, stamina, presence, scope, temperament, calmness, and way of going, all of which they successfully demonstrate in our hunter and equitation rings. I feel they have really enriched and enhanced the hunter and equitation performances with all of the qualities mentioned above.

As judges witnessing this change, we have in no way lessened our expectations, but instead look forward to a lot of new and exciting prospects continuously emerging in the pre-green and green divisions, which are filled with winning per-formances!

Randy Roy is licensed by Equine Canada as a senior judge ("S") and by the USEF as a registered judge ("R") in hunters, jumpers, and hunter-seat equitation. He also has an "R" in the USEF hunter breeding division and senior status ("S") in Equine Canada as both a hunter and jumper course designer. The author of seven equine books, he is the only Canadian to have judged at all four of the prestigious Indoor Shows—Harrisburg, Washington, Madison Square Garden, and the Royal Winter Fair.

8

Lili 2007

Hunter Classes over Fences

Jumping Form

The Ideal Hunter

What are the components of an ideal performance in a hunter class over fences? First, the ideal horse will meet each fence at the correct takeoff spot for a perfect arc over the obstacle. Its jump will be "snappy" and athletic, with the forearms held at or above a parallel line to the ground, the joints of the front legs tucked tightly in front of its chest, and the neck and back arched over the fence (figs. 8.1 A & B). It will begin its round at a pace suited to the size of the fences and sustain this pace for the entire trip, staying straight through its body when negotiating fences on a straight line and bending in the direction of travel on the corners of the ring.

That's the ideal, but in judging you rarely observe this flawless performance, so let's look at faults you may see while judging a hunter class over fences and consider the degree of penalty for each.

Form Faults Associated with Long Spots

The worst error in a class over fences is a "risky" fence in which the horse leaves the ground dangerously far from the base of the obstacle (figs. 8.2 A & B). An animal that realizes it has left the ground too far from the base of a fence may try to put its feet back on the ground on the near side of the obstacle and crash through the fence; or a horse may flail its legs in an effort to propel itself in the air and barely clear the obstacle. Another drastic alternative is "diving": the horse stretches its front legs so far forward in an effort to clear the rails that it appears to be diving toward the ground (figs. 8.3 & 8.4). Any of these desperate actions should keep a horse out of the ribbons unless

8.1 A & B Seen from an oblique view, the horse demonstrates excellent form in a rounded topline, high and even knees, and tightly folded legs (A). This front view of a horse that has just passed the rails and is beginning its descent shows the attentive, yet relaxed expression desirable in a hunter (B).

the class is so small or the trips so bad that you have no other choice.

"Reaching" and "cutting down" are less dangerous methods of dealing with a risky spot, but are still major faults. In "reaching," a mild form of diving, the horse tries to clear the obstacle by stretching its front legs forward—beyond their normal position in the air—often in a quick frantic movement (fig. 8.5). In "cutting down," the horse unfolds it legs early on the far side of the fence, landing closer to the center of the fence on the far side than its takeoff was to the center on the near side (figs. 8.6 A & B). Cutting down demonstrates lack of scope, since a more athletic horse in the same situation would leave from the long distance, make its arc higher than the size of the fence demanded (though appropriate to the takeoff spot), and land as far from the fence on the far side as it took off from the fence on the near side.

Unless the horse that cuts down also carries a rail to the ground with its hind feet, you should penalize this fault

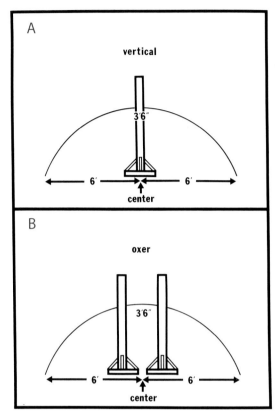

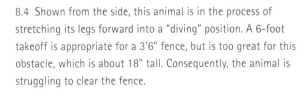

8.2 A & B The diagram shows the approximate proper takeoff distances at verticals (A) and oxers (B) measuring 3'6" or higher. For fences under 3'6" the horse should leave the ground and land approximately 5 feet from the center of the fence. If a horse leaves the ground much farther away than these measurements, it could have a "risky" fence.

8.3 The hooves are pointed forward when a horse is "diving" over the obstacle.

8.4 Shown from the side, this animal is in the process of stretching its legs forward into a "diving" position. A 6-foot takeoff is appropriate for a 3'6" fence, but is too great for this obstacle, which is about 18" tall. Consequently, the animal is struggling to clear the fence.

8.5 Taken on a cross-country course, this photo is an excellent example of "reaching." Notice that the horse is straining with its back legs while reaching forward with its front legs to clear the obstacle. The horse will generally stretch its front legs forward, then yank them back toward its chest in a quick movement to propel itself forward, clearly distinguishing "reaching" from other form faults.

less severely than reaching. The reasoning is that in reaching, the horse risks catching its front limbs on the obstacle and possibly flipping over in the air. In cutting down, the horse risks catching its hind limbs on the obstacle—a fault that has much less potential danger for the rider and horse. (As a rule, front-end errors are more heavily penalized than hind-end errors.)

In a class consisting only of the horses mentioned, you would pin as follows: sixth, the horse that tried to put its feet back on the ground on the near side of the fence and crashed; fifth, the horse that flailed its legs but cleared the fence; fourth, the horse that dove over the fence; third, the horse that reached; and second, the one that cut down. The

8.6 A & B When a horse "cuts down," the takeoff spot is much farther from the fence than the landing spot. This horse is leaving the ground at least 6 feet from the obstacle (A), but is landing about 2 feet from it (B). The sharp downward angle on landing is the reason it is called "cutting down."

8.7 A–C Shown from a side view, this horse is "hanging" its left leg. The takeoff spot looks a little close, and the rider is tipped forward with her leg slipped back, adding weight to the front end and making it more difficult for the horse to raise its legs evenly over the fence (A). The reason this horse is hanging is more difficult to discern. The rider's position is good, but the animal has managed to drop its left leg considerably. Sometimes horses simply can't keep their balance at takeoff, due to the footing or other factors, and end up hanging a leg (B). An overly deep takeoff spot is definitely the cause of this horse hanging both of its front legs. The takeoff spot is too close to the fence for the horse to be able to fold its legs properly (C).

winner would be the athletic horse that compensated for the long spot with an even arc.

Form Faults Associated with Short Spots

When a horse leaves the ground from a spot too close to the fence—whether the rider has placed it there or the horse happened to meet that spot through lack of rider assistance—the animal should compensate for the deep spot by bringing its hocks well under its body on the takeoff stride and rocking backward slightly more than it would for a medium spot, so that its legs will be away from the rails. A talented, athletic horse will get its rider out of trouble this way, but a lazy or untalented one will hit the top of the fence with its front feet.

Even worse than the horse that doesn't mind touching the fence is the one that hangs its legs down toward the fence when placed at a deep spot. Not only is hanging visually unattractive, but it should be penalized severely for safety reasons: a horse that hangs its front legs could catch one or both of its forelimbs on the top of the obstacle and have a serious accident (figs. 8.7 A–C). Front and hind legs should be neatly tucked while jumping so there is no danger of the animal entangling itself in the rails. You should penalize a horse that hangs even if it doesn't touch the rails, for the *Rule Book* directs that "Judges must penalize unsafe jumping and bad form over fences, whether touched or untouched."

In judging only these horses that have taken off from deep spots, place third the horse that is lazy with its legs and hangs. Pin second the horse that remains in good form but has a front-end touch, and place first the horse that rocks back at takeoff and copes with its placement in an athletic manner.

Another form fault you may see when a horse meets a fence from a spot too deep is "propping." A horse that props appears to be pushing back from the fence during the approach to the obstacle and at takeoff, in an effort to get its front legs away from the rails (figs. 8.8 A–F). When a rider attempts to drive a horse past a reasonable takeoff spot, the horse may prop to set itself up to jump in good form despite the rider's signals. Propping may also be caused by a weak rider who allows the horse to slow down at every fence, so the animal becomes accustomed to making the smallest effort possible to get over the fences. In its slightest form, propping is not heavily penalized, for it is not a dangerous fault but only an interruption in the horse's forward flow of energy at takeoff. However, if the horse chronically props, as in the case of the weak rider who lets the horse prop at every fence, the penalty should be great, for chronic propping is a manifestation of the horse's general unwillingness to go forward.

Other Form Faults

You may see other form faults while a horse is airborne, such as a horse that "lies on its side" by tilting in midair so that one of its sides is inclined toward the ground and the other toward the sky (figs. 8.9 A–C). Penalize this fault severely, since it shows a marked lack of balance and can be quite dangerous: if the rider's weight shifts radically toward the down side, the horse may be unable to land on its feet.

Less serious than inclining to one side is "twisting" over a fence, in which the horse remains upright in the air, but writhes during its flight path in order to let the front and hind limbs clear the fence (figs. 8.10 A–E). A horse may twist for one of several reasons: an overfaced animal may be struggling to clear the fences; a horse with a physical disorder, such as a navicular or a back problem, may be incapable of a straight jumping effort; or a lazy horse placed at a deep spot may twist instead of rocking back on its hocks to clear an obstacle. Whatever its cause, twisting receives a severe penalty.

Minor Form Faults

The faults we have considered so far—hanging, diving, reaching, cutting down, lying on the side, and twisting—are serious enough to keep a horse out of the ribbons. Now we will consider less serious faults that will also affect your placement of horses in a class.

8.8 A–F The horse is "propping" by pushing away from the fence on the approach (A). Its front legs are together just before takeoff (B), rather than remaining in the rhythm of the stride. The forward energy of the horse is hindered at takeoff (C) because the horse has been pushing its body away from the fence on the approach to the obstacle. In comparison, a normal approach to the fence has continuous impulsion and a separation of the front legs in the final stride (D), power in the takeoff (E), and a sense of unhindered forward thrust as the horse forms an arched path over the obstacle (F).

8.9 A–C Shown jumping a cross-country obstacle, this horse is "lying on its side," with the axis of its body tilted far toward its left side (A). This horse is also "lying on its side," but in a subtle way (B) that becomes more apparent when compared to another horse jumping the same fence without any tilt in its axis (C). Although the horses in A and B are tilted toward their left side, the tilted axis can be toward either direction.

8.10 A–E A horse can twist toward its right side (A) or left side (B) in the air. When seen from the hind view in a sequence shot, this horse twists its front legs to the left (C), continues through the air (D), then twists its hind legs to the left (E) to clear the fence from an overly deep spot.

8.11 The open knee and fetlock joints in the air are considered "loose form."

of chest between the forelegs while airborne. Neither leg position presents a threat to the rider's safety, so you only need to consider these faults in a class where the trips are so similar in quality that you must use style as the deciding factor.

Form of the Back and Neck

Form over fences does not depend entirely on the horse's use of its legs, but involves the back and neck as well (fig. 8.12). When we speak of a horse "using itself," we mean that the animal elevates its body in the air in an arched manner, so the back and neck look rounded rather than flat and stiff (fig. 8.13). An arched neck and back are signs of an athletic or "scopey" horse, and horses that have this athletic look accompanied by good leg formation should place above horses that have tightly folded legs and a flat appearance of the back.

An interesting observation was made by a professional horseman who said he found that horses that use their backs well often hang their legs, and horses that use their legs well are often flat in their backs. From his point of view, he preferred to own the horse that used its back well and was lazy with its legs, reasoning that an agile back shows good scope, and when the fences become higher, the horse will have to use its legs as well as its back to clear them and at such times will jump in good form. On the other hand, he felt that the flat-backed horse showed a lack of scope and, even though it may look fairly nice with its legs tucked neatly in front of its chest at a 3'6" obstacle, would never be a "big-time" horse.

Although there may be some truth to this observation, as a judge you must consider the performance the horse actually makes, rather than conjecture as to how nice the horse might be in the future over larger fences. All else

A horse with legs not folded tightly when it jumps shows "loose form" (fig. 8.11). You may end up pinning a horse with loose form in moderately stiff competition if everything else about its trip is top-notch and its legs are only loose, not dangling down from its shoulders as in hanging. However, in a good class of athletic jumpers and excellent movers, a horse with loose form will suffer in the pinning.

Another fault you may see over fences is a horse carrying its legs very close to each other or very far apart. Some horses' legs are so close together in the air that one hoof appears to be wrapped around the other, while other horses' legs are so wide apart that they display an expanse

8.12 Good form is exhibited in the rounded topline of this athletic bay. His knees are held high, but his fetlock joints could be more tightly closed to achieve perfect form.

8.13 The chestnut horse demonstrates a flatter style of jumping than the bay in figure 8.12. A flat-backed horse can make it easier for an equitation rider to maintain good form, but a round-backed horse is preferable in the hunter ring.

being equal, the horse that jumps with a rounded back and its knees down should not be pinned above a flat-backed horse that has its legs tightly folded in front of its chest.

In classes in which the fences are extremely small for the horses, the animals will be unable to have a very round appearance in the back and neck and the tight form that should accompany this; over such low jumps, their front legs will almost touch the ground on the far side of the fence while their hind legs are still pushing off on the near side. Out of necessity, you may end up pinning such a class more on the horses' general way of going and the spots they meet at the fences than on form faults. However, in competitions in which the fences are 3'6" or higher for horses, the obstacles will be large enough in proportion to the animals that you will be able to consider all the form faults discussed in this book, including how the horses use their backs and necks.

Flight Path

Ideal Flight Pattern

Sometimes a horse's form—that is, its use of its legs, back, and neck—may be attractive, but the animal commits other errors over the fence by wavering from the ideal flight pattern. The flight pattern of a horse begins as the animal leaves the ground on the near side of the obstacle and ends as the horse's feet touch the ground on the far side (see figs. 8.2 A & B). Ideally, the horse's landing spot and its takeoff spot should be equidistant from the center of the fence. To simplify the explanation, if a horse leaves the ground 6 feet from the center of the fence, it should land on the far side 6 feet from the center of the fence.

In addition, the horse should approach the middle of a fence without wandering off a straight line, jump the fence without drifting off that line in the air, and land on the same

8.14 A & B This sequence shot shows a horse drifting to its right over the fence. The animal takes off at the center of the obstacle (A), but drifts about 3 feet in the air so that it peaks over a different portion of the fence (B). Despite this, the horse manages to maintain great style in its front legs, which is not usually the case when a horse drifts across the fence panel.

line. On hunter courses, a horse that deviates from this ideal path commits a flight pattern fault. (The exception is usually a handy hunter class, in which the placement of a previous or upcoming fence may require the horse to jump the current fence at an angle or at some place other than the middle of the fence. These classes are now rarely held, however.)

Maintaining a Line

One of the major flight pattern faults is "drifting," in which the horse leaves the ground on the centerline, "drifts" in the air either to the right or left, and lands off the centerline (figs. 8.14 A & B). Drifting is penalized because it is a lateral evasion of the rider's aids that can result in injury to the rider if the horse drifts so far across the fence that the rider's leg catches on the standard.

Another fault is the horse jumping on a line that is not in the middle of the obstacle—that is, approaching, jumping, and landing on a straight line that is either left or right of the middle of the fence. This is not as bad as drifting, but it, too, can cause injury to the rider if the horse jumps too close to the standard (figs. 8.15 A & B).

In scoring, a horse that drifts should be penalized more than a horse that jumps left or right of the center but remains on a straight line before, over, and after the fence. A basic precept of mounted equestrian sports is that a horse should be forthright in its work and not attempt to evade the rider's legs by dropping behind or wandering between them. Therefore, the horse that jumps off center, but remains straight, is considerably better than the horse that wanders across the fence, taking advantage of the few seconds in the air to evade the rider's control.

Even Arc

Whenever a horse has an uneven flight pattern, in which it

8.15 A & B Seen from both the side (A) and front view (B), this horse is jumping far left of center. Notice how close the rider's foot is to the standard in the second photo.

leaves and lands at different distances from the center of the fence, it should be penalized. Some horses will "over-jump" their fences, with their landing distance being greater than their departure distance from the center of the obstacle; while others will "cut down" on the far side of the fence, making the landing distance shorter than the distance of their departure from the center of the obstacle.

Overjumping the fence is associated with an anxious horse that uses the period of time the rider releases it in the air to gain momentum. Although the rider may be able to control the horse's pace until takeoff, few riders have the talent to control a horse well in midair; thus, an anxious horse will seize the occasion to take advantage of the rider in the air, will land far from the fence with a great deal of momentum, and, having been able to stretch its neck forward during the rider's release, will keep its neck outstretched, preventing the rider from collecting it from this long, pulling frame. Reflecting anxiety and disobedience in the horse, overjumping is severely penalized.

Cutting down has already been discussed, but it is mentioned here again because it is the opposite of overjumping the fence. In cutting down, the horse lands closer to the fence than it departed the ground before the fence (see figs. 8.6 A & B). Compared to an anxious horse that overjumps fences, a horse that cuts down is preferable, for cutting down signifies lack of scope, but not bad temperament.

Rhythm

Not only should the flight pattern be considered, but also the rhythm the horse displays as it leaves the ground, flies through the air, and lands. "Getting quick off the ground" is characterized by the horse's front feet quickly patting the ground on the takeoff stride, rather than maintaining the same rhythm the horse had as it approached the fence. A horse that gets quick off the ground is usually a high-strung or "hot" horse that makes other errors related to its temperament—such as overjumping the obstacles. Getting quick demonstrates anxiety in the animal and is heavily penalized in keeping with other faults that relate to nervousness in the horse.

In contrast, "dwelling off the ground" (that is, at takeoff) and "dwelling in the air" are associated with horses of dull, lazy temperament. When a horse dwells off the ground, its jumping ability is hindered by the lack of momentum before it leaves the ground, and the horse's flight and landing may be dangerous. In contrast, a horse that dwells in the air already has completed the crucial takeoff thrust and generally will have enough momentum to make a safe (though not necessarily attractive) landing. For this reason, dwelling in the air is preferable to dwelling off the ground. In comparing these faults associated with dullness to faults associated with nervousness, the faults indicating anxiety are worse because an anxious horse is a greater threat to the rider's safety than is a lazy animal.

Pace and Impulsion

Definitions

In simplest terms, pace equals speed, and impulsion equals thrust. They go hand in hand to a certain degree because as a horse increases its pace, its thrust also increases, both on the flat, as the animal pushes off the ground harder to achieve greater speed, and over fences, when the greater pace allows the horse to launch its body weight more easily. However, there is a point at which a horse needs more impulsion, but not more pace, in order to turn in a first-rate performance— that is, simply going faster will not improve the quality of the round, but having more impulsion will.

For instance, in courses involving tight turns, such as a handy hunter course, a horse cannot create sufficient thrust off the ground at the fences by simply going faster, for the acuteness of the turns restricts the pace. However, a rider can create more impulsion in the horse by adding leg and balancing the horse with the hands so that the horse's engine—its hindquarters—will push harder while the rider's hands will restrict the horse from gaining speed. (See chapter 10, "Equitation on the Flat," and chapter 11, "Equitation over Fences," for a more detailed discussion of the rider's control of the horse's impulsion.)

Pace is related to horizontal motion in the horse, for the horse that is asked to go forward by the rider's legs and is unrestricted by the rider's hands will stretch forward into a longer stride, create a faster speed, and move in a flatter frame. In contrast, impulsion is related to vertical motion, for a horse that is asked to go forward by the rider's legs and is restricted by the rider's hands will have a more vertical motion to its strides; while the rider's legs create more energy, the rider's restricting hands cause that energy to be used in upward, thrusting motion.

The Correct Pace

There is no set speed at which every horse should be going when approaching fences. The pace depends upon many things, such as the size of the fences, the horse's length of stride, and the way the course is set. The best rule in judging pace is, "Use your common sense." Does the horse look as though it is going too fast or too slow? Does the round appear dangerous because of excessive speed, or dull because of too little pace? If the answer to any of these questions is "yes," then the horse's pace is inappropriate for the course.

The Correct Impulsion

Judging proper impulsion is considerably more difficult than judging proper pace. Basically, we can equate impulsion with the horse's athletic ability. Does the animal use its hocks well as it takes each stride so that its hindquarters are well under its body? Does the animal rock back onto its hocks when it jumps, or does it simply "jump off its front end," using as little push power from its hocks as possible? If the horse doesn't have impulsive, athletic strides and good, solid thrust off the ground at each fence, it doesn't have enough impulsion. Although impulsion will not be marked separately on the judge's card, it will come into play when considering "way of going" and will be evident in the markings concerning the horse's jumping form, which inevitably suffers when the animal lacks sufficient impulsion.

Bending

Since much more time is spent going between fences than actually jumping them, the way a horse travels between the obstacles is extremely important and gains more importance as a deciding factor between horses as the competition gets stiffer. To make a horse look its best on course, the rider must keep the animal straight in its body on straight lines and bent in the direction of travel on bending lines (figs. 8.16 A–C).

In a typical hunter course, the horse will be asked to negotiate two straight outside lines, two straight diagonal lines, and five curving lines, which include the beginning and ending circle (fig. 8.17). Since a large part of every course is performed on curving lines, a chronically unbent animal will not be successful in top-notch competition.

Balance, Vision, and Impulsion

Besides the fact that the unbent horse produces an unattractive performance, there are a few safety reasons for penalizing the animal. As it negotiates corners with its head cranked to the outside, it carries most of its weight on its inside legs. This means it is traveling off-balance, which can cause serious problems in good footing as well as bad.

When a horse is unbalanced around corners, it has difficulty jumping fences close to them and will sometimes "jump off one leg." Occasionally, a horse will even run through a fence, because its head is turned so far to the outside that it can't see the obstacle toward which it is galloping.

Also associated with the unbent horse is the problem of maintaining enough forward momentum to "make the distances" between the fences. A horse that is not bent around a corner will lose impulsion and shorten its stride by leaning toward the inside of the curve—two faults that make it nearly impossible for the horse to travel to the next fence in the correct number of strides.

As for the aesthetics involved in judging the unbent horse, the combination of a short-strided, unbalanced, and stiff animal is hardly a winning one.

The Numbers

Now, on to the controversial matter of the "correct number

8.16 A–C The horse's vision, balance, and length of stride are compromised when it is not bent in the direction of travel (A). In contrast, when the horse is properly bent, the rider and horse are aligned on the same axis, providing good balance, vision, and continuous momentum on the approach to the upcoming obstacle (B). Compare the properly bent horse to this animal that is drifting to the outside of the turn (C). Drifting causes the path to the upcoming obstacle to become longer than intended, making it difficult for the rider to find the proper takeoff spot at the fence, and leaves the horse unbalanced at takeoff, with too much weight on one side of its body.

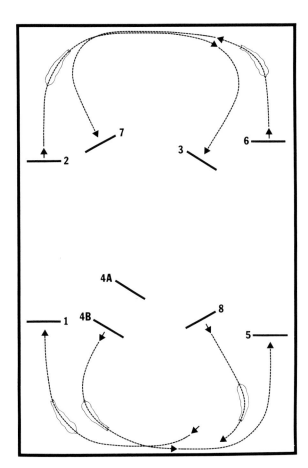

8.17 Five bending lines are shown in this diagram of a typical hunter course. Since much of every course is performed on curves, a chronically unbent animal should be heavily penalized.

numbers" meaning the correct number of strides based on the 12-foot or 13-foot stride). The answer is this: if a horse has good form over fences, maintains a suitable pace for the size of the obstacles, and moves well between fences, then it should not be penalized for having added strides.

The problem of riding a course in the numbers is not so great in the hunter division as in the equitation division, for the closer the fences are set, the more crucial it becomes to stick to the designated number of strides. This is not because of the distance between two fences on a line, but because of the distances between these fences and other fences that precede or follow them, since related segments of a course can be drastically affected by the addition of strides. In hunter classes, however, besides negotiating obstacles that have a distance of four strides or less between them, the small horse is not likely to suffer in the quality of its performance from the addition of a single stride. Even for a line of two fences set four strides apart, a small horse can put in an extra stride and look quite nice. The four-stride distance only becomes a problem for a small horse when it is followed by a maximum-length in-and-out. The problem arises when the horse waits to add the fifth stride and has neither the necessary impulsion, nor the long spot, to get through the in-and-out in the designated one or two strides, whichever the case may be.

You should not feel obliged to excuse the erratic performance of a small horse, for it is the rider's responsibility to pick a suitable horse for the competition. If a rider intends to show on the Florida circuit or in the indoor shows in the fall, then he or she must recognize that most big shows are setting the distances based on a 13-foot stride and must keep this in mind when choosing a mount.

Although a horse should not be penalized for adding or deleting strides if those options are appropriate within the

of strides" between fences on a line. In A-rated shows today, the fences are set with a given number of strides intended between them. Each stride may have been figured at 12 feet, or, in major competitions, at 13 feet. The question arises each year, "What about the small-strided horse? Should it be penalized for not making the line in the numbers?" (with "the framework of a suitable pace and the horse's natural length of stride, you must not excuse faults that result from the horse's size. For example, a small horse may be overfaced by the size of the fences and show its lack of ability at that height by flattening its back in the air or twisting to clear the rails. Similarly, a large horse may not be jumping fences at an appropriate height to demonstrate good form in the air and may be sloppy with its legs, never seeming to reach a peak because its hind legs are still on the ground when the horse is at the zenith of its arc over the fence.

As far as pace is concerned, a large horse usually has an advantage, since it appears relaxed as it casually covers ground. A small horse, on the other hand, often goes beyond appearing brilliant to looking rushed if it attempts the long distances; or, if it tries the other option of adding a stride, it may struggle to jump the fences from a lesser pace.

If a large and a small horse turn in comparable trips, however, you can pin the horses according to your personal taste, for a small, brilliant horse may be more appealing to you than a large, casual horse—or vice versa. As long as the trips are considered equal in every other way, you can pin the one you personally prefer.

Changing Leads

Landing on the Lead and Flying Changes

Many hunter classes are lost by horses that won't go around corners of the ring on the correct lead. I believe the smartest solution for the rider is to teach his horse to land out of the air onto the correct lead at the end of each line by using the outside leg aid while the horse is airborne—the same aid that is used for the basic canter depart. However, both landing on the proper lead and performing a flying change are

correct, and a rider is free to use whichever solution he or she prefers.

Counter Canter vs. Cross Canter

As for the horse that lands on the incorrect lead and refuses to perform a flying change, the animal will take one of four options: stay on the counter canter around the entire corner; switch leads in front but not behind, resulting in a cross canter around the entire corner; cross canter for a few steps before switching completely onto the proper lead; or, cross canter the corner and switch back onto the counter lead on the approach to the upcoming fence.

Although a horse traveling on the counter canter is not properly balanced on corners, it is preferable for a horse to remain on the counter lead than to maintain a cross canter through the entire corner, for the cross canter is disjointed in appearance, affects the rider's ability to place the horse properly at the upcoming fence, and causes the horse to be unbalanced. Further considering balance at takeoff, it is preferable for a horse to cross canter the corner and switch back onto the counter lead just before the fence than to attempt to jump the fence out of the cross canter.

However, in comparing the horse that cross canters a few steps with the horse that maintains the counter canter around the entire corner, the horse that cross canters and switches would be preferable, for the animal would be on the proper lead for at least part of the time and would be better balanced for takeoff.

In judging the class, then, the horse that landed on the correct lead after each line and the horse that properly performed the flying changes would be considered equal. However, in top competition, the horse that lands on the correct lead might place higher because its round would look smoother without the interruption of the flying changes.

Following the first- and second-place pinning of these two horses, the next would be the horse that cross cantered a few steps then switched to the proper lead. In fourth place would be the animal that remained on the counter lead around the entire corner and on the approach to the upcoming fence. Fifth place would go to the horse that cross cantered the corner and switched back to the counter lead on the approach to the fence; and in sixth place would be the horse that cross cantered the entire corner and jumped the fence out of a cross canter.

Breaking Gait

Besides counter cantering or cross cantering the corners, the horse might break gait from a canter into a trot rather than perform a flying change. A break in gait is a serious fault in both classes over fences and on the flat and is worse than a counter canter or cross canter. Breaking gait demonstrates the horse's unwillingness to go forward from the rider's leg and is penalized in accordance with other faults related to lack of forward motion. It would only be pinned above severe behavioral faults, such as refusing at a fence or rearing, and other faults that imply danger to the rider, for instance an extremely fast pace or a knockdown (which is considered worse than a break in gait because of the involvement of the horse's legs with the rails).

Habitual Switching of Leads on Lines

Another error involving leads in the show ring is the switching of leads between fences on a line. This fault normally occurs when a horse is trying to save itself from meeting an overly deep takeoff spot; but it can be the result of an animal's habit of jumping off only one lead. Whether it is an indication of the rider's poor placement of the horse at the fence or of the horse's poor coordination, it should be penalized.

The Dishonest vs. Honest Horse

Dishonest and Unsafe

A "dishonest" horse is one that attempts to evade its rider's commands, and in so doing, threatens the safety of the rider. The worst fault a horse can exhibit in competition is the lack of honesty, for just as this is a major character flaw in a human, so is it in a horse.

Excessive Forward Motion

Although the dishonest horse is usually associated with the lack of forward motion (that is, rearing, refusing to jump a fence, balking at the in-gate or anywhere else in the ring, or attempting to back without having been asked to do so), dishonesty is also associated with horses that use extreme forward motion to frighten or displace the rider. When a horse bolts during a performance—that is, runs away with its rider at some point during the course—it should be heavily penalized, with the severity of the penalty keeping the horse out of the ribbons if at all possible.

Shying, in which the animal quickly moves away from some object in or around the ring, is a mild form of bolting, which lasts usually only a second or two and involves sideways, rather than forward, movement. Shying can be a minor disobedience or a major one, according to how much the animal has reacted to the object that frightened it and depending on the particular situation.

For instance, a tense horse that persistently shies away from objects in and around the ring should be greatly penalized for not exhibiting the obedience and working attitude we are looking for in a good hunter. However, a horse with a basically good working attitude might shy slightly when an unusual incident occurs, such as a gust of wind blowing down the umbrella over the judge's stand. In this case, the animal is simply surprised, and its reaction is not an indication of its basic attitude toward work. Therefore, the circumstance would call for only a slight penalty, particularly since the animal was subject to a situation that its competitors did not have to deal with when they jumped the course. However, if other faults occur on the course following such an incident—such as the horse speeding up or shying from other objects—then the judge must penalize these faults, for there is only so far one can go in giving the horse the benefit of the doubt.

Lack of Forward Motion

Equally as dangerous as a runaway horse is one that rears, for in both cases, the rider and horse can be seriously injured. Rearing, the ultimate expression of the horse's unwillingness to go forward, should be severely penalized. As in the case of bolting, rearing should keep the competitor out of the ribbons if at all possible, for these disobediences are more potentially dangerous than any other faults the horse can commit.

A refusal at a fence also demonstrates the horse's unwillingness to go forward from the rider's leg, which may present a physical threat to the rider if the horse stops so abruptly that it slings the rider forward into the rails. An honest horse will find some way to help the rider get to the other side of the fence, even from a difficult spot, while a dishonest horse will simply stop on the near side rather than put forth the effort.

Although traditionally the *Rule Book* has considered the penalty for a refusal equal to that for bolting, most judges penalize bolting (running away) more severely because it is commonly believed to be the more dangerous fault of the two. (However, if a refusal results in the fall of a rider, or if the horse leaves the arena while bolting, the penalty is elimination.) Also, according to the *Rule Book* prior to 1991, a refusal should have been penalized equally with a knockdown; but in reality, a refusal is penalized more heavily than a knockdown by the majority of judges. The reason is that judges realize an honest horse will attempt to jump a fence, although it may knock it down in doing so, while a dishonest horse will refuse to try to jump the obstacle. Most horsemen appreciate a horse with "heart," that is, a horse that will at least give it a try. In keeping with this attitude, most horsemen hate a "stopper," the horse that won't put forth the effort to try to jump the fence and always looks for a way out.

It is commonly accepted that there is more inherent danger to a rider mounted on an unwilling, dishonest horse than to a rider on a well-intentioned animal that doesn't put forth quite enough effort to clear an obstacle. Therefore, while a horse that has its feet close enough to the fence to bring a rail down presents some threat to the rider's safety, most judges agree that the danger involved in riding a stopper is greater.

Following the 1991 USEF Convention in Baltimore, Maryland, the *Rule Book* changed from designating specific penalties for a refusal, bolting, and knockdown to listing them along with many other errors. The rule now states, "The following faults are scored according to the judge's opinion and, depending on severity, may be considered minor or major faults." This allows judges to use their "horse sense" in penalizing these errors.

Honest but Unsafe

Next, we'll consider the horse that does not intend to harm its rider but nonetheless performs in an unsafe manner. The horse that falls into this category is often the nice horse ridden by an inadequate rider.

Too Fast, Too Slow

When a rider becomes anxious about a class over fences, he or she may charge around the course in an effort to get over the obstacles in "any old way." The result is a horse that approaches the fences with too much pace, making the round appear dangerous.

At the other extreme is the rider who uses too little leg on his horse, resulting in the animal approaching each fence so slowly that it looks as though it will land on a fence before the course is completed. Since both the overly fast and overly slow rounds are incorrect, horses that demonstrate these extremes should be severely penalized, with the round that exhibits excessive speed being penalized more than the round that is excessively slow; for again, danger is the deciding factor, and a rider is less likely to be injured in a round that is too slow than in one that is too fast.

Knockdowns

In good company, a knockdown will keep a horse from being pinned, but occasionally during a show, a judge must pin a horse with a knockdown for lack of enough horses in the class to allow any options. As stated in the *Rule Book* prior to 1991, a knockdown with any part of the horse's body in front of the stifle should be penalized twice as much as a knockdown with any part of the horse's body behind the stifle. This was in keeping with the rule for touches, in which a front touch was penalized twice as much as a hind touch. Although these specific designations were removed in 1991, most judges still penalize twice as much for front end knockdowns or touches as for the same errors in the hind end.

When you are watching a knockdown, the reason behind the severity of the penalty for this fault may not be obvious, for a horse may roll a rail yet remain in good form and make a safe landing. However, the penalty for the knockdown is based on the show ring's simulation of fences in a hunt field—fences that are usually fixed and could present great danger to the horse and rider if the horse caught its feet on the unyielding obstacle. The catching of front feet on a fence presents a much greater chance of an accident than does involvement of hind feet, since the horse could flip over if its front end became hung in the fence. Even in the show ring, where the fences give way to pressure, a horse can become entangled in the rails during flight and on landing and have an accident. Therefore, given the show ring's simulation of hunting obstacles and the possibility of an accident occurring even when the rails give way, the penalty for a knockdown is deservedly severe.

Summary

As noted, some basic characteristics of a dishonest horse are: bolting, rearing, refusing to jump, balking at the in-gate, or backing up without having been given the command to do so. In contrast, an honest, but unsafe horse will commit faults such as: going around the course excessively fast, due to an anxious rider; going excessively slow, due to a passive rider; or knocking down a rail, which judges usually consider preferable to a refusal because it shows the horse to be one that is honest in its intentions, rather than a dishonest "quitter."

As a general rule, a horse that shows honesty in its approach to jumping a course of fences should place above a horse that has dishonest characteristics, for a rider is safer on a horse that tries to please him than on one that attempts to thwart his commands.

Conformation Classes

General Observations

In judging conformation classes, you are considering the horse's physical makeup as it relates to both performance and soundness. Since much of the available information on this topic has been written by veterinarians who deal daily with the negative results of poor conformation, you should not only use your firsthand experience as a horseman, but also make an effort to read veterinary books and journals in order to be competent to judge these classes.

Before we delve into the specifics of judging horses on the line, let's establish some generalities. First and foremost, a judge should consider a horse's *structural composition*— that is, its body proportions and joint angles—since a horse that is well-proportioned and has the proper angles will have the greatest chance of being sound, balanced, and athletic.

Problems of proportion—such as a short neck, long back, or small hindquarters—are heavily penalized. So, too, are angular problems—such as a steep shoulder, a hip or hind leg that is too straight, sickle hocks, or pasterns that are overly upright, to name a few.

Your second consideration is *physical defects*—malformations, resulting from poor structural composition or from injury, that have the potential for producing lameness. Those that appear to be a result of poor structural composition are more heavily penalized than those that are apparently a result of injury. The reason for this is that a horse with a defect related to poor structural composition will continually put stress on the affected area, making recovery difficult, if not impossible. On the other hand, a horse that has a defect as a result an injury that was not related to poor conformation will only have the severity of the injury itself to contend with during recovery, without additional conformational stress.

Thirdly, we need to distinguish *defects*—such as a splint, capped elbow, bucked shin, capped hock, curb, bog spavin, bowed tendon, bone spavin, thoroughpin, sidebone, osselets, and ringbone—from *blemishes,* which are malformations that do not cause unsoundness. Such things as windpuffs, a cupped indentation in a horse's neck, and superficial scars are blemishes and are the least penalized of conformation faults because they are not a hindrance to the horse's quality of performance or serviceability.

Finally, consider the horse's *soundness.* According to the *USEF Rule Book,* "Unless specific division rules state otherwise, all animals except stallions and mares in breeding classes must be serviceably sound for competition purposes, i.e. such animal must not show evidence of lameness or broken wind."

Although most people can detect a horse that limps and understand the necessity of penalizing this unsoundness, few people are knowledgeable concerning "broken wind." In its old interpretation, *broken wind* was synonymous with the term *heavy.* Heavey means that the horse has grown fibrous tissue in the air spaces of its lungs that makes it difficult for the animal to exhale. When a horse is heavey, it uses the following internal sequence to force the air out of its body: it abruptly lifts the abdominal muscles, which push the intestines forward, pressing the diaphragm into the lungs and forcing the air out. Since the heavey condition affects the horse's ability to exhale, the animal retains too much carbon dioxide and can't get enough air out or allow a sufficient amount of fresh air to come in. Therefore a heavey horse will pant in an effort to catch its breath and will display dilated nostrils, as well as the violent upward abdominal motions. On a "good day," which is usually cool and clear, a heavey horse may be able to jump a course of eight fences without having severe problems; however, in a hot, dusty environment, the horse can be in distress after two or three fences. Since competition in an arena is intended to showcase horses capable of carrying a rider hunting, if you are able to detect a heavey horse while it is jogging in a conformation class, the animal must be disqualified from placing because it is serviceably unsound.

A heavey condition is not the only cause of respiratory sounds on exhalation, for on occasion you will hear a horse making noise as it exhales with "false nostrils." The false nostril (or "alar fold") is an extra flap of skin between the outer nostril and the passageway through which the horse breathes. (You can see part of the false nostril as you stand facing the animal, and if you run your finger between the outer and inner nostril, you will find that the two join only a few inches from the opening to the nose.) A horse that makes noise with this flap has learned that it can control the muscles to the nose and does so only on occasion as a habit, rather than on a regular basis as a result of a physical defect. You can detect this fault as a vibration in the nostrils as the horse makes a blowing sound through its nose. It is a fault akin to ringing the tail or pinning the ears in that it represents a horse's lack of relaxation, willingness, and concentration on its work. As an indication of a less than desirable attitude, "false nostrils" is slightly penalized; but it should not be considered an unsoundness.

Another noticeable breathing sound is "roaring," which can be detected during inhalation. The rattling breathing of a roarer is caused by paralysis of the airway in the horse's head. The constriction occurs where the airway passes through the back of the animal's mouth, before it reaches the trachea. A roarer makes a whistling sound during inhalation and a fluttering sound during exhalation as the air crosses the animal's vocal cords. As long as the horse does not have to exert itself too much, the roaring condition may not severely hinder its performance. For instance, a roarer might be able to go around three courses of eight fences back-to-back and not be in distress, while a heavey horse usually cannot exert itself that long without having severe problems. However, both the roarer and the heavey horse would be in trouble in the hunt field. Although the heavey condition is worse than roaring, both are unsoundnesses affecting stamina and must be penalized equally by denying the horse a ribbon. Thus, when the term "broken wind" is used in the *Rule Book*, it not only encompasses the older meaning of "heavey," but also the respiratory unsoundness known as "roaring."

Since we will be dealing with many specifics throughout this chapter, it is important to keep in mind these general observations:

1   Good proportions and proper joint angles (that is, the animal's structural composition) are the most important features of a conformation horse. Therefore, good proportions and angles accompanied by a mild defect or blemish should pin above poor proportions and angles with no defects or blemishes.

2   Defects that are related to poor structural composition should be more heavily penalized than those that are solely a result of injury; and because defects have the potential to cause unsoundness, they should be more heavily penalized than blemishes, which do not affect soundness.

3   Unsoundness of a horse's legs or respiratory unsoundness (except for "false nostrils") must prevent a horse from being pinned.

Throughout this chapter, mention will be made of structural faults and injury as they relate to specific defects in the horse. Although poor nutrition is a third cause of abnormalities in the horse, I have chosen not to discuss nutrition as it relates to defects, since the vast majority of trainers who enter animals in conformation classes have sufficient knowledge of equine nutrition to provide for the basic dietary needs of their animals. For the most part, then, defects in the conformation horse will be a result of injury or structural predisposition rather than nutritional deficiency.

In order to present the following information in such a way that the reader can appreciate the relative penalties for the faults, I have listed comparative defects in order of severity—ranging from most to least serious—as often as possible. Although these comparisons give a general guide for judging, when in the show ring you must take into consideration the degree of severity of the defects on the specific horses being judged and pin accordingly.

A Comparative Guide to Judging Defects

Listed from most to least serious:

1   ringbone
2   osselets
3   sidebone
4   bone spavin
5   thoroughpin
6   bowed tendon
7   bog spavin
8   curb
9   splint
10   capped hock
11   capped elbow
12   bucked shins

These comparisons have been determined considering the worst possible effects of each of these defects (that is,

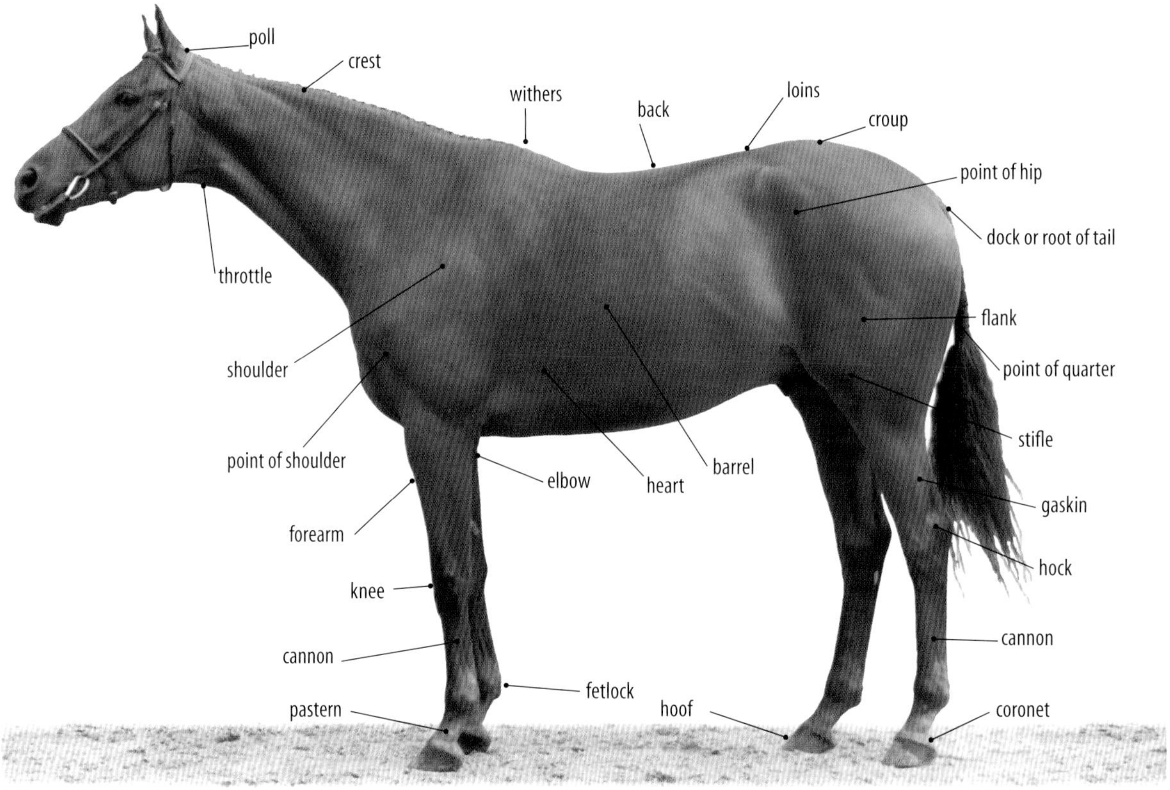

9.1 This is an excellent example of a top quality conformation horse, with the basic body parts labeled for reference.

the degree of unsoundness that each can cause at its worst and the horse's chance of recovery) and the degree of severity that could be present and still render the horse sound for jogging. These comparisons are also limited to the outward perception of the flaw, since a judge does not have access to X-rays.

A System for Judging Conformation

Side View, Near Side

As stated in the *USEF Rule Book,* the criteria for judging a conformation class are "quality, substance, and soundness." Begin judging a strip class by standing far enough away from the side of the first horse in line that you can form a general opinion of the animal's proportions and angles. Since it is easy to overlook conformation faults unless you have a system of examination, you may want to use the procedure outlined here, beginning with a side view on the near side of the animal.

Start at the poll of the horse and run your glance along the animal's topline—that is, the crest, withers, back, and croup to the dock—to see if the topline is smooth (fig. 9.1). The crest should be slightly arched and athletic-looking. If it is unusually muscular and studdish, it is penalized more than if it is flat and weak, since an overly muscular neck is less yielding and flexible than a flat neck and contributes less to the animal's bending, flexion, and balance. The withers should fit smoothly into the topline, and the top of the shoulder should blend into the withers. Any excess protrusion of bone from the shoulder or withers is penalized. The animal's back, from the middle of the withers to the area in the loins just above the point of the hip, should be approximately one-third the length of the horse's body from chest to hindquarters (see fig. 9.5). An overly long back is penalized for the weakness it indicates. The croup should be curved, not pointed; the hip should blend smoothly into the loins and croup; and the horse's tail should fit naturally into the topline and sit high, rather than drooping off the horse's rump.

After examining the topline, consider the horse's depth of body in the chest, barrel, and flank, and notice any malformation of the horse's frame that would diminish this space in which the internal organs lie. Throughout the body, the animal should appear rounded or "filled out." This doesn't mean the horse should look obese, as though it isn't in work; but if the animal is thin, with its shoulders, ribs, and hips poking out and the flesh sinking in around them, then penalize it. (Actually, the person responsible for the care of the horse ought to be penalized!)

Now that you have examined the topline and depth of body, look at the horse's head. The animal's head should fit the body, rather than being abnormally large or small. The throttle should be well-defined and smoothly connect the head to the neck. The neck must be of a sufficient length and arc to provide the horse with a means of balance while jumping; both a short neck and a ewe neck (commonly called an "upside-down neck") are heavily penalized, for they restrict

9.2 A ewe neck, being muscular along the underside instead of at the crest, gives the lower part of the neck a convex appearance.

the horse's ability to keep its balance and thus they affect the animal's athletic ability as a whole (fig. 9.2). A short neck is penalized more than a ewe neck because, unsightly as a ewe neck is, if it is long it contributes more to bending and balance than does a short neck.

The horse's shoulder must be long and sloping. A shoulder that is too steep and short is heavily penalized because it restricts the horse's length of stride and smoothness of gaits. A line from the middle of the withers to the point of the shoulder and down to the elbow should form approximately a 90-degree angle (figs. 9.3 & 9.4).

The angle of the hip must be sufficiently acute to keep the hind leg from falling too straight from the stifle joint. The connection of the ilium and femur should be at approximately a 90-degree angle. The horse's haunches must not appear hiked up or dropped down from the animal's front portion; the croup should be approximately the same height

9.3 The proper shoulder and hip angles of this horse allow freedom of movement and prevent excess weight from being placed directly on the animal's limbs.

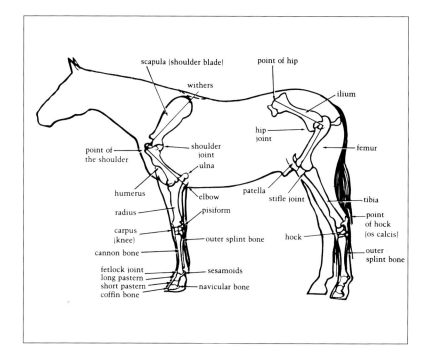

9.4 Compare the steep shoulder and hip angles in this drawing to the correct angles shown in fig. 9.3. You can see that more pressure is placed downward on the limbs when the angles are too wide. Notice also how the change of the angles has affected the horse's silhouette.

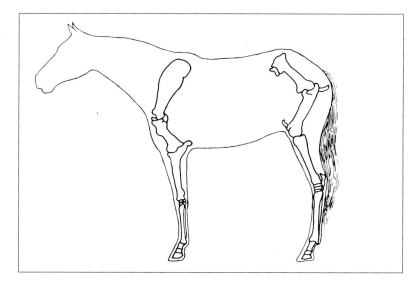

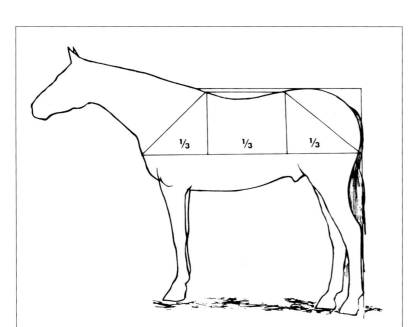

9.5 This horse's croup is the same height as its withers, and the animal is standing properly positioned so that its correct conformation is evident in the direct line through the point of the quarter, the point of the hock, and the back of the fetlock. The trapezoid shows the length of the horse's back to be correctly one-third the length of the horse's body.

as the withers (fig. 9.5). (In young horses, the haunches will sometimes grow sooner than the withers, and as the horse matures, the forehand will grow to match the haunches. Although you would make note of the tall haunches in a class of young horses, you should not penalize it as severely as you would when judging an older animal.)

From this side perspective, notice the horse's stance. When properly positioned by its handler, a horse stands with its legs square in front and with at least one hind leg placed with the point of the hock and back of the fetlock on an imaginary line that extends straight from the point of the quarter to the ground (see fig. 9.5).

If an animal stands with its front or hind feet too far under or with its feet camped in front or behind, it should be penalized (figs. 9.6 A & B). Standing under in front is more heavily penalized than camping in front because standing under overloads the forelimbs, causing excessive wear to the bones and fatigue of the ligaments and tendons, and predisposes the horse to falling, while camping in front may indicate a soundness problem, such as navicular, but does not present a safety problem.

When a horse stands too far under behind, you should look for the structural fault "sickle hocks" and related defects—bone spavin, curb, and cow hocks. (Sickle hocks, bone spavin, curb, and cow hocks will be discussed in the sections "Side View, Hind Leg [Near Side]", and "Rear View.")

If the animal stands camped out behind, look for upright pasterns that might be the cause. Since a hunter must engage its hocks to jump safely, a horse that stands under behind, with its hocks too far underneath its body, is preferable to one that camps behind, with its hocks built back of its body.

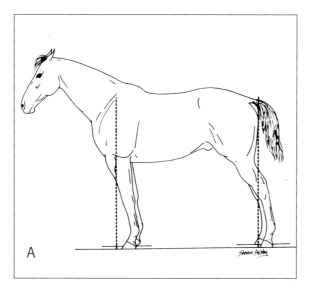 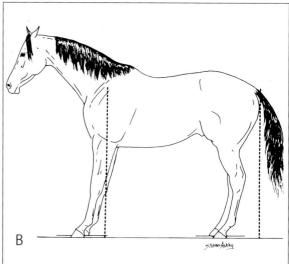

9.6 A & B The drawings show a horse standing under in front and camped behind (A), and another standing camped in front and under behind (B).

Side View, Front Leg (Near Side)

Move closer to the horse to visually examine its legs. Starting with the near front leg, examine the animal from foot to elbow. Check the hoof to see if it is in proportion to the size of the animal and if it properly connects with the leg on the same angle as the pastern (fig. 9.7). Although a horse that has foundered will not likely enter a conformation class, you should notice any ripples or "rings" on the hooves that would indicate this problem (fig. 9.8). Since the rings are only an outward indication of some type of internal turmoil and cause no unsoundness themselves, they should be slightly penalized. (The sign that would confirm founder is the dropped sole of the foot. However, since you must not pick up the hoof during this examination, you therefore cannot penalize for the dropped sole, since it may or may not accompany the rings.)

In the area of the coronary band and just above, check for signs of sidebone, low ringbone, and high ring-

bone. Sidebone—a hardening of the cartilages of the foot into bone, caused by concussion—can be found on the outside, inside, or both sides of the foot just above the heels (fig. 9.9). Although sidebone often develops as part of the natural aging process, a horse that has this condition is heavily penalized because: (1) the animal no longer has the cartilage cushion necessary to minimize trauma from jumping; (2) the bone formation can cause mechanical interference to the foot action; and (3) acting as bone, rather than as a cushion, the formation can fracture.

The defects "low ringbone" and "high ringbone" are so named because of their location on the horse's leg. Low ringbone—a bulging ring around the coronet—affects the coffin joint. High ringbone—a bulging ring approximately 1 inch above the coronet—affects the pastern joint, which, of course, is higher up the horse's leg (figs. 9.10 A & B). (Although "low ringbone" and "sidebone" are found in the area of the coronary band, low ringbone is differentiated visually as a forma-

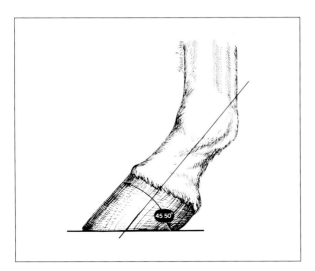

9.7 This front foot and pastern are correctly angled at 50 degrees.

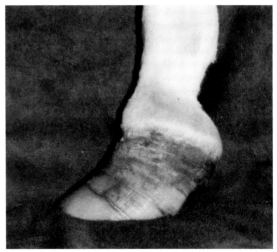

9.8 Founder rings are very noticeable on this animal because their dark color is contrasted against a white hoof. On a horse with a dark hoof, the same growth pattern and rippled appearance would suggest founder, but the dark coloration of the blood seen through the hoof wall would not be so obvious, if it were apparent at all.

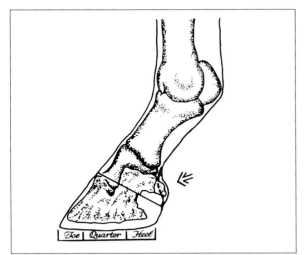

9.9 Sidebone may be detected visually in the area just above the horse's heel and can be found on either side or both sides of the foot. The dotted line shows a horse's normal shape in this area, while the solid line indicates the bulge of sidebone.

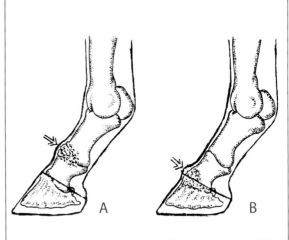

9.10 A & B High ringbone occurs in the pastern joint and can be seen approximately 1 inch above the coronet (A), while low ringbone (known also as pyramidal disease or "buttress foot") affects the coffin joint and is found at the coronet (B).

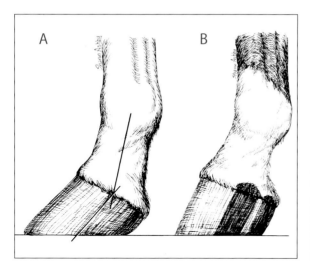

9.11 A & B When the foot axis is not the same as the pastern axis, the difference in angulation is called a "broken foot." Notice in the first drawing that the pastern is extremely steep (A). When both the foot axis and pastern axis are excessively steep, the horse is said to have a "club foot" (B).

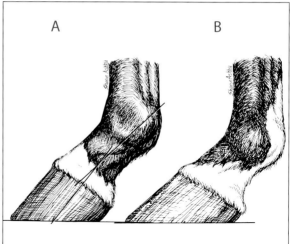

9.12 A & B In this "broken foot," "the hoof is on a proper axis and the pastern is too sloping, a formation known as a "coon foot" (A). When both the foot and pastern angles are too closed, the horse has a "sloping foot" (B).

tion that circles the entire coronary band, while sidebone is seen only on the sides of the foot, at the portion of the coronary band above the heels.) Both low and high ringbone can lead to degenerative arthritis in the involved joint, or can cause the joining of the bones on each side of the joint into a single piece. Ringbone, whether high or low, should be penalized more heavily than sidebone.

Observe the slope of the horse's pastern, which should match the angle of the hoof. (The ideal pastern and hoof angle is about 50 degrees in the front legs and slightly more upright in the hind legs. The difference between front and hind angulation should not be greater than 5 degrees.) If a horse has an overly upright pastern, the result will be a shorter, less athletic stride and excess concussion to the bones in the leg and foot (figs. 9.11 A & B). In contrast, an overly sloping pastern will produce a longer stride, but it will

be weak and cause excess pressure to be placed on the heel and the soft-tissue supporting structures in the back of the leg (figs. 9.12 A & B). In scoring, penalize the upright pastern more heavily than the overly sloping pastern because of the limiting effect the steep pastern has on the horse's length of stride.

Move your eyes to the area of the fetlock and examine the horse for osselets and windpuffs. Osselets appear as a bulge on the front of the fetlock, extending at least halfway around the joint in most cases (fig. 9.13). The bulge under the skin is caused by a deposit of calcium, formed as a result of trauma that produced arthritis in the fetlock joint and inflammation of the joint capsule. A horse with osselets should be pinned above an animal with ringbone and below a horse with sidebone—although we hope that no horse in the class will have any of these serious faults!

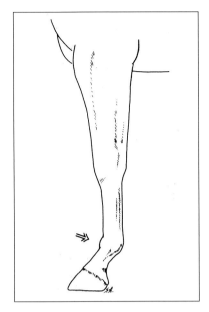

9.13 Osselets appear as a bulge on the front of the fetlock and usually extend at least halfway around the joint.

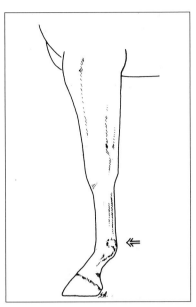

9.14 Found on the side of the fetlock joint, a windpuff is a blemish seen in many hardworking horses. Since it does not cause lameness, it should only be mildly penalized.

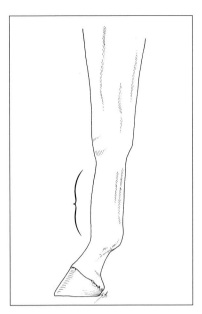

9.15 Bucked shins are penalized mildly, for although the blemish left after the horse has returned to soundness may be unsightly, it does not present a problem of recurrent unsoundness.

A windpuff, which is a swelling on the side of the fetlock joint, is found either on the inside or on the outside of the front (or hind) legs (fig. 9.14). It is seen in many hardworking horses and does not cause lameness. Being a blemish, a windpuff is penalized only in the mildest degree.

Moving up the leg to the cannon bone, look for a bucked shin, which is a swelling on the front of the cannon bone generally caused by concussion and related to speed and fatigue (fig. 9.15). Bucked shins usually are found in the forelimbs, rather than hind limbs, and the condition generally occurs in both forelegs at the same time (although this is a defect mainly found in racehorses and rarely seen in hunters, unless they came from the track). If a bucked shin is present in only one limb, direct trauma to the area is most likely the cause.

Since a horse with bucked shins can have complete recovery if rested for a proper length of time, this defect is not considered a serious fault. "Complete recovery" means a return to soundness without recurring problems, although the swelling on the front of the cannon bone may remain as a blemish. Bucked shins are penalized less than any of the other defects mentioned in this chapter.

In the area between the fetlock and knee, look for splints. A splint is a bony growth usually found about 3 inches below a horse's knee on the inside of a front leg, but it may be found at other locations on both the inside and outside of the legs along the splint bones (see figs. 9.34 A & B). Caused

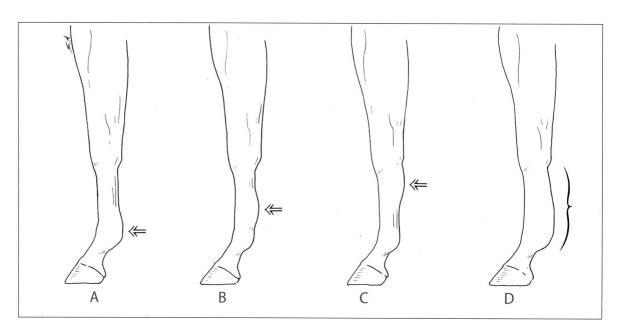

9.16 A–D Found between the fetlock and knee, a bowed tendon is classified as low (A), middle (B), or high (C), or it may involve all three areas (D).

by hard training, interference (or another type of blow to the leg), or poor conformation, splints most often appear in the forelegs. They frequently develop from hard work that causes a disturbance in the ligament between the inside or the outside splint bone and the cannon bone, which results in new bone growth. When seen in a conformation class, a splint should not be considered a serious defect unless it is related to poor structure or is located toward the back of a splint bone so that it is obviously impinging upon a tendon or ligament. Although you look for splints on the outside of the near foreleg at this point in the examination, you'll usually be able to see both inside and outside splints more clearly when viewing the horse from the front.

A bowed tendon—another of the serious defects not likely to be found in a conformation class—appears in the area between the fetlock and knee (figs. 9.16 A–D). A bowed tendon is caused by severe strain to the tendon sheath, which results in development of scar tissue. Although the condition can be present in the hind limbs, it is generally an injury of the forelegs and is most often seen in horses with overly sloping pasterns. With a chronic problem, the horse may be sound walking and trotting, but will go lame in hard work. When judging the bowed tendon, consider it to be worse than a bucked shin, capped elbow, capped hock, splint, curb, or bog spavin, but preferable to thoroughpin, bone spavin, sidebone, osselets, and ringbone.

Just below the knee, check for the horse being "cut out under the knee" or "tied in behind the knee." Both of these conditions are structural weaknesses that cause the tendons behind the leg to be pulled around a curve within the knee by the muscles above. This action, similar to a rope running through a pulley, prevents a straight line of force as the

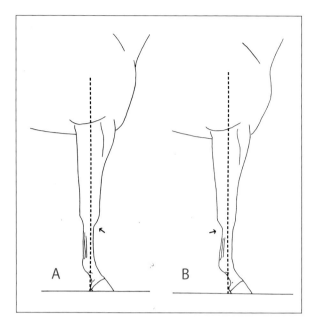

9.17 A & B "Cut out under the knee" (A), and "tied in behind the knee" (B).

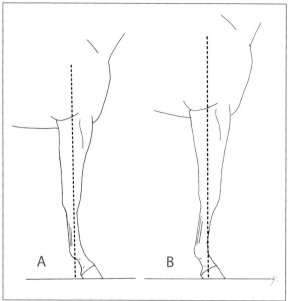

9.18 A & B "Calf knee" (A), and "bucked knee" or "over in the knee" (B).

horse places the foot during motion. Since "cut out under the knee" and "tied in behind the knee" have the same negative effect, they receive equal penalty (figs. 9.17 A & B).

If the knee is set too far back ("calf knee") or if it hangs over the front of the cannon bone ("bucked knee" or "over in the knee"), penalize the horse, since these structural faults cause weight to be distributed improperly down the leg and can lead to unsoundness (figs. 9.18 A & B). Calf knees are more severely penalized than bucked knees, because they are more likely to lead to unsoundness during hard work. Comparing these faults to those above, calf knees and bucked knees are worse than legs being tied in below the knees or cut out under the knees.

Look for a bulging contour of the knee that suggests "degenerative joint disease," commonly referred to as DJD

or "carpitis" (fig. 9.19). If a horse's knee is unusually shaped when compared to a normal knee on the other leg, suspect DJD. Although you cannot determine the extent of DJD without using X-rays, you must heavily penalize any indication of this defect, for it is a progressive disease that is worse than any of the other knee abnormalities discussed in this chapter.

After examining the knee, consider the horse's forearm and the manner in which the leg attaches to the body. The forearm should be well-developed, with more emphasis being placed on this quality in mature horses than in young ones. As for the attachment of the leg to the body, the leg should extend straight down from the joint so that the horse's weight is equally distributed between the front and back of the leg (fig. 9.20).

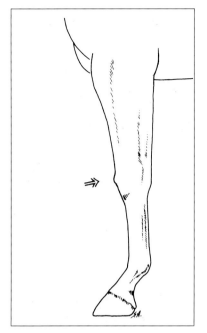

9.19 Degenerative joint disease (DJD or "carpitis").

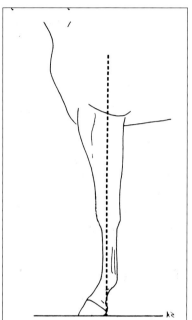

9.20 A horse's foreleg should extend straight down from the joint, as in this example.

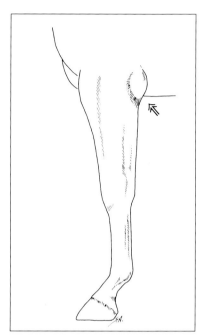

9.21 "Capped elbow" or "shoe boil."

Look in the area of the elbow for any swelling of a "capped elbow" (also called "shoe boil"), which is bursitis in the elbow usually caused by the shoe on the foot of the affected limb hitting the elbow while the horse is lying down (fig. 9.21). A "capped elbow" is not heavily penalized in comparison with most of the defects in this chapter (see "A Comparative Guide to Judging Defects"), since it is due to injury rather than a structural fault in the horse.

Having examined the outside of the left foreleg, begin the same process on the inside of the right foreleg by standing across from the horse's barrel on the near side, so you can see the inside of the right foreleg on an oblique angle. Once again, start with the foot and work up, looking for the previously mentioned faults and penalizing those you find.

Side View, Hind Leg (Near Side)

Once you have finished looking at the inside of the right foreleg, move toward the back of the horse so you can view the left hind leg from a side perspective. Many of the desirable features of a front foot should be present in a hind foot: the foot being the proper size for the horse's body and on the same angle as the pastern; the foot being neither overly steep, nor overly sloping; and the hoof wall being smooth, showing no signs of founder rings. Moving upward to the coronary band, where sidebone and ringbone can be found in the forelegs, look for any abnormalities, although the incidence of these particular defects in the hind legs is rare.

The slope of the hind foot and pastern should differ slightly from that of the forefoot and pastern. While the

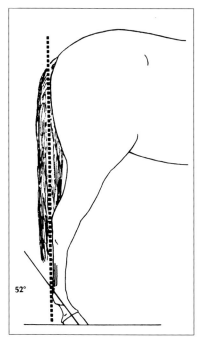

52°

9.22 The slope of the hind foot and pastern should be slightly more upright than 50 degrees. The difference between angulation of the front and hind limbs should not exceed 5 degrees.

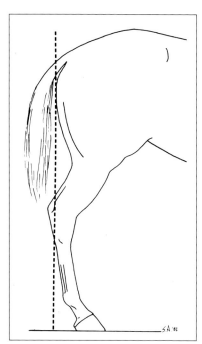

9.23 Sickle hock.

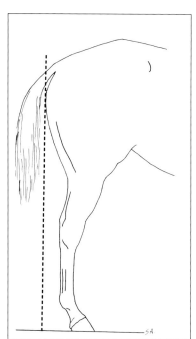

9.24 Straight hind leg.

slope of a front foot should be about 50 degrees, the hind foot should be slightly more upright (fig. 9.22). As stated earlier, the difference between front and hind angulation must not exceed 5 degrees. In scoring the hind legs—just as in scoring the front—penalize pasterns that are excessively upright more than those that are too sloping.

Although osselets are not common in the hind legs, windpuffs are found frequently in both the front and hind legs in the fetlock area. Again, windpuffs do not produce lameness and should be mildly penalized.

Splints and bowed tendons, found in the area of the cannon bone on the front legs, are rarely seen in the hind

legs. Directly above the cannon bone, however, is the hock area, in which many problems can develop.

A "sickle hock" is a structural fault characterized by the angle of the hock joint being so acute (when viewed from the side) that the horse is standing under from the hock down (fig. 9.23). A sickle hock is often responsible for the development of bone spavin and curb and is a very undesirable feature in the hind limbs.

In a "straight hind leg," the hock joint is so erect (when viewed from the side) that it causes excess concussion to the leg (fig. 9.24). This structural fault can cause bog spavin (a swelling of the hock joint capsule from trauma) and upward fixation of the patella (a condition in which the horse's hind leg is locked in extension, or, in milder cases, the hind leg "catches" as the horse moves). Comparing a straight hind leg to a sickle hock, the horse with the sickle hock should be more heavily penalized.

Besides these structural faults, there are also a number of defects that may appear in the hock area. At the front of the hock, look for "bog spavin," which, as mentioned earlier, is a swelling of the hock joint capsule usually caused by trauma (fig. 9.25). Bog spavin may result from trauma associated with conformation—as in the case of a horse that is too straight in the hock—or from trauma brought on by jumping a horse while it is too young, jumping too often, or stopping or turning a horse quickly. In some cases, bog spavin has two accompanying swellings, one on the outside of the leg and one on the inside. These swellings are sometimes confused with thoroughpin, which actually occurs higher in the hock area.

"Thoroughpin" is a more serious defect than bog spavin, for although bog spavin can cause lameness due to the irritation within the joint, thoroughpin is a progressive condition in which adhesions form around a tendon in the hock, which finally results in complete loss of the gliding capability of the tendon within its sheath. Thoroughpin can be found just in front of the point of the hock at a level slightly higher than the point where secondary bog spavin swellings occur (fig. 9.26).

On the point of the hock, look for a "capped hock," the least serious of all hock faults that will be mentioned. A capped hock is bursitis caused by trauma to the point of the hock and is usually incurred through the horse kicking a wall or the tailgate of a trailer (fig. 9.27). The condition is characterized by a swelling at the point of the hock and may be accompanied by curb (discussed next). A capped hock is

preferable to the other hock faults because, although it can be a defect (that is, can cause unsoundness, particularly if the horse continually reinjures the hock), it is usually only a blemish (that is, the swelling remains visible, but does not cause unsoundness, after the inflammation has subsided).

Just below the point of the hock, look for signs of a "curb"—an inflammation of one of the ligaments in the hock, usually caused by extreme exertion or by trauma from kicking stable or trailer walls (fig. 9.28). On a horse with sickle hocks or cow hocks, however, curb is often a result of poor structure. In judging, penalize a curb more heavily than a capped hock, but less than a bog spavin, thoroughpin, or bone spavin (discussed below). After considering the major hock problems best detected from a side view, look at the horse's gaskin to see whether or not it is well developed and at the proper angle (see figs. 9.1, 9.3, & 9.4). If the gaskin is too steep, it should be penalized for causing excess pressure to be exerted directly down on the hind leg.

Once examination of the left hind leg is complete, step back into place next to the horse's barrel where, from an oblique viewpoint, you can begin the same process with the off hind leg, starting with the foot and working up. All of the aforementioned faults that can be seen from this vantage point should be penalized.

In addition, look for "bone spavin" on the inside of each hind leg on the lower part of the hock (figs. 9.29 & 9.30). A bone spavin, frequently called a "jack spavin" or "jack," begins with inflammation of the covering of the bone or of the bony tissue itself. The inflammation is usually caused by trauma associated with jumping a horse while it is too young, jumping too often, or stopping a horse quickly, or by trauma related to poor conformation such as sickle hocks, cow hocks, or thin hocks. The inflammation results in new bone growth that, in some cases, merges the lower two joints of the hock on the

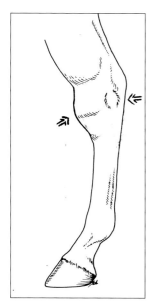

9.25 The arrow on the left indicates the position and swelling of bog spavin. The arrow on the right points to a secondary bog swelling. Compare the position of secondary bog spavin to the position of thoroughpin in fig. 9.26 (right).

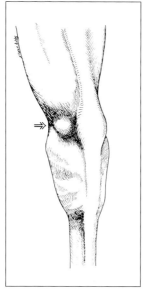

9.26 Thoroughpin.

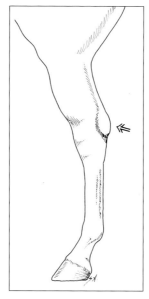

9.27 Capped hock.

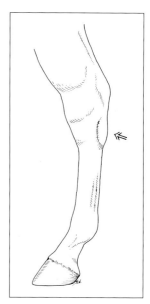

9.28 Curb.

9.29 In this view of the horse's hind legs from a front perspective, notice the difference in the shape of the normal hock on the left and the hock on the right with bone spavin (indicated by arrow).

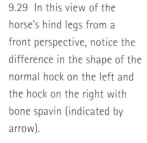

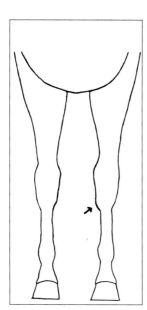

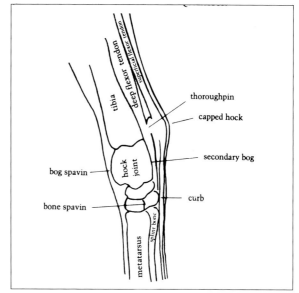

9.30 The locations of conformation faults in and around the hock, as viewed on the inside of the right hind leg.

inside of the hind leg. The horse will generally become lame during the bone growth process involving these joints, but may return to soundness once the merger of these joints is complete. However, the percentage of horses whose joints fuse, allowing them to become sound again, is not very high. In comparative scoring, bone spavin is penalized more heavily than any of the other hock defects (thoroughpin, bog spavin, curb, and capped hock) because if the involved joints do not fuse, the horse may become permanently lame.

Front View

While you are walking from the side to the front of the horse, notice the animal's general expression and attitude. Ideally, a horse should have wide-set, intelligent-looking eyes that have a kind expression. An eye that is cloudy, indicating partial or complete loss of sight, is penalized at the judge's discretion.

While an animal is being shown on the line, it should be relaxed enough to stand still, but appear attentive, "wearing its ears well" by carrying them pointed forward rather than "pinning the ears" back, which is an indication of a bad attitude. Long, floppy ears are mildly penalized because they detract from the overall picture of elegance that an ideal strip horse should have.

Stand in front of the animal on an imaginary centerline that bisects the horse (generally, you can see past the person showing the animal, but if not, ask him or her to move slightly to one side so you can get a good view). Consider the breadth of the horse in proportion to the depth of its body, making sure the chest is sufficiently wide, as well as deep, to give plenty of room for the heart and lungs. A well-formed chest should have an upside-down V shape that indicates proper musculature in the attachments of the front legs to the body and of the neck to the chest (fig. 9.31).

Next, look at the forelimbs to see if the horse stands squarely or if it toes out or in (figs. 9.32 A & B). In judging the forelimbs, most to least serious would be: an entire leg turned out, an entire leg turned in, toes turned out, and toes turned in. The reason for this is that an entire leg out or in is worse than only toes out or in; and, because of the possibility of interference between the forelimbs, an out-turned position is worse than an in-turned position in the front legs. (In the rear end, however, an out-turned position is preferable because it allows the hocks to remain under the horse, while an in-turned position places the hocks to the outside of the horse and weakens its jumping effort.)

Look at the horse's right forefoot (in front of your left hand as you face the animal) and notice whether or not the foot is symmetrical, as it should be (fig. 9.33). Continuing up the leg, look for sidebone, ringbone, osselets, windpuffs, and splints, since the new perspective may bring a previously overlooked abnormality to light. Viewed from the front, the bones in the legs should have substance, rather than looking thin and brittle. The forearms should be muscular and the legs should join smoothly with the chest. Once you have completed examination of the horse's right foreleg, go through the same procedure with the left foreleg.

It is usually easier to find splints from the front view than from the side (figs. 9.34 A & B). When a splint is present, check for a "bench knee," a structural fault in which the cannon bone is offset toward the outside of the imaginary line (extending vertically from the point of the shoulder joint to the ground) that should be bisecting the foreleg (fig. 9.35 A). Lacking support from the cannon bone, the inside splint bone carries an abnormally heavy load, and the result is often inside splints.

Other structural faults found in this area are "knocked knees" and "bowed knees." In "knocked knees," the horse's

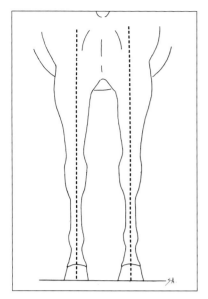

9.31 Between the forelegs of a horse, a well-formed chest has an upside-down "V" shape, indicating proper musculature.

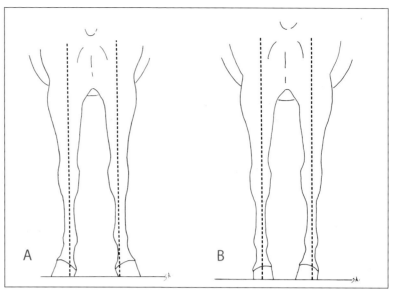

9.32 A & B Toes turned out (A), and toes turned in (B).

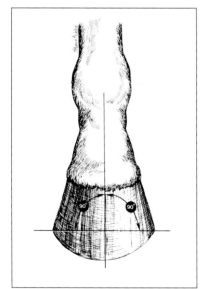

9.33 A symmetrical foot.

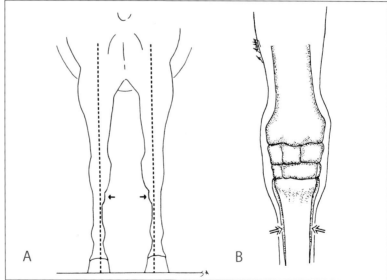

9.34 A & B Since this horse has bench knees (see fig. 9.35 A), it is not surprising that there are splints on both forelegs (A). However, splints frequently occur in only one leg and may appear at other locations along the inner or outer splint bones, which are directly to the rear and sides of the cannon bone, as seen in this front view of a foreleg (B).

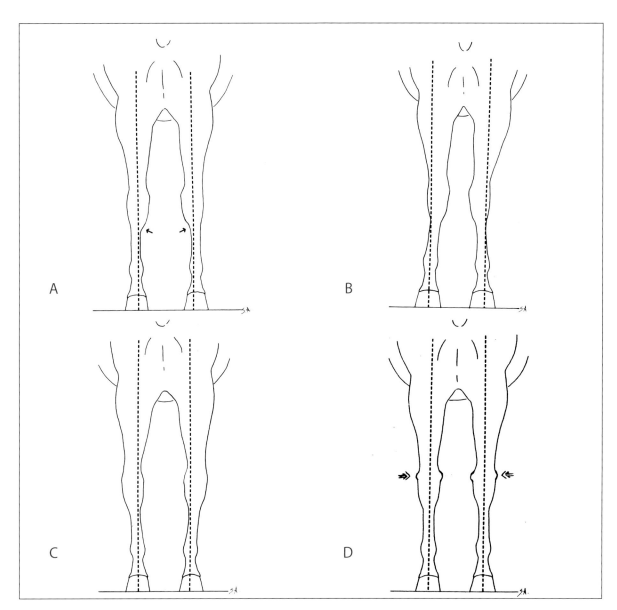

9.35 A–D Bench knees (A); knocked knees (B); bowed knees (C); unclosed epiphyseal line (D).

forelegs bend in toward each other at the knees, so that the bones above and below the knees, as well as the knees themselves, lean inward (fig. 9.35 B). In "bowed knees," the forelegs bend outward at the knees, so the bones above and

below the knees, as well as the knees themselves, lean outward (fig. 9.35 C). Both knocked knees and bowed knees cause the horse's weight to be distributed unequally down the legs; but knocked knees are more heavily penalized because they are usually accompanied by "toe-out" conformation, suggesting interference, while bowed knees are usually accompanied by "toe-in" conformation, which does not cause interference. Bench knees would be less penalized than the other two faults because it is a less radical deviation from the proper leg structure.

From this front vantage point, look for a bulge on both sides of the upper portion of the knee. This silhouette, in which the bulge is usually larger on the inside than the outside of the knee, indicates an unclosed epiphyseal line (fig. 9.35 D). This is the least penalized of knee abnormalities, especially when the horses being judged are quite young, for the condition improves with age.

After examining the forelimbs, glance toward the hind legs to look for bone spavin, which may be easier to detect from this front view than from the prior oblique view (see fig. 9.29). You may also find splints on the hind legs, although they are uncommon in the rear end.

Side View, Off Side

Move to the off side of the horse and stand far enough away to get an overview of the animal. You have already determined the general quality and substance of the horse from the near side, but must check the off side for blemishes, such as a cup in the neck or a body scar.

Side View, Front Leg (Off Side)

Look for the same structural faults, defects, and blemishes outlined in "Side View, Front Leg (Near Side)," examining the outside of the foreleg on the off side of the horse, then the inside of the foreleg on the near side of the horse.

Side View, Hind Leg (Off Side)

Look for the same structural faults, defects, and blemishes outlined in "Side View, Hind Leg (Near Side)," examining the outside of the hind leg on the off side of the horse, then the inside of the hind leg on the near side of the horse.

Rear View

When the horse is viewed from the rear perspective, the point of the quarter, point of the hock, ergot, and center of the foot should be on the same vertical line (fig. 9.36). You can easily detect two structural faults from the rear view: "bowed hocks" and "cow hocks." In "bowed hocks" the horse's hind legs bend outward, placing the hocks too far to the outside of the body (fig. 9.37 A). Since the hocks are not properly aligned beneath the haunches, the horse's jumping effort will be weak. In addition, when a horse has good conformation in front, but bowed hocks behind, the fault is likely to cause interference between front and hind limbs. Thirdly, the bowed hock formation causes excessive strain on the outside of the hind limbs, which may lead to unsoundness. These three problems—weak jumping effort, interference between front and hind limbs, and potential unsoundness—cause bowed hocks to be the most undesirable structural fault of the hind limbs.

"Cow hocks" is a fault in which the hocks are too close together and turned in so they point toward each other slightly, rather than being parallel (fig. 9.37 B). By placing excessive strain on the inside of the hind legs, cow hocks often cause bone spavin. In comparing structural faults of the hind end, cow hocks are preferable to sickle hocks and bowed hocks; but when cow hocks and sickle hocks appear together, as they often do, this combination would be worse than sickle hocks alone, but still preferable to bowed hocks.

Each hock should appear well-developed and symmetrical from this rear view—a perspective that may further enforce findings you had from the side and front views con-

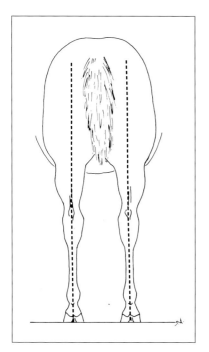

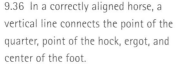

9.36 In a correctly aligned horse, a vertical line connects the point of the quarter, point of the hock, ergot, and center of the foot.

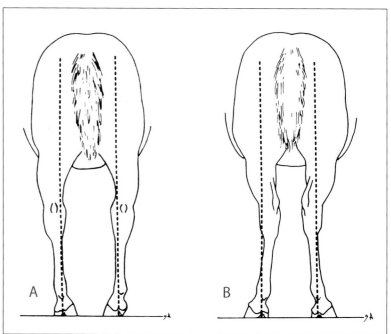

9.37 A & B When a horse has bowed hocks, its toes tend to point inward (A). With the opposite formation, cow hocks, the horse's toes will generally be turned outward (B).

cerning spavins, thoroughpins, curbs, or capped hocks. Run your eyes up the horse's left hind leg, then right hind leg, to check for any abnormalities already discussed that you might have missed when looking from other perspectives.

Once you have completed examination of the first horse in the line, go through the same procedure in judging each of the other horses. In all classes over obstacles, all horses being considered for an award must be jogged for soundness in the judge's order of preference prior to being judged for conformation. Two more entries than the number of ribbons offered must also be jogged if there are sufficient entries.

Model and Breeding Classes

Model and Breeding classes use the same basic criteria as Conformation classes, with one major exception. The jog, which is used only to determine soundness of the horse in Conformation classes, becomes very important in Model and Breeding classes as the only test of the horse's athletic ability. Since you haven't had the opportunity to watch the horses perform as you would in judging a Conformation class, you must pay close attention to the jog as an indicator of the accuracy of your judgment about the horses' conformation.

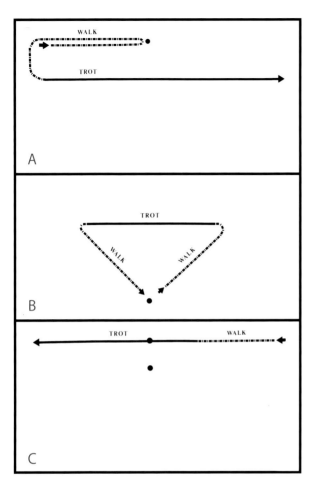

9.38 A–C The diagram shows patterns commonly used in the Hunter Breeding Division, with the dots representing the position of the judge during each pattern. Portions of the patterns performed at the walk are designated by interrupted lines, while trot segments are represented by solid lines. The third pattern (C) is often used in Futurity classes.

There are three systems of judging the way a horse moves, all of which were devised to examine the horse from the front, hind, and side views (figs. 9.38 A–C). In fig. 9.38 A, the horse moves at a walk toward the judge, turns just in front of the judge and walks away, then turns again and jogs the length of the arena, giving the judge a final side view. In fig. 9.38 B, the horse walks away from the judge on the first leg of the triangle, trots the second leg, then walks toward the judge on the third leg. In fig. 9.38 C, the horse walks the first third of the length of the ring, then trots the remaining two-thirds. The judge must start by standing on the line about half-way down the ring, move to the side as the horse trots by, then move behind the horse as it trots away. This is the quickest method, but it requires a judge capable of immediate, correct impressions and a lively step. The first method (see fig. 9.38 A) is probably the easiest for a novice judge.

The jog will be your only chance to see if the horse moves straight, has a good length of stride, and demonstrates rhythm and coordination in its motion. A good handler can minimize a horse's structural problems by standing the horse in a position that shows the animal to its best advantage. But once that horse has to jog, its structural problems will become apparent to the judge who has a keen eye to detect them. If the horse you thought looked great turns out to paddle, be short-strided, or show some other problem you didn't anticipate, then reconsider that horse's structure. The horse can only paddle if its foot isn't put on straight, and the well-structured but short-strided horse may prove to be the obese animal that is literally "too fat to move."

The jog, then, not only should be viewed as a test of soundness in a Model or Breeding class, but should be considered as the ultimate test of the theory you have used in judging the horses in the line-up. For this reason, in Model and Breeding classes you judge the conformation of the

A horse that is built well should move well. You are looking for the good athlete—the horse that will be capable of turning in good performances over fences for many years to come—not for the overly fat, "hot-house" variety horse that has no blemishes but shows little promise as an athlete.

horses first, then jog the animals (or, in the case of brood-mares and foals, walk the animals), and finally move the horses into the proper position for pinning.

It is important to keep in mind the intended use of the horse when judging Model and Breeding classes. If your Breeding stock shows some wear and tear from pasture life—such as a skinned place or the lack of a polished coat or perfect weight—you are more forgiving than if the same were true of your Model horse, which should show every sign of being at its peak as a performance animal. When judging non-Thoroughbreds, be sure to judge the horse's appearance based on the task it will be required to do. You would not pin high the heavy-set non-Thoroughbred horse with delicate Thoroughbred legs, but would look for a horse that had enough bone to support its heavier body.

When you judge a horse's conformation, your main consideration should be how the horse's build will affect its ability to perform. If it is breeding stock you are judging, then you are considering the horse's "performance" in terms of the quality of the traits it is capable of transmitting to its offspring—that is, a well-balanced structure that promotes soundness and athletic ability.

If you are judging young horses in a Model or Breeding class, then "performance" is seen in more immediate terms. The jog should be crucial in your assessment of a young horse, for it is a major indicator of the animal's general athletic ability. After all, what is a horse worth that doesn't cover enough ground? You don't want to pin a horse high that has a limited future as a hunter.

Lili
2007

Equitation on the Flat

Position

"Put your heels down!" is heard frequently in equitation lessons, not simply because this command produces a certain look, but because it causes the rider to be more securely fixed on his horse and gives him a position from which he can be more effective. When a rider's heels are down, he has allowed his weight to drop as far as it can and, consequently, he'll be much less likely to fall off than a person who doesn't exert this downward pressure.

It is important that the weight not only be distributed downward, but also that it be distributed equally on each side of the horse. When a rider leans to one side, causing his weight to shift off the horse's center, he is apt to fall off on the side he is leaning toward if the animal suddenly moves in the other direction. If he remains in the center of his horse, however, he'll be able to stay on through balance and not become unseated unless the horse has a major mishap, such as falling and rolling over.

The concept of staying on through balance and downward weight distribution becomes clearer if the rider is compared to a sack of grain laid over a donkey's back. The bag of grain has no muscle to hold it on and only stays in place because the grain has settled equally on each side of the donkey. So it is with a rider who sits in the middle of his horse and does not allow his weight to shift more to one side than the other.

Unequal weight distribution presents a balance problem not only for the rider but also for the horse. When a rider leans to one side, the horse invariably leans in that direction, too. Sometimes you'll see a competitor trying to push his horse away from his leg while he is leaning toward the

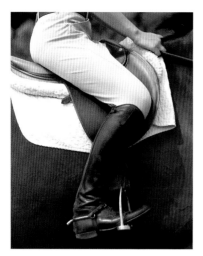

10.1 In this properly positioned leg, the rider's knee and toe are on the same vertical line, and the rider's calf is against the horse. The stirrup is on the ball of the foot, and weight is properly placed in the rider's heel.

10.2 A & B This rider's toe and knee are incorrectly turned out and the back of the rider's calf is against the horse (A). In contrast (B), the inner knee has contact with the saddle and the inner calf with the horse, so that these pressure points provide stability for the rider.

leg he is using, so that his off-center upper body is moving the horse inward, counteracting the leg aid as it attempts to push the horse outward.

It is essential, then, for the rider to remain in the center of his horse, for the sake of his own and his horse's balance, and for him to keep his heels pressed down at all times, so he will be securely fixed on his mount no matter what problem arises. These two principles are so basic to the rider's safety that a person who does not sit centered on his horse or press his heels downward during all phases of competition should be heavily penalized in every level of equitation.

In addition to the ankle being pressed downward, it should also break slightly toward the horse's side, bringing the rider's calf into contact with the animal. A small portion of the sole of the boot will be visible to the judge because the side of the foot that is away from the horse is upturned

as the inner side of the foot is depressed (fig. 10.1). Although the rider's toe will naturally be farther from the horse than his heel, the toe should not be turned out so far that the rider uses the back of his calf, rather than the side of it, and lets his knee be pulled away from the saddle (figs. 10.2 A & B). This position—toe out, back of calf active, and knee out—should be heavily penalized because it takes the rider's security away as it pulls his leg from the saddle.

Lack of security in the leg causes a multitude of problems in the upper body. In general, a rider whose leg is thrust too far forward will be riding with his upper body "behind the motion," and, in, extreme cases, will be pounding on his horse's loins with his seat and pulling on the horse's mouth as he uses his reins to support his upper body (fig. 10.3 A). In contrast, a rider whose legs are too far back will be "ahead of the motion," and, in an extreme case, will be leaning on his

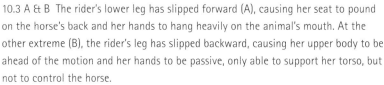

10.3 A & B The rider's lower leg has slipped forward (A), causing her seat to pound on the horse's back and her hands to hang heavily on the animal's mouth. At the other extreme (B), the rider's leg has slipped backward, causing her upper body to be ahead of the motion and her hands to be passive, only able to support her torso, but not to control the horse.

10.4 In "at the girth" position—that is, positioned on the horse's flesh just behind the girth—the rider's leg provides a sound foundation for the upper body.

hands to support his upper body and letting his horse move in an overly long frame because his hands and torso are rendered so passive that he cannot use them to balance the animal (fig. 10.3 B).

Since the leg thrust forward does not touch the horse's side, it is of no use in communicating with the animal; therefore, this leg position is severely penalized. A leg drawn back too far is weak, but is not penalized as seriously because it can communicate somewhat with the horse. Compared with these major leg faults, the ideal rider's leg is positioned just behind the horse's girth, with the steady leg providing a sound foundation for the upper body (fig. 10.4).

Finally, there are riders whose legs appear to be in the correct position when viewed from the side, but who from the oblique or rear view can be seen not to have contact with the horse (figs. 10.5 A & B). These riders appear balanced as long as their horses are cooperative, but will be pulled out of position if their horses become strong. This is often the case with a rider who is on a high-strung horse and is afraid to add leg pressure for fear of the horse becom-

ing even more keyed up. Although the rider may appear to be positioned correctly from the side, he is actually committing a serious fault in not having his leg on the horse, for the leg is one of the prime sources of control of the animal. It is preferable, however, for the rider to have this fault of seeming to have a good leg position, but not actually having the leg on the horse, than to have either of the other two faults mentioned—that is, leg kicked forward or drawn back too far. This is because in the case of the well-positioned, but inactive leg, the rider is at least supporting his own weight from his leg, and his upper body is not being thrown out of balance with the horse. A rider can learn to use his leg properly at this point, whereas riders who have their legs too far forward or back must first correct these errors and the many accompanying faults before they can learn to use the leg properly as an aid.

In summary, the major faults of the lower leg, ranging from most to least serious, are: legs too far forward; legs too far back; and legs that appear to have proper angles when viewed from the side, but are not actually against the horse.

10.5 A & B Although this leg looks correct from the side while the horse is at a standstill (A), seen from a rear view, it is apparent that the rider's calf is not properly placed on the horse's flesh (B). When the horse moves, the rider's unstable leg will swing back and forth, making the error obvious to an onlooker from the side view, too.

This last fault can best be seen during the canter, in which the motion of the horse's stride will generally cause the rider's leg to swing back and forth.

Now move up to the knee, thigh, and buttocks to consider faults that may occur in these areas. The knee should remain close to the saddle at all times, acting in conjunction with the rider's calf and thigh to produce a secure and effective leg. When a rider's knee is pulled away from the saddle, you should look for two possible causes: either the rider is improperly using the back, rather than side, of his calf against the horse (fig. 10.6), or the rider's conformation does not fit his animal's.

A long-legged rider on an animal too narrow-bodied for him will often exhibit this fault of the knee being away from the saddle, for he finds he must turn loose at the knee in order to press his lower leg against his horse. In the case of a mismatched horse and rider, it is preferable to see a

10.6 The back of the lower leg, rather than the inside of it, comes into contact with the horse when a rider's knee and toe are turned out. In this position, the rider must grip with the calf to steady the leg, since it is impossible to receive any stability from the saddle if the knee is pulled away from it.

gap at the knee than the other option the rider would have, which would be to keep his knee close to the saddle and not have his lower leg on the horse. Of course, the answer to this dilemma is that the rider should compete on an animal that suits him and not on one too small or too thin; but if you are faced with pinning two riders with this problem of being poorly mounted, the one who keeps his lower leg on the horse, but has his knee off, should place above the one who has his knee close to the saddle, but his lower leg off the horse's side.

Moving upward visually, notice the rider's thighs and buttocks at various gaits. At the walk, you may see a rider using these portions of his body to push his horse forward, rather than motivating the horse properly with his legs. This obvious movement in the rider's seat is penalized because the thighs and buttocks should be following the horse's movement at the walk, rather than creating the impulsion.

At the sitting trot, many competitors have a problem keeping their thighs and buttocks relaxed, and they either bounce each step or slow their horses down to keep from bouncing. A well-positioned, relaxed rider who knows how to shorten and lengthen his horse's frame will not have to cut the animal's pace in order to sit the trot, but will be able to collect the horse—while maintaining the rhythm of the working trot—and sit quite comfortably and still, having altered the horse's center of gravity back toward his seat through collection of the animal's frame. Tension in the thighs, buttocks, and stomach, as well as a lack of knowledge concerning collection, is the cause of bouncing; and riders usually try to conquer this problem by gripping with their legs to hold themselves on, rather than letting their weight and balance follow the horse's movements and effortlessly keep them in the saddle.

In judging the sitting trot, call for a "working trot sitting"—not a "slow, sitting trot"—and penalize riders who evade the test by cutting the pace. If you request that stirrups be dropped for this test, ask the riders to cross them, so the irons won't bang against the horses' sides (fig. 10.7).

At the sitting trot, the rider's pelvis angle should be slightly closed—just a couple of degrees in front of the vertical, the same as for the walk. If the rider allows his upper body

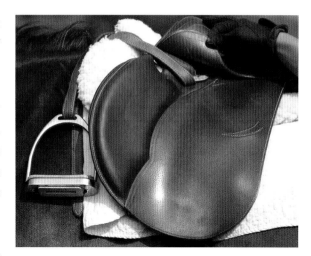

10.7 It is very important for the stirrups to be crossed properly, as shown, with the leathers lying flat, rather than the leathers being a lumpy source of bruising for a rider's sensitive inner thigh. When requesting work without stirrups, give the riders time to cross the leathers so the stirrup irons won't bang against the horses' sides.

to go behind the vertical, he should be penalized for the forced appearance that accompanies this error; and an even greater penalty must go to the rider who is at the other extreme, closing his pelvis too far forward so he is ahead of the motion, with his upper body rendered ineffective (fig. 10.8).

When asked to perform the posting trot, the rider will close his pelvis at an angle no greater than 20 degrees in front of the vertical. This hip closure will cause the rider to be posting on his thighs and crotch, rather than on his buttocks (fig. 10.9).

At the canter, the pelvis returns to the angle of the walk and sitting trot—only a few degrees in front of the vertical—as the rider's body adjusts from the horizontal motion of the horse's trot to the more vertical motion of the canter (fig. 10.10). When the rider's pelvis angle opens from the position of the posting trot to that of the canter, he is no

10.8 At the sitting trot, the pelvic angle should not be closed any more than shown in this photo. The rider's leg is correctly positioned the same without stirrups as with them—ankle flexed, calf against horse, and knee close to saddle. Although the rider's position is very good, her eyes are down a bit and the horse is slightly overflexed at the moment this photo was taken.

10.9 This is the picture of perfection at the working trot rising. The rider's upper body is inclined about 15 degrees in front of the vertical so that she is with the motion of her horse as it demonstrates impulsion, balance, and relaxed submission in a beautiful medium frame. (At the rising trot, a rider's upper body can be a few degrees more vertical or inclined than shown, but should never fall behind the vertical or be inclined forward more than 20 degrees.)

10.10 At the canter, the rider's body should be only a few degrees in front of the vertica. The deep seat and well-positioned upper body enable this rider to perform the half-halt successfully, helping to maintain the horse's lightness and balance. The upper body could be even a little more erect, but not on or behind the vertical.

longer on his crotch, and his buttocks and thighs can be used to absorb the shock of the canter. Tension in the buttocks and thighs will result in noticeable bouncing of the rider during each stride. This fault should be penalized for it shows that the rider's base of support—his seat—is ineffective, as opposed to a deep, relaxed seat that would indicate support for the rider's upper body and control of the horse.

Although a good rider's thighs and buttocks are relaxed, this does not mean they are physically unfit, for a rider with a weak seat slides back and forth in the saddle as the horse moves, while a fit rider's thighs and buttocks are sunken into the saddle, so horse and rider are at one during the walk, sitting trot, and canter.

Upper Body—From the Pelvis Up

Next, consider the upper body: back, shoulders, neck, head, eyes, and arms. Take note of the torso angulation at each of the gaits and penalize riders who are either behind or ahead of the motion of their horses. As previously mentioned, if the rider's balance problem begins in the leg, a forward leg position accompanied by a behind-the-motion upper body is worse than a leg too far back accompanied by an in-front-of-the-motion upper body. If, however, the rider's leg is positioned correctly and is effective, but the rider's upper body is either ahead of or behind the motion, the degree of penalty for the improper torso angulation would depend on the adverse effect on the horse's performance or the indication of a weakness in the rider's aids.

Besides counting off for these general balance faults, look for specific upper-body faults, such as a loose back, roached back, swayback, rounded shoulders, shoulders forced back too far, a neck stretched forward, a set jaw, or a head cocked to one side. The worst of the errors that can occur in the rider's back is a "loose back," which is a slinging movement in the rider's waist as the horse moves forward. This fault at the trot is usually caused by the rider not stretching upward in his back on an animal that has a particularly springy trot, so that the horse's movement slings the rider's body, making him look weak and sloppy.

At the canter, the loose back indicates that the rider is fixing his arm in an effort to restrict the horse's length of stride, but the arm is not reinforced by a strong back (which may be traced even further to the lack of a secure leg position). As the rider tries to restrain his animal, the horse is maintaining the lengthy stride by pulling the rider's waist forward. If the rider could keep his back still, he could correctly perform the half-halt, and the animal would go in a more collected frame and not produce this loose-backed

10.11 With a round curve along the entire length of her spine, this rider demonstrates a "roached back." Both unattractive and ineffective, a roached back is heavily penalized.

appearance in the rider. A loose back should be penalized heavily, for just as a poor leg position indicates an ineffectual leg, the loose back indicates an ineffectual back.

Another fault that may be found in the back is a "roached back" (also called a "rounded back"). This fault is a combination of buttocks that are tucked under and shoulders that are rounded (fig. 10.11). Although the roached back can be effective when accompanied by an extremely short stirrup—as for steeplechasing or flat racing—it is not a strong position when accompanied by the proper equitation-length stirrup, which hits just below the rider's ankle when he drops his stirrups and hangs his leg in a relaxed manner. Since the roached back is both ineffective and unattractive, it is heavily penalized.

A third fault found in this area is the "swayback" (also called a "hollow back"), characterized by the rider closing

10.12 With shoulders forced backward and buttocks protruding toward the rear of the saddle, the rider demonstrates a "swayback." This fault makes the rider look stiff and inhibits proper use of the back during half-halts.

10.13 "Rounded shoulders" weaken the effectiveness of the rider's back and detract from an elegant appearance.

his hip angle too much and carrying his buttocks too far behind him and his shoulders too far back (fig. 10.12). The acute angle of the pelvis causes the rider to lose much of the power of his back that is necessary for control in a variety of movements, from the half-halt to sharp turns on tight jumping courses. The swayback is definitely preferable to the loose back because at least it is stationary and has some strength. In comparing the swayback and roached back on the flat, although both of these faults show a weakness, the swayback generally is pinned higher because it is less unattractive visually and is usually accompanied by fewer position faults.

"Rounded shoulders," which may appear without the rider having his entire back roached, is a position fault usually found in long-waisted riders, who may also carry themselves with rounded shoulders when off a horse (fig. 10.13). Ideally, the back should be used subtly to keep the animal balanced—

for example, the back should act in conjunction with the rider's hands and legs during half-halts or on tight turns. In contrast, riders with rounded shoulders are limited in their use of the back and are not in as much control of their animals as those who keep the back straight and are able to use it fully.

The opposite of rounded shoulders is a position in which the rider has "forced-back shoulders" (fig. 10.14). Usually, this fault is present in a rider who is either swaybacked, as mentioned before, or who naturally has rounded shoulders and is forcing them back in order to have what he believes to be the correct appearance in an equitation class. Again, the shoulders being out of line with the rest of the upper body causes the back to lose some of its strength; however, this forced-back position of the shoulders is preferable to rounded shoulders because it is a somewhat stronger position from which the rider can work.

10.14 Young riders often respond to a coach's command to sit up straight by "forcing their shoulders back." This also creates a swayback in the rider.

10.15 The "neck stretched forward" and "set jaw" diminish the upper body's effectiveness and create an unattractive appearance.

Moving up to the area of the neck and head, look for a "neck stretched forward," out of line with the rest of the rider's torso, and a "set jaw," in which the rider has his jaw thrust forward (fig. 10.15).

Since the neck and head are upward extensions of the rider's torso, any excess inclination of them should be penalized for diminishing the strength of the upper body. When viewed from the side, the rider's head and neck should be in line with the upper body as though the rider's torso had been pulled upward from the top of the head by a string. In addition, a rider should not cock his head to one side or the other, for this, too, is a distortion of the straight and strong upper body desirable in a rider (fig. 10.16).

You should also notice the rider's use of his eyes during an equitation class on the flat. Throughout the class, the rider should be using his eyes to look slightly ahead of where

he and the horse are so that he can anticipate: (1) the path he will take according to where other horses are in the ring or where jumps, standards, or other objects within the ring are set; and (2) any adjustments he might need to make concerning extension, collection, bending, and so forth, according to the specific tests, the shape and size of the ring, and the traffic pattern of the other competitors.

The rider should turn his head slightly toward the direction of travel on corners and face straight ahead on the straight sides of the ring. If he exaggerates the turning of his head while traveling around corners so that he is almost looking over his shoulder, he should be penalized for "looking too far ahead," a fault that indicates he is thinking too far ahead and is not concerned enough with the horse's immediate performance (figs. 10.17 A & B). The rider must be capable of concentrating on what he is currently doing as well as on what

10.16 When the rider's head is tilted to one side, it subtly affects the balance of the horse. The degree of penalty for a "cocked head" depends on related errors in the rider's position and horse's performance.

10.17 A & B This rider is looking too far ahead on a turn (A), gazing over her shoulder at a 90-degree angle toward the direction of the turn. In comparison (B), she looks ahead properly, at about a 45-degree angle toward the direction of the turn.

he will have to do—dealing sufficiently with the present and planning sufficiently for the future—if he wants to succeed in the show ring (or anywhere else, for that matter!)

Worse than "looking too far ahead" is "not looking soon enough." A rider who doesn't look soon enough is so absorbed in what is presently happening that he doesn't look ahead of where he is to plan for what he'll have to do next. Ideally, a rider should use peripheral vision to get an idea of what is going on everywhere in the ring and should use this knowledge to pick the best paths to show himself to the

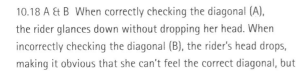

10.18 A & B When correctly checking the diagonal (A), the rider glances down without dropping her head. When incorrectly checking the diagonal (B), the rider's head drops, making it obvious that she can't feel the correct diagonal, but instead must search for it. (I find it amusing that the rider seems to be looking at the horse's right fore, while the horse appears to be looking at its left fore. Maybe together they can figure it out!)

judge and stay out of trouble. By noticing a group of horses misbehaving in another area of the ring, the competitor can determine approximately how long it will take these horses to catch up to him. Then he can plan to avoid the impending trouble by circling behind the group—giving them another circuit around the ring before they catch up once again—or by moving to the rail or inside track of the ring to let the horses pass, with this decision depending on which path the horses are taking when the rider views their problem. Sometimes escape from this type of situation is impossible, especially when the class is packed. However, a smart rider will keep his eyes active enough to avoid most of these situations and, in addition, will plan passes in front of the judge by looking for holes in the herd into which he can slip and be seen alone, to his best advantage.

Besides the rider's eyes being used to plan ahead, they can also be subtly used to check leads or diagonals. After the

beginner stage, a rider should not have to look down to check a lead or diagonal; he should be able to feel it. However, if a rider is uncertain without visual assurance, he can keep his head in normal position and cast a quick glance downward at the horse's shoulder (figs. 10.18 A & B). Glancing for a moment should not be penalized in equitation classes; but when the rider tilts his head downward or leans over to look for a lead or diagonal, he should be penalized for lacking sensitivity and sophistication.

Finally, consider the rider's hands, the effectiveness of which will be greatly determined by the rider's leg, seat, and use of his upper body. As mentioned before, if the rider's leg position is incorrect, it will generally be evident in his upper body. For the rider with his legs kicked forward, the hands will generally be used as a support mechanism as the rider attempts to pull himself up at the posting trot, rather than pushing himself up from his leg (see fig. 10.3 A).

10.19 If a rider fixes the hands on a horse that pulls, the animal will continue to travel on its forehand, counterbalancing its front end against the rider's weight. When intimidated by a pulling horse, a rider may remove leg and seat pressure, in an effort to placate the animal, and lean on the hands to support the upper body. This position is insecure, ineffective, and unattractive.

For the rider with his legs too far behind him, the hands will be used to support his upper body weight as he leans forward onto them to catch his balance (see fig. 10.3 B). These are the worst hand faults—the first being abusive to the animal's mouth, and, consequently, the more serious of the two; and the second exhibiting a completely passive hand that is unable to control the animal. When I call these two hand faults "the worst," I am putting them in perspective with other hand faults the rider could commit without intentionally trying to abuse the horse. Of course, a rider who jerks his horse in the mouth or wrings the bit from side to side in an intentionally abusive manner is in an entirely different category. These types of abusive behavior are not to be tolerated by the judge, and if they are considered abusive to the point

of "cruelty," you should deal with them accordingly, as provided for in the *USEF Rule Book*.

Next in the line of hand faults is what is commonly called a "fixed hand." This term is used for riders who do not follow the motion of the horse's head during the gaits, but who set their hands in an immobile position. The look of the fixed hand is one of rigidity, in which the rider appears to be holding the horse's head in place (fig. 10.19). (This fault could more appropriately be called a "fixed arm," for it is not the hand alone that is unresponsive as much as the entire arm, which should be following the motion of the horse's head.) The fixed hand is often seen in a rider on a high-strung animal as he attempts to restrain the horse from getting faster. In this case, the horse will try to escape the fixed hand either by pulling its head in toward its chest, behind the bit, or by fighting the rider's hands, trying to pull the reins out of them. Accompanying faults seen in riders with a fixed arm on a tense horse are: an insecure leg position as the rider attempts to hold his legs away from the horse's sides in hope the animal may slow down from the lack of leg pressure; the rider holding his seat out of the saddle as he tries to avoid any pressure against the horse's back that might cause it to go even faster; and a low hand as the rider attempts to balance himself on his hands, since he doesn't have the leg or seat security from which to support his upper body.

The problem of the fixed arm is not restricted to riders on tense horses, but is seen also in riders on dull horses that pull. The dull horse that leans heavily on its front end will often cause a rider with a weak leg, seat, and upper body to fix his hands to support the horse's front-end weight. In this case, the rider is lacking the means to half-halt his animal and make it carry its own body weight. Although this type of horse is the opposite from the tense one mentioned above, its rider may have many of the same position faults—insecure leg, seat out of the saddle, and a low hand.

In summary, hand faults found in an equitation class are, from most to least serious: hanging on a horse's mouth for balance (abusive hands); leaning on the hands for balance (passive hands); and fixing the hands, rather than following the motion of the horse's head. In high-level equitation classes, riders will have their horses in a more collected frame than competitors in lower levels. In order to achieve this collection, the rider performs a series of half-halts that require a momentary fixing of the hands and cause the horse to have less motion in its head and neck. Thus, a hand that can properly produce the half-halt (in conjunction with the leg) should not be mistaken for the insensitive, fixed hand that sets against the horse for lack of a proper half-halt. The greatest indication that the rider has a fixed hand is the horse's reaction. Even if the horse's head is positioned low and the neck is slightly flexed, if the animal travels with its mouth open, pulls on the bit, or drops behind the bit, you should check to see if a fixed hand is the cause.

Ideally, the hands should be persuasive with an animal, so the rider can accomplish what he wants without the animal looking distressed. The hand should not be severe, causing the horse to react abruptly, nor should it be so passive that it allows the horse to travel unchecked on a long frame. Instead, the hand should subtly balance the horse in all gaits with such finesse that it is an "invisible aid."

In proper position, the hands are just over and slightly in front of the withers, and, when viewed from the side, in a direct line from the rider's elbow to the horse's mouth (fig. 10.20). If the rider's reins are too long, he will not have sufficient control of his horse; this is especially noticeable when the horse becomes "strong" and the rider ends up with his hands in his stomach as he tries to slow the animal down. In

10.20 In proper position, the hands are just over and slightly in front of the withers and in a direct line from the rider's elbow to the horse's mouth. The forearms and wrists should be straight, and the thumbs just inside the vertical and only a couple of inches apart.

contrast, if the reins are held too short, the rider's upper body and seat will be pulled ahead of the horse's motion..

The long rein results in an uncontrolled performance at worst or an imprecise one at best; while an overly short rein—usually associated with an aggressive or anxious rider—draws the rider's seat out of the saddle, so he cannot feel the subtleties of the horse's movements, such as the sequence of the feet, lateral suppleness, and impulsion. The degree of penalty for reins too short or too long depends upon the effect each has on the rider's position and on the horse's performance (figs. 10.21 A & B).

Conclusion

From the discussion of faults in the lower and upper body, some generalities can be derived concerning position errors. First, the most serious position errors are those that negatively affect the rider's balance. Second, since a rider's bal-

10.21 A & B An overly long rein connects the horse's mouth to the rider's stomach (A). The rider's greatest source of strength lies in the part of the back that is just behind the elbows.

A direct line of force from the horse's mouth to the rider's elbows can be reinforced by the rider's back, making it possible to have a great deal of control when needed (B).

ance and effectiveness are greatly determined by his leg position, the worst position errors are those that allow the lack of secure contact between the rider's legs and the horse's sides.

Many riders attempt to communicate with their horses predominantly through their hands, rather than through their legs, and find themselves limited in what they can accomplish. If the rider cannot keep his legs against the horse at all times without the horse overreacting, then he has chosen the wrong animal for the job and should look for a mount on which he can compete without being intimidated into removing his leg. As a judge, you are not supposed to justify the lack of leg contact by thinking, "Well, the rider is on a hot horse." Instead, you should penalize this lack of leg contact severely and leave it to the competitor either to solve the problem on his current mount or else compete on another horse.

Having taken note of the general balance of each rider and, specifically, how leg position affects this balance, consider the interaction of all body parts and pin riders who are the most securely positioned, balanced, coordinated, sensitive to their animals, and disciplined in their attitude toward performance. Riders should not be smiling throughout a flat class—as they are sometimes advised to do by misinformed coaches—but should have a look of concentration on their faces, for you are considering skill and quality of performance, not personality.

Performance

General Observations

"Performance" is what the rider is able to accomplish with his horse based on security of position and proper use of his aids.

10.22 A & B As the rider performs the sitting trot, the horse demonstrates lack of impulsion (A) with its high head carriage and short steps. In contrast (B), the bay is filled with impulsion, taking long, powerful steps and remaining balanced and on the bit as the rider performs the sitting trot without stirrups.

Just as the rider must exhibit a look of concentration on his work, the horse also should have this disciplined appearance throughout the performance. The animal should be moving ahead in a forthright manner, minding its own business rather than looking out of the ring or paying attention to other horses within the arena. If a horse becomes somewhat distracted during a flat class—lifting its head for a moment—but the rider gets the horse back to work, the penalty should not be great, unless the distraction results in bolting, breaking gait, or some other major fault during the class.

In judging performance, note how riders deal with problems that crop up during the class. For instance, if two riders are having trouble with spooky horses, the rider who is assertive and works his horse forward out of the problem should receive less penalty than the rider who is passive and lets the horse continue to shy away from objects and drop behind the leg.

Especially in judging beginner classes, consider not only what the rider is able to do, but also what he is trying to do. For example, in a division of very young riders, one who is obviously trying to bend his horse, but is unable to get it bent properly from head to tail, should place above one who is seemingly unaware that his animal is supposed to be bent and is content to let his horse lean to the inside on every corner. Although neither rider performed well, the one who showed knowledge of bending and kept trying to correct his animal should place above the one who was unaware of his error. If a third rider in the class is able to bend his horse correctly, he will, of course, be given highest place, since the reward for good intentions should not exceed the reward for a good performance.

Impulsion and Cadence

One of the most important aspects of performance, either on the flat or over fences, is impulsion. Impulsion is not the speed or "pace" at which the horse is going, but is the push power or "thrust" the animal has as it takes each step (figs. 10.22 A & B). Accompanying this thrust, the horse must have a steady cadence in each of the gaits. Impulsion, then, is best described as "rhythmic thrust."

At the walk, the rider's legs should cause the horse to keep a definite forward rhythm. This is sometimes referred to as a "marching rhythm," although I find this terminology misleading because I associate it with a high-stepping movement, which the walk is not. However, the word "march" also suggests a regular cadence; and it is in this sense that the horse's proper walk is compared to a march.

In judging any flat classes, you should consider the cadence of the gaits to be very important. Riders who treat the walk as a "time out" should be penalized for not correctly performing the test. This penalty should carry the same weight as that for riders who slow their mounts down for the sitting trot, for in both cases, the test is performed very badly.

In all gaits, the horse should be pushing from its hind legs in a regular cadence; if a horse plods or rushes, penalize the rider for not creating and maintaining the proper impulsion.

10.23 The horse is "on the bit," balanced, and relaxed at the canter. The rider's position is also very good, except for the hands, which are too flat. The forearms and wrists should be straight, with the thumbs just inside the vertical and only a couple of inches apart.

On the Bit

Getting a horse "on the bit" begins with the rider creating impulsion in the animal's rear end, for when the hocks are engaged, the horse will seek the bit with its head and neck. By half-halting the animal periodically, the rider can restrict it from elongating its frame, so the horse will remain on the bit in a medium frame, rather than extending into a long frame in reaction to the rider's maintenance of leg pressure (fig. 10.23).

Once the horse is on the bit, it should stay there, not drop "behind the bit" by bringing its head in toward its chest. Though both a horse that is behind the bit and one that is "pulling" present a problem, the animal that chronically travels behind the bit is committing the greater fault, for it is entirely evading the hand by not moving forward from the leg onto the bit (figs. 10.24 A–C).

Worse than a horse that pulls or drops behind the bit is one that raises its head in the air, escaping "above the bit"

(fig. 10.25). This fault is seen mostly in horses whose necks are built upright, for the steep conformation encourages the horse to use an upward route whenever it wants to avoid hand pressure. However, when seen in a horse with a properly constructed neck, the raised head usually signifies an emotional reaction to the rider—such as anger or panic—for if the horse were mildly resisting the hands, it would tend either to pull on or drop behind the bit because of its conformational predisposition, rather than take the more uncomfortable upward route. You should severely penalize horses that go "above the bit," because they are evading the rider's hands, legs (the horse will not move forward from the leg to the bit), and seat (an upraised head causes the horse's back to invert, making it impossible for the rider to sit comfortably).

10.24 A–C Compare the chestnut horse traveling "behind the bit" (A) to the same horse "on the bit" at few steps later (B). A momentary loss of contact is not a big problem, but a horse chronically behind the bit is. At the other extreme is a horse that is "pulling" (C). However, this bay will not succeed at gaining speed or disturbing its rider's balance because this gentleman has a remarkably sound position. The horses are in a long frame because the photos were taken during an under-saddle class.

10.25 This horse is trying to evade the rider's hands by lifting its head and traveling "above the bit." Instead of burying the hands, the rider should maintain a direct line between the elbows and the horse's mouth. Sustained pressure on the corners of the mouth encourages the horse to lower its head, whereas a low hand uncomfortably acts on the bars of the mouth and drives the head up even more. This photo was taken in an over-fences class, which accounts for the martingale—illegal in a flat class.

Bending

Besides looking for proper impulsion and the horse being "on the bit," notice whether or not the rider bends the horse around the corners of the ring. "Bending" is the part of performance on the flat that demonstrates the rider's ability to make his horse supple from side to side (while impulsion reflects the rider's ability to create forward rhythmic thrust of the horse's energy). When a rider cannot bend his horse, he is at a great disadvantage in competition because the unbent animal is poorly balanced around corners, including not only the ends of the ring, but also any tests that involve curves, such as circles, half-turns, or serpentines.

A properly bent horse is molded around the rider's inside leg according to the shape of the turn. That is, the animal is bent from head to tail to the same degree as the acuteness of the curve it is negotiating. In basic terms, when the animal is circling to the left, its entire body is bent to the left—its head is turned slightly in the direction in which it is traveling; its body is bent from head to tail; and its inside legs are on one track, while its outside legs are on another (fig. 10.26).

At the other extreme is the horse that travels around corners as stiff as a board—with its head "cranked" to the outside and its shoulders and haunches leaning toward the middle of the ring. This lack of bending is heavily penalized because it restricts the horse's vision, shortens its stride, and threatens its balance and, consequently, the safety of the rider. Even a very young rider should be aware of the importance of bending and be penalized for holding a pony's head toward the rail with an outside hand, rather than holding the animal's body to the rail with pressure from the inside leg (fig. 10.27).

Smooth Transitions

Another concept that should be familiar to riders in even the young age groups is the smooth transition between gaits. In

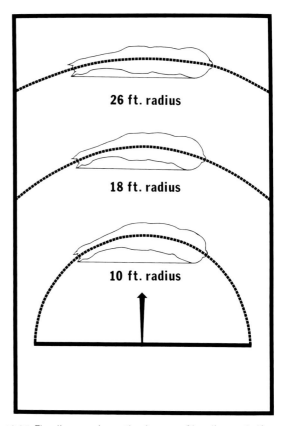

10.26 The diagram shows the degrees of bending on half-circles of varying radii. Although each horse's spine appears to match the pattern of the bend, this is a visual deception. The part of the spine from the withers to the dock is restricted by the shoulder, rib, and hip bones, and thus is not as flexible as the spine in front of the withers. Although this restriction prohibits the backbone from being bent uniformly from head to tail, the horse will appear uniformly bent because the soft tissues surrounding the shoulder and hip permit some lateral flexibility, which allows the outside plane of the rib cage to follow the pattern of the turn.

younger riders, poor transitions are often blatantly apparent during upward changes of gait, whereas more experienced riders, usually adept at upward transitions, are more likely to commit errors in downward changes.

10.27 On a corner, you will often see a young rider leaning inward while pulling the animal's head to the outside in an effort to keep it on the rail. The strength of the outside rein is negated by the effect of the rider's weight being thrust to the inside of the ring. This is only a mild example of the error, which is often acutely obvious in children this age. (Compare to fig. 2.16.)

The biggest problem for beginners is the transition into the canter, whether it be from the trot or walk. Many young riders hang their upper bodies over one of the shoulders of their horses to try to make them take the correct lead. This is a major mistake, for the competitor is attempting to engage the canter with his upper body instead of his leg and, by leaning forward, is thrusting his own weight on the horse's front end, making it more difficult for the horse to lift its forehand into the canter sequence. As mentioned several times before, the rider's leg is all important, and a fault that involves an ineffective leg is a serious one.

With advanced riders, however, the problem of smoothly performing an upward transition usually has been con-

quered, and the horse requires but a simple leg aid, accompanied by a balancing hand, to engage the canter. In downward transitions, however, riders are often concerned with promptness at the expense of smoothness, and they abruptly "slam on the brakes" into the downward transition, so the horse stops with its haunches out behind, its nose poked out in front, and most of its weight thrust on its forehand.

A poor downward transition is a serious fault at the advanced level, for it means that the rider abandons his leg when he wants his horse to slow down, and the passive leg aid will pervade the animal's performance both on the flat and over fences. Correctly, the rider should prepare for the downward transition by performing a half-halt—that is, by momen-

10.28 A & B This horse is forced into "overflexion" (A) by the rider's behind-the-motion upper body position, driving seat, and pulling hands. Even when the rider's aids are correctly positioned (B), the hands can be too heavy and draw the horse into "overflexion." This is a common fault seen in the show ring today, even at the top levels of equitation.

tarily adding both hand and leg pressure to collect the animal—then he should perform a series of half-halts (with the number of half-halts depending on the particular horse) to further slow the animal down, so the transition is smooth and balanced.

In comparing a poor upward transition with a poor downward transition, the poor upward transition is the greater fault, for it is a more basic command. For instance, if a rider asks his horse to canter from the trot and the horse trots faster and faster before breaking into the canter, this would be an elementary-level mistake on the part of the rider, who did not teach his horse to respond immediately from the leg aid. As has been stressed throughout this text, it is essential for the horse to move willingly forward from the rider's legs, for any hesitancy to do so (such as balking, refusing at a fence, or rearing) spells danger for the rider.

An abrupt downward transition indicates either that the rider is allowing the horse to drop behind his leg, or that the rider must be rough in order to control his horse. Unless the horse is out of control, however, an abrupt but prompt transition is better than a very late transition.

Flexion and Collection

"Flexion" is the contraction of the horse's neck that results from the rider pressing the horse onto the bit with his legs and half-halting the horse with his hands. When a horse is flexed, its head moves inward toward the vertical and its neck becomes more arched. This aspect of flexion is visually obvious to the novice, who often assumes that this appearance is caused by hand pressure alone. As a result, uneducated riders attempt to hold the horse's head down with a fixed hand in order to achieve a flexed look (figs. 10.28 A & B).

Nothing could be less correct than this forced flexion, for flexion properly starts with the horse's engine—its haunches—not with its mouth. When a horse moves forward with impulsion, it is thrusting its energy into the rider's hands. If unrestricted by half-halts, the horse will extend its stride or break into an upper gait. By half-halting, the rider can ask the horse to elevate the front portion of its body, rather than let the horse drive its weight downward into the ground and travel "strung out" on the forehand (figs. 10.29 A–F).

When a half-halt is properly accomplished, the horse maintains its impulsion from behind, but collects itself in front, and during this accordion-like procedure, the neck takes on a flexed appearance. Half-halts should create lightness in the horse as it carries its own weight rather than leaning on the rider's hands to support the weight of its head and neck.

The entire picture of the horse traveling with its hocks well under its body and its neck flexed is called "collection" (that is, the animal is "collected" from both ends), whereas the contracted appearance of the horse's neck alone is "flexion." The degree of collection necessary for a class depends upon the difficulties of the tests. In a class that calls for walk, trot, and canter both directions, a horse can travel in a medium frame (that is, with moderate collection) and perform quite well; but in a class that calls for further testing—such as counter canter, simple changes, or the like—the horse must be collected into a shorter frame to assure the rider's success in these tests of precision (figs. 10.30 A–C).

Extension

"Extension" is the horse's lengthening from a medium stride into a long stride through increased impulsion. The USEF Show Jumping Talent Search Class calls for a working trot rising "showing a lengthening of stride," which is intended to test the rider's ability to create more impulsion in the horse and to control this extra thrust with a sensitive hand. Sensitivity of the hand is particularly important in this test, for a good rider can feel if the animal is about to go from the trot into the canter and will support the horse's front end with the hand, so the animal won't break into a canter sequence (figs. 10.31 A & B).

During a USEF Talent Search Class, a horse should be traveling in a collected frame for the series of high-level tests on the flat. For a lengthening of stride at the working trot rising, the rider's upper body should be only a couple of degrees in front of the vertical, so the rider's weight, being behind the horse's motion, can act as a driving aid each time the rider sits. However, the rider's weight should be used so subtly that you cannot see it forcing the horse forward. When the forcing is apparent, it is a fault called "pumping."

Riders who perform the test poorly increase the animal's pace, rather than its impulsion, when asked to lengthen the stride and end up with a quick, medium-strided horse instead of a rhythmical, long-strided animal.

Severe Performance Faults

The worst performance faults in an equitation class are those that show that the rider is not in control—such as a horse that runs away with its rider (bolts) or stops at any point in the ring and refuses to go forward (balks or rears). If a horse's behavior appears to be a threat to its own rider or other competitors, you should excuse the rider from the ring.

Preferable to dangerous behavior, but still heavily penalized, are faults in which the rider does not perform the test. For instance, if you ask a rider to back his horse and the animal does not take even one step backward, or if you ask a rider to stop his horse and the animal moves around instead of standing immobile, you should severely penalize the rider for not performing the test.

Although not as bad as a "dangerous performance" or "not performing the test" at all, "breaking gait" is still a major error, because by momentarily switching to an incorrect gait, the rider does not perform the test in its entirety. When young or inexperienced riders commit this error, it usually is a downward break from the canter to the trot

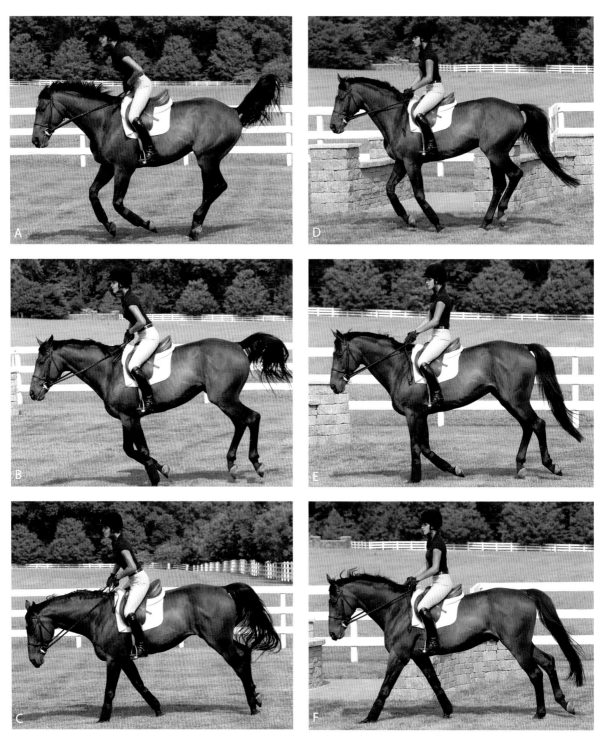

10.29 A–F With long reins and an upper body tipped forward (A–C), the rider is enabling the horse to travel "strung out" at the canter. In contrast, when the rider is in the proper position and collects her horse into a medium frame (D–F), the animal is well-balanced, relaxed, and light on its forehand.

10.30 A–C The same horse is shown in a short frame at the counter canter (A), a medium frame at the canter (B), and a long frame at the canter (C). As the reins become longer, it is more difficult to stop or steer the horse, and the animal's forehand becomes increasingly heavier.

10.31 A & B When asked to lengthen the pony's stride, this young rider correctly presses with her legs and keeps a steady hand so that the pony's steps demonstrate elevation (A) and extension (B). An older rider would be expected to have the horse in a more collected frame and keep the upper body just a few degrees in front of the vertical during lengthening.

from lack of enough leg support; experienced riders are more likely to break gait upward from the trot into the canter during extension.

Quality of Performance

After weeding out competitors who commit severe performance faults, compare the performances of the remaining riders. (Unless the class is terrible, severe performance faults will keep those who committed them out of the ribbons.) You should pin the class by considering each rider's position as it relates to the quality of performance.

"Quality of performance" is not the quality of the horse as a hunter, but is what the rider is able to accomplish on his horse. In equitation classes, if one rider does an excellent job on a mediocre horse, he should pin above another rider who does a poor job on a wonderful horse, for you are judging the rider's capabilities alone.

This doesn't mean that the quality of the horse doesn't matter, for what the rider is able to accomplish often depends on the horse's ability. For instance, if a good rider gets on a rough-moving animal on the flat, the performance may look choppy when compared to that of other good riders on better movers. Although the rider need not have the fanciest hunter in the world to get a ribbon in equitation, he should choose a horse that does not have severe locomotion, conformation, or disposition problems, which will continually put him at a disadvantage.

Tests on the Flat

Test 1
Halt (4 to 6 seconds) and/or back.

To properly perform the halt, the rider presses the horse forward with a supporting leg through the downward transition, so that the animal keeps its hocks engaged as it moves to the halt. By using a series of half-halts, the rider maintains lightness in the animal's forehand during the transition. The final picture at the halt should be of a horse standing squarely and on the bit, ready to respond to the rider's next request.

A very poor transition to the halt is marked by the horse pulling against the rider's hands and trailing its hocks behind—i.e., a horse that is "strung out." The horse may open its mouth in resistance, or may set its jaw and pull very hard. These errors result from the rider's hands being too strong in relation to his legs, which is an error in basic concept that should be heavily penalized. Even at the most elementary level, the rider must demonstrate the leg as the primary aid and the hand as a secondary, complementary aid. As the rider progresses to the point where collection of the horse is expected, he should not allow the hand to overpower the legs—an easy mistake to make when collection is first introduced.

The error of an overpowering hand may not be marked by such a severe reaction as a resistant, pulling horse. Instead, the horse may stay light on the bit, but "slam on the brakes" with its front feet and leave its quarters stringing out behind as it performs a downward transition to the halt. Again, the horse should move forward into the halt, so that when it reaches immobility, it is standing square, on the bit, and ready to react to the rider's next command.

Once the horse reaches the halt, it should stand quietly for several seconds, so there is no question about the animal's obedience. As the rider reaches the halt, he can square his horse's legs by pressing the horse forward, never by backing the animal. The reason for this is that the hocks should be engaged by forward thrust, not by moving the horse's body backward to position it correctly over them. The rider should square the legs in the final step of the downward transition, rather than halting for a second or two, then moving forward a step, which would be considered an interruption in the required 4- to 6-second immobile stance.

The halt is a useful test, for it points out the balance of the rider's aids during the downward transition. This test can be used by itself, but it is frequently seen in conjunction with the test of backing.

Backing a horse correctly is an art. Just as fine dancers exude energy even while they stand upon a stage, a rider must also create this sense of energy in his horse as it stands poised to back. The readiness of the animal is caused by the rider's legs, which subtly signal the animal to anticipate movement. In conjunction with pressure from the legs, the hands keep a steady feel of the horse's mouth, so that if the animal begins to move forward, it will be restricted. Prior to the actual backing movement, then, the rider must use his legs to create this anticipation in the horse, yet be sensitive enough to feel whether the horse is going to stand or move about; he must be ready with a restricting hand in case the horse starts to move too soon.

Once the horse is alert and ready for motion, the rider adds more leg to encourage the horse forward onto the bit and increases his hand pressure to prevent the animal from stepping forward. Pressed into the restricting hand by the rider's leg, the horse, unable to move forward, begins to step backward. As the horse starts to go in reverse, the rider's leg and hand pressure ease up to reward the animal for moving backward. (The hand and leg should exert the minimal amount of pressure necessary to accomplish the required number of backward steps in a steady rhythm. If the rider is "overriding" his horse by using too much hand and leg, he should be penalized.) As soon as the backward steps are completed, the rider increases leg pressure and decreases hand pressure, so the horse moves forward. The animal should return to its original position in the same number of steps.

Requiring very good rider coordination and sensitivity to the horse's energy, backing is often poorly performed even at the highest level of equitation competition. Especially in classes of very young riders, you will see competitors pulling their horses backward, using a great deal of hand and very little leg— the opposite of what you are looking for in a good backing test.

A poor backing performance usually results from the rider's lack of coordination or lack of practice on the horse he is showing. From most to least serious, the performance faults associated with backing are: (1) the horse raising its head and/ or opening its mouth and refusing to step backward; (2) taking one or more steps forward before it backs; (3) backing crook-

edly; (4) taking the incorrect number of steps backward (if you have specified the number of steps); (5) not backing with the feet stepping in diagonal pairs, but rather sliding backward in a sloppy fashion; and (6) being unwilling to go forward immediately following the backward steps.

Although these faults are listed from most serious to least serious in a general sense, their penalties would depend on the degree of disobedience in each specific case. For instance, a horse that drags its feet backward reluctantly, rather than stepping backward in diagonal pairs, is worse than a horse that hesitates slightly after backing before it moves forward into its original place. However, a horse that slides backward reluctantly would pin over a horse that not only hesitates to go forward after backing, but absolutely refuses to do so without being forced by its rider.

Performances that should be pinned high are those that demonstrate willing obedience of the horse as it starts to move forward onto the bit and, finding a restrictive hand, steps backward the correct number of steps as specified by the judge. This test should be flowing, so there is no hesitation between the backward motion and resumption of forward motion into the original position. The horse's head should remain low and its mouth closed, not gaping in resistance. Its feet should move in diagonal pairs in a steady rhythm; and once the proper number of steps has been completed, the horse should willingly go forward into its original position, returning in the same number of steps as it took going backward. From head to tail, the horse should remain straight and not resist by throwing its haunches to one side or the other.

Throughout the backing test, the rider's body must be erect—on the vertical—so that he stays with the horse's motion as it moves backward. His eyes should be looking straight ahead, not cast downward watching the horse as it performs the test (figs. 10.32 A–F). The hand and leg aids

10.32 A–F Backing correctly with its legs moving in diagonal pairs, the horse stays round as it moves its right fore and left hind backward (A & B), then its left fore and right hind backward (C & D) and continues with its right fore and left hind again (E & F). When the prescribed number of backing steps are completed, the horse should move forward into the starting position in the same number of steps. The exception would be if the backing test were followed by a test such as trotting over a fence, in which case the horse could pick up the trot immediately following the backward steps.

increase pace from
canter (10-12 mph) to
hand gallop (14-16 mph)

X

hand gallop is
established by
this point and
sustained the
length of ring

upward transition
into canter

X

X
halt

10.33 Hand gallop and halt.

should be so subtle that they are invisible to the judge. Any pulling or kicking by the rider is heavily penalized.

Test 2
Hand gallop.

The "hand gallop" is distinguished from the "gallop" in that the hand gallop is less extended and is a three-beat gait, while the gallop, which calls for much greater pace and extension, causes each hoof to be placed separately and creates four beats. The "hand gallop" is so called because it is a "gallop in hand"; in other words, the rider restricts the horse's extension with his hands and prevents the animal from extending into a four-beat rhythm.

The hand gallop should be executed at 14 to 16 mph; however, it is best judged as a pace greater than that of the normal canter, but not so great as to appear unsafe for the size of the ring in which the horse is showing. You must be careful not to ask for this test in rings that are very small or that have unsafe footing, for the small ring restricts the proper pace, and poor footing could cause an accident.

When individual testing is designated, the hand gallop (Test 2) is usually used in conjunction with the halt (Test 1). Prior to individual testing, instruct the riders to pick up a canter just before a specified corner, hand gallop their horses down the following long side of the ring, and halt just before the upcoming corner (fig. 10.33). In this way, each rider can make an upward transition into the canter, assume two-point position, and increase his horse's pace around the corner, so the animal will be at the proper speed by the beginning of the long side.

In equitation classes, the halt should be performed without use of a pulley rein (the very powerful emergency rein aid in which the rider presses one hand on the horse's mane, just in front of the withers, and pulls back with the other hand to stop an uncontrollable horse). The ideal halt is prompt but smooth, with the horse keeping its hocks under its body, rather than throwing them out behind and "slamming on the brakes" in front. Once the horse has halted, it should stand immobile for several seconds before moving back into line with the other competitors.

Smoothness and control are important elements in this test. The rider performs the upward transition into the canter in "three-point position"—his legs and seat making three points of contact with the horse—while his upper body is inclined about 2 to 3 degrees in front of the vertical. Following the upward transition, the rider assumes two-point position—his two legs being in contact with the horse while his seat is held out of the saddle—and he inclines his upper body about 20 degrees in front of the vertical. The rider increases the pace to the proper speed along the corner and maintains this pace down the long side. To perform the halt, he sinks into three-point position during the downward transition, with his body returning to only a few degrees in front of the vertical. If the rider drops his upper body behind the vertical and hauls on the horse's mouth, he is severely penalized for roughness.

Test 2 can be used as a group test, but the number of horses galloping at one time should be limited for the sake of the competitors' safety and easy viewing by the judge. (Eight horses is the number allowed in the hunter division, and although it is not specified for the equitation division, it is a reasonable guideline). When asking for a group hand gallop, be sure not to let the test last too long. The chance of the horses misbehaving in a dangerous manner is greatly increased as the test is prolonged.

In group testing, scan the ring to see if each horse has reached the appropriate pace and, if you call for the halt, scan the ring again to check for fidgety animals unwilling to stand immobile. It will be impossible to see every horse's downward transition, but try to be aware of any riders having trouble with an uncooperative horse, especially those just shy of riding a runaway. As in all cases, lack of control is severely penalized.

Test 3

Figure eight at trot, demonstrating change of diagonals. At left diagonal, rider should be sitting the saddle when left front leg is on the ground; at right diagonal, rider should be sitting the saddle when right front leg is on the ground; when circling clockwise at a trot, rider should be on left diagonal; when circling counter clockwise at a trot, rider should be on the right diagonal.

The description of Test 3 emphasizes the importance of diagonals during the figure eight at the trot. Diagonals have this importance because they affect the horse's balance at this gait. We are mainly concerned with the horse's outside foreleg at the trot because: (1) the outside legs reach farther than the inside legs when a horse is on a circle because the outside legs are tracking a larger circle; and (2) the rider's upper body, inclined forward with the motion of the horse at the trot, can greatly affect the horse's forehand. If the rider lifts his weight as the horse's outside foreleg goes forward, he frees this leg to reach its maximum extension; and, if he sits when this leg hits the ground, he adds weight at the moment the horse is best able to handle it. Thus, by keeping the proper diagonal—rising when the outside foreleg goes forward and sitting when it is placed on the ground—the rider is aiding the animal in keeping its balance around curves at the trot.

THE BIG PICTURE
Two-Point and Three-Point Position
"If sitting made a horse go faster, jockeys would sit."

Throughout the country, there seems to be a misunderstanding about when two-point position and three-point position are appropriate. Two-point position, when the rider's two legs are on the horse and seat is out of the saddle, lightens the horse's back and enables it to gallop and jump more freely. Many riders appear unaware of the purpose of two-point position and remain seated on their horses' backs on course, using their seats instead of their legs to motivate the animal forward.

If sitting made a horse go faster, jockeys would sit. The truth is that the farther removed the rider's weight is from the horse's back, the easier it is for a horse to reach and maintain pace on course. By bringing the stirrups up a notch or two from flatwork position and rising into two-point, the rider drives more weight into his heels, causing his calf muscles to be more flexed and, consequently, providing better "glue" at the faster gaits. In addition, the forward inclination of two-point puts the rider at the proper angulation for takeoff, so he doesn't have to throw his upper-body forward to catch up to the horse's motion over the fence.

Not only do I see riders incorrectly in three-point position on course, but also incorrectly in two-point position during equitation classes on the flat. The *USEF Rule Book* states in the hunter seat equitation section, "At the walk, sitting trot, and canter, body should be a couple of degrees in front of the vertical; posting trot, inclined forward; galloping and jumping, same inclination as the posting trot." The canter, then, should be performed in the same position as the walk, which is certainly not two-point position.

The purpose of sitting at the canter on the flat is initially to feel the sequence of the horse's feet as it goes into the canter so that you don't let the horse pick up the wrong lead, which is a fault that often casts a rider to the bottom of the class. You should continue to sit during the canter to maintain a round, balanced frame so that each stride is controlled. This prevents the horse from gaining momentum and increasing weight on its forehand as the class progresses. Control is especially important when there are many horses cantering together in a class.

Related to the confusion about when to use two-point and three-point position is the frequently seen habit of riders posting during the downward transition from the canter to the walk. Both upward and downward transitions should be performed with the rider sitting—there are no exceptions. Sitting during transitions enables the rider to feel the sequence of the horse's footfalls and puts him in a better position to control the balance of the horse, keeping the hocks engaged and the forehand light.

At the top level of competition, you don't see the improper usage of two-point and three-point; but at the mid-level and lower-level, these mistakes are rampant throughout the United States. These two positions are so basic to the rider's success over fences and on the flat that it would be wonderful if we had a better national understanding of their purposes.

10.34 A & B The figure eight is performed incorrectly if the rider crosses the center point on diagonal lines (A). When performing this figure correctly, the rider straightens his horse for a few steps on the centerline before changing the animal's bend toward the direction of travel (B).

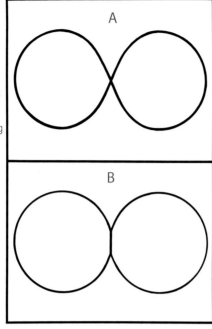

In judging this test, note the shape of the figure the horse is making. Riders often make the mistake of performing the figure eight as the number eight is written, with diagonal lines connecting two arcs (fig. 10.34 A). The correct figure is composed of two adjoining circles of equal size, with a small straight segment along the centerline at which the circles join—which is where the horse straightens its body for a few steps in order to gradually change its bend from one direction to the other (fig. 10.34 B).

Riding two circles of equal size requires thinking ahead. An intelligent competitor will map out his path beforehand, so you should allow a little planning time before the test for those with the foresight to use it. It is best if, before judging this test, you designate the *centerline*, along which the horse should approach the figure. You can either stand at the end of the line or, if the judge's box is centered on the long side of the

arena, begin the instructions with, "Using the judge's stand as a centerline, perform a figure eight...." The rider can then choose his *center point*—the exact place at which the transitions will occur. (The rider should plan to emphasize the center point by sitting the trot down the centerline and posting as he starts his figure at the center point. Although going from the walk or halt into the posting trot could also designate the center point, changing from the sitting trot to the posting trot is the smoothest means of designation. The rider must signal the end of the test by halting at the center point.)

Once the rider has planned where his center point will be, he should map out a path for the first circle and then the second, looking for stationary reference points (preferably one for each quadrant of each circle) to help him stay on his path. If he sees that he will be unable to keep the second circle the same size as the first—a jump is in the way, for instance—he should go back and plan another path that will allow the circles to be of equal size.

While performing the test, the rider should keep his reference points in mind and concentrate on going from one to the next, demonstrating impulsion, bending, the proper frame for the test, and the correct diagonals. As you watch the test, you'll see which riders have planned their routes, for lack of forethought will result in mistakes such as a near collision with an object in the ring, the formation of ovals instead of circles, or one circle being larger than the other. The more obvious the lack of planning, the heavier the penalty you assess.

From most to least severe, the faults you will often see in Test 3 are: (1) wrong diagonals; (2) an imprecise figure—such as the figure performed as the number eight is written, the circles being unequal in size, ovals being performed instead of circles, or the rider missing the center point; (3) lack of bending; and (4) a rhythm that is too dull or too quick, lacking in steady impulsion.

Test 4

Figure eight at canter on correct lead, demonstrating simple change of lead. This is a change whereby the horse is brought back into a walk or trot (either is acceptable unless the judge specifies) and re-started into a canter on the opposite lead. Figures to be commenced in center of two circles so that one change of lead is shown.

In Test 4, emphasis is placed on the proper leads at the canter and the correct changing of leads. Although the change may occur through either the walk or the trot, the walk is traditionally correct and, being considered greater in difficulty, should receive slightly higher marks if the performances are executed with equal accuracy and smoothness.

The shape of the figure eight is the same at the canter as at the trot—two adjoining circles of equal size. During the lead change, a horse should take only a few trotting or walking steps. The ideal is two steps (in either gait) during the change, which is the most prompt change possible; but if the horse needs more steps to balance itself in order to change leads smoothly, the rider can allow it to take four or six steps between leads. (The steps must be in multiples of two for the horse to have the proper sequence of feet to pick up the new lead. Six steps are the outside limit and should be used only for young horses, which take that long to get their balance; older horses should be better trained, using only two or four steps during the change.)

As in the figure eight at the trot, the rider plans his test and marks the beginning and end of it clearly for the judge by picking up the canter from the sitting trot (or from the walk or halt) to designate the beginning of the figure, and by halting at the center point to mark completion of the test. For the changing of leads, the horse should pick up the new lead as the rider's shoulder is over the center point of the figure. This means that all walking or trotting steps should occur before the horse reaches the center point, so the rider must anticipate how many steps his horse will need between leads and perform a downward transition the necessary distance from the center point.

The most heavily penalized faults in a figure eight test at the canter are, from most to least serious: (1) incorrect leads; (2) an imprecise figure; (3) lack of bending; (4) a rhythm that is too dull (so the horse canters in four beats instead of three) or a rhythm that is too quick; and (5) a late change, in which the rider misfigures the number of steps his horse will need to take between the leads and crosses the center point still walking or trotting.

Test 5

Work collectively or individually at walk, trot, and/or canter.

This test has already been discussed in depth in the sections on "Position and Performance."

Test 8

Question(s) regarding basic horsemanship, tack and equipment, and conformation.

This test encourages riders to possess basic knowledge about equine sport and sometimes produces amazing answers. Even among competitors with the most polished appearance, it is not uncommon to find that they cannot identify the type of bit in their horses' mouths or locate the pommel of their saddles. Literature from the United States Pony Clubs can provide judges with a stockpile of questions and competitors with a wealth of knowledge.

The web address, www.ponyclub.org, will bring up the association's web site. Pony Club publications are available through this site, with the "Bookstore" link appearing to the right of the association's name on the homepage. Click on "Reading List/Standards," then "D1 and D2 Recommended Titles" to locate one of the association's most useful texts, *The United States Pony Club Manual of Horsemanship: Basics for Beginners through D Level.* In Part 4, chapters 11 and 12, there is information on parts of the horse, the various colors of horses, conformation, and tack. It will provide basic information that all riders should know. (This is the first of a three-volume collection that replaces the British Horse Society's *Manual of Horsemanship for the United States,* a single volume that was a practical guide for riders for many years.) For more details concerning this book, go to www.amazon.com and search by title. This site provides the Table of Contents and an excerpt that includes both text and photos.

Test 9

Ride without stirrups (riders must be allowed option to cross stirrups).

In the test of riding without stirrups, you are looking for riders who show no change in position when their stirrups are removed, but who appear as stable and effective as they did with their irons. Competitors should appear well-balanced in their upper bodies and not depend upon reins for balance when the stirrups are missing. The leg must be in the same position as with stirrups, with the ankle retaining its angular appearance. There should be no wiggling of the leg at the trot or swinging of the leg at the canter that could cause the horse's performance to be adversely affected.

When calling for tests without stirrups, allow riders sufficient time to cross the stirrup leathers so the irons won't bounce against the horses' sides.

Test 11

Dismount and mount individually.

Test 11 is used to determine if the rider can mount by himself without pulling on the horse's mouth or poking the animal in the side with the toe of the boot.

To dismount, the rider puts both reins in his left hand—along with a clump of mane that will keep him from inadvertently pulling on the horse's mouth during the dismount and will assure fixed rein pressure, preventing the horse from walking forward as the rider is getting off. The rider can dismount in either of two ways: by dropping the outside stirrup and swinging the outside leg over the croup to the near side, then dropping the near stirrup and sliding down the horse's side, or by dropping both feet out of the stirrups and vaulting to the ground on the near side. Either way is acceptable.

Landing on the ground facing the horse's near side (at which point the test of dismounting is completed), the rider then turns to face the horse's rear end, still holding the reins and mane in the left hand. Grasping the back of the stirrup iron with his right hand and turning it toward himself, the rider inserts his left foot in the iron and turns the toe of his boot into the girth, so it won't press into the horse's flesh as he mounts (fig. 10.35). The rider's right hand is then free to grasp the cantle of the saddle and, aided by one or two bounces on his right foot, the rider can pull himself up above the saddle and swing his right leg over the horse. He should not land heavily on the horse's back, but should gradually sink into the saddle and separate his reins into the proper position for riding while finding the stirrup iron by feel, rather than looking for it or reaching down to position it on the foot. (In order to separate dismounting from mounting more distinctly, the rider may move to the front of his horse following the dismount and stand facing the same direction as his horse, then turn

10.35 Mounting correctly, the rider holds the reins taut enough to prevent the horse from walking forward; grasps the mane to keep from pulling on the animal's mouth when mounting; and turns the toe of the boot into the girth, rather than pressing it into the horse's flesh.

and begin the mounting process. This break between mounting and dismounting is not mandatory, however, for once the rider's feet have touched the ground, the dismounting phase has ended and the mounting phase can immediately begin.)

Test 12
Turn on the forehand.

The turn on the forehand is a schooling exercise executed from the halt and is employed to teach the horse obedience. The hindquarters of the horse should move in regular, quiet steps in a circle around its forehand. This movement may be executed through 90, 180, or 360 degrees.

The turn on the forehand can be performed in either of two ways: the horse moving away from the direction it is bent (basic) or the horse moving into the direction it is bent (advanced). A competitor is correct whether he bends his horse outward or inward; but whichever way he chooses, he must stick to that method throughout the turn and not let the bend of the horse slip from one direction to the other.

If a railing were on the horse's right side, the animal would have to move its haunches to the left to complete a 180-degree turn ("half-turn") on the forehand (figs. 10.36 A & B). The horse's neck in the basic turn is bent slightly toward the rail with a right indirect rein. The rider's right leg is drawn back about 4 inches behind the normal left-leg position in order to activate the haunches into sideways movement, and because of this leg position, the horse's body will remain basically straight from withers to tail, rather than being bent around the rider's right leg. However, the bending in the horse's neck and the motion of the animal's legs during the turn will make the horse appear slightly bent from head to tail. (Fig. 10.36 A reflects this bent appearance in the body of the middle, "moving" horse, while the first horse has only its neck slightly bent as it is positioned to begin the turn, and the last position shows the horse straight from head to tail as the rider straightens the animal in the final step of the turn.)

While the rider's right hand maintains the bend in the neck and his right leg pushes the haunches to the left, his left hand and leg restrict the horse from stepping forward or backward, or moving hurriedly to the left. The horse's steps should be cadenced, with the right foreleg stepping in place (not stuck to the ground and twisting), the left foreleg stepping around the right foreleg, and the right hind leg crossing the left hind leg. It usually takes four steps to make a half-turn on the forehand on a willing horse, but the number will vary somewhat according to each animal. Therefore, don't be concerned with the specific number of steps as much as with the maintenance of a steady rhythm throughout the test and with the successful completion of the turn.

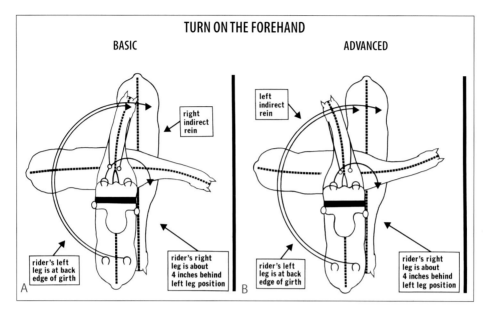

10.36 A & B In the basic turn on the forehand, the horse is bent away from the direction of travel (A). In the advanced turn on the forehand, the horse moves toward the bend (B). The diagrams show the aids of the rider and movement of the horse's legs during the basic and advanced turns.

For the more advanced turn on the forehand, the horse's neck will be slightly bent to the left as the animal stands with the railing on its right side (fig. 10.36 B). The rider uses a left indirect rein, but his legs are positioned the same as above, with the right leg slightly back and the left leg in normal position. The rider presses with his right leg, and the horse's body bends slightly around the rider's left leg as the animal moves to the left—into the bend. The horse's feet step in the pattern described above. This method of turning on the forehand is more difficult than the first because it requires the horse to move into, instead of away from, the direction it is bent.

At the intermediate stage of riding, the emphasis is on making the horse supple through movements such as leg-yielding and shoulder-in, both of which require the horse to move away from the direction it is bent (although in the leg-yield, the horse is only slightly bent in its poll; while in the shoulder-in, the horse is bent from head to tail). In advanced riding, however, we expect greater control over the horse,

so the animal will not only willingly move away from leg pressure, but also will be obedient enough to remain bent when asked to move toward the direction in which it is bent. Movements such as the advanced turn on the forehand, turn on the haunches, half-pass (two-track), travers (haunches-in), renvers (haunches-out), and modified pirouette are tests of the horse's obedience and the rider's ability to keep his horse balanced when it is moving toward the direction in which it is bent. When performing each of those movements correctly, the horse will remain bent in the direction of travel throughout the test and keep a steady and impulsive rhythm, staying solidly on the bit.

A rider who is knowledgeable and coordinated enough to do the advanced turn on the forehand should be given credit for his sophistication. Even though we speak of these turns as "basic" and "advanced," the turn on the forehand in either form should be reserved for more experienced riders in the 14- to 17-year age group, for younger riders rarely understand this test.

Although I have explained at length the difference between the basic and advanced turns, the most important aspect of the turn on the forehand is not the direction in which the horse is bent, but how willingly the horse moves from the rider's leg. Ranked from most to least serious, performance faults frequently committed during a turn on the forehand are: (1) the horse backing, rather than moving sideways—a fault akin to other serious faults involving evasion behind the rider's leg; (2) the animal moving sideways for a step or two, then halting and refusing to complete the test until the rider forces it to do so; (3) the horse walking forward a step before submitting laterally to the rider's leg; (4) the horse changing its bend during the exercise from the original direction in which it was bent; and (5) the animal grinding its pivotal foreleg into the ground, rather than stepping in the rhythm of the walk. Although a horse should not walk forward as an evasion of the rider's aids during this test, the pivotal forefoot may move slightly during the turn so the horse is tracking a small half-circle with the pivotal foot, rather than stepping in place. There is no rule as to the size of this half-circle, but generally speaking, a turn in which the pivotal foot remains within a 9-inch radius is acceptable.

Throughout the turn on the forehand, the horse's neck should remain in a steady, slightly flexed position, and the judge should penalize a horse that shows resistance to the rider's aids by raising or lowering its head or by pulling on or dropping behind the bit. The penalty for these disobediences is determined by the accompanying errors, since all are related to the horse's unwillingness to obey the rider's leg—an unwillingness that begins in the haunches.

For the turn on the forehand performed in the opposite direction, the pivotal foot would be the left foreleg and the rider's aids would be reversed.

Test 13
Figure eight at canter on correct lead demonstrating flying change of lead.

For a flying change, the rider asks his horse to switch leads at the completion of the first circle of the figure eight without breaking into either the walk or the trot. The initial circle is usually performed to the right; but if a horse is better at switching from the left to the right lead, then the rider can make the decision to start with a circle to the left and not be penalized, provided you do not specify otherwise in your instructions.

When a rider performs the test starting with a circle to the right, on approaching the end of this circle, he begins to even out his hand and leg positions to straighten the animal and uses a series of half-halts to "set up" the horse for the change. Keeping the animal from leaning toward the upcoming direction of travel—by using a supporting left leg and left bearing rein—and drawing the right leg back about 4 inches behind the girth as the horse reaches the center point of the figure, the rider signals the horse to change leads with pressure from his right leg and sensitively controls the horse's forward movement with his hands, so the horse doesn't run from the leg aid.

To do a flying change, the horse must be well-balanced, not drifting toward the outside of the first circle, since this would thrust excess weight onto the side of the horse which must be light for the change. As the horse switches leads, it should not fall into the new direction, but rather should lift its front end slightly and switch in one fluid motion of the front and hind limbs—the horse landing on the new lead all at once. Just after the switch, the rider must bend his horse in the new direction of travel, so the animal will be balanced around the circle.

Performance faults seen during the figure eight with a flying change of lead, from most to least serious, are: (1)

the rider not getting his horse to switch to the new lead and allowing the animal to counter canter or cross canter the entire second circle; (2) rider allowing the horse to remain on the original lead past the center point, so the horse counter canters a portion of the second circle before switching to the new lead; (3) the rider getting his horse to switch partially at the center point, so the horse cross canters a few steps before changing entirely to the new lead; and (4) the rider allowing his horse to speed up during the switch or letting the horse bounce a few steps leading into the change.

The figure eight with a flying change is a difficult test that should be reserved for advanced equitation riders.

Test 14

Execute serpentine at a trot and/or canter on correct lead demonstrating simple or flying changes of lead.

This is another test of the rider's understanding of diagonals and leads, involving more changes than required in the figure eight tests.

When you call for a serpentine, specify the gait or gaits, type of lead changes (if applicable), and the number of loops—generally three or four loops (fig. 10.37). The loops begin and end as the rider's shoulder crosses the centerline. A serpentine commences at one end of a centerline (chosen by the competitor or designated by the judge) and ends at the other end of that line, with the loops on each side of the centerline being equal in proportion.

To start the test, the rider sits the trot to the point at which the serpentine is to begin. He then designates the centerline by posting on the correct diagonal, if the test is performed at the trot, or picking up the proper lead, if the test is performed at the canter. He bends his horse in the direction

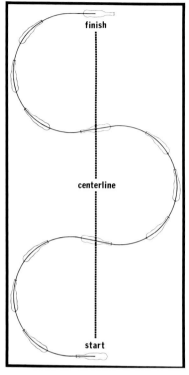

10.37 A bird's-eye view of a three-loop serpentine shows the horse correctly bent in the direction of travel on the loops and straight in the body as it crosses the centerline.

of travel around the loops and straightens the animal for a few steps as it approaches, crosses, and departs the centerline. The rider's shoulder should be directly above the centerline when he halts to mark completion of the serpentine. (If you ask for two serpentines—one at the trot and one at the canter—the rider should not halt after the first, but should go directly into the canter from the trot, by sitting the trot for a few steps before the centerline and picking up the canter as his shoulder passes over the centerline.)

If you ask for simple changes, the walking or trotting steps should occur prior to the centerline, so the horse can pick up the new lead as the rider's shoulder crosses the centerline. Flying changes also occur as the rider's shoulder crosses the centerline.

Faults that can be committed during the serpentine are, from most to least serious: (1) performing the incorrect number of loops; (2) not getting the correct diagonals at the trot or correct leads at the canter; (3) not having the horse bent in the direction of travel around the loops; (4) over-shooting the centerline during the change of diagonals or leads or at the beginning or end of the test; and (5) rough transitions or lead changes.

The serpentine is an appropriate test for all levels beyond the absolute beginner. It can be a simple test for a young rider (for example, performing a three-loop serpentine at the posting trot) or an advanced test for a sophisticated rider (such as, performing a four-loop serpentine demonstrating flying changes of lead). Consider the competitors' level of ability as a group and choose the appropriate test.

Test 15

Change leads on a line demonstrating a simple or flying change of lead.

Precision, straightness, and willing submission of the horse are your main concerns in judging Test 15. You should specify whether the riders are to perform simple or flying changes. If you call for simple changes, each rider makes his own decision as to the use of the walk or trot, unless you specifically call for one or the other. In judging all tests of precision, you mark higher those performances that show forethought—ones in which you see the competitor has marked off mentally the places where he should make the changes you are requiring. For instance, if you ask for two simple changes, the competitor should mentally divide the ring into three equal sections down the line, noting stationary objects in or around the ring that will help him mark each section (fig. 10.38). The trotting or walking steps should occur prior to the rider's mental marker, so he can

perform the upward transition as his shoulder is directly above the marker. Flying changes also should occur as the rider's shoulder crosses the marker. It doesn't matter which lead the horse begins on—unless you have specified the initial lead in your instructions.

When this test is used as a flat test alone, the rider begins with an upward transition into the canter at the beginning of the line to mark the start of the test. If the test is used in conjunction with jumping tests, however, the rider should complete the last fence, collect his horse, and turn down the line without making a downward transition (or flying change) until the first marker for the changing of leads.

Faults you may see in this test, from most to least severe, are: (1) overshooting the points at which the leads should be changed—which indicates either lack of planning or lack of control; (2) drifting off the centerline, which shows the rider is not using his hands and legs to limit the animal's lateral movement properly; and (3) making rough transitions during the simple changes, or a rough switching of leads in the flying changes.

Of course, if a rider overshoots his designated points for lead changes so far that the horse performs only part of the test—if it runs out of room before picking up the final lead, for example—he deserves the heaviest penalty, since he has not performed the given test.

Test 16

Change horses. (Note: this test is the equivalent of two tests.)

When you ask riders to change horses for further flat testing, be sure one rider will not be at a disadvantage due to the build of the horse he or she is asked to ride. For instance, if you ask a girl of medium height, whose horse has a medium

10.38 The diagram shows the division of a line for "two simple changes"—that is, three leads. It doesn't matter which lead the rider starts on, but he must alternate leads down the line, never picking up the same lead in succession. "X" marks the initial upward transition into the canter and the points at which the leads are changed. The dotted lines designate where transitions occur during simple changes through the walk or sitting trot. The rider should mark completion of the test by halting while still on the line.

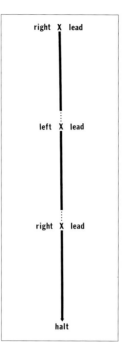

right **X** lead

left **X** lead

right **X** lead

halt

build, to switch with a tall boy on a very large animal, the girl will have the advantage because she can still look nice on the large horse, while the boy will look ridiculous on a horse too small for him. To do justice to the competitors, try to switch them onto horses that suit their builds, so the awful picture of a mismatched horse-rider combination will not get in the way of judging each rider's position and quality of performance.

The test of switching a rider onto a strange horse is used to determine the rider's ability to cope with an animal at the spur of the moment, without the benefit of practice time. If one rider is attempting to deal with a strange horse in the proper way, but must be a little rough to achieve results, he should place above another rider who is afraid to assert himself on an unfamiliar animal and looks as if he is trying to survive rather than compete. However, if a third rider gets the proper results using invisible aids, he should be placed above the other two; for, ideally, you are looking for a rider as relaxed and effective on a strange horse as he was on his own.

Test 17

Canter on counter lead. (Note: no more than 12 horses may counter canter at one time.)

Test 17 is used to determine an advanced rider's degree of coordination and sensitivity and his ability to maintain obedience in his horse.

The counter canter calls for the horse to take the outside lead, rather than the inside one it normally uses to maintain its balance on corners. Traveling counterclockwise, the horse would be on the right lead for the counter canter; moving clockwise, it would be on the left lead.

The rider's position is extremely important in maintaining the counter lead. To take the right lead while moving in a counterclockwise direction, the rider should have his left leg about a hand's breadth behind the back edge of the girth to give the aid for the canter depart, to maintain impulsion, and to keep the horse's haunches from swinging left. He should put his right leg just behind the back edge of the girth—to keep the horse's body bent to the right—and position his hands in a right indirect rein so that the horse's neck is properly bent, that is, slightly toward the leading right front leg (fig. 10.39 A).

The rider's right hand and leg work together to keep the horse bent to the right, while the left hand (used as a slight bearing rein against the horse's neck) and left leg work together to prevent the animal from leaning toward the inside of the ring and switching leads. The rider's upper body is positioned on the vertical throughout the test, so his weight can act in conjunction with his left leg to drive the horse forward, preventing it from four-beating, breaking gait, or switching leads. However, you should penalize the rider if he noticeably presses the horse forward with his seat, for his leg aid should be predominant. To perform the

Do not prolong this test, for it is difficult in itself, and the problem of horses trying to pass each other while on the counter lead makes it even harder. When watching the counter canter, notice any animals that are strung out, for they are the most likely to switch leads; and, if they do, you shouldn't miss it.

Faults you may see in Test 17 are, from most to least severe: (1) the rider never getting the horse on the counter lead; (2) allowing the horse to break gait or switch leads; (3) letting the horse travel strung out on its forehand, or letting the horse four-beat the canter from lack of impulsion; and (4) bending the horse toward the inside—instead of the outside—of the ring.

Test 18
Turn on the haunches from the walk.

The *USEF Rule Book* describes the turn on the haunches as follows: "The horse's forehand moves in even, quiet and regular steps around the horse's inner hind leg while maintaining the rhythm of the walk. In the half turn on the haunches, the horse is not required to step with its inside hind leg in the same spot each time it leaves the ground, but may move slightly forward. Backing or loss of rhythm are considered a serious fault. This movement may be executed through 90 degrees, 180 degrees, or 360 degrees."

Just as the advanced method of performing the turn on the forehand requires the horse to move into the bend, so does the turn on the haunches. If the horse is walking with the railing on its right side, it will have to pivot to the left to complete a 180-degree turn ("half-turn") on the haunches (Fig. 10.40).

First, the rider bends the horse's neck slightly away from the rail with a left indirect rein placed farther to the left than

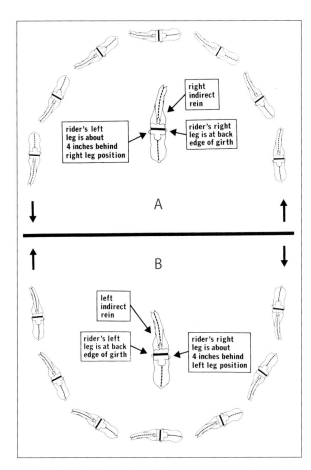

right
indirect
rein

rider's left
leg is about
4 inches behind
right leg position

rider's right
leg is at back
edge of girth

A

B

left
indirect
rein

rider's left
leg is at back
edge of girth

rider's right
leg is about
4 inches behind
left leg position

10.39 A & B A bird's-eye view of the counter canter shows the rider's aids and the direction of the horse's bend for counterclockwise (A) and clockwise (B) movement. The horse should be bent from head to tail slightly toward the outside (leading) foreleg on the ends of the ring. (Theoretically, the horse is no longer on the "counter lead" on the long sides of the arena because the horse is equally balanced on either lead when traveling on a straight line. However, the horse must maintain the outside lead both on the ends and long sides of the ring during this test.) The horse's body should become straighter on the long sides of the ring, so there is only a hint of bending to the outside.

counter canter in the other direction, the rider reverses his aids (fig. 10.39 B).

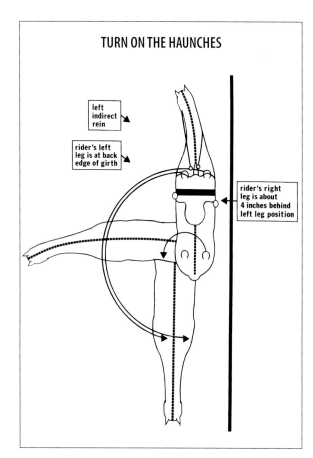

TURN ON THE HAUNCHES

left indirect rein

rider's left leg is at back edge of girth

rider's right leg is about 4 inches behind left leg position

10.40 During a turn on the haunches, the horse moves into the bend. The diagram shows the aids of the rider and movement of the horse's legs during the turn on the haunches moving counterclockwise. For clockwise movement, the aids are reversed.

normal indirect rein position, so the left rein can act as a subtle leading (opening) rein while the right rein restricts forward movement and can be used as a bearing (neck) rein if necessary. Then, exerting pressure with his right leg—placed about a hand's breadth behind the position of the left leg—the rider displaces the horse to the left, causing its right foreleg to cross its left foreleg and its right hind leg to step around its left hind leg in the rhythm of the walk.

Ideally, the left hind leg would march in place, so that as the horse turned, its left hind foot would turn and step on its previous footprint. However, maintenance of enough impulsion to keep the hind feet marching in the rhythm of the walk, with the pivotal foot landing on the same spot each step, is nearly impossible. Therefore, it is acceptable for the pivotal foot (in this case, the left hind leg) to move slightly with each step, so the walk rhythm will be maintained by the pivotal foot making a small half-circle rather than stepping in place. The smaller this half-circle the better, and, as a rule of thumb, the radius of the turn made by the pivotal foot must not exceed 9 inches.

While moving during the turn on the haunches, the horse should remain bent from head to tail in the direction of travel, for the combination of the rider's right leg (placed 4 inches behind the girth) pushing the horse toward the rider's left leg (placed at the back edge of the girth) causes the horse to be wrapped around the rider's left leg—that is, bent from head to tail—as the animal steps around the turn. (Fig. 10.40 shows the bend from head to tail in the middle [moving] horse; while the initial position shows a horse only bent slightly in its neck—as the rider prepares it for the first step of the turn—and the final position shows a straight animal as the rider straightens the horse during the last step of the turn.) For the turn on the haunches in the opposite direction, the pivotal foot would be the right hind leg and the rider's aids would be reversed.

Faults that can be committed during the turn on the haunches, from most to least severe, are: (1) the horse backing, rather than moving sideways; (2) not remaining bent in the direction of travel; (3) hesitation between steps before finishing the test; and (4) walking forward for a step.

In this test, notice that more emphasis is placed on the horse remaining bent toward the direction of travel than in the description of the turn on the forehand. This is because in the turn on the forehand—a basic exercise—emphasis is placed on the horse's willingness to move from the rider's leg, with the bending (which can be in either direction) having secondary importance; the turn on the haunches, however, is an advanced exercise, and the only way it can be performed correctly is for the horse to move into the bend.

Although I have used a railing in the description of both the turn on the forehand and haunches, both tests can be asked of riders without any railing present.

Test 19

Demonstration ride of approximately one minute. Rider must advise judge beforehand what ride he plans to demonstrate.

Test 19 allows a rider to demonstrate the level of his skill by making up his own test. Since it takes time to plan a series of movements on the flat that best show one's abilities, it is advisable for the competitor to have worked out his plan prior to the horse show and committed at least one plan (if not several alternate ones also) to memory. The rider should attempt movements that best display his education and skill and not attempt movements so difficult for his level of riding that he is likely to make major faults. (Movements are not limited to other tests in Tests 1–19 but may also include schooling movements, such as shoulder-in, two-track, extended trot, etc.)

Test 19 is a wonderful test that should be used more often. It allows riders of outstanding ability to show their skills to the fullest, while it enables less talented riders in the same class to choose movements within their limitations. Test 19 is interesting for spectators and judges to watch and for competitors to perform because it allows more individuality than any of the other tests.

Equitation Over Fences

Position over Fences

General Observations

In judging equitation classes over fences, as in classes on the flat, begin by focusing on the position of the rider's lower leg. You are looking for riders whose deep ankles reflect the downward distribution of their weight and whose lower legs stay fixed on their horses' sides at all times, between fences and in the air (figs. 11.1 A–E).

In the area of the thighs and buttocks, your emphasis is on the rider's ability to use two-point and three-point position appropriately. Two-point position, commonly called "galloping position," is used for a variety of purposes: racing, hunting, galloping cross-country, and showing in hunter or equitation classes over fences. The term "two-point position" means that only the rider's two legs are in contact with the horse, for his seat is held out of the saddle to free the animal's back (see fig. 11.1 A). When using two-point position between fences in hunter or equitation classes, the rider should incline his upper body approximately 20 degrees in front of the vertical, so he will be with the motion of the horse. (When two-point is used for competition involving greater speed—such as flat racing—the rider's upper body is inclined more forward to match the change in the horse's center of gravity.)

Three-point position—involving the rider's two legs and his seat—offers greater security than two-point and allows the rider's aids to be used more strongly (figs. 11.2 A & B). Three-point position is used in jumper classes that require tight turns and equitation classes that have simulated jumper courses—such as the USEF Show Jumping Talent Search Class and some Medal and Maclay classes. In

11.1 A–E It takes many hours of practice, both with and without stirrups, to achieve a leg as steady as the one captured in this sequence. On the approach to the fence (A & B) at takeoff (C & D), and in the air (E), the rider's weight stays in her heels and her leg position remains steady.

11.2 A & B To make a tight turn (A), the rider has sunken her seat into "three-point position" (B), giving her a stronger base from which to control this powerful horse.

"extreme three-point" position, the rider fixes his seat bones firmly in the saddle and keeps his upper body on the vertical, giving himself maximum control of his horse. Since this position tends to rob the round of fluidity and subtlety, riders should use it only if absolutely necessary—that is, if a rider realizes that without the use of this position, he will not be able to negotiate a particularly tight turn with precision.

Preferable to the "extreme three-point" position, in which the rider's upper body is vertical and seat is fixed in the saddle, is a "modified three-point" position, in which the rider sinks his crotch into the saddle for the third point of contact (figs. 11.3 A & B). By opening his body halfway between two-point angulation and the vertical—that is, about 10 degrees in front of the vertical—he can increase the strength of his upper body as a restricting aid. In modified three-point, the rider places some weight on his horse's back, but is better able to lighten the animal's front end than when he is in two-point position, so he can ride trappy courses with precision. Although equitation courses never demand "extreme" or "modified" three-point throughout, these positions can be useful to the rider in negotiating a tricky turn or an unusually short distance between fences.

No matter what degree of inclination the upper body has, the rider's back should stay straight from the base of

11.3 A & B The rider sinks her crotch into the saddle, lowering her center of gravity into a "modified three-point position" (A). Her body angle could be even more open—10 degrees in front of the vertical—so that her upper-body weight could better reinforce her hands. As the horse moves from the turn to a straight approach to the fence, the rider rises once again into "two-point position" and is inclined 20-degrees in front of the vertical (B), freeing the horse's back on the approach to the upcoming fence.

the spine to the back of the rider's head, and should not show evidence of any of the upper-body errors previously discussed: loose back, roached back, swayback, rounded or forced-back shoulders, stretched-forward neck, set jaw, or cocked head. The rider's arms and back should work together, with the back supporting the arms' restraining efforts during half-halts. Otherwise, the rider may be dislodged if the horse pulls between fences (fig. 11.4).

Approaching the Fence and in the Air
Legs Too Far Forward

A rider whose leg position is insecure during the approach to a fence will have difficulty staying with the motion of his horse as it jumps. At takeoff, his legs will not be able to give his upper body support and his torso may fall back, causing his legs to shoot forward. This combination of a forward

11.4 The rider is properly using her back to reinforce her hands and arms in the half-halt, so that she remains in control of the horse. Notice the direct line from elbow to bit, which enables her to employ her back properly. Her leg, however, has slipped back a little, slightly compromising the effectiveness of her upper body.

leg position and the upper body behind the horse's motion in the air is called "getting left." You should penalize this fault very heavily, for it is the most serious airborne mistake a rider can make. It radically affects the horse's balance and causes abuse to the animal's back and usually its mouth as the rider falls backward in the air. A rider who manages to grab the mane and keep himself from "catching his horse in the mouth" redeems his performance a little; but getting left in any degree is a serious fault, for when a horse jumps, the rider must go with it, for his own and the animal's safety.

An insecure leg position is not the only cause of getting left, for on occasion a rider with a secure leg will make this error when his horse leaves the ground earlier than expected. More often, though, the riders you'll see getting left are beginners who have not yet developed either a sound leg position or a good eye for finding a distance to a fence (figs. 11.5 A–C).

Another fault that may appear with a forward leg position—both on the approach to and in the air over a fence—is a roached back. A rider whose leg is thrust forward may hover over his horse's front end in an effort to counterbalance his upper body against his leg. This "jack-knifed" position indicates an ineffectual leg and back, as well as a lack of balance and security, and should be heavily penalized (fig. 11.6).

11.5 A–C Seen in a sequence over a cross-country jump, the rider is still in the saddle at takeoff (A), falling behind the motion of the horse in the air (B), and extremely "left in the air" on landing (C). Due to the arc of a jumping horse, the saddle will serve as a launching pad for the rider who sits erect on top of a fence.

11.6 With a rounded back attempting to counterbalance a leg that has slipped forward, the rider is in a "jackknifed" position.

If a rider with a forward leg position doesn't counterbalance himself by inclining his upper body above his leg, he may keep his upper body behind the horse's motion on the approach to the fence, then throw his torso forward in the air, to catch up to his horse's motion. As the rider pivots on his knee to move from behind the motion to in front of the motion, his leg is too far forward on the approach to the fence and too far back in the air (figs. 11.7 A & B). Sudden upper body movement—commonly called "jumping up on the horse's neck"—has an unbalancing effect on the animal as it leaves the ground and becomes airborne.

Although you should give a major penalty for jumping up on the neck in an equitation class, the jackknifed position mentioned previously deserves an even heavier penalty. While a rider who throws his upper body onto his horse's neck and lets his legs swing back is ahead of the horse's motion, one who jackknifes over a fence, letting his legs kick forward and his seat drop back into the saddle, is behind

11.7 A & B The rider's leg moves from being braced forward on the approach (A) to sliding back at takeoff (B). When this fault is accompanied by the upper body being behind the motion on the approach, then thrown forward at takeoff, it is know as "jumping up on the neck."

the motion. Since the rider ahead of the motion in the air is less likely to interfere with or physically abuse his horse, you shouldn't penalize him as heavily. Of course, you'll pin both of these riders lower than one who stays with the motion of his horse at all times.

11.8 A & B At takeoff (A) and in the air (B), the rider's leg is too far back, causing the upper body to drop ahead of the horse's motion, a position known as "perching."

For pinning purposes, the worst of the faults connected with a leg positioned too far forward is "getting left." Next is leaning the upper body forward over a leg that is kicked forward. Least severe of the three is approaching the fence with the leg forward, then pivoting on the knee to catch up with the horse in the air.

Legs Too Far Back

Not only do legs thrust forward cause problems, but so do legs drawn too far back along the horse's sides. A major form fault resulting from legs too far back is "perching," in which the upper body is ahead of the horses's motion at takeoff and in the air (figs. 11.8 A & B). Perching is penalized because it throws excess weight onto the horse's front end as the animal is taking off from the ground and is airborne; it diminishes the rider's control, since he is ahead of the motion; and it affects the animal's balance, causing jumping faults such as front-end rubs and hanging (figs. 11.9 A & B).

A perching rider is particularly at risk aboard a horse that is prone to stopping at fences: when the rider gets ahead of his horse, a quick stop is likely to sling him forward into the jump. (This is why riders on green horses or stoppers should ride defensively by staying with—or, in extreme cases, behind—the motion on the approach to an obstacle.)

Although a rider usually perches because he is anxious to get over a fence, his putting his upper body ahead of the horse's motion in no way drives the animal over the obstacle. In fact, it has the opposite effect, since the rider's upper-body weight bearing down on the horse's forehand makes the animal question its ability to lift its front end off the ground and consider stopping or cheating (adding a stride at the base of the fence). However, perching is preferable to the faults connected with legs positioned too far forward (getting left, jackknifing the body, and suddenly shifting from behind to in front of the motion at takeoff), because the rider who perches is less radically out of balance than is one committing any of these other errors.

11.9 A & B These riders demonstrate how "perching" can cause the horse to "rub" a rail (A) or "hang a leg" in the air (B).

Form Faults Not Necessarily Related to Leg Position

Not only may riders whose legs are too far forward roach their backs to counterbalance themselves, but a rider with a good leg position may also roach his back, in which case the rounded back is usually an indication of assertive riding (fig. 11.10 A). The opposite fault is a swayback (or hollow back), which is seen mainly in beginners who are forcing their bodies into position in an effort to maintain their balance in the air (fig. 11.10 B). As long as a rider's leg position is good, the swayback and roached back should only be penalized mildly, for although both detract from the elegance of the rider's appearance, neither affects the horse's balance significantly.

"Ducking," another upper-body fault, is characterized by the rider snapping his torso forward in the air so that his head is alongside the horse's neck at the zenith of the animal's arc (fig. 11.11). Like perching, ducking is fre-

quently a sign of an anxious rider—one who thinks he needs to do something with his upper body to get his horse over the fence. Also like perching, ducking has an effect just the opposite from the one intended; as the rider snaps forward in the air, he interferes with the horse's balance, making it more difficult for the animal to jump. For pinning purposes, ducking is worse than perching, since it is a more radical form of the rider being ahead of the horse's motion.

Looking back over the form faults discussed so far in this chapter, you would rank them, from most to least severe, as follows: (1) getting left over the fence—which is especially bad if the rider also catches the horse in the mouth; (2) jackknifing the body by kicking the legs forward and roaching the back on the approach to and in the air over an obstacle; (3) being behind the motion of the horse on the approach to the fence, then pivoting on the knee to catch up in the air; (4) ducking; (5) perching; and (6) roaching or hollowing the back.

11.10 A & B A "roached back" (A), often indicative of an assertive rider, is not a serious fault as long as the rest of the rider's body is positioned correctly and used effectively. The "swayback" (B), usually associated with beginners, but demonstrated here by an advanced rider, is also a minor error in the context of an overall good position. However, the stiffness of the swayback suggests a lack of relaxed communication between horse and rider that may lead to other errors during the round.

Hands

While airborne, the rider has three appropriate options for hand position: (1) primary release—the basic release, in which the rider grabs his horse's mane as the animal jumps, giving himself both support for his upper body and assurance that he won't catch his horse in the mouth or get left in the air, no matter what happens; (2) secondary (or crest) release—the intermediate-level release, in which the rider rests his hands approximately a third of the way up the horse's neck, just below the mane, and presses down to provide support for his upper body and freedom for the horse's head and neck (figs. 11.12 A–F); and (3) jumping "out of hand"—the advanced method of release, in which the rider maintains contact with the horse's mouth as the horse leaves the ground, is airborne, and lands, so he can control the animal in the air (figs. 11.13 A–C).

Grabbing the mane is fine for beginners, but a rider past this stage should master the crest release, which will enable him to support his upper body by pressing into the horse's neck, rather than by hanging onto the mane. Once he masters the crest release, he may attempt jumping out

11.11 "Ducking" not only impairs the rider's vision and thrusts excess weight on the horse's forehand in the air, but also throws the horse off balance from side to side. The animal will usually lean away from the side to which the rider is ducking in an effort to counterbalance the rider's upper body weight.

11.12 A–F In a proper "crest release," the rider moves the hands forward at takeoff (A), presses them down about a third of the way up the neck (B), and has enough slack in the reins to avoid interfering with the horse's use of its head and neck as a balancing mechanism in mid-air (C). The downward pressure of the crest release, used in conjunction with heels pressed downward and a secure leg position, are the glue that hold the rider on the horse over the fence. Safety is compromised when a rider's weight is not pressed downward at takeoff (D), in the air (E), and on landing (F).

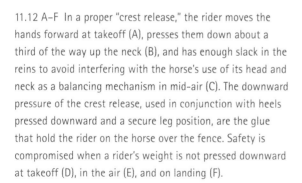

11.13 A–C When "jumping out of hand," the rider moves the hands forward at takeoff (A), but does not move them as far forward in the air as during the crest release, so that rein contact is gently reestablished in flight (B). This contact is sustained both through the air and on landing (C). For advanced riders, jumping out of hand permits subtle control of the horse.

THE BIG PICTURE

Don't Be Cruel to a Heart That's True

"I often see the nicest people who don't realize that their heavy,
unrelenting hands are a source of cruelty to the horses they ride."

I've been judging about 30 years, and although the sport as a whole has progressed, I still see inadvertent acts of cruelty in the show ring from riders who do not release their horses' necks in the air. It surprises me that such a basic principle has been overlooked in any rider's education.

The horse uses its head and neck to counterbalance the rest of its body in the air so that it can travel a successful arc that keeps its limbs away from the obstacle it is jumping. When a rider doesn't release enough at takeoff, the horse's balance is threatened, so the animal pulls hard against the reins to try to stretch its head and neck out as it fights to keep its balance. This means that the rider's weight is fully on the horse's mouth, which is as comfortable for the horse as it would be for you if you had about 100 pounds or more hanging on your mouth.

- The horse that stops at fences is the horse that gets no release.
- The horse that runs to fences in a panic is the horse that gets no release.
- The horse that crashes through the fences is the horse that gets no release.

A while ago, I was interviewed for Rick Lamb's radio program, "The Horse Show," and was asked, "If you could wave a magic wand and change just one thing, what would it be?" My answer was that I would like to stop everyone from hanging on their horses' mouths.

I often see the nicest people who don't realize that their heavy, unrelenting hands are a source of cruelty to the horses they ride. They don't think of the horse as a living, feeling creature that is dependent upon them for guidance, but simply concern themselves with controlling the large animal that is intimidating to them.

The truth is that if you have a horse that runs to the fences, you've probably caused that fault by not easing off the horse's mouth at takeoff. A horse needs to know a couple of strides away from the fence that you're not going to hang on its mouth in the air. You accomplish this by easing the hand pressure slightly as you near takeoff, then making sure you are not restricting the head and neck with your reins as the horse leaves the ground.

Whether you grab the mane, use a crest release, or jump out-of-hand, you must allow the horse to stretch its head and neck as much as it needs to counterbalance the rest of its body. There is nothing scarier for a horse than an unrelenting hand, especially at takeoff. For your safety and that of your horse, release the head and neck at takeoff and allow the horse to sustain this extension of the neck until landing.

11.14 A & B Horses naturally use their necks for balance in the air, and a "fixed hand" that restricts this instinct will frustrate and intimidate an animal, causing it to "lose heart." While fixing the hand may be an obvious error (A), it can also be more subtle, so that you only notice the fault in the horse's slightly opened mouth and restricted extension of its neck (B).

of hand. This advanced release is necessary for riding difficult equitation courses that require the rider to be in control of his horse at each moment, even while airborne. At the top of the horse's arc in the air, the rider's hand should be in either a direct line from the rider's elbow to the horse's mouth or above this line, but should never be below it.

If the rider makes the mistake of under-releasing, or "fixing the hand in the air," he threatens the horse's balance, and the animal quickly learns that for its own safety, it should stop at the fence rather than attempt to jump it (figs. 11.14 A & B). In judging, impose a severe penalty on the rider who under-releases, causing his horse to struggle for balance. In the realm of rider errors over fences, only getting left deserves a heavier penalty, for it is the only fault that makes it harder for the horse to keep its balance in the air.

Between fences, the rider's reins should be short enough for him to steer his horse easily—not so short that they cause the horse to overflex or the rider's body to be pulled forward, but not so long that the rider carries his hands in his lap (fig. 11.15).

11.15 This is a good rein length on course—not so short as to draw the rider ahead of the motion and not so long as to render the aids ineffective.

Eyes

The rider's eyes are his means of plotting his path from fence to fence and judging distances to the fences. When he uses his eyes properly, the rider looks ahead of where he is in the ring to line up his next set of fences, so he can travel on a logical path between obstacles.

Riders should envision a course as a series of lines (fig. 11.16 A). For instance, in fig. 11.16, fences 1 and 2 form the first line, fences 3 and 4 form the second line, fences 5 and 6 form the third line, and fences 7 and 8 form the final line.

In properly using his eyes while riding this typical hunter course, the competitor looks toward fences 1 and 2 by point A, toward fences 3 and 4 by point B, toward fences 5 and 6 as he again reaches point A, and finally toward fences 7 and 8 as he gets to point B. Although the rider cannot visually line up the fences while he is still on the corners, the fact that his eyes are actively searching for a line enables him to find that line at the earliest place possible and gives him enough time to find a good distance to the fence.

The rider's ability to "find a good distance to a fence"— that is, to see as he approaches an obstacle how much he must adjust the horse's stride so the animal's feet will be placed at the correct distance from the fence for takeoff—is a combination of innate talent and practice. Some riders have a gift for finding a good distance several strides away from the fence and are naturally inclined to make the necessary adjustment of the horse's stride; while others think distances are elusive— easy to see on some occasions and very difficult at other times. (For this less talented rider, lots of practice adjusting the horse's stride between poles set on the ground, as well as practice over actual courses, will help him develop a better "eye" for a fence.) Whether the rider has natural talent or not, he must look to the upcoming fence soon enough to have time to adjust his horse's stride, for even those riders who judge dis-

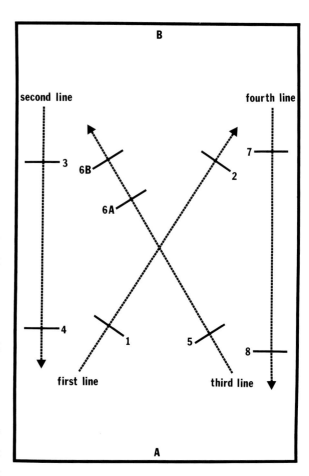

11.16 A A course seen as a series of lines.

tances with ease will make mistakes if they allow their horses' behavior or other circumstances to distract their eyes from the obstacles (figs. 11.16 B & C).

Having examined use of the eyes in connection with riding a very basic course, let us look at a more difficult course—one composed of several lines that have been used in Medal and Maclay finals in past years (fig. 11.17). Walking this course beforehand, the rider should realize that if he tries to travel between fences 1 and 2 on a straight line (as

11.16 B & C The rider should be looking through the horse's ears at takeoff (B) and in the air (C).

shown by the dotted line in the diagram), he'll have to angle his horse so acutely across both fences that he'll risk a refusal or a runout. The better option is to ride straight over fence 1, keep the horse on a bending line around the turn, and jump fence 2 straight also.

From fence 2 to 3, the rider again can jump either on a bending line or on a straight line that angles his horse across both fences. Here the straight-line option presents two problems: (1) the angle at which both fences would have to be jumped is acute, and (2) the horse might think it is being steered into the railing on the far side of fence 3. The better option again would be the bending line: the horse jumps fence 2 straight across and takes a bending line between the fences that lets it jump fence 3 straight also. The bending line also gives the rider an advantage in placing the horse at the fence for takeoff: if the horse is not covering enough ground between fences, the rider can shave the corner and get to the third fence at the right point in the horse's stride; and if the animal is going to get to the fence too soon, the rider can use an inside leg to push the horse to the outside of the bend and make extra room for its stride.

Since the turns come quickly in this course, the rider should look for fence 2 while airborne over fence 1 and for fence 3 while in midair over fence 2. While the rider focuses on each upcoming fence, peripheral vision will keep him from wandering off his intended path between fences.

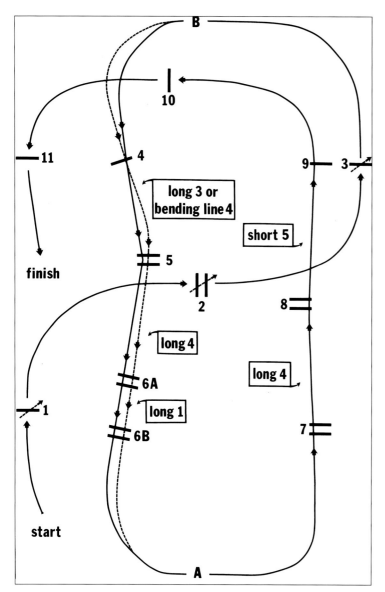

11.17 A course composed of typical lines from the Medal and Maclay finals.

A few strides before point B, the rider begins looking for fence 4. Since this fence is not on the track but inside the ring, the rider should look toward the fence earlier than usual, for he needs time to plot his turn, line up the fences, and find a good distance to fence 4.

As mentioned in chapter 8, the number of strides a horse should take between two fences often depends not only on those particular fences, but also on the fences that precede or follow them. The educated rider will realize that the most impressive route he can take for fences 4, 5, and 6a and 6b is to go straight between 4 and 5, turn in the air over fence 5 so the horse lands facing fences 6a and 6b, and move forward on a long stride into 6a, making it possible for the animal to go through the maximum-length in-and-out (6a and 6b) in one stride. He should shave the corner on the approach to 4 so his horse will be lined up to jump from the middle of 4 to the right-hand side of 5. In the air over fence 5, he looks toward fences 6a and 6b, with his hands and legs holding the horse straight between 5 and 6a so it won't lose precious footage by wandering to one side. (Note that centrifugal force will cause the horse to drift toward the left side of this line. The rider's hands and legs should compensate for this tendency.)

If the rider were on a short-strided horse and afraid his animal could not make the turn over fence 5 and have enough stride to get to fence 6a on time (since a turn in the air causes loss of momentum, which can be a serious problem on a short-strided horse), then he might consider adding a stride between fences 5 and 6a. However, this addition of a stride would cause lack of momentum that would spell trouble for the horse in the maximum-length in-and-out.

Suppose the rider tried to solve this problem another way—by adding a stride between fences 4 and 5, so he could ride on a bending line between them and approach fence 5 straight (see dotted line in fig. 11.17). This would allow his horse to land facing fence 6a, so the animal would have taken off and landed straight, not losing any momentum in the air and, consequently, making the approach to fence 6a on a long stride possible. This option presents a satisfactory solution; but when comparing the difficulty of the options, you should realize that it is much harder for a rider to turn in the air over fence 5 than to take the bending-line option, which avoids the difficulty of reversing the direction of travel while airborne. The most difficult option is called the "winning option," for if everything else about the trips is equal, this difference in difficulty breaks the tie. For this reason, a competitor should not show a horse that has an extremely short stride if he wants to win in high-level competitions, for the horse's lack of an athletic stride will prohibit the rider from choosing the winning option.

After fences 6a and 6b, the rider looks for his next line by point A. Between fences 7 and 9 he must find as straight a line as possible, for the way these fences are set encourages a horse to drift. Since this line also involves going from a long distance to a short one, riding it well requires changing the horse's frame from an extended to collected one.

As the rider reaches point A, he should look to line up fences 7, 8, and 9, turning his horse for the approach to fence 7 as soon as he sees the right side of 8. Since the distance between 7 and 8 is long, the rider should move his horse forward in long strides from point A, so he will give himself the best opportunity to find a long spot to 7—which will enable the horse to leave long, land long, and cover the ground between 7 and 8 more easily.

For fences 7, 8, and 9, the line that allows the most fluid yet precise performance goes from the left side of fence 7 to the right side of 8 and back to the left side of 9. The distance between 8 and 9 is short, so between these fences the rider should bring his body back closer to the vertical, where his back can support his hands as he asks his horse to collect for the shorter strides necessary here. (If he realizes the horse is going to get to fence 9 too deep anyway, he can give the animal a little more room by using his left leg to press the horse toward the right side of the fence.)

As the rider lands over fence 9, he should keep his hands up, rather than collapsing onto them, so he can quickly collect his horse for the immediate approach to fence 10. Fence 10 is difficult because the turn to it is acute and the fence is set off the railing—a position that courts a runout. Active eyes that look for fence 10 while in midair over fence 9 and for fence 11 while airborne over fence 10, and an active hand and leg that collect and steer the horse are the keys to successful turns between these last three fences. (These turns are an example of places in a course at which the rider might need to resort to three-point contact in order to be precise.)

Throughout a course, the rider's eyes are inseparably linked with the execution of his plan. If he uses his eyes poorly—if, for instance, he looks too late toward upcoming lines—he'll overshoot turns and/or miss distances. These are major errors that indicate he is not "riding out a plan" and that he doesn't appreciate the importance of putting his horse at a safe takeoff point at every fence. You should penalize such mistakes heavily.

Landing

As a rider lands over a fence, his leg should maintain the same fixed position it held during the approach to the obstacle and in the air. His seat should remain out of the saddle, so it won't interfere with the animal's balance, and his upper body should stay with the horse's motion to the ground, rather than being ahead of or behind it (fig. 11.18).

The worst leg fault a rider can commit on landing is letting the leg slip forward. This causes his seat to be thrust backward, behind the horse's motion, as the animal lands—a fault called "dropping back" (figs. 11.19 A & B). As he drops back, the rider may yank his horse in the mouth and/ or hit it in the back with his seat; and for these abuses, as well as for the unsafe position the rider puts himself in by being radically behind the

11.18 The rider is correctly keeping her heel down, leg on, and seat out of the saddle during landing.

horse's motion, you should penalize this fault severely. (A rider whose leg slips forward only on landing isn't considered to have gotten left, since "getting left" refers to the rider being behind the horse's motion at takeoff and/or at the peak of the jumping arc. The results of dropping back are similar to those of getting left; but dropping back is not penalized as severely because it presents a lesser chance of an accident, since the horse is almost on the ground when the fault occurs.)

Just as getting left and the leg slipping forward on landing are related, perching and the leg slipping backward on landing are related. Perching on takeoff and in midair places undue weight on the horse's front end, and the rider who perches at these points will generally maintain this overly forward position on landing. You will see him fall forward onto his hands for support, unable to support his upper body with his leg during landing (figs. 11.20 A & B). As perching

11.19 A & B The rider's leg is slipping forward on landing, causing her seat to "drop back" into the saddle (A). Whether or not the rider's leg shifts in the air, if the seat touches the saddle before landing, the rider must be penalized for dropping back. If the grip of the legs is lost so that the rider slides backward in the air (B), it is called "sliding in the tack." This is a more severe error than simply dropping back.

is preferable to getting left, the leg that slips backward on landing is preferable to the leg that slips forward, for the rider is at least with his horse as the animal lands, neither catching the horse in the mouth nor falling onto its back.

Performance

General Observations

In an equitation class over fences, a rider should enter the ring with an aura of purpose, having prepared his horse by warming up over a few fences in the schooling area and prepared himself by formulating his strategy for negotiating the obstacles. He should pick up a posting trot and maintain it until the horse completes the first quarter of the circle, at which time the rider sits the trot for a step or two and picks up the canter (fig. 11.21). Immediately, he should assume two-point position and increase his horse's rhythm until the animal reaches a pace that is suitable for the size of the fences and the distances between them.

It is important for a rider to make his circle big enough, for a small figure will limit the horse's length of stride, as well as pace, and encourage the animal to lean inward to catch its balance. Necessary pace adjustments—such as squeezing the horse forward if it is too dull, or half-halting if it is trying to lengthen stride and increase its pace—should be made during the circle, with the pace for the entire course being established before the horse completes the circle, so the rider can concentrate on maintaining the proper pace, rather than on establishing it, throughout the course.

If the course is set in such a way that the rider cannot make the standard circle at the end of the ring, he must find

11.20 A & B With his leg having slipped backward at takeoff (A), the rider relies upon his hands, rather than his leg, to be his main means of support as the horse is landing (B).

another path that will allow him to accomplish the circle's aim—to establish pace. If he fails to do so, penalize him.

According to the *USEF Rule Book*, the competitor may also circle at the completion of the round—which not only makes the trip more flowing, but also trains the horse to obediently pass the out-gate, rather than encouraging it to stop there. The final circle should be made at the same pace at which the round was ridden; and the downward transition that takes place before the horse leaves the ring should be forward and smooth, with the horse's hocks coming under it as the animal goes from the canter to the walk.

In equitation over fences, you seek many of the same qualities as in a performance on the flat: impulsion, bending, the horse being on the bit, collection in keeping with the difficulty of the test, and a look of discipline in both horse and rider. You should see no kicking, yanking, or clashing of aids (that is, aids working against one another); instead, the rider's legs, hands, and weight should be coordinated so well that they become "invisible aids" with the horse seeming to move around the course of its own volition. (Each competitor spends only a few seconds airborne during a class over fences, while the large remaining portion of the round is on the flat—that is, between fences. Consequently, flatwork often makes the winning difference in competitions over fences as well as those entirely on the flat.)

Penalize riders whose coordination of aids is poor according to the area in which they are weak; assess the greatest penalties for weaknesses related to leg position and assign less heavy penalties to other faults, following the order of severity described in the previous chapter on position. Consider the rider's position and use of aids as they affect the horse's performance between fences and in the air; but don't penalize a rider for his horse's poor form unless the rider's position or actions seem to be the cause.

For instance, if a horse doesn't fold its legs tightly over a fence, but the rider has made no error that would seem to have caused this fault, you should not mark the rider lower for his horse's loose jumping form. If, however, the rider

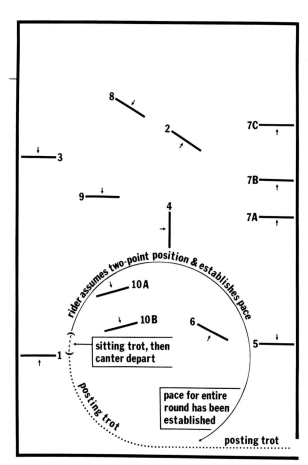

8

2

7C
↑

3
↓

7B
↑

9
↓

4
→

7A
↑

rider assumes two-point position & establishes pace

10 A
↓

10 B
↓

6
↗

5
↓

sitting trot, then
canter depart

1
↑

posting trot

pace for entire
round has been
established

posting trot

11.21 The initial circle allows the rider to establish pace for
the entire round. One of the major mistakes made by beginners
is making the circle too small, so the horse never reaches the
proper pace before the first fence.

perches on his horse and puts it at a deep takeoff spot, his
excessively forward position and poor placement of the horse
could reasonably be considered responsible for the horse's
poor jumping form, and the rider would be penalized.

Since it is the rider's responsibility to place the horse
at a good takeoff spot, you should severely penalize riders

who place their horses poorly, for a bad spot creates risks
for both horse and rider. A rider who "misses the distance"
and drives his horse into a poor spot deserves the greatest penalty, for he has not only chosen poorly, but has also
forced his horse into this difficult position for takeoff. If a
rider realizes the spot is not going to be good and unsuc-
cessfully tries to adjust, the penalty you assess him for the
bad spot shouldn't be as great as your penalty for the rider
who seemed unaware his spot was bad and kept driving his
horse into it. If a third competitor sees the spot is not going
to be good and is successful in correcting it, but a little rough
in doing so, penalize him less than either of the previous two.
Finally, if a fourth rider sees he will not be able to get to the
correct spot without an adjustment and manages to make it
subtly, give him the best marks of the four.

Besides being responsible for the correct takeoff spot,
the rider should be in control of the horse's leads during a
course. If a horse is approaching a corner on the counter
canter, the rider should ask the animal to do a flying change,
so the horse will be balanced around the turn. (If the rider
has difficulty performing the flying change, it would be
smart for him to practice landing out of the air onto the correct lead, thereby avoiding the entire issue of flying changes
in most instances. By applying an outside leg in the air, the
rider can generally cause his horse to land on the inside lead;
after a few practice sessions, most horses will land on the
correct lead every time they're asked, as long as the rider is
diligent about giving the aid and does so whenever the horse
must land on a certain lead—that is, whenever the animal is
negotiating a turn within the course or approaching a corner of the ring.)

Both the horse that performs the flying change prior to
the corner and the horse that lands on the proper lead after
a fence are correct; but horses that cross canter or coun-

ter canter the corners are incorrect. Penalize a cross canter around an entire corner more than a counter canter around an entire corner, for although the counter canter causes the horse to be unbalanced on the corner—and encourages the horse to drift to the outside of the turn on the approach to the fence—it is a normal sequence of the horse's feet and, therefore, does not look disjointed; whereas a cross canter around the entire corner causes the horse to be unbalanced, threatens the rider's safety when the horse attempts to jump from this disjointed gait, and looks terrible.

You should, however, pin a rider whose horse cross canters only a few steps before switching to the correct lead above a rider whose horse counter canters the entire corner. The issue is balance: the horse that cross canters briefly before switching is on the correct lead for most of the corner and is balanced for takeoff, but the horse that counter canters through the corner is unbalanced all the way around the turn and tends to drift to the outside on the approach to the upcoming fence.

Tests over Fences

Test 6
Jump low obstacles at a trot as well as at a canter. The maximum height and spread for a trot jump is 3' for horses, 2' for ponies.

By asking a rider to trot a fence within a course, you can further test his control of the horse and his timing to the fences. The rider should look for a distance to the obstacle and adjust the horse's steps to help the animal meet the proper takeoff point. The decision to sit or post the trot on the approach should be left up to the rider. When a trot fence is being

judged, neither the sitting nor posting option should be considered preferable, for both options are equally difficult.

Faults that can be committed by riders during Test 6 are, from most to least severe: (1) allowing the horse to refuse the fence; (2) "getting left" in the air; (3) letting the horse break gait on the approach to the fence—for instance, the common error of allowing the horse to canter the last step or two at a "trot fence"; and (4) "jumping on the horse's neck"— that is, getting ahead of the horse's motion at takeoff.

Test 7
Jump obstacles on figure eight course.

Use this test to measure the rider's ability to get the horse to land on the correct lead after a fence, to perform flying changes, or to jump fences on an angle (figs. 11.22 A & B).

As the first course is set (see fig. 11.22 A), the best option is to land on the proper lead out of the air, rather than attempt flying changes on the turns. To go from fence 1 to fence 2, the rider should apply left leg pressure in the air over fence 1, asking the horse to land on the right lead so that it will be balanced on the approach to fence 2. In the air over fence 2, he should use right leg pressure to ask the horse to land on the left lead, to assure a balanced approach to fence 3.

Although landing on the left lead is the better option after fence 3, a horse that lands on the right lead can perform a flying change at point A and still have a smooth performance, since there is enough space between fences 3 and 4 for either option. (The rider should make a flying change just as his horse starts into a corner. If the change occurs after the horse is in the turn, mark it as having been made late.)

Negotiating fences 4, 5, and 6, the rider should ask the horse to land on the left lead over fence 4 and on the right

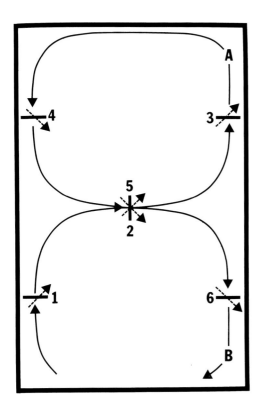

11.22 A In Course A, the solid line traces the logical path for negotiating these obstacles, while the dotted line shows the option of jumping fences at an angle—a poor option in this case, because the fences are set so close to the railing.

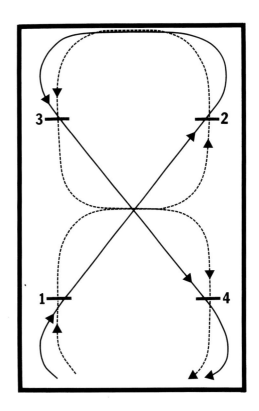

11.22 B In Course B, the solid line marks the path for jumping obstacles on an angle, while the dotted line shows the route that would be taken if the rider decided to demonstrate flying changes across the center line.

lead over 5. He again has the option of landing on the right lead over 6 or performing a flying change (by point B) if his horse doesn't land on the proper lead.

A rider who cannot get his horse to land on a particular lead is at a great disadvantage in this test, since a horse that lands on the wrong lead must either counter canter to the next fence—and have its balance threatened—or collect and perform a flying change, which costs precious footage in competition where the distances are set long. In addition, when a rider has to concern himself with a flying change, his concentration on the distance to the upcoming fence is interrupted.

When the fences are set next to the railing (see fig. 11.22 A), the flying change is the only option for a rider who can't get his horse to land on a desired lead dependably; but when the fences are set away from the railing (see fig. 11.22 B), the rider may choose either to perform a flying change on the center-line or to jump the fences at an angle, with no change of leads across the middle of the ring. Both options have their drawbacks, for although flying changes disrupt length of stride for a few seconds and make finding a good distance to the next fence more difficult, jumping fences at an angle increases the likelihood of runouts and knockdowns. Since angling the fences is the riskier choice, you should give credit to the rider who carries out this more difficult option successfully.

Test 9

Ride without stirrups (riders must be allowed option to cross stirrups).

Not only should a rider appear as secure without stirrups as with them, he should also be able to "get the job done" as well. Without stirrups in a class over fences, the rider's body should be positioned generally the same as it was when he had his feet in the irons. The only significant difference is that without support from his stirrups, it is acceptable for the rider to maintain a "modified three-point" position between the fences, rather than two-point—that is, his crotch will be touching the saddle, and his body will be inclined 10 degrees in front of the vertical, rather than 20 degrees. At the fence, however, he must hold his seat out of the saddle during takeoff, while in the air, and on landing, so he won't interfere with the horse's back. (The rider may also use "extreme three-point" position at particularly difficult places in the course, such as during tight turns or short distances; but he should not maintain this extreme position—with his upper body on the vertical and seat riveted in the saddle—during the entire course.)

Test 9 is not frightening to an experienced, fit athlete who believes he can turn in a trip without stirrups that is comparable to one with them; but it can be an alarming test for a weak, inexperienced rider who is afraid he will not be able to stay on without stirrups. For this reason, Test 9 should be reserved for advanced riders. (See also "Equitation on the Flat: Tests".)

Test 10

Jump low obstacles at a walk as well as at a canter. The maximum height and spread for a walk jump is 2'.

When a rider asks his horse to jump from the walk, he must maintain a marching rhythm to the obstacle so that the horse won't stop in front of the fence due to lack of impulsion. He must also keep the horse straight to the fence and focus on a point beyond the obstacle, subtly driving the animal toward the focal point so that it is clear that the rider wishes to go over the obstacle. The horse should maintain the walk until takeoff, not breaking into a trot or canter the last step or two.

Faults that can be committed during Test 10, from most to least severe, are as follows: (1) allowing the horse to refuse the fence; (2) "getting left" in the air; (3) letting the horse break gait on the approach to the fence; and (3) "jumping up on the horse's neck," ahead of the motion at takeoff.

Test 16

Change horses. This test is the equivalent of two tests.

Although Test 16 is popular in high level competitions, such as the Medal and Maclay finals, it should be used with discretion, for a young rider on a strange horse is a combination that lends itself to uncertain results. The fact that the rider was forced to get on an unfamiliar horse in order to complete the competition is legally questionable in the event the child is injured; and, in addition, there is the problem of fairness in putting riders on horses that may not be trained as well as their own.

Since it is common knowledge that horses must be trained in order to give proper responses to the rider's aids, it should also be recognized that the rider who has put in the most time and effort on his mount and has refined his animal's responses to the aids will be at a disadvantage when he has to compete on another rider's horse that is not trained as well and therefore is not as responsive to the rider. Although the better rider would be able to improve his competitor's horse if given time to work the animal, it can hardly be expected of the rider to remake the horse while competing over the course and to produce the beautiful round he is capable of making on his own mount. In effect then, the lesser rider is given the advantage during a switch, for he is handed the better-trained horse and can "cash in" on his competitor's talent and effort.

Much is left up to fate in Test 16, for many of the rider's considerations in planning his performance on his own horse are wasted when he has to get on another person's horse. For instance, the smart rider will have chosen a horse that suits his build and dressed himself to look attractive on that horse; but when he is asked to switch onto another animal, his build may not suit the horse's conformation and his clothing may look ugly with the horse's coloring. If his competitor has been lucky enough not to have these problems, then the mismatched horse-rider combination is at a disadvantage even before the ride-off has begun.

Since Test 16 is being used today, however, we must consider what it is intended to prove. The idea behind this test is that a good rider can switch onto various horses and ride them all well, while a mediocre rider may be able to ride his own horse well but will not be capable of getting on a strange horse and turning in a trip of equal quality.

When you call for this test, judge the rider's position and performance by the criteria you use when considering riders on their own horses. Riders who get into a problem with a strange horse but attempt to correct it should place above those who have trouble but passively allow the horse to be in control. This theory holds true whether the rider is on his own horse or on an unfamiliar animal: the rider who recognizes a problem and attempts to correct it should be rewarded for his knowledge and effort by being pinned above the rider who does nothing when placed in a similar situation. Of course, better than these two would be the rider who turns in such a good trip on a strange horse that he looks as though he's ridden the animal all his life. This would be the ideal rider in Test 16.

What to Expect from Equitation Riders

Beginners

As mentioned numerous times throughout this book, the most important feature of a rider's position is his leg. In judging a class of beginners on the flat or over fences, reward riders who have worked hard to develop good leg position and who use their legs properly to propel the horse forward—squeezing, rather than kicking the animal. All abuses (for example, yanking the horse in the mouth, kicking it in the sides, or getting left over the fence) are severely penalized, for it is at this elementary level that riders must learn to be sensitive to horses as living beings, and nothing brings this home as well as losing a class. Intentional abuse, such as jerking or kicking out of anger, should be penalized more than inadvertent abuse, for example, getting left in the air and grabbing mane in an effort to stay off the horse's mouth.

As for use of the crop, it is better if a rider can keep his horse going forward without the use of a stick; but it is preferable for a beginner to use his stick to keep the horse moving than to hesitate to use it and let the horse break gait (on the flat or over fences), add a stride between fences, or stop at an obstacle. As long as the rider uses the stick properly—that is, on the horse's flesh just behind the rider's leg; in degree appropriate to the severity of the disobedience; and timed properly with the occurrence of the fault—the use of the stick is not a major fault in a class of beginners. If a rider uses the stick anywhere in front of the saddle, however, he should be severely penalized for improper use of this artificial aid.

Generally speaking, beginners should not wear spurs, for most of them don't have the stationary leg position to be able to wear spurs without accidentally abusing the horse.

THE BIG PICTURE
The Engine Is in the Rear
"...the front legs only go where the hind legs push them."

When horses refuse to go forward, it is not uncommon to see the crop applied to the front, rather than the rear of the animal. A blow on the neck is startling, not motivating, and can cause a horse to run sideways in fear, rather than move forward as desired. It may let the horse know it has done something wrong, but in no way helps to correct the problem.

A horse's engine is in the rear—its hind legs. When the crop is properly applied in a tactful way, just behind the rider's calf, it motivates the horse to push forward with its hind legs, which is the direction the rider wants the balking horse to go, whether through a puddle or over a fence.

Part of the problem in applying the stick behind the calf may be the rider's reluctance to switch the reins into one hand so the crop can be applied with the other. When a horse balks, especially in front of a fence, fear can overcome a rider so that he no longer thinks clearly about the proper response. He simply applies the stick somewhere on the shoulder of the horse as a punishment, without giving any thought to motivating the horse's source of power—the haunches.

It is also common to see a rider holding the reins tightly after a horse balks. This restricts the horse, rather than encouraging it to move forward. The correct response would be for the rider to drive the horse forward with his legs, spur, and stick applied behind the calf, while easing off the rein pressure to encourage the horse to go forward. The rider should also keep his body slightly behind the motion of the horse and may even use his seat as a driving aid, to guarantee that the horse continues forward past the point at which it balked.

The more advanced a rider becomes, the more he realizes how important the hind legs of the horse really are, for the front legs only go where the hind legs push them. Everything we do as riders should be with the hind legs foremost in our minds. This is often difficult because we are normally much more aware of the things in front of us, within our line of sight, than the things behind us—"out of sight, out of mind."

Through concentration, however, you can learn to keep the hind legs foremost in your thoughts, so that even the slightest loss of energy in the haunches is recognized and dealt with appropriately. The application of the crop toward the rear of the horse indicates an understanding of the function of the horse's hind end. Even the youngest rider should be cognizant of where the engine is located in his equine vehicle.

However, if a beginner wears spurs and uses them properly—that is, uses them only when needed and doesn't stab the horse in the sides, but rather presses the spurs into the flesh—he should not be penalized.

If the rider uses voice commands—such as "whoa"—to slow the horse down, his voice should be so soft that it is audible only to the horse, not to the judge. Loud commands should be penalized at even this beginning level, for equitation is founded on the concept of nonverbal communication between rider and horse. Most annoying is the competitor who provides a running commentary during his performance. His accounts are intended to convince onlookers that it is not he and his poor job of riding, but rather the horse that is responsible for the terrible performance. Comments such as, "Come on, Salty. We've done this lots of times before," uttered as the horse stops at the fence, indicate that the rider is not concentrating on his performance, but is unduly concerned with what spectators think of him as he finds himself in this embarrassing situation. Penalize the orator severely.

Clucking to encourage a horse forward should be used discreetly, for a rider who clucks around the entire course demonstrates the ineffectiveness of his leg. A cluck from a rider at a single difficult place in the course should not be penalized; but if clucking is noticeably a habit, it should be faulted. In comparing the cluck to talking, however, talking is ten times worse, for it is completely out of the realm of what the rider should be doing.

In all levels of equitation competition, riders must be able to get the proper diagonals and leads. If a beginner picks up the wrong diagonal or lead but corrects the mistake immediately, he should be penalized only mildly, for it is obvious he knows what he should be doing. If, however, a beginner goes around the ring for long periods of time and does not realize he is on the wrong diagonal or lead, he must be severely penalized.

When performing the canter depart, the beginner must not lean over his horse's shoulder to throw the horse on the lead or to check for the correct lead. In checking both leads and diagonals, he should keep his upper body in the center of the horse and tilt only his head (or, preferably, keep his head up and let his eyes glance down) to check the motion of the horse's leg—the outside foreleg for diagonals, the inside foreleg for leads. Give a heavier penalty to the rider who leans over his horse's shoulder to "throw it on the lead," than to one who leans to check the diagonal or lead.

In judging beginners, you are looking for riders who have a clear understanding of "reward" and "punishment." In simplest terms, punishment is the use of any of the natural or artificial aids, and reward is the lack of punishment. When the rider squeezes the horse forward with his leg (natural aid), or encourages the horse forward with his stick (artificial aid), he is punishing the horse for not going forward at the desired pace. As soon as the horse achieves the proper pace, the rider relaxes his aids as a means of reward. Similarly, if the rider squeezes his hand muscles (natural aid) in an attempt to slow the horse down, then the hand is a punishment. As the horse slows down, the hand muscles relax as a reward to the animal. It is important for a beginner to practice the separation of driving aids—such as the leg and stick—from restraining aids—such as pressure on the reins—so he won't "clash aids" by simultaneously asking the horse for opposing responses.

In higher levels of riding, the concept of reward and punishment becomes more difficult for the rider to comprehend when he is told to collect his horse by using what would appear to be two opposing aids—leg pressure, to create impulsion in the haunches, and hand pressure, to half-halt the horse in order to balance its front end. However, a talented rider, through much "trial and tribulation" on the flat, will eventually understand how the principles of reward and punishment hold true at even the highest level of riding; and, using this knowledge, he will be able to produce the maximum quality performance with minimum anxiety in the horse.

When judging the beginner, however, we are not expecting collection, but are mostly concerned with the rider's basic understanding of reward and punishment as it relates to simple tasks. A beginner should know not to use the gas pedal (leg) and brakes (hand) at the same time. He should realize that to turn a horse to the right, he must ease off of the left rein, and vice versa. Basically, he must understand how to avoid fighting himself, so he can prevent the clashing of aids from leading to a battle with his horse.

In all levels of riding, a good motto is: "Do only what it takes to get what you want." This is particularly pertinent to beginners, who are apt to kick or jerk before they have attempted to squeeze.

Intermediate Riders

By "intermediate riders," I don't mean competitors who show in classes restricted by 12 wins or less; rather, this term is used loosely to encompass all riders past the beginner stage, but not up to an advanced level. By the intermediate stage, a rider's position should be well founded, offering security and allowing him to be effective. Not only should he be able to perform at the walk, trot, canter, and hand gallop around the ring, but also he should be capable of riding basic school figures, such as a serpentine or figure eight with a simple change of leads.

At this stage, the rider should not have to resort to his stick to reinforce a weak leg, but should only go to the stick if the horse commits a serious error—such as refusing a fence or persistently adding a stride at the base of obstacles. If he has any doubt his horse will approach each obstacle willingly, he should wear spurs (as well as carry a stick) so he can use this more subtle aid before resorting to the obvious.

An intermediate rider should check the diagonal or lead by glancing, rather than tilting his head, if he is not able to feel whether he is right or wrong. If the rider picks up the wrong lead or diagonal, he should be severely penalized for making these elementary mistakes—although he can redeem himself somewhat if he immediately notices the error and corrects it. (Since it is easier for a rider to feel he has the wrong lead or diagonal on a corner—because the turn makes the lack of balance more obvious—you should penalize a competitor who travels on the wrong lead or diagonal on the straightaway and does not notice his mistake until he is in the corner more than one who is able to recognize the problem while still on the straightaway.)

At the intermediate level, a rider should be able to keep his horse on the rail by holding it there with his inside leg, rather than leading it there with an outside opening rein. He should be able to bend his horse, keep a steady rhythm at the various gaits, make smooth upward and downward transitions, and maintain contact on the animal's mouth and sides on the flat and between fences.

During a course, he should try to place his horse at a safe takeoff spot, rather than let the horse get there "any old way," as beginners—who are mainly preoccupied with staying on—are likely to do. On course, he should look as though he is trying to ride out a plan. At this stage, the crest release, rather than grabbing mane, would be appropriate in the air.

Advanced Riders

You should expect a great deal more from advanced riders than from intermediate-level competitors. Not only should an advanced rider be able to maintain steady contact with the horse's mouth and sides, he should also collect his horse into a medium frame for the basic flat tests—walk, trot, and canter—and lengthen or shorten the frame for more difficult tests, such as those required in the USEF Show Jumping Talent Search Class or included in Tests 1–19.

Emphasis on performance increases at this level because many advanced riders have attractive, as well as secure, positions, so the deciding factor becomes quality of performance. On the flat, an advanced rider's horse should move forward with impulsion and stay on the bit at all times. From head to tail, it should be slightly bent in the direction of travel on the corners of the ring and straight in its body on the long sides of the arena. An incorrect diagonal or lead is inexcusable at this level, for the rider should feel the error coming and correct the problem before it is visible to the judge. Even one step of the wrong diagonal or lead, showing lack of feeling in the rider, is penalized. An advanced rider should concentrate on his horse's source of power—its haunches—and keep the hocks engaged by coordinating leg pressure and half-halts. If the rider is insensitive in doing this, his horse's angry expression will point out the problem to you.

When riding a course of fences, the advanced competitor should have a plan and adhere to it as much as possible, only making alterations where unforeseen problems necessitate them. You should take into consideration the riders' strategies when comparing two trips of similar quality and give credit to the one who chooses the more difficult options in a course. Riders at this level should be "jumping out of hand," so they can control their horses in the air as well as on the ground, making the difficult options feasible.

In addition to displaying all the desirable features discussed in the equitation chapters, the advanced rider's performance should demonstrate one more significant quality: empathy between horse and rider. When watching horse and rider, you should feel that they are working together for a common goal, that the animal is not just being obedient to a master, but that it is performing with "heart," trying to please the person whose words it cannot understand, but whom it understands just the same.

13

The Judge's Card

Numerical Scoring

There are three types of symbols used in marking the judge's card: abbreviations, hieroglyphics, and numbers. Limited time and space make these symbols necessary, for if you try to use longhand, you will not have as much time to watch the performance and your card will be messy and confusing.

Abbreviations are made up mostly of consonants suggesting the word or words that describe an error—such as "Tw" for *twist,* or "LF" for *loose form.* When using abbreviations, capitalize only the first letter of a word, so that it will be clear whether your consonants are part of one word, as in the case of "Twist," or of two words, as in "Loose Form" (see list of abbreviations beginning on p. 335).

Hieroglyphics are pictorial representations of your comments. These lines, dots, arrows, and other symbols will not only save space but also make the card easier to read than if you try to use abbreviations alone.

At the completion of each round, when you have finished using abbreviations and hieroglyphics to record your observations, give the performance a numerical score (figs. 13.1 A & B). If the score is 75 or above, place it on a separate sheet of paper and write the rider's number next to the score, so that at the end of the class you will immediately be able to give the results to the announcer (fig. 13.2). If you do not have enough scores above 75 to pin the class, refer to your card and list the next highest scores until you reach the number of placings you need (eight numbers for classes requiring a jog and six for classes not requiring a jog, unless the prize list states otherwise). At the other extreme, if you have an abundance of horses scoring above 75, you can adjust your cutoff point higher during the class.

JUDGES' SCORECARD
CLASSES OVER FENCES

CLASS NO. 12
Large Junior Hunter

1	2	3	4	5	6	7	8	9	10
71	73	42	54	48	39	29	27		

NO.	1	2	3	4	5	6 n8	7	8	9	10	11	12			TOTAL
54	—	∧	—	—	—	╭—	—	—					Gm		81
39	—	—	—	∧	—	∧⌐	¢	—					Fm		68
71	—	—	—	—	—	— —	—	—					Em		92
66	∧	⅔∧	—	—	1	⌐—	—	®					Fm	®	45
27	—	—	—	—	∧	—1	—						Pm	+1	55
73	—	—	—	—	—	— —	—	—					Gm		90
42	—	—	—	╭	— —	—	—						Gm		85
101	—	—	(fall)	—	—	— —	—						Fm	Ⓔ	E
29	⌐	—	⌐	⌐	—	⌐⌐	—	⌐					Gm	Ⓖ	60
48	—	—	—	—	∧	— —	—	—					FM		80

A

JUDGES' SCORECARD
CLASSES OVER FENCES

CLASS NO. 15
Equitation Over Fences (15-17)

1	2	3	4	5	6	7	8	9	10
73	71	29	42	54	39				

NO.	1	2	3	4	5	6 n8	7	8	9	10	11	12			TOTAL
54	—	⊥↓∧	—	—	—	╭—	—	—					GP		79
39	—	—	—	∧	—	∧⌐	¢	—					FP		72
71	—	—	—	—	—	— —	—	—					GP		90
66	∧	⅔∧	—	—	1	⌐—	—	®					FP	®	45
27	—	—	—	—	∧	—1	—						FP	+1	55
73	—	—	—	—	—	— —	—	—					EP		92
42	—	—	—	╭	— —	—	—						FP		80
101	—	—	(fall)	—	—	— —	—						PP	Ⓔ	E
29	—	—	—	╭	— —	—	—						FP		85
48	⌐	⌐	—	—	∧⌐	—	⌐	—					PP	Ⓖ	67

B

13.1 A & B The mock card A above shows symbols and scores as they might appear in a Large Junior Hunter class. Compare these symbols and scores to those in B, which shows the same trips when scored as an Equitation over Fences class. Notice that the horses' general way of moving and specific form errors over fences affect the hunter scores in A, while the riders' general position between fences and specific position errors over fences affect the equitation scores in B.

Many shows provide a walkie-talkie or head-set, so the judge can call in the placings to the announcer. If, however, you have to send the results through a runner, write down your list again and send the copy, so that you will have a list in hand for the jog. Do not write the results at the top of your card until you have finished judging the jog, for a lame horse will change all the placings below it.

Basically, numerical scoring is patterned after the scoring system used at schools:

90s	Excellent A
80s	Good B
70s	Fair C
60s	Poor D
50s	Failing F

Think of a score of 90 as a "basic ceiling," with only a horse of exceptional ability—that is, one that is both an excellent jumper and an excellent mover—being able to score above this mark. You also want to think of 95 as an "absolute ceiling," so that your scores will not reach too close to the real ceiling of 100. By trying to cap the scores at 95, you still have a little room in case you are faced with scoring a number of outstanding trips in the 90s. (This is a problem only at the largest shows in the country.)

Reserve scores above 90 for horses of excellent quality that turn in wonderful trips. For horses that have inherent limitations, the scores should never move above 90. Some examples of this are horses that are good jumpers and good movers, but are not excellent in either category; horses that

#12 Large Jr.	
#	Score
71	92
73	90
42	85
54	81
48	80
39	68
29	60
27	55

#15 Equitation O/F	
#	Score
73	92
71	90
29	85
42	80
54	79
39	72
48	67

13.2 It is helpful to have a separate sheet of paper on which the top scores can be listed in proper pinning order. The sheet on the left shows the pinning list for the Large Junior Hunter class in fig. 13.1 A, while the sheet on the right shows the pinning list for the Equitation Over Fences class in fig. 13.1 B.

are excellent movers, but only adequate jumpers; and horses that are excellent jumpers, but only adequate movers. With the very best trip each of these could turn in, their scores would never go beyond 90. When ridden well, these are the horses that score in the 80s.

To score in the 70s, a good horse—that is, a good jumper and good mover—would have to make some substantial errors. Untalented horses, however, can easily fall into the 70s. A poor mover would not have to have many jumping faults to reach the 70s, and a horse with chronically poor form in the air would have no trouble falling to the 70s or below.

The 60s and 50s represent very bad trips. Most judges have a set of predetermined scores to use for common major errors. I have provided a chart comparing these predeter-

mined scores for hunter and equitation classes, since the division rules differ. Asterisks (*) identify equitation scores that differ from hunter scores.

Note: According to the *USEF Rule Book,* in the Equitation Division, "The following constitute major faults and can be cause for elimination: (a) a refusal; (b) loss of stirrup; (c) trotting while on course when not part of a test; and (d) loss of reins." However, I have never known any of these to be penalized by elimination. Usually, they are scored as follows.

Hunter	Equitation
Trotting on course 60	Trotting on course 60
Very poor trip 51–59	Very poor trip 51–59
Dangerous fence 55	Dangerous fence 55
Adding a stride in an in-and-out 55	Adding a stride in an in-and-out 55
	*Loss of stirrup 55
	*Loss of reins 55
Knockdown 50	*Knockdown (penalized at judge's discretion)
1 Refusal 45	1 Refusal 45
2 Refusals 35	2 Refusals 35
3 Refusals *Elimination*	3 Refusals *Elimination*
Fall *Elimination*	Fall *Elimination*
Off course *Elimination*	Off course *Elimination*

For "trotting on course" to receive a 60, there must be a clear break from the canter, not just a skip behind. The late Gene Cunningham, a well-respected horseman and judge, used to say, "If you can't post to it, it isn't a trot." A skip behind—that is, a break of gait in the hind feet, but not in the front—is penalized at the judge's discretion.

For a "very poor trip" to receive a score between 51 and 59, it should be so bad that if you deducted points for all the errors, the score would be 50 or less. You stop at 50 to make sure you don't score a bad trip below one that had a knock-down (exception: equitation classes) or refusal.

When an automatic score of 55 is assigned because of the way a single fence was jumped, the obstacle must have been jumped so dangerously that it made you gasp! This is not just a risky spot but one that nearly "bought the farm" for the rider's family.

Other than giving these predetermined scores for major errors, you arrive at a numerical score based on the deduction of points for each error committed. Do not deduct for the error as it occurs, but use the symbols previously discussed to "draw a picture" of the way the course is ridden,

so that later you can bring each trip to mind if you need to-for instance, if two or more horses have the same score and you have to break the tie. At the end of each trip, starting with a score of 90, deduct points for errors committed. Use a 5.point deduction for a medium-deep spot as the standard around which all other scores are based.

For horses that are in the category of excellent jumpers and movers, scores above 90 will be based on "plus points." These are additional points added to reflect the quality of performance. Again, you are thinking of 95 as an "absolute ceiling," so do not get carried away and score too high when you get your first really good trip in a class.

Too many horses scoring in the 90s is not the usual

THE BIG PICTURE
The Evolution of Hunter Seat Competition
By George H. Morris

In the old days, two types of judges were invited to horse shows. Those most often asked were very socially accepted people, who—it was hoped—also knew something about horses. Contrary to belief, lots of those men and women were exceptional horsemen and horsewomen; they had been brought up all their lives to participate in many different horse sports. Not quite so frequently, the others who were asked to judge were local professionals who were also (almost) socially acceptable. These men (rarely women) were usually good, solid horsemen of the old school who had worked their way up to prominence. Because of the social whirl surrounding even a one-day show (let alone the long major shows!), "party manners" were a prerequisite to an invitation.

Nowadays things are different. Horse showing has become a very serious, competitive, and expensive sport. The social aspect, while still evident, has definitely taken a back seat to the game at hand. It is for this reason that show management, though still prone to ask the fun friend, is under a great deal of pressure to invite a "popular" judge. This man or woman is conscientious, knows his job well, and keeps more of the people happy more of the time than some of the less "popular" judges. The big problem in judging today is nobody's fault. The most talented and progressive teachers, trainers, and riders are too busy showing to have much time to judge. The judges, therefore, are sometimes just a bit behind the newest and, perhaps, the best ways of doing things. I say "perhaps" because sound and progressive techniques can often be misrepre-sented, misunderstood, or exaggerated. In this instance, some of the old beats the new.

Over the years, the sport of showing hunters has changed a great deal. We used to see lots of middleweight and heavyweight horses, both Thoroughbred and half-bred. These horses had lots of bone and strong quarters, were good gallopers, and could often jump a big fence. Then, the overwhelming number of horses showing as hunters became lightweights. Although these horses often were "pretty," moved well, and jumped low fences in good form, they generally didn't have the substance to do too much more. Funnily enough, through the importation of European Warmbloods, we are again seeing bigger horses coming back into the hunter ring and competing successfully. The pendulum swings!

Hunters go differently today, too. Up until the mid-1950s, the emphasis was on pace and a brilliant, long jumping effort. Most of the horses were not schooled; they bordered on being runaways. Woe to the fellow on a mediocre jumper who came in "wrong." He usually stood on his head! Horses in under-saddle classes went on loose reins, cutting their corners. Contact and bending? What on earth were they talking about!

Today we want balance and precision. Speed? Why, that is hardly noticed. Eight jumps exactly alike, working on straight lines and bent turns is what wins the blue ribbon. The schooling of horses has finally come into its own. Time marches on and things get better. Now it's the "short option," not your life!

The Hunter Seat Equitation Division has changed dramatically, too. Of course, the training of a rider always has to precede the training of his horse. The animal can do only what the rider asks him to do. Again, the big turning point came in the first half of the 1950s. While the forward seat had been around for half a century, few riders were among the "enlightened" until after the Second World War. Heels down, eyes up, lean forward, follow the mouth were techniques foreign to those "seat-of-the-panters" who only knew the old "hunting" seat. The '60s and '70s saw the influence of dressage. And the forward seat can now be considered a balanced seat—neither too forward nor too backward—and most classic in appearance. Truly we have a unique American style coupled with marvelous control. And this is due in large part to our Equitation Division.

Where will judging and showing go from here? Not likely to anything radically new. Horses will be horses, and riders will be riders, and good sound basics will prevail. We'll always have to be on guard against the trendy, the mannered, and the exaggerated. After all, only the horse will really know. And he'll always tell us...if we were born to listen.

George Morris began his stellar career by winning the Medal and Maclay Finals at age 14. He went on to achieve success as an international competitor and coach, as well as becoming a USEF judge with "Big R" status in hunters, jumpers, and hunter-seat equitation. Between 1958 and 1960, he rode on eight winning Nations Cup teams and was a member of the gold medal team in the 1959 Pan American Games and silver medal team at the 1960 Rome Olympics. His students have medaled in the 1984, 1992, 1996, 2004, and 2008 Olympic Games. He currently serves as chef d'equipe of the U.S. Equestrian Team and in 2007 received the coveted USEF Lifetime Achievement Award.

problem for judges. Most will be dealing with a number of scores in the 80s and 70s, or possibly below. It will suffice to put a series of plusses if you find you have too many horses scoring the same. (For Classics, just hold up your score, even if it is the same as an earlier one, for the announced score is the average from the two or three judges present. Even at small shows that hold a Classic-type competition using only one judge, there is no problem in holding up the same score as for a previous trip because the final score will be the average of each horse's scores for the two rounds).

It is helpful in judging classes over fences to put a circle around a major error—such as a refusal, a knockdown, an added stride in an in-and-out, trotting on course, or elimination—and to make note of it in your space for comments following the trip, so that you will make "double sure" not to overlook the error in tallying your score. If the competition is terrible and/or the class very small, you may have to pin a horse that has a major fault, such as a knockdown or refusal, but generally these faults would put a hunter out of the ribbons. Of course, an eliminating fault—such as a third refusal or a fall—must not be pinned even if there are ribbons left over.

In numerical scoring, as with everything else, practice makes perfect. If you use this system all the time, you will not feel uncomfortable when your score is displayed to the public during a Classic.

Back-to-Back Classes

Back-to-back classes are two hunter classes in the same division and section that are held simultaneously in a ring. The rider can perform over the first course, stay in the ring, then perform over the second course; or he can leave after the first trip and come back later to ride the second course. This format is intimidating to novice judges, for it requires scoring intermittently on two cards.

Here are a few tips to make judging back-to-back classes easier:

1   Number your cards with a large "1" or "2" in the top left-hand corner so that you can easily locate each card for the first and second trip.

2   At the top of each card, draw a line representing the first fence, placing it at the correct angle in the ring and drawing an arrow to show the direction in which it should be jumped. Also, write what type of fence it is. This will help you know if the horse is starting over the wrong fence or if you are about to score the performance on the wrong card.

3   Write the courses out at the top of the cards. For instance, outside-inside-outside-inside would tell you the horse should jump the line of fences next to the rail, a diagonal line, a second line of fences next to the rail, and a final diagonal line. Even simpler is a course with an outside line, two diagonal lines, and a final outside line. It can be marked outside-8-outside, with the "8" describing the shape formed by the two diagonal lines (figs. 13.3 A–D).

4   If you are judging a class and think a horse is performing over the wrong course, but are not sure, keep scoring the animal wherever you started writing. You can check your cards at the end of the trip to see if the horse was off course or if you started scoring on the wrong card. If the error was yours, go ahead and write the horse's number on the proper card, assign a numerical score, and transfer the symbols later as you have time. Remember to strike the number and symbols from the wrong card so that you won't pin the horse in the wrong class.

5   Keep a small notebook on hand that you can use for judging back-to-back classes, so that the first round is always on a page to the left and the second round on the page to the right. At the top of each page, mark "#"

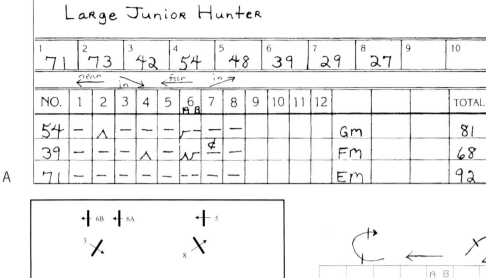

NO.	1	2	3	4	5	6 A B	7	8	9	10	11	12				TOTAL
54	—	∧	—	—	—	⌐—	—	—					Gm			81
39	—	—	—	∧	—	∿⌐	¢	—					Fm			68
71	—	—	—	—	—	——	—	—					Em			92

A

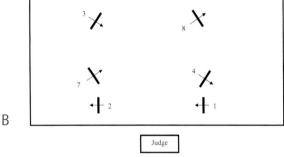

B

13.3 A–D Another way to remember the course is to show the direction each line is jumped by marking in the space above the boxes where the fence numbers are shown. The markings in A represent the course in B. This notation is particularly useful in equitation and jumper classes, where the courses are more complicated. The markings in C represent the course in D.

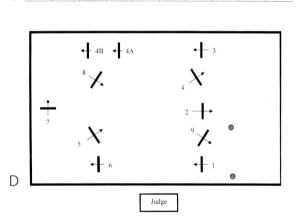

to the left and "score" to the right, so that after each round you can enter the rider's number and numerical score on a ladder in pinning order.

General Impressions

In both hunter and equitation classes, there will be space on the judge's card for "comments" just after the numbered boxes

designating each jump. For hunters, this space should be used to mark the horse's general way of going: "EM" for excellent mover, "GM" for good mover, "FM" for fair mover, and "PM" for poor mover. Coupled with the specific markings in the boxes, these comments give you the complete story of the horse's performance. For horses that are only "fair" or "poor" movers, deduct points in addition to the points deducted for jumping errors. A "poor mover" would receive about a 10-point deduction; a "fair mover" would receive about a 5-point deduction; a "good mover" would receive no deducted points; and an "excellent mover" would receive from about 1 to 3 "plus points" according to how well it moved.

In judging equitation classes, the area for "comments" is used to remark on the rider's basic position, which includes not only how he sits but how he uses his aids: "EP" for excellent position, "GP" for good position, "FP" for fair position, and "PP" for poor position. These general impressions enable you to consider not only the riders' position over the fences but also their basic riding ability on course. "Poor position" describes the rider who has few, if any, of the basics; "fair position" describes the rider who has a minimal number of position errors or whose angles are good, but who is weak or a little loose; "good position" describes the rider who is basically correct and effective in the use of his position; and "excellent position" describes the rider who is built beautifully, has the correct position, and is effective with his aids—a rider with "style." Riders with a "fair" or "poor" position should have points deducted in addition to those reflecting their position over fences. A "poor" rider receives about a 10-point deduction, a "fair" rider receives a 5-point deduction, a "good" rider receives no point deduction, and an "excellent" rider receives between 1 and 3 "plus points" according to the quality of his riding.

You can make comments to help yourself remember each horse or rider, but never write the riders' or horses' names. If an exhibitor asks to see a judge's card, a name beside a number might give the impression that the judge is relying on a competitor's reputation, as well as on the performance, to pin the class. Markings that designate physical appearance (such as "Tl Gl" for "tall girl," or "Bg Gry" for "big gray" horse) or that indicate chronic problems (such as "LL" for "loose legs") are beneficial in helping the judge recall particular riders.

Competitors Expectations of a Judge

Since hunter seat riding has become such an expensive and competitive sport, riders, trainers, and owners tend to be more vocal about poor judging than in years past. They come to the show with the expectation that the best performances will be pinned, and if they feel the judge is incompetent or dishonest, they are angry that their money and efforts are being wasted.

Competitors should be able to expect three things from a judge: knowledge, accurate scorekeeping, and honesty. Knowledge is not simply knowing the rules set forth by the USEF, but also understanding the various aspects of performance of horse and rider and how they should be scored.

Accurate scorekeeping—the ability to maintain an accurate and easily readable judge's card—is extremely important. If a judge can't keep track of comments concerning each horse, confusion will ensue, especially during a large class. For classes over fences, each fence should be scored; but for flat classes, the less written the better, for you need viewing time.

Finally, judges must be honest, not swayed by personal friendships or politics. They should put the interests of the sport above their own and have the character to make impartial decisions and stand by them.

You may find the following lists of abbreviations and hieroglyphics helpful in marking a judge's card. Since there is no official set of marks that judges are required to use, each judge makes up his or her own system for scoring. The lists are a compilation of marks submitted by several judges, and the examples that follow some of them are provided to show where certain marks are placed in relation to others—that is, above, to the side of, or below.

Faults over Fences

Good Spot	—	
Long Spot	⌐	
Cutting Down	⌄	Example: ⌐⌄
Reaching	⌐→	
Diving	⋀↘	
Dangerous	Ⓓ	

(i.e., "risky," as in flailing legs or other desperate and unorthodox jumping attempts)

Quick off the Ground	Q	Example: ⌐Q
Deep Spot	⋀	
Very Deep Spot			
Refusal	Ⓡ	Example: ⓇⓇ—
Elimination	Ⓔ————	Example: ⓇⓇⒺ——
Hanging One Leg	⌐	Example: ⌐⋀
Hanging Two Legs	⊓	Example: ⊓|
Loose Form	LF	Example: LF
Dwelling in the Air	Dw	Example: Dw⋀
Flat-Backed	—	Example: ⌐—
Hollow-Backed	⌣	Example: ⌣—

Propping at Base of Obstacle	∧	Example:	∧∧
Twisting	Tw	Example:	Tw ∧
Lying on Side	LoS	Example:	LoS ∣
Drifting in the Air to Left	↖	Example:	↖ —
Drifting in the Air to Right	↗	Example:	— ↗
Rail Knocked Down with Any Part of Horse's Body in Front of Stifle	Ⓚ	placed to right of obstacle Example:	∧ Ⓚ
Rail Knocked Down with Any Part of Horse's Body Behind Stifle	Ⓚ	placed to left of obstacle Example:	Ⓚ —
Rail Touched with Any Part of Horse's Body in Front of Stifle	•	placed to right of obstacle Example:	— •
Rail Touched with Any Part of Horse's Body Behind Stifle	•	placed to left of obstacle Example:	• —
Standard or Wing Knocked Down with Any Part of Horse, Rider, or Equipment	SⓀ	Example: ↖ SⓀ	
Standard or Wing Touched with Any Part of Horse, Rider, or Equipment	S•	S•	

Faults between Fences

Propping on Approach to Obstacle	⋏⋏	Example: ⋏⋏⋀
Breaking Gait	Ⓑ	Example: horse breaks gait behind (i.e., "skips") Ⓑ⋮
Cuts a Corner of Ring	¢	
Not Bent	− β	
Weaving on Approach to Fence	⸮	Example: ⸮ ⋀
Bulging on Approach to Fence: Bulges Right	)	or Bulges Left (
(each symbol placed to left of fence)		Example:) — or (—
Wrong Lead (counter canter)	Ⓧ L	
Cross Canter	Ⓒⓒ	
Rough Lead Change	⸮ch	
Adding Strides between Fences	(+ No.)	Example:
Omitting Strides between Fences	(− No.)	Example:
Head Up	H ♩ ↑	
Mouth Open	mo	
Pulling	Pu	
Strung Out	⟷	

Manners and Way of Going

Pace

Even Pace (correct)	Ev
Slow Pace	Sl
Fast Pace	Fs
Erratic Pace	Er

Locomotion

Excellent Mover	Em
Good Mover	Gm
Fair Mover	Fm
Poor Mover	Pm

General Impressions

If a horse habitually commits an error, such as holding its head in the air during a large part of the course, or has a major error, such as a refusal, this should be noted on the right side of the card, just after the box for the last fence.

Equitation Symbols

Basic Symbols

Toe	T
Heel	H
Leg	Lg

Seat	S
Eye	I
Head	Hd
Hand	Hn
Back	Bk
Rein	Rn
Stirrup	Stp
Bad	Bd
Good	Gd
Short	Sh
Long	Lng
Backward	↰
Forward	↷
In (placed to right of word)	← Example: Ln ← ("leans in")
Out (placed to right of word)	→ Example: T → ("toes out")
Up	↑
Down	↓
Weak	Wk
Strong	St
Rough	≷

Smooth	Smo
Loose	Ls
Stiff	Stf
Little	x
Very	v
Not	—
Lead	Ld
Diagonal	Dg

Position in the Air

Good Position	Γ
Perching	/
Ducking	∧
Jackknifing	<
Dropping Back	D B
Left in the Air	Ⓛ
Roached Back	⌐
Swaybacked	⌣
Fixed Hands	FHN
Open Hands	OHN

Eyes Down	I↓
Heel Up	H↑
Toe Out	T→
Leg Out	Lg→

Position between Fences

Behind Motion	Bm
Ahead of Motion	Am
Late Eye (looking too late to upcoming fence)	late I
Bad Eye (poor timing to a fence)	Bd I
Leans for Leads (leans to check leads on corners)	LL
Leg off Horse's Side	∧

Additional Faults

Other errors can be designated by using a combination of the above symbols. You can also use markings from the list of hunter symbols when necessary. For example, if a rider does not bend his horse around the corners of the ring, you would mark the error the same as you would during hunter classes: −B

Glossary

Ahead of the motion   An overly forward position of the rider's upper body at a particular gait.

Aids   The rider's means of communication with his horse. "Natural aids" include the rider's legs, hands, weight, and voice. "Artificial aids" include crop, spurs, bit, martingale, and any other type of equipment that reinforces the rider's body commands.

At the girth   The position of the rider's leg in which the calf rests just behind the back of the girth.

Backing   The horse walking backward for several steps; also known as "backing up" or "reining back."

Bascule   The extension of a horse's head and neck outward and downward to counterbalance its hindquarters over a fence.

Behind the girth   The position of the rider's leg in which the calf is about 4 inches behind the back edge of the girth.

Behind the motion   An overly vertical position of the rider's upper body at a particular gait.

Bending   Positioning the horse's body so that it is curved to the left or right.

Bounces   A series of small fences with no strides between them.

Built up in front   This term describes a horse whose forehand is slightly taller than its haunches and/or whose neck attaches high upon its shoulder.

Cavalletti   Closely-spaced poles on the ground, which are used to regulate the horse's rhythm and length of step.

Centerline   An imaginary line extending down the length of the arena and bisecting the ring.

Chipping in   The horse adding an extra step at the base of the fence just prior to takeoff.

Cooler   A wool blanket used to cover a horse on a chilly day. When the cooler is used following work, the horse's sweat passes through the fibers and beads up on the top of the blanket, leaving dry fibers next to the animal's body to keep it warm.

Combination   Two or more fences with distances between each pair of fences being 39'5" or less when measured from the base of an obstacle on the landing side to the base of the next obstacle on the takeoff side. A "double combination," also known as an "in-and-out," is made up of two fences; a "triple combination" is made up of three obstacles; and a "multiple combination" contains more than three obstacles.

Counter canter   A schooling and competition movement in which the horse canters on a turn in one direction while traveling on the lead to the outside of the turn. For example, the horse canters clockwise while traveling on the left lead.

Cutting in   A horse leaning its shoulder toward the inside of a turn so that it makes a turn that is tighter than the rider desires.

Daisy cutting   The movement of the horse's feet close to the ground as the animal swings its legs forward correctly.

Dictate the rhythm   To use the rider's aids to create and maintain a particular tempo of the horse's footfalls.

Disobedience   The refusal of a horse to jump a fence.

Distance   The footage between two fences. A "long distance" measures longer than the standard striding between fences, while a "short distance" measures less than standard striding. A long-to-short distance is the combination of the two measurements with the long distance coming first in the line. A short-to-long distance is the combination of the two measurements with the short distance coming first in the line.

Diving over a fence   A form fault in which the horse stretches its front legs forward as it clears the rails, rather than tucking its legs neatly in front of its chest. This error usually results when a rider places his horse at a takeoff spot that is much too far from the fence.

Drifting   The movement of the horse to the left or right, either while working on the flat or while jumping over a fence.

Dropping back   The rider allowing the angle of his hip to open too early over a fence so that his buttocks hit the saddle while the horse is still airborne.

Dull horse   An animal that requires a great deal of pressure from the rider's legs before it reacts with a forward response.

Engaged hocks   A movement of the horse's hind legs in which the hock joint has a circular motion and stays well underneath the horse for most of the cycle. When a horse "loses engagement," the hock joint has a flat motion causing the joint to be behind the horse much of the time.

Equitation division   A category of classes at horse shows in which the rider's ability alone is judged. Hunter seat equitation riders compete either over fences or on the flat and are judged on their position and their ability to produce an accurate performance on their horses.

Falling out of frame   An abrupt change from the horse being balanced and collected to being unbalanced and strung out.

Feeling good   The horse being full of energy and often wanting to run or buck.

Fences   Obstacles over which a horse jumps in schooling or competition. They are also referred to as "jumps."

Flatwork   Exercise of the horse that does not involve jumping fences.

Flying change   A complete alteration of sequence in the order of the horse's footfalls at the canter, hand-gallop, or gallop without a break in gait. The horse begins on one sequence or "lead" and, in a moment of suspension of all four feet, switches to the other lead.

Forehand   The horse's front end, including its forelegs, shoulders, neck, and head.

Form   The style in which a horse jumps a fence. When a horse jumps in "good form," its topline forms a convex curve and the horse is said to be "using itself" over the fence. When the topline is level, the horse is "jumping flat"; and when the topline forms a concave curve, the horse is "jumping inverted."

Frame   The degree of collection of the horse as determined by the animal's length of body and step, elevation of its forehand, and engagement of its haunches.

Gaits   The various sequences of foot movements of the horse. The walk is a four-beat gait; the trot is a two-beat gait; the canter and hand-gallop are three-beat gaits; and the gallop is a four-beat gait.

Good eye   The rider's ability to accurately determine what corrections must be made to the horse's stride in order to reach the correct takeoff spot at each fence.

Green horse   This term loosely refers to any inexperienced horse. Technically, however, a "green horse" is a horse of any age in its first or second year of showing at Regular Member competitions of the USEF or the Canadian Equestrian Federation in any classes that require horses to jump 3'6" or higher. When shown in a Green section, a horse in its first year of showing must show as a First Year Green horse and a horse in its second year of showing must show as a Second Year Green horse.

Ground pole   A jump pole that has been placed on the ground.

Gymnastics Closely-set fences designed to improve a horse's athletic abilities.

Half-halt A technique in which the rider's hands and legs are coordinated so that they cause the horse to collect slightly and move with less weight on its forehand.

Hands An increment of 4 inches used in measuring horses and ponies. The measurements are taken from the ground to the animal's withers with a special measuring stick during official measuring sessions at USEF recognized horse shows. In the Junior Hunter Division (for riders under 18 years of age), the horses are often divided into "sections" based on height. Horses that are 16 hands or over are placed in the Large Junior Hunter section; while horses measuring less than 16 hands compete in the Small Junior Hunter section. Hunter Pony sections are also determined by height.

Haunches The horse's hind legs and hips.

Herdbound The horse's desire to stay near other horses, rather than work alone.

Home The in-gate or out-gate of a show arena, which remind the horse of going back to the barn.

Hot horse An animal with an overly sensitive, nervous temperament.

Hunter division A category of classes at horse shows in which the performance of the animal is judged, with scoring based upon the horse's jumping style and way of moving.

Impulsion The force a horse uses as it pushes off the ground each step.

Isolated distance The distance between fences on a two fence line. (See *related distances.*)

Jumper division A category of classes at horse shows in which the animals' faults over fences are scored with a designated number of points for each particular error. In jumper classes, the fences are brightly colored and are high enough to challenge the horses to clear them. The object of most jumper classes is to test the horses' ability to jump the fences without any errors within a given amount

of time. In the case of ties, the time taken to complete a course is usually a factor in placement of the animals.

Jump off A round of competition following the initial round in a jumper class.

Junior rider An individual who has not reached his eighteenth birthday as of December 1 of the current competition year.

Knockdown The changing of the height of a fence through contact with any part of the horse or rider, so that the part of the fence which establishes the height of the obstacle rests on a different support from the one on which it was originally placed.

Lateral movements Exercises which promote suppleness of the horse from side to side.

Lead The sequence of the horse's feet at the canter, hand-gallop, or gallop. When traveling on the left lead, the horse's left foreleg is the last leg to strike in the sequence; when traveling on the right lead, the horse's right foreleg is the last to strike.

Line A segment of a course of fences. The term "line" refers to: (1) fences set either on a long side of the arena (an "outside line") or across the diagonal of the arena (an "inside line" or "diagonal line"); or (2) fences set on either a straightaway ("straight line") or a curve (`bending line").

Longeing Exercising a horse in a circle on a long line held by a person at the center of the circle.

Maclay Finals The Alfred B. Maclay Finals (also known as the ASPCA Horsemanship Finals) is a national equitation championship class.

Mechanics of jumping Standardized procedures that result in the rider's or horse's correct performance over a fence. "Mechanics" refers to learned techniques, as opposed to "feel," which refers to innate ability.

Medal Finals The USEF Hunter Seat Medal Finals is the prestigious equitation competition that determines the USEF's national equitation champion each year.

Numbers   The correct number of strides to be taken between two fences. Usually referred to as "the numbers."

Overfacing the horse   Asking the animal to do something it is either emotionally or physically incapable of doing. This usually refers to asking the horse to jump a course that is too complicated or which has fences that are high enough to discourage the horse at its particular level of training.

Oxer   A fence that is constructed on two vertical planes. An "ascending oxer" is composed of a slightly lower element on the near side of the oxer than on the far side (usually about a 3-to 6-inch difference). A "square oxer" consists of a near and a far element that are equal in height.

Pace   The speed at which the horse is traveling.

Poll   The point directly between the horse's ears.

Pony   An animal measuring 14.2 hands or less. To compete in the Large Pony Hunter section, an animal must not exceed 14.2 hands; to compete in the Medium Pony Hunter section, an animal must not exceed 13.2 hands; and to compete in the Small Pony Hunter section, an animal must not exceed 12.2 hands.

Popping the shoulder   The horse's shoulder falling to the outside or inside of the uniform curve of a bend.

Posting trot   The rhythmic rising and sitting of the rider as the horse performs the trot. The rider should rise when the horse's outside foreleg (toward the rail of the arena) goes forward; he should sit when it moves backward and strikes the ground.

Puller   A horse that constantly tugs on the reins.

Punishment and reward   Punishment is the application of the rider's natural or artificial aids; reward is the cessation of the rider's aids.

Quick horse   An animal that overreacts to the rider's aids by rushing forward.

Recognized competitions   All competitions which are under the auspices of the United States Equestrian Federation, Inc (USEF).

Related distances   The measurements between fences on a line composed of three or more elements. The way the distance rides between the first two fences will affect the way the distance or distances can be ridden between the remaining fences.

Rhythm   The recurring pattern of the horse's footfalls, such as a three-beat cadence of the footfalls at the canter; or the repeated accent on a particular beat, such as the canter having an accented third beat (dah, dah, *dum*).

Rub   The horse touching a fence with its legs while in the air, without lowering the height of the obstacle.

Running into the canter   The horse increasing the speed of its trot until it has to canter.

Running out at a fence   An error in which a horse avoids jumping an obstacle by veering away from or passing it.

Running under a fence   The horse taking short, quick, additional steps just before takeoff.

Rusher   A horse that anxiously hurries to a fence, rather than waiting for the rider's commands.

School horse   An animal used for training students at a riding academy.

Schooling   The horse and rider practicing either on the flat or over fences.

Side reins   Longeing equipment made of leather and elastic, which attaches between the horse's bit and girth on both sides of the animal.

Standard   The part of a fence which is used to support the poles and, in the case of a "wing standard," to give extra width to the obstacle. The poles, or "rails," rest in cups which are attached to the standard.

Stick   A riding whip, crop, or bat.

Stride   Each full sequence of the horse's footfalls at the canter, hand-gallop, or gallop. The sequence begins with a hind foot, followed by a diagonal pair of feet striking together (except at the gallop, in which they strike separately). Finally, the remaining forefoot strikes, completing the stride.

Strong horse   An animal that pulls hard on the reins, usually in an effort to increase its pace.

Strung out   A method of traveling in which the horse's frame is overly long and the animal moves with sloppy motions.

Takeoff spot   The place at which the horse leaves the ground to jump a fence. When the horse leaves the ground too far from the obstacle, it has left from a "long spot." When the horse leaves the ground too close to the obstacle, it has left from a "short spot" or "deep spot."

Tempo   The frequency of the horse's footfalls.

Three-point position   The rider's body making contact with the horse at three places: his two legs and his seat.

Throwing a horse on the lead   The rider making a horse pick up a particular lead by slinging his upper body in the direction of the desired lead.

Timing   The rider's ability to place his horse correctly for take-off at a fence.

Topline   The uppermost parts of the horse's body, all the way from the top of its head (poll) to the top of its tail (dock).

Transitions   The periods of change between one gait and another. When changing from a slower to a faster gait, the horse performs an "upward transition." When changing from a faster to a slower gait, the animal performs a "downward transition."

Triple bar   A fence composed of three planes with gradually ascending heights from the near to the far side.

Two-point position   The rider's buttocks raised out of the saddle so that only his two legs make contact with the horse.

Under-saddle classes   Hunter classes in which the horse competes on the flat only. The animal must be shown at the walk, trot, and canter both directions in the arena. Sometimes the judge will also ask competitors to show at the hand-gallop. The animal is judged on its way of moving and its manners.

(USEF) United States Equestrian Federation, Inc.   The governing body that oversees recognized competitions in America and serves as the National Equestrian Federation of the United States for world-wide competitions.

Upper body   The rider's parts above his buttocks.

USEF Show Jumping Talent Search Finals   The United States Equestrian Federation Talent Search Finals are split into East Coast and West Coast competitions. These equitation finals are intended to encourage young riders capable of successfully showing jumpers. The courses are more difficult than those of regular horsemanship classes and are constructed similar to jumper courses.

Verticals   Fences that are built straight up-and-down, on a single plane.

Wall up the horse's energy   To restrict a horse's drifting to the outside of a turn through the use of the rider's legs, hands, and weight.

Withers   The boney ridge above the horse's shoulders.

With the motion   The correct inclination of the rider's upper body at a particular gait, allowing the rider to remain balanced on his horse while the animal is in motion.

Work-off   A test which takes place after the first round of competition. It usually consists of individual testing of a few riders who are being considered for top placings.

X fence   A small obstacle composed of two crossed rails that form the shape of the letter "X."

Index